New Threats and New Actors in International Security

New Threats and New Actors in International Security

Edited by

Elke Krahmann

NEW THREATS AND NEW ACTORS IN INTERNATIONAL SECURITY
© Elke Krahmann, 2005.

First published in 2005 by
PALGRAVE MACMILLAN™
175 Fifth Avenue, New York, N.Y. 10010 and
Houndmills, Basingstoke, Hampshire, England RG21 6XS
Companies and representatives throughout the world.

PALGRAVE MACMILLAN is the global academic imprint of the Palgrave Macmillan division of St. Martin's Press, LLC and of Palgrave Macmillan Ltd. Macmillan® is a registered trademark in the United States, United Kingdom and other countries. Palgrave is a registered trademark in the European Union and other countries.

ISBN 1–4039–6697–4

Library of Congress Cataloging-in-Publication Data

New threats and new actors in international security / Elke Krahmann (ed.).
    p. cm.
Includes bibliographical references and index.
ISBN 1–4039–6697–4
    1. International relations. 2. Security, International. 3. Terrorism. 4. Arms control. I. Krahmann, Elke.

JZ5595.5.N48 2005
355'.033—dc22   2004054713

A catalogue record for this book is available from the British Library.

Design by Newgen Imaging Systems (P) Ltd., Chennai, India.

First edition: January 2005

10 9 8 7 6 5 4 3 2 1

Printed in the United States of America.

Contents

Preface   vii

Contributors   viii

Abstracts   x

Part I   Introduction

1. From State to Non-State Actors: The Emergence of
   Security Governance   3
   Elke Krahmann

Part II   Civil War

2. The New Conflict Managers: Peacebuilding NGOs and
   State Agendas   23
   Loramy Conradi Gerstbauer

3. Humanitarians and Mercenaries: Partners in Security Governance?   45
   Christopher Spearin

Part III   Terrorism and Transnational Crime

4. Drug Traffickers, Terrorist Networks, and Ill-Fated
   Government Strategies   69
   Michael Kenney

5. Targeting Money Laundering: Global Approach or
   Diffusion of Authority?   91
   Eleni Tsingou

Part IV   HIV/AIDS

6. HIV/AIDS: The International Security Dimensions   111
   Stefan Elbe

7. NGOs as Security Actors in the Fight against HIV/AIDS?   131
   Carrie Sheehan

Part V   Small Arms and Light Weapons

8.   The Proliferation of Small Arms and Light Weapons   155
     Mike Bourne

9.   NGOs and the Shaping of the European Controls on Small
     Arms Exports   177
     Holger Anders

Part VI   Conclusion

10. New Threats and New Actors in Security Governance:
     Developments, Problems, and Solutions   199
     Elke Krahmann

Selected Bibliography   213

Index   223

Preface

New threats and new actors are changing the nature of security in the twenty-first millennium. This book attempts to examine the relationship between these two phenomena by bringing together experts from both fields. As such this volume is a collective effort. It has benefited from the contributions of a broad range of scholars from the United States and the United Kingdom covering research on civil war, terrorism, transnational crime, HIV/AIDS, and small arms proliferation as well as the progressive involvement of NGOs and private firms in the making and implementation of security policies.

The idea for this volume first originated with a panel proposal put together by Dr. Stefan Elbe and me. Our aim was to encourage an exchange between academics that worked on different aspects of a transformation from state to non-state threats and actors in global security. To our mind, it was clear that the spread of transnational threats such as terrorism, transnational crime, and HIV/AIDS was directly related to the growing role of private actors in the provision of security. However, little research appeared to have been conducted on this relationship. Fortunately, our idea was supported by the International Studies Association (ISA) that generously funded a workshop on this theme during the ISA Annual Convention in Portland. From there it was a short step toward this book that presents the findings of our workshop and a number of other contributions to close the gaps in our research.

I would like to thank all the contributors who joined our discussion and made this volume possible. In addition, I would like to acknowledge the publication of an earlier version of Michael Kenney's chapter under the title "From Pablo to Osama: Counter-terrorism Lessons from the War on Drugs" in *Survival* 45, no. 3 (2003). Further thanks go to two anonymous reviewers who provided valuable comments and helped transform our separate contributions into a coherent volume. Finally, I am grateful to the German Academic Exchange Service and the United States Institute of Peace, as well as the Department of Politics at the University of Bristol and the Center for European Studies at Harvard University for financial and organizational support for my editing of this book.

Elke Krahmann

Contributors

Holger Anders is European Information Officer for the International Action Network on Small Arms as well as a Ph.D. candidate at the University of Bradford, U.K. His research interests include the small arms trade, proliferation, and transnational crime, and he has published various articles in the *European Security Review* and the *Royal United Services Institute (RUSI) Newsbrief*.

Mike Bourne is Researcher at the Centre for International Cooperation and Security (CICS) at the University of Bradford, U.K. He researches on arms transfers, illicit trafficking, and conflict, with a particular focus on small arms proliferation and control, and has contributed among others to Abdel-Fatau Musah and Niobe Thompson, Niobe, eds., *Over a Barrel: Light Weapons & Human Rights in the Commonwealth* (London: Commonwealth Human Rights Initiative, 1999) and *Implementing the Programme of Action on Small Arms* (London: IANSA, 2003).

Stefan Elbe is Senior Lecturer in International Relations in the Department of International Relations and Politics at the University of Sussex. He is an expert on the security implications of HIV/AIDS and is the author of *Strategic Implications of HIV/AIDS* (Oxford: Oxford University Press, 2003) and "HIV/AIDS and the Changing Landscape of War in Africa," *International Security* 27, no. 2 (2002).

Loramy Conradi Gerstbauer is Assistant Professor of Political Science and Director of Peace Studies at Gustavus Adolphus College in St. Peter, Minnesota. Her research focuses on peace work of nongovernmental organizations (NGOs), transitional justice issues, and postwar reconciliation. She has published previously in *Peace Review* and the *Brandywine Review of Faith and International Affairs* and is currently completing a manuscript about the contribution of faith-based NGOs to peacebuilding.

Michael Kenney is Assistant Professor of Public Policy at the School of Public Affairs at Pennsylvania State University, Harrisburg and currently fellow at the Center for International Security at Stanford University. Among others, he has published articles in *Survival* and *Transnational Organized Crime* and is currently completing a book on the Colombian drug trade and U.S. and Colombian drug enforcement policies.

Elke Krahmann is Lecturer in International Relations at the University of Bristol, U.K. She has published on governance and transnational relations in foreign and security policy including *Multilevel Networks in European Foreign Policy* (2003) and articles in *Cooperation and Conflict, International Affairs, Global Governance,* and *Review of International Studies*. Currently she is working on a USIP-funded project on the privatization of security.

Carrie Sheehan is a Ph.D. candidate in the School of International Service at American University in Washington, DC. Her research focuses on nontraditional security issues and U.S. foreign policy. She is presently completing her dissertation, "Securitizing the Pandemic: Framing International HIV/AIDS Policy."

Christopher Spearin is Assistant Professor of National Security Studies and Deputy Director of Research at the Canadian Forces College, Toronto, Canada. His research concerns non-state actors and conflict, the privatization of security, change in state security sectors, and human security. His work has been published in a variety of forums, including *International Politics, Contemporary Security Policy, International Peacekeeping, Civil Wars, Journal of Conflict Studies*, and *Canadian Foreign Policy*.

Eleni Tsingou is Postdoctoral Research Fellow at the Center for the Study of Globalization and Regionalization of the University of Warwick. Her main research interests include the role of non-state actors in global financial governance, the politics of banking regulation and policy approaches in the fight against money laundering.

Abstracts

From State to Non-State Actors: The Emergence of Security Governance
Elke Krahmann

Non-state threats and actors have become key factors in contemporary security. However, little research has been conducted on the relationship between the two. This chapter seeks to provide an overview and theoretical framework for the analysis of the growing role of non-state actors—both as the cause of new security threats and as security providers. Specifically, it argues that both developments can be conceptualized as part of a shift from "government" to "governance" in security. The result appears to be the emergence of a system of security governance in which new transnational threats are addressed by overlapping networks of state and non-state security actors at the national, regional, and global levels.

The New Conflict Managers: Peacebuilding NGOs and State Agendas
Loramy Conradi Gerstbauer

In the past decade, NGOs have been hailed as the new conflict managers for their emerging role in peacebuilding in violent conflicts. Many relief and development organizations have come to realize the impact of their presence and their provision of aid in conflicts, and they have decided to be purposeful about that impact by adding peacebuilding to their mandates. For the most part, the NGO and peacebuilding literature has praised the advent of NGOs in peacebuilding. This chapter provides a more critical analysis of NGO peacebuilding; just as development NGOs are interdependent with the government agencies that fund them, the new NGO mandate of peacebuilding is heavily influenced by state interests in post-conflict settings. The dilemmas this raises for NGO peacebuilding work are discussed.

Humanitarians and Mercenaries: Partners in Security Governance?
Christopher Spearin

In light of the threats humanitarian NGOs face in the post–Cold War, weak state environment, many NGOs have turned to International Private Security Companies (PSCs), a form of modern-day mercenarism, in order to satisfy their security requirements. On the one hand, this development reflects the increasing role played by non-state actors in international affairs. On the other hand, the chapter contends that these actors cannot escape the dominance of state-centric activity. Additional operational and managerial constraints also exist that will impact upon the efficacy of the NGO–PSC relationship. Moreover, attempts to handle problems resulting from the interaction between NGOs and PSCs will lack coherency and uniform direction into the foreseeable future.

Drug Trafficking, Terrorist Networks, and Ill-Fated Government Strategies
Michael Kenney

In wars on drugs and the terrorism, states confront daunting adversaries, transnational networks of traffickers and terrorists that carry out illegal activities while avoiding government efforts to destroy them. These illegal enterprises share numerous similarities, including compartmentalized structures, flat decision-making hierarchies, and an aptitude for organizational adaptation. While the United States and its counterterrorism allies have achieved important results against al Qaeda, similarities among traffickers and terrorists, and lessons from two decades of Colombia's war on drugs, suggest a number of difficulties in dismantling terrorist networks. If policy makers hope to achieve lasting victory in the war on terror, they must move beyond supply-reduction policies and devote greater diplomatic, political, and economic resources to addressing the 'demand side' of terrorism.

Targeting Money Laundering: Global Approach or Diffusion of Authority?
Eleni Tsingou

This chapter investigates the policy processes and practices that make up anti-money laundering measures and argues that at the center of the problem is the tension between the cost of dealing with money laundering and the benefits of containing financial crime. This dilemma is analyzed through an assessment of public–private interaction and the issue of private responsibility in the implementation of public policy goals.

HIV/AIDS: The International Security Dimensions
Stefan Elbe

This chapter argues that the global AIDS pandemic is no longer solely an international health issue; it is also becoming a global security issue. This argument is substantiated by outlining the human, national, and international security dimensions of HIV/AIDS. Scholars and policy makers must recognize these security implications in order to arrive at a more comprehensive understanding of the nature and extent of the contemporary pandemic; in order for the level of the international response to become commensurate with the extent of the global challenge posed by the AIDS pandemic; and because the security sector, as a high-risk group and vector of the virus, can make a responsible contribution to international efforts to reduce the transmission of HIV/AIDS. The chapter concludes by outlining the broad policy implications that follow from such an analysis.

NGOs as Security Actors in the Fight against HIV/AIDS?
Carrie Sheehan

This chapter examines the role of U.S.-based international health and development nongovernmental organizations (NGOs) in the fight against HIV/AIDS globally. It begins with an overview of the development of U.S. policy toward the security dimensions of HIV/AIDS and then examines whether NGOs working on HIV/AIDS are addressing the pandemic both in words and actions as a security threat. It finds that while NGOs rarely publicize or discuss the security aspects of the HIV/AIDS pandemic, they nevertheless actively promote human security through their work with civilians and traditional security in their more limited work with militaries.

The Proliferation of Small Arms and Light Weapons
Mike Bourne

Half a million people are killed with small arms and light weapons (SALW) every year. The proliferation of SALW fuels conflict, terrorism, and crime and is a key challenge to international security. This chapter examines the nature of that proliferation, with a particular focus on the flow of SALW to conflicts, and the roles of non-state actors. It examines the nature of the interaction between state and non-state actors in the supply of SALW to conflicts, and explores the implications of key determinants of rebel groups arming patterns.

NGOs and the Shaping of the European Union Conventional Arms Regime
Holger Anders

This chapter looks at current changes in relations between governments and non-governmental advocacy actors with respect to policy formulation on security policies. In particular, the chapter focuses on such changes within the context of the arms export control regime that emerged over the last years in the European Union. It is demonstrated, that this development saw the close involvement of nongovernmental actors. The chapter argues that, despite the increasing prominence of nongovernmental actors in the field of arms export controls, governments remain firmly in control of processes of policy formulation.

New Threats and New Actors in Security Governance: Developments, Problems, and Solutions
Elke Krahmann

This chapter aims to integrate the findings presented in this volume and to provide some answers to the question of the nature of the relationships between state and non-state actors and threats in contemporary security governance. In addition, it seeks to position these answers within the theoretical context of the shift from government to governance outlined in the introduction to this volume. In particular it suggests that the evidence and conclusions presented by the contributors to this volume can be understood in relation to three concepts: the emergence of "security governance"; the problems or "governance failures" that can arise from it; and the role that standards of "good governance" can play in resolving these failures.

Part I

Introduction

Chapter 1

From State to Non-State Actors: The Emergence of Security Governance

Elke Krahmann

Non-state threats and actors have become key factors in contemporary security. However, little research has been conducted on the relationship between the two. The aim of this book is to address this gap by examining the growing role of non-state actors—both as the cause of new security threats, such as civil war, transnational crime, terrorism, infectious diseases, and the proliferation of small arms, and as security providers, including nongovernmental organizations (NGOs), private security companies, and international regimes.

Since the end of the Cold War the notion that the state is the primary unit of interest in security studies has increasingly been challenged. Statistics show that today many more people are killed by ethnic conflicts, HIV/AIDS, or the proliferation of small arms than by interstate wars. Moreover, non-state actors are progressively complementing states in the provision of security. This chapter suggests that both developments can be understood as part of a shift from "government" to "governance" in security. This shift is characterized by the changing nature of threats in contemporary world politics and the ways in which they are addressed. In particular, the following seeks to illustrate the emergence of a system of security governance in which the making and implementation of security policies is shared among overlapping networks of state and non-state actors at the national, regional, and global levels.

The concept of security governance can thus serve as an overarching theoretical framework for the contributions to this volume that brings together experts on new threats and new actors. It seeks to examine how private actors have become one of the main sources of insecurity in the contemporary world, but also how non-state actors play a growing role in combating these threats.

New Threats and New Actors

Many will assert that neither civil war, transnational crime, infectious diseases, or the proliferation of small arms are new phenomena, nor is the involvement of non-state actors, such as NGOs and private firms, in security policy. Before one can turn to an analysis of the transformation of security since the end of the Cold War, it is therefore necessary to examine why this volume talks about "new" threats and "new" actors.

Changing threat environment. To understand the changing nature of threat in contemporary global security one needs to define what is understood as security threat. A general reading of the term suggests that a security threat can be defined as an event with potentially negative consequences for the survival or welfare of a state, a society, or an individual. However, already this simple attempt at defining a security threat indicates the complexity of the concept. First, this definition suggests that a security threat refers to a possible future event. Our assessment that something represents a threat thus depends very much on the probability attributed to an event. Some negative events might be considered to be so unlikely that they are not considered a security threat anymore, such as a civil war in the United States or a military conflict among the member states of the European Union. Second, a security threat is characterized by the intensity of its potential effects, that is, whether it endangers the survival or merely the welfare of human beings. Some threats, such as infectious diseases and weapons of mass destruction affect the welfare and survival of humans in a very immediate manner. Others, such as threats to the environment or the livelihood of peoples, affect the survival of humans in a more indirect way. Third, a security threat is defined by the geographical scope of its effects. Nuclear war, for instance, not only poses a danger to entire regions, but to life on earth in general. Conversely, the effects of civil wars are commonly limited to states or subregions. Finally, the nature of a security threat can be classified by its object. Threats are be differentiated according to whether they are directed at a collective, such as a state, an ethnicity or a religious group, or at individuals.

The preceding analysis illustrates that a security threat is as much a subjective as an objective category. Some aspects of it, such as the intensity and scope of a particular threat, can be assessed on the basis of technical data and evidence. The reach of a ballistic missile, for instance, can be measured. Others, such as an assessment of the probability of an ethnic conflict or the use of weapons of mass destruction in a border conflict, are inherently subjective and based on an understanding of the individuals involved in taking these decisions.

As a consequence of the complexity and subjectivity of threat assessment, our understanding of what presents a security threat in the twenty-first century has changed considerably. In particular, the end of the Cold War has led to a fundamental reassessment of key security threats. The following section examines some of the primary security concerns of today.

Contemporary security threats. During the Cold War the primary national and international security threat indisputably was nuclear war between the United States and the Soviet Union. With the fall of the Berlin Wall in 1990 and the dissolution of the Warsaw Pact, this threat has suddenly disappeared. However, rather than leading to a period of unprecedented security, it has been replaced in the minds of decision makers and the general public by a multitude of new security threats, such as terrorism, the proliferation of weapons of mass destruction, civil war, and ethnic conflict.

What makes these the primary security threats of the new century? The above section has argued that what is a key security threat is inevitably based on subjective assessments. Thus, the end of the Cold War did not lead to the elimination of nuclear war between the major powers as the first and foremost security threat because of the dismantling of all their nuclear weapons. In fact in 2003, both the United States and Russia still retained between 7,000 and 8,000 nuclear warheads.[1] The threat of a global nuclear exchange has primarily decreased because of trust in the changed foreign policy imperatives of these two countries. Similarly, the degree to which new security threats such as terrorism are considered of prime importance today is not only dependent upon the proliferation of weapons of mass destruction which might be used in a terrorist attack, but also on subjective estimates of the probability of such action, likely targets, scope, and intensity.

The range of factors involved in defining a security threat makes the ranking of threats a difficult and very political choice. Since the resources of governments and international organizations are limited, they have to decide whether to make a threat with limited scope and intensity, but high probability, a priority or a threat with global reach and deadly consequences, but a comparatively low likelihood.

Among the new security threats identified by contemporary governments, terrorism is the most limited in terms of intensity, that is, the number of peoples directly affected by death or injury. Empirical data on the degree of threat posed by terrorism shows that terrorism causes relatively few deaths if compared to other security concerns such as interstate war, civil conflict, or infectious diseases. Even on a global scale, numbers of terrorist casualties varied merely between 12 and 704 per year from 1968 to 1997.[2] In more recent years, the number of global deaths caused by terrorist attacks averages to less than 2,000 annually. In addition, most terrorist attacks are very limited in their scope. Typically only people in the immediate neighborhood of an attack will be affected. However, since September 11, 2001 terrorist attacks have been attributed a growing likelihood. Moreover, recent data show an increase in the lethality of individual terrorist incidents.

In the wake of September 11 there has also been a re-evaluation of the threat of international proliferation. The potential of weapons of mass destruction, that is chemical, biological, and nuclear weapons, reaching the hands of terrorist groups like al Qaeda has received particular attention. The sarin gas attacks by the Japanese Aum sect in Tokyo in 1995 and the anthrax letters mailed to Congress in 2001 have illustrated the relative ease with which chemical agents can be manufactured by amateurs. Equally likely is the development of nuclear weapons by countries such as North Korea or Iran. The scope and intensity of the danger posed by the use of weapons of mass destruction is very high. They can not only destroy cities, but also entire regions and countries. However, the likelihood of their deployment is unclear. Biological and chemical weapons are notoriously difficult to control, and nuclear weapons invite massive retaliation. Weapons of mass destruction have rarely been used even by the most determined actors.[3] Traditionally, nuclear weapons have primarily been obtained for defensive purposes. Indeed, the nuclear stalemate between the United States and the Soviet Union has been credited by some with the preservation of the "long peace" that characterized the Cold War in Europe.[4] However, the actors who would employ weapons of mass destruction and the nature of these weapons appear to be changing. Suicide terrorists are presumably less concerned about their ability to control biological, chemical, and nuclear weapons and more willing to take the risks involved in using them. Moreover, weapons of mass destruction are becoming more easily obtainable and deployable. So-called "dirty bombs" of nuclear material do not require sophisticated knowledge or material and the United States is studying the development of a new class of low-yield nuclear weapons for use in limited warfare rather than as a deterrent.[5]

Statistically the most dangerous form of proliferation is the spread of small arms and light weapons. There are currently 600 million small arms and light weapons in circulation affecting every part of the world. Used in wars as well as homicide, small arms kill over half a million people per year. Moreover, during the 1990s, small arms emerged as the weapon of choice in 47 out of 49 major conflicts, most of them civil wars.[6] The link between small arms proliferation and civil conflict is particularly lethal since the number of intrastate wars has been increasing progressively since 1945.[7] In the 1970s there were annually between 15 and 20 major civil conflicts per year, in the 1980s this had increased to between 20 and 30, and since the 1990s it lies between 25 and 35. Conversely the number of interstate conflicts has been rarely above five per year during the same period.[8] Civil war scores high in terms of scope and intensity as well. Civil war not only affects large regions from Africa to South America and Southeast Asia, it also ranks high in terms of threats to both the survival and the welfare of the peoples involved with both immediate and long-term consequences to life and prosperity.

Nevertheless, the credit of being the deadliest threat in contemporary security does not go to any form of human conflict, but to HIV/AIDS. The threat from this disease is not geographically limited, it leads to death within on average ten years, and the probability of adult infection ranges between 0.1 percent in Australia, 0.5–0.7 percent in North America, and 7.5–8.5 percent in sub-Saharan Africa. In 2003, 3 million people died of HIV/AIDS.[9] Furthermore, because of the long gestation period of the illness, HIV/AIDS has serious effects on the well-being of the infected and their relatives.

The preceding sections have indicated that none of these contemporary security threats are "new." Concerning terrorism, proliferation, and civil war, data has been collected since the 1940s or 1960s. Nevertheless, it can be argued that all of them have achieved a new quality. The following section examines what distinguishes the new security threats of today from those that dominated the Cold War era.

Nature of the "new" threats. If a security threat is generally defined by its probability, scope, intensity, and object, the central security concerns of today are characterized by a number of changes in some of these dimensions that differentiate them from the threat of interstate war that defined the theory and practice of international security during the Cold War period. In particular, the new security threats appear to have a higher probability, a more variable scope and intensity, and a new object. Moreover, all of them are transnational security threats challenging the authority and reach of individual states. Examining each of these aspects in turn, it can be suggested that although these threats are not entirely "new," they have a number of characteristics that set them apart from traditional security concerns of the last century and appear to be especially dangerous today.

One of the main features common among the security threats discussed in the preceding section is their higher probability. Although a nuclear war was considered the primary security threat of the Cold War period, its historical frequency was rather low. In the twentieth century, there was only in one instance, namely during World War II, when nuclear weapons were employed in a military conflict. What ensured the priority of nuclear war among security policy-makers was not its likelihood based on previous experience, but rather its potentially devastating effects on the survival and welfare of peoples around the globe.

New threats, such as terrorism, transnational crime, civil conflicts, and HIV/AIDS are much more pervasive and probable. In comparison with interstate war, civil conflicts have not only been on average about five times more frequent, but the number of internal conflicts has also been steadily increasing since the end of World War II, while the occurrence of intrastate war has been relatively stable. Similarly, the number of terrorist casualties appears to have been on the rise since the 1960s, reaching its peak with 4,548 in 2001.[10] Although a latecomer, HIV/AIDS by far exceeds these numbers with a steady increase from 2 million deaths globally in 1999 to 3 million in 2003.[11] The statistical chance of any individual being directly affected by one or several of these threats during their lives today is considerably higher than the threat of nuclear war has been during the Cold War period.

In addition, the new security threats are more diverse in terms of their scope and intensity and thus appear to be more difficult to assess. Many of the effects of civil war, transnational crime, terrorism, and HIV/AIDS are not immediately apparent, but can only be measured in the long term. Moreover, their consequences on the lives of peoples are frequently indirect. These consequences include the displacement of large sections of a population, the damaging of the economy, the shortening of life expectancies and the withholding of foreign investment.

The third and most critical common feature of contemporary security threats is the fact that they do not target states, but societies and individuals. The new threats, such as civil war, terrorism, and transnational crime, the proliferation of small arms, and HIV/AIDS, are transnational. Using the same technologies and means of transport that have benefited the globalization of trade and finance, these transnational security threats illustrate that global integration can not only lead to new opportunities, but also new dangers. Specifically their ability to cross national boundaries with little hindrance undermines the security provisions established by a system based on sovereign nation-states.

Transnational threats are particularly unsettling because they do not fit into the analytical frameworks that had been developed during the Cold War.

Governments and international organizations have had to realize that their established security arrangements, such as large standing armed forces and the protection of national borders, are unsuited for the fight against transnational threats. However, not only do governments have to adapt their strategies to address these security threats, but national borders and sovereignty which provided the basis for national and international security in the past are now frequently proving an obstacle. Transnational threats are thus requiring a reconsideration of security and how it can be achieved. The following section suggests that non-state actors play a crucial role in this transformation.

New actors. Non-state actors have not only contributed to the emergence of new security threats such as terrorism and transnational crime, they are also playing a growing role in the provision of security. This section examines the nature and capabilities of non-state actors which enables them to help address contemporary security threats either in collaboration with governments or independently.

Types of non-state actors. Non-state actors formally can be grouped into two categories—private actors and intergovernmental organizations. The former includes a variety of forms such as private companies, charities, local pressure groups, as well as national and international NGOs. The latter refers to multilateral institutions formed by sovereign nation-states. This book focuses in particular on three types of actors that have become key actors in contemporary security: NGOs, private military companies, and international institutions.

Nongovernmental organizations are one of the largest groups of non-state actors engaged in security. They are typically defined as voluntary, nonprofit organizations that operate at the national, regional, and global levels. NGOs include multilateral associations, such as the International Red Cross, international organizations, such as Médecins sans Frontières, and a multitude of regional or national NGOs, such as the American Refugee Committee. As the following chapters will illustrate, NGOs contribute directly and indirectly to security by offering services such as humanitarian aid and conflict reconciliation or by lobbying governments and international organizations in areas such as arms control and HIV/AIDS research.

Private military companies are more limited in their number and services, but have proliferated exponentially since the end of the Cold War. Commonly, the literature on private military companies distinguishes three types of firms based on the services that they offer.[12] The term "mercenary firms" has been employed to denote private military companies that provide private soldiers and directly engage in national or international conflicts such as Sandline International, which was involved in the civil wars in Angola or Sierra Leone. "Private military firms" has been used to refer to companies that offer military training and strategic advice such as the Virginia-based Military Professional Resources Inc. (MPRI), and "private security firms" has been used to describe firms which provide military support, including logistics, base maintenance, and transportation such as Halliburton. Typically, however, companies offer a range of services across these categories and the terms private security and private military companies are therefore used interchangeably in this book.

Finally, the number and role of international regimes and organizations have expanded in global security since the Cold War. Both can be formally distinguished in that the term "international regimes" is most often used to refer to multinational institutions that take the form of intergovernmental agreements or treaties. Examples include nonproliferation regimes such as the Australia Group, the Missile Technology Control Regime, the Nuclear Suppliers Group, and the Wassenaar Agreement. International regimes typically do not have an institutional organization, but are directly implemented by the member states. Conversely, international organizations like the North Atlantic Treaty Organization (NATO), the United Nations, and the European Union have independent organizational and administrative capabilities.

Characteristics of the "new" actors. As with the security threats identified above, neither NGOs nor private military companies or international organizations are in fact "new" actors. Nevertheless, it can be argued that all three types of actors have not only proliferated disproportionally over the past two decades, they have also significantly expanded their contribution to the making and implementation of security policies. NGOs, for instance, have become key actors in the provision of human security in the post–Cold War interventions in the former Yugoslavia, Somalia, and Iraq. Private military companies increasingly offer military support services for national armed forces as well as in international peacekeeping since the mid-1990s. International organizations, such as NATO and the European Union, have extended their functional and geographical scope since the fall of the Iron Curtain to include new members in Central and Eastern Europe and address a new range of security threats.

What makes NGOs, private military companies, and international regimes and organizations "new" actors in contemporary security is that they are challenging the "monopoly" of the nation-state in the legitimate provision of security that had developed over the past centuries and appears to have reached its prime during the Cold War. Today it is widely accepted that NGOs and international organizations play important roles in global security. Moreover, some of these actors lay claim to a higher legitimacy than states because they are not operating in the interest of a single nation. Most crucially, NGOs, private security companies, and international organizations appear to be more suited to address contemporary security threats because they can operate across state boundaries by building on national chapters and multilateral cooperation. Similarly, many governments have been forced to recognize that a system based on national sovereignty can be rather ineffective when it comes to fight transnational proliferation, crime, terrorism, or HIV/AIDS. Since the new security threats predominantly target individuals and not states, governments find that substate actors such as NGOs and private military companies can help provide security at this level. Moreover, because threats such as terrorism and the proliferation of small arms are operating transnationally, many nation-states accept that multilateral cooperation through international regimes or organizations has become more important.

The changing nature of security threats and actors is not only transforming the making and implementation of security policies, it also has serious implications for the theoretical analysis of security. In particular, these two interlinked developments suggest that the study of security needs to be broadened beyond the state as the primary unit of analysis—both in terms of its object and subject. The following section examines the widening and deepening of the concept of security and the emergence of security governance as a framework for the analysis of contemporary international relations.

Implications for International Relations Theory

Having its origins as a separate field of study in the last century, theorizing in international relations and security studies has crucially been influenced by the experience of the two world wars and the superpower confrontation that followed it. As a consequence, many theoretical approaches to security studies have tended to focus on the threat of nuclear war and the role of states and their alliances in maintaining international security. Since the end of the Cold War, interstate war appears to have been replaced by a multitude of new transnational security threats. Moreover, as the preceding sections have suggested, the making and implementation of security policies is becoming increasingly fragmented among a multiplicity of actors, including states, international organizations, NGOs, and private military companies. International relations theory has reflected these transformations through three developments in particular: the broadening of the notion of security, the emergence of the concept of security governance, and the analysis of transnational networks. This section examines each of these new theoretical developments in turn.

Redefinition of security. Already in the 1980s, some authors pointed out the need to reexamine the meaning of security.[13] However, in particular since the end of the Cold War the concept of security has become increasingly contested in international relations theory.[14] At the heart of this debate have been attempts to deepen and widen the concept of security from the level of the state to societies and individuals, and from military to nonmilitary issues.

This challenge to the state-centric notion of security that had dominated the discipline builds upon the argument that the end of the superpower confrontation has significantly reduced the likelihood of interstate war, whereas the threat from civil war, transnational crime, terrorism, and infectious diseases appears to have increased. As has been outlined in the preceding sections, annually many more casualties are incurred by subnational and transnational threats than from major power conflicts. In 1999, for instance, about 32,000 individuals were killed in interstate wars. However, more than 900 people were killed through terrorist attacks, up to 39,000 were killed in civil conflicts, and no less than 2.8 million were killed by AIDS.[15] The changing balance becomes even more striking in the data provided by the Stockholm International Peace Research Institute (SIPRI) which records on average 30 major conflicts per year between 1990 and 2000, yet SIPRI observed only 8 interstate wars during the entire ten-year period.[16]

Academics remain divided over the utility of a more inclusive notion of security.[17] Stephen Walt, for instance, has argued that broadening of the concept of security will "destroy its intellectual coherence and make it more difficult to devise solutions to any of these important problems."[18] And Ole Wæver has warned that the "securitization" of an issue, that is, it being identified as a national or international security issue, "tends to lead to specific ways of addressing it: threat, defense, and often state-centred solutions."[19] Nevertheless, a broader understanding of security has by now come to be widely accepted not only in international relations theory, but also among policy makers. The field of international relations today includes an ever-increasing number of studies on environmental security, human security, and HIV/AIDS as a security issue.[20] These studies argue that examining new security threats need not detract from the analysis of interstate war, but rather complements it. In fact, understanding the security effects of environmental degradation, underdevelopment, and diseases can help explain and resolve intrastate and interstate conflicts.

Moreover, by adopting a broad definition of security, international relations theory responds to important changes in the security policy-making process. Politicians, the military, and the general public are increasingly recognizing that crime, terrorism, environmental degradation, and infectious diseases are endangering not only individual, but also national security. This transformation is widely reflected in the national security estimates in the United States and other countries. Moreover, international organizations, such as NATO and the Conference for Security and Cooperation in Europe for instance, have expanded the scope of their security functions to include the fight against terrorism, international peacekeeping, refugee resettlement, and the promotion of civil society among others. Even the European Union that was conceived of as an economic organization is defining a growing array of its concerns in terms of security, including immigration and development aid.[21]

From government to security governance.   At the same time as governments and international organizations have extended their security concerns, however, limited resources, lack of expertise in nontraditional areas of security, and divergent interests among the United States and European governments have facilitated the fragmentation of security policy-making. As the following chapters will illustrate, in addition to national governments and international organizations, a variety of private actors ranging from charities to private security companies have emerged in local, regional, and global security dealing with issues such as humanitarian aid, human rights monitoring, refugees, and military protection.[22]

While in the area of security the relations between diverse groups of actors have traditionally been conceived in terms of alliances, the fragmented but overlapping networks which structure the collaboration among the growing range of state and non-state security actors are more adequately described by the concept of governance. Contrary to "government" which refers to a system of centralized political control within the state, "governance" denotes a fragmented mode of policy making that includes state and non-state actors at the subnational, national, and international levels.[23] Gordenker and Weiss thus define global governance as "efforts to bring more orderly and reliable responses to social and political issues that go beyond capacities of states to address individually. Like the NGO universe, global governance implies an absence of central authority, and the need for collaboration or cooperation among governments and others who seek to encourage common practices and goals in addressing global issues."[24]

The characteristics of governance arrangements vary widely. Most are concentrated around sets of states that share specific geographic, economic, and cultural similarities. However, even within these sets, governance is fragmented among governmental and nongovernmental actors at the national and international levels. While states continue to play a central role in global governance, international organizations, NGOs, and multinational corporations increasingly participate in the formulation, implementation, and monitoring of international policies, rules, and regulations.[25] Moreover, in the absence of a central authority in the international system and shifting balances of power, the relationships between governmental and nongovernmental actors at the national and international level are frequently complex and horizontal.[26]

Several factors that involve the emergence of new threats and new actors have been identified as causes for a shift from government to governance in security. The first factor has been budgetary pressures that have encouraged the outsourcing and privatization of state security functions in a bid for improved efficiency.[27] The second factor is a growing awareness of global problems and new security threats, such as transnational crime, terrorism, and migration, which can only be resolved through international cooperation.[28] The third factor is globalization, specifically increased transnational contact, which appears to be creating or exacerbating many of these problems.[29]

Specifically, the shift from government to governance in security can be observed in the fragmentation of political authority among state and non-state actors in seven key dimensions: geography, function, distribution of resources, interests, norms, decision making, and policy implementation.[30] With the help of these seven dimensions a framework for the analysis of policy-making arrangements can be established that distinguishes between "government" and "governance" as ideal types. This theoretical framework helps to conceptualize the emergence of security governance since end of the Cold War.

The first dimension suggests that government and governance can be distinguished in terms of the geographical scope of policy-making arrangements. Government can thus be defined as centralized modes of governing based on the state as the key unit, whereas governance is characterized by the fragmentation of political authority among regional, global, and transnational private entities. In security, geographical fragmentation has particularly involved the delegation of security functions from the state to the regional level, such as NATO and the European Union, to the global level, such as the United Nations, and to private actors, such as NGOs and private security companies.[31]

The second dimension proposes that policy-making arrangements can vary between functional centralization and differentiation. A shift to security governance is thus indicated by the issue-specific division of labor in recent international peacekeeping missions such as in the former Yugoslavia where the United

Nations or NATO provided military security, while NGOs dealt with humanitarian aid, and private security companies offered logistical support.[32]

The third dimension implies that the distribution of resources can also be understood in terms of centralization and fragmentation. In centralized arrangements all or most resources that are required for the making and implementation of policies are ideal-typically held or channeled by the government. Conversely, in fragmented governance arrangements, resources are dispersed among a range of public and private actors who have to coordinate their efforts in order to resolve common problems. In global security, it can be argued, this dispersion of capabilities has been fostered by the broadening of the notion of security to include new issues such as refugees and the environment where non-state actors have accumulated considerable experience as well as by the increasing cost of a more comprehensive security policy.

The fourth dimension suggests in addition a distinction between centralized and differentiated interests. It contends that the underlying premise of central government is that individual preferences can and should be subordinated to the common interests, whereas the notion of governance implies an acceptance of the heterogeneous and sometimes conflicting nature of interests and seeks to ensure that each actor can pursue them as uninhibited as possible. The emergence of security governance can thus be identified in the weakening of the transatlantic alliance and a shift toward "coalitions of the willing" after the end of the Cold War. Both developments are a response to the more localized and long-term consequences of the new security threats that, in spite of their transnational repercussions, allow governments to resist direct involvement unless they believe their immediate security interests are concerned. In addition, the increasing number of non-state actors introduces new interests into the security policy-making process such as the religious or ethical imperatives of NGOs.

In addition, the fifth dimension identifies diverging norms underlying government and governance, either promoting a strong state or prioritizing the self-determination of public and private actors. Three norms have traditionally supported the central authority of the state vis-à-vis national and international actors: sovereignty, command and control, and the ideal of redistribution. The opposing principle of differentiation is represented in the increasing limitation of national sovereignty, self-government, and marketization. In security the weakening of the norm of national sovereignty could be particularly observed in the intervention in Kosovo to counter Serb "ethnic cleansing" as well as more recently in the war against Iraq. In both interventions, self-government and the commercialization of security have been growing features as illustrated by the involvement of NGOs in both countries and an estimated 15,000 private military personnel in Iraq.[33]

Finally, the difference between government and governance also applies to policy decision making and implementation. Decision-making processes that are centralized within governments are typically hierarchical, democratic, and consensual. Governance, on the contrary, is defined by horizontal relations among state and non-state actors, negotiation, and structural inequality. Similarly, policy implementation in government is centralized, authoritative, and, if necessary, coercive, while governance involves decentralized implementation, self-enforced policies, and voluntary compliance. In global security, the rise of governance is thus illustrated by the proliferation of non-state actors engaged in major international interventions and the emergence of civil–military cooperation (CIMIC) as a concept and policy-making arrangement.[34]

Governance and networks. Characteristic of the shift from government to governance is the development of new networked forms of coordination among state and non-state actors. Networks are defined as sets of actors who share an interest in a specific issue area and are linked to each other through stable formal or informal relations.[35] They can include domestic, transnational, and international linkages.[36] Moreover, networks allow for a mixture of relations ranging from hierarchical to horizontal, and from government to market.[37] The basis of network relations is typically the exchange of information, money, political support, or commitments for cooperative behavior among the involved actors.

Networks are particularly suited for political coordination in global and security governance for several reasons. First, due to the inclusion and frequently dominance of informal relations, networks are flexible and can adapt comparatively quickly and easily to new actors or demands. While formal institutional linkages require considerable time and resources in order to be established in national law or international regimes, informal relations can be set up instantaneously among actors who have an interest in an exchange or collaboration on a particular issue. New actors can enter into these relations on the basis of their capabilities and open channels of communication. New issues or problems can be responded to by forming new networks among affected actors or by transforming existing networks in order to enlarge their scope or capabilities.

In security, new networks have thus emerged and old networks have been adapted in response to the end of the Cold War. A prime example of changing networks is the transatlantic security community. In particular, NATO has transformed from a collective defense to a collective security organization, expanded its functions from military defense to peacekeeping and peacemaking, and incorporated new members in Central and Eastern Europe first through informal relations and later through formal enlargement. Moreover, the Atlantic Alliance has established informal civil–military relations with NGOs and other private actors during its interventions in Bosnia and Herzegovina, and Kosovo.[38] During each of these interventions new operation-specific networks have developed among state and non-state actors engaged in the region in order to coordinate their interests and functions such as the provision of military security, mine clearance, humanitarian aid, and reconstruction.

Second, by moving beyond traditional institutional relations among states or among state and non-state actors, networks can stretch across national boundaries and sovereignties. Networks thus can address transnational security threats such as terrorism, transnational crime, HIV/AIDS, and small arms proliferation more effectively. Often these networks involve formal cooperation in transnational organizations such as, Interpol or international regimes such as the Nuclear Suppliers Group. However, equally often they build on transnational private linkages most notably within charitable federations such as the International Red Cross and Red Crescent Societies, Médecins sans Frontières, CARE, Amnesty International, or Human Rights Watch, which have national chapters in different countries, or collective organizations such as InterAction.

Third, through decentralization and horizontal relationships networks promote subsidiarity, that is, the making and implementation of policies by those who are directly involved or affected. Networks thereby encourage the development of differentiated solutions for a complex world rather than the imposition of centrally directed, uniform policies. Moreover, networks foster the use of local knowledge and resources, which benefits the long-term advancement of affected communities. Finally, drawing on local groups, personnel and assets is frequently more cost-efficient than using centralized capabilities. In security governance, states and international organizations such as the United Nations, thus increasingly attempt to develop "civil society" in the form of local or regional groups that can help with security issues and reconstruction after conflicts. In addition, NGOs and private military companies employ to a large degree local personnel wherever they are operating.

However, networks do not develop only among state and non-state actors concerned with providing security. Transnational crime, terrorism, and the proliferation of small arms increasingly also use networks as operating system. These "dark networks"[39] benefit from the same characteristics that help states and non-state actors to coordinate their efforts to combat these threats: flexibility, transnational relations, local knowledge, and efficiency. Similar pressures thus facilitate similar structures among new threats and new actors in security governance.

Content of the Book

To examine the complex relationship between new threats and new actors in contemporary security this book is divided into four parts: civil war, transnational crime and terrorism, HIV/AIDS, and the proliferation of small arms. The first part specifically examines the contribution of non-state actors to international peacekeeping. In Chapter 2, "The New Conflict Managers: Peacebuilding NGOs and State Agendas," Loramy Gerstbauer provides a compelling analysis of the emerging role of NGOs in conflict and post-conflict environments. She suggests that many relief and development organizations have come to realize the impact of their presence and their provision of aid in conflicts. Consequently, they have decided to add peacebuilding to their mandates. However, Gerstbauer points out that NGO conflict management activities are not uncontroversial. Just as development NGOs are interdependent with the government agencies that fund them, the new NGO mandate is heavily influenced by state interests in post-conflict settings. This raises a number of dilemmas for NGOs ranging from the challenge of maintaining neutrality when working alongside or in cooperation with armed forces to balancing the influence and interests of donors and recipients.

In Chapter 3, "Humanitarians and Mercenaries: Partners in Security Governance?," Christopher Spearin picks up on this theme by analyzing the emerging partnership between peacebuilding NGOs and private security companies.

Particularly he raises the question whether the employment of private security by NGOs will lead to a new humanitarian order through which all those in need of assistance will receive aid promptly and effectively. Spearin argues that, although there are good reasons for this partnership, there are also a number of problems such as the image of the "mercenary" and the cost of private security. In the end a trade-off will have to be made.

The second part of the book turns to terrorism and transnational crime as key security threats for the new millennium and the contribution that private actors can make to address these threats. In Chapter 4, "Drug Trafficking, Terrorist Networks, and Ill-Fated Government Strategies," Michael Kenney offers a unique analysis of the similarities between terrorist networks and the transnational drug trade. As a consequence, Kenney explains, the existing "head hunting" approach to the war on terrorism threatens to repeat critical mistakes in the anti-drug initiatives of the 1990s. Specifically, Kenney argues that by focusing its military, law enforcement, and intelligence capabilities on a handful of organizations and individuals, the U.S. government runs the risk of weeding out the most notorious enterprises and providing opportunities for lesser known, more technologically sophisticated operations to materialize.

Chapter 5 "Targeting Money Laundering: Global Approach or Diffusion of Authority?" by Eleni Tsingou explains why combating money laundering is central to contemporary security, notably as a means of undermining terrorist and transnational criminal activities. Yet, Tsingou argues, in particular private financial institutions perceive a tension between the cost of dealing with money laundering and the benefits of containing financial crime. Fostering private corporate responsibility in the form of self-regulation and the implementation of public policies thus becomes a central concern in security.

The third part of the book analyses HIV/AIDS as a global security threat and the role of nongovernmental actors in addressing it. In Chapter 6, "HIV/AIDS: The International Security Dimensions," Stefan Elbe sets out convincingly why the global AIDS pandemic is no longer solely a health issue, but also contains human, national, and international security dimensions. Elbe contends that only by recognizing these security dimensions we can arrive at a more comprehensive understanding of the nature and extent of the contemporary AIDS pandemic and to develop suitable responses.

This analysis is complemented by Chapter 7, "NGOs as Security Actors in the Fight against HIV/AIDS?," by Carrie Sheehan that examines how HIV/AIDS is addressed. Sheehan observes that there is currently a proliferation of NGOs working in developing countries on the HIV/AIDS pandemic. However, Sheehan illustrates that while many states, think tanks, and international organizations today perceive HIV/AIDS as a national and international security issue, NGOs do not. The result is a disconnection between the actors addressing the HIV/AIDS pandemic at the policy level and the, frequently non-state, actors implementing HIV/AIDS programs.

The final part of the book discusses the role of non-state actors in the proliferation of small arms and light weapons as well as their contribution to the establishment of effective non-proliferation regimes. Chapter 8, "The Proliferation of

Small Arms and Light Weapons," by Mike Bourne turns to small arms and light weapons (SALW) proliferation as a security threat and explains how non-state actors, such as brokers, transporters, transnational criminal organizations, as well as criminalized state officials contribute to the global spread of SALW. Bourne specifically highlights the collaboration between non-state and state actors in the spread of SALW and their diversion from the legal sphere into illicit circulation.

In Chapter 9, "NGOs and the Shaping of the European Union Conventional Arms Regime," Holger Anders offers an insightful examination of how NGOs influenced the creation of the European Union regime on conventional arms. Anders argues that transnational networks of NGOs, researchers, and campaigners were able to shape public policies on small arms by consistently mobilizing and generating political and public support for their policy preferences, and by closely interacting with government officials across Europe. Thus, Anders demonstrates how non-state actors could facilitate and contribute to governmental policy coalitions, and insist on the inclusion of certain dynamic elements in the European regime.

The conclusion of this book seeks to summarize the findings presented in the preceding chapters and discusses the advantages and problems that have been identified with regard to the growing role of non-state actors in security and the collaboration between state and non-state agents.

In particular the conclusion raises the question whether the shift from government to governance is a suitable solution to the emergence of transnational security threats that cannot be addressed within the traditional system of nation-states. Moreover, the conclusion discusses whether the growing influence of private actors is a sign of the emergence of a global civil society or whether private actors are merely tools for state intervention.

Notes

1. Hans M. Kristensen, "Russian Nuclear Forces," http://projects.sipri.se/nuclear/russia.pdf, and "US Nuclear Forces," http://projects.sipri.se/nuclear/usa.pdf.
2. RAND-MIPT, "Terrorism Database," http://db.mipt.org/.
3. Instances include the use of mustard gas by Italy in World War I and Iraq against its Kurdish population between 1983 and 1988, the atom bomb by the United States in 1945, and various biological agents by Japan in World War II.
4. John Lewis Gaddis, *The Long Peace: Inquiries into the History of the Cold War* (Oxford: Oxford University Press). John Mearsheimer has even suggested that nuclear proliferation could enhance post–Cold War security. See John Mearsheimer, "Back to the Future: Instability in Europe After the Cold War," *International Security* 15, no. 4 (1990): 5–56.
5. Paul Harris, "Bush Plans New Nuclear Weapons," *Observer*, November 30, 2003.
6. United Nations Small Arms Programme, http://disarmament.un.org:8080/cab/salw.html.
7. Heidelberg Institute on International Conflict Research, *Conflict Barometer 2003*, 5, http://www.hiik.de/en/barometer2003/Conflict_Barometer_2003.pdf.
8. Ibid.
9. World Health Organization (WHO), "AIDS Epidemic Update 2003," http://www.who.int/hiv/pub/epidemiology/imagefile/en/.
10. RAND-MIPT, "Terrorism Database," http://db.mipt.org/.

11. UNAIDS, *AIDS Epidemic Update 2003* (Geneva: UNAIDS/WHO, 2003).

12. Peter W. Singer, "Corporate Warriors: The Rise and Ramifications of the Privatized Military Industry," *International Security* 26, no. 3 (2001): 186–220; Garry Cleaver, "Subcontracting Military Power: The Privatisation of Security in Contemporary Sub-Saharan Africa," *Crime Law and Social Change* 33, no. 1–2 (2000): 131–49.

13. Richard H. Ullman, "Redefining Security," *International Security* 8, no. 1 (1983): 129–53.

14. Stephen M. Walt, "The Renaissance of Security Studies," *International Studies Quarterly* 35, no. 2 (1991): 211–39; Emma Rothschild, "What is Security?," *Daedalus* 124, no. 3 (1995): 53–98; David A. Baldwin, "The Concept of Security," *Review of International Studies* 23, no. 1 (1997): 5–29.

15. UNAIDS, *Report on the Global HIV/AIDS Epidemic* (New York: UNAIDS, 2000), http://www.unaids.org/epidemic_update/report/glo_estim.pdf.

16. See SIPRI Yearbooks from 1991 to 2001 (Oxford: Oxford University Press).

17. Keith Krause and Michael C. Williams, eds. *Critical Security Studies: Concepts and Cases* (Minneapolis: University of Minnesota Press, 1997).

18. Walt, "The Renaissance of Security Studies," 213.

19. Ole Wæver, "Securitization and Desecuritization," in *On Security*, ed. Ronnie D. Lipschutz, 46–86 (New York: Columbia University Press, 1995), 65.

20. See for instance, Thomas Homer-Dixon, *Environment, Scarcity, and Violence* (Princeton, NJ: Princeton University Press, 2001); B.R. Allenby, "Environmental Security: Concept and Implementation," *International Political Science Review* 21, no. 1 (2000): 5–21; Roland Paris, "Human Security. Paradigm Shift or Hot Air?" *International Security* 26, no. 2 (2001): 87–102; Peter W. Singer, "AIDS and International Security," *International Security* 44, no. 1 (2002): 145–58.

21. Ian Manners, *European [Security] Union: From Existential Threat to Ontological Security*, Working Paper No. 5 (Copenhagen: COPRI, 2002), http://www.copri.dk/publications/workingpapers.htm.

22. See for instance, OXFAM, *Oxfam International Annual Report 2002* (Oxford: Oxfam, 2002); ICRC (International Committee of the Red Cross), *Annual Report 2002* (Geneva: ICRC, 2002); International Rescue Committee, *International Rescue Committee Annual Report 2002–2003* (New York: International Rescue Committee, 2002); MRPI (Military Professional Resources Inc.), *Overview*, http://www.mpri.com/channels/int_overview.html.

23. Ernst-Otto Czempiel, "Governance and Democratization," in *Governance without Government: Order and Change in World Politics*, ed. James N. Rosenau and Ernst-Otto Czempiel, 250–71 (Cambridge: Cambridge University Press, 1992), 250; Leon Gordenker and Thomas G. Weiss, "Pluralizing Global Governance: Analytical Approaches and Dimensions," in *NGOs, the UN, and Global Governance*, ed. Leon Gordenker and Thomas G. Weiss, 17–47 (London: Lynne Rienner, 1996), 17.

24. Gordenker and Weiss, "Pluralizing global governance," 17. For similar definitions see Lawrence S. Finkelstein, "What Is Global Governance?" *Global Governance* 1, no. 3 (1995): 367–72, 368; Commission on Global Governance, *Our Global Neighbourhood: The Report of the Commission on Global Governance* (Oxford: Oxford University Press, 1995), 2–3; Oran Young, *International Governance: Protecting the Environment in a Stateless Society* (Ithaca, NY: Cornell University Press, 1994), 53.

25. James N. Rosenau, "Change, Complexity, and Governance in Globalizing Space," in *Debating Governance. Authority, Steering and Democracy*, ed. Jon Pierre, 167–200 (Oxford: Oxford University Press, 2000), 172–73; Commission on Global Governance, 2–3; Gearóid Ó Tuathail, Andrew Herod, and Susan M. Roberts, "Negotiating Unruly

Problematics," in *An Unruly World? Globalization, Governance and Geography*, ed. Andrew Herod, Gearóid Ó Tuathail, and Susan M. Roberts, 1–24 (London: Routledge, 1998), 14.

26. Rosenau, "Change, Complexity, and Governance," 189; Finkelstein, "What is global governance?," 367; Gordenker and Weiss, "Pluralizing Global Governance," 17.

27. Giandomenico Majone, "From the Positive to the Regulatory State: Causes and Consequences of Changes in the Mode of Governance," *Journal of Public Policy* 17, no. 2 (1997): 139–68, 142.

28. James N. Rosenau, "Governance, Order and Change in World Politics," in *Governance without Government: Order and Change in World Politics*, ed. James N. Rosenau and Ernst-Otto Czempiel, 1–29 (Cambridge: Cambridge University Press, 1992), 3; Tuathail et al., "Negotiating Unruly Problematics," 12.

29. Gordenker and Weiss, 20; Bernard Zangl and Michael Zürn, "The Effects of Denationalisation on Security in the OECD World," *Global Society* 13, no. 2 (1999): 139–61, 140.

30. Elke Krahmann, "National, Regional and Global Governance: One Phenomenon or Many?" *Global Governance* 9, no. 3 (2003): 323–46.

31. Damian Lilly, *The Privatization of Security and Peacebuilding* (London: International Alert, 2000); Rosenau, "Change, Complexity, and Governance," 169–200; Alexander Cooley and James Ron, "The NGO Scramble: Organizational Insecurity and the Political Economy of Transnational Action," *International Security* 27, no. 1 (2001): 5–39; Robert Mandel, *Armies Without States: The Privatization of Security* (Boulder, CO: Lynne Rienner, 2002).

32. Larry Minear, Ted van Baarda, and Marc Sommers, *NATO and Humanitarian Action in the Kosovo Crisis*, Occasional Papers (Providence, RI: The Thomas J. Watson Jr. Institute for International Studies, 2000).

33. Peter W. Singer, "Warriors for Hire in Iraq," *Brookings Institution*, April 15, 2004, http://www.brook.edu/views/articles/fellows/singer20040415.htm; *New York Times*, "Families Find Iraq Earnings Carry a Price," April 15, 2004.

34. On Civil Military Cooperation in Kosovo see http://www.nato.int/sfor/cimic/cimic.htm; see also NATO, *NATO Civil-Military Cooperation (CIMIC) Doctrine*, AJP-09, 2000, http://63.104.169.22/PDF/AJP-09.pdf.

35. M.M. Atkinson and W.D. Coleman, "Policy Networks, Policy Communities and the Problems of Governance," *Governance* 5, no. 2 (1992): 154–80.

36. Margaret Keck and Kathryn Sikkink, *Activists beyond Borders: Transnational Advocacy Networks in World Politics* (Ithaca, NY: Cornell University Press, 1998); Elke Krahmann, *Multilevel Networks in European Foreign Policy* (Aldershot: Ashgate, 2003).

37. Paul Kenis and Volker Scheider, "Policy Networks and Policy Analysis: Scrutinizing a New Analytical Toolbox", in *Policy Networks. Empirical Evidence and Theoretical Considerations*, eds. Bernd Marin and Renate Mayntz, 25–62 (Frankfurt/Main: Campus, 1991), 42.

38. "Cimic Reconstruction," *NATO Review* 49, no. 1 (2001): 21. http://www.nato.int/docu/review/2001/0101–06.htm.

39. Jörg Raab and H. Binton Milward, "Dark Networks as Problems," *Journal of Public Administration Research and Theory* 13, no. 4 (2003): 413–39.

Part II

Civil War

Chapter 2

The New Conflict Managers: Peacebuilding NGOs and State Agendas

Loramy Conradi Gerstbauer

The number of nongovernmental organizations (NGOs) of all types, including international, domestic, development, human rights, has dramatically increased in the last decades. Of this overall trend, Lester Salamon exults: "a veritable associational revolution now seems underway at the global level that may constitute as significant a social and political development of the latter twentieth century as the rise of the nation state was of the nineteenth century."[1] As this chapter will explore below, there are multiple explanations for this trend. Insofar as this growth of NGOs may be pegged to changes in the behavior of nation-states, one might argue that NGOs have taken on functions that states have failed at or are ill-suited to manage. Alternatively, it can be argued that states are purposefully, particularly through financing, encouraging NGOs to take on certain responsibilities when it is in the interest of those states not to become directly involved.

One of the areas where NGO work has blossomed is in peacebuilding. Though most of the literature in conflict resolution has focused on efforts of state actors or international governmental organizations, such as the UN, NGOs are increasingly gaining attention for work in conflict amelioration. It has been argued that the kinds of security threats and conflicts faced today are ones that NGOs are particularly well suited to address. Moreover, the prevalence of civil war and complex humanitarian emergencies as well as the increasing attention on poverty and disease as security issues have led many relief and development NGOs to the realization that their traditional relief and development mandates would be jeopardized if they failed to address the violent conflict and potential violent conflict in their environs. Many relief and development organizations have come to realize the impact of their presence and their provision of aid in conflicts, and they have decided to be purposeful about that impact by adding peacebuilding to their mandates.

For the most part, the NGO and peacebuilding literature has praised the advent of NGOs in peacebuilding. This chapter provides a more critical analysis of NGO peacebuilding, particularly questioning the relationship between NGOs engaged in peacebuilding and nation-states. Are NGOs better suited than states to take on these peacebuilding tasks, as some of the literature claims? To what extent are NGO agendas influenced by states? The following draws from the literature on relief and development NGOs and concerns that this literature raises about NGO interactions with state actors in relief and development work to address the dilemmas that arise for humanitarian NGOs as they take on peacebuilding mandates. This is useful for understanding NGOs and their operations, NGOs in relation to the states, and how both are influenced by changing dynamics in conflict and security issues.

Although there continues to be debate about what constitutes an NGO, definitional concerns can be quickly disposed of.[2] By NGOs this chapter refers to nonprofit, private organizations that work for public purposes. Its focus is on western NGOs working in humanitarian relief and development operations internationally and the western donor governments that fund them.

This chapter begins with the evolving literature on humanitarian NGOs and their relationships to donor governments and then moves to the new mandate of peacebuilding, how it developed, and the challenges it raises for the state and NGO relationship.

NGOs and Development Aid

Explanations for the proliferation of NGOs. Why have the numbers of NGOs grown so dramatically, and particularly for this chapter, the number of humanitarian or development NGOs? Explanations vary, but one dominant view is that increasing democratization and growth of civil society have led to an increase in the number of civil society organizations such as NGOs. Kriesberg points to four trends that provide a context for the expanding NGO population: growing democratization, proliferating transnational organizations, increasing global integration, and converging and diffusing values such as human rights and consumerism.[3] With regard to the first two trends, the growth of participatory governmental institutions in both domestic and international contexts is both a consequence and cause of NGO growth domestically and internationally. NGOs lobby and advocate for democratic reforms, and increasing freedom allows for the formation of NGOs that can contribute to government accountability. Integration and converging and diffusing values are attributed to changes in technology as well as to the international interaction fostered by the first two trends.[4]

A second explanation for growth in the number of NGOs, not incompatible with the first, is that our rapidly globalizing world and the turbulent changes it evokes renders the state inadequate and incapable to deal with these challenges. The lack of the state has led to the functional necessity of NGOs to fulfill certain tasks. Rosenau has dubbed this as an era of turbulent change where issues are so complex, uncertain, and rapidly moving that states can not effectively deal with them. The nature of authority and power in the international system is being reshaped by transnational issues such as drugs, massive migration and refugee flows, the global information network, warfare, human rights, global environmental degradation, HIV/AIDS, and economic interdependence. These are not all new issues, but their transnational nature is, and the negative effects of these issues have increased with modernization and globalization.[5] These transnational threats to national and international security reflect a level of functional interdependence that has progressed farther than our global political institutions can handle. In other words, the political and legal structure of a nation-state system is incongruent with the interdependence and interaction occurring among individuals, states, and international and transnational actors globally.[6]

By this account, the growth of NGOs comes in part from the failure and inability of governmental entities to address needs in a globalizing world. Thus, NGOs are citizen forums designed for mutual support in provision of goods and services as well as a lobbying force to which governments, intergovernmental organizations, and corporations must be held accountable. This explains why the last few decades have seen a particular growth of NGOs focused on human rights issues, women's issues, development, and the environment.[7] On the other hand, while NGOs may fill up spaces where governments fail or which governments ignore, this does not preclude the idea that states may actually encourage NGO growth and cooperate with NGO activity.

The relationship between NGOs and governmental bodies is complex. NGOs work against, with, and for states and intergovernmental organizations.[8] As Smillie states, NGOs originated as "supplements, complements, alternatives, critics, and watchdogs to governments."[9] Much of the international relations literature on NGOs examines NGOs as advocacy and issue-framing organizations that can influence states.[10] Paul Ghils argues that international NGOs act in three principal ways: as pressure groups or "shapers of opinion," for example, by pressuring governments; as actors in competition with and critical of states and intergovernmental organizations; and as autonomous actors, for example, by running their own aid operations.[11] This chapter argues that these roles can be subsumed under two categories: advocates, who pressure and critique states, and service providers, who work for, or complementary, to the state. Increasingly it is recognized that these service providers are not necessarily "autonomous" as Ghils describes them, but rather can operate as agents of the state. Thus, a third and less popular explanation for NGO growth is that the number of NGOs has increased because state actors find them to be useful agents of government agendas and policies and thus promote, support, and fund them.

All three of these explanations for the increase in NGOs—increasing democracy, failure of the state to meet needs, and active promotion by states—have validity, though this chapter will suggest that in the world of development NGOs which are primarily service providers, the third explanation has much merit. In fact, it argues that engagement in peacebuilding will likely swing relief and development NGOs more heavily to the advocacy side and thus could alter the relations they have with state agencies.

Development NGOs as agents of the state. Edwards and Hulme throw doubt on the assumption that NGOs are truly autonomous actors, operating independently of state agendas. In their edited volume focusing on NGOs working in international development, Edwards and Hulme caution against glorification of the NGO's "magic bullet" power in a time when NGOs are increasingly relied on by governments and intergovernmental organizations to deliver services from the north to the south.[12] During the 1980s, the total funds transferred by and through "northern" NGOs increased at twice the rate for international aid as a whole.[13] In the relief and development field, the "New Policy Agenda" that developed in the 1980s dictated that NGOs are the preferred channels for service provision in substitution for the state. NGOs are viewed as vehicles of democratization and civil society building in the developing nations, while giving aid dollars directly to the beneficiary state creates a bloated state bureaucracy that works against the New Policy Agenda's goal of reduction of the state, market reforms, and privatization. Thus, northern governments increasingly seek to direct their foreign aid dollars through nongovernmental channels.[14] Partly for this reason, service-providing NGOs have experienced a growth spurt, and some worry that this growth may undermine the very strengths that the NGOs offer. Rather than independent actors, some NGOs are in danger of becoming delivery mechanisms for governments.[15]

This relationship between humanitarian NGOs and governments in developed countries did not arrive on the scene in the 1990s but has evolved over a long period. NGOs have historically been used as an extension of nation-state interests abroad. They can act as complements to or surrogates for their home governments, for example, by providing aid to allies after World War II or during the fight against Communism. It is not coincidental that many relief and development NGOs originated in the immediate aftermath of World War II when the United States sought to rebuild Asia and Europe. In the 1960s, the U.S. government redirected its aid efforts to meet basic human needs of the poor and the U.S. Agency for international Development (USAID) was created; government funds to NGOs increased as did the strings attached to the aid, such as excluding work with the South African liberation movements or programming in Cuba. Special funds were developed for special need areas or with special thematic emphases such as the Philippines after Marcos, gender or environmental programming, and peacebuilding. The development of these special funds, even if conceived in collaboration with NGOs, meant that governments were dictating more and more where and how NGOs would carry out their work.[16]

Brian Smith confirms that the literature on NGOs does not address the deep paradoxes that exist in the cooperation between governments and NGOs, failing to note variations in style and political orientation within the NGO world and failing to acknowledge that NGOs have any political or ideological agendas.[17] He argues that it is primarily because NGOs are viewed as a political that they have been politically useful.[18] Thus, one might argue that rather than NGOs developing as a natural outcome of state or market failures, they developed as a product of deliberate state policies.[19] Governments benefit from the relationship because working with NGOs promotes the New Policy Agenda, but also for many unstated reasons as well. Some of these might include government spending imperatives such as agricultural surplus, a desire to legitimate aid giving to the public, and provision of alternative channels or access to politically risky areas.[20] While governmental relief dollars have been directed through NGOs to allies, NGOs have been sources of intelligence and informal diplomats for government agencies. For example, the role of the large relief and development organization CARE as a component of U.S. policy against President Nasser in connection with the Suez crisis in 1956 is well documented, as is the pro-government role of U.S. NGOs in Vietnam and Korea during those wars.[21]

Despite the collaboration of NGOs and governments, until recently the aura of autonomy persisted around humanitarian NGOs. The questioning of this autonomy has arisen largely as a critique of the effectiveness of NGO aid, and as a challenge to the NGOs' supposedly superior effectiveness in comparison with government aid programs. After all, the public argument sustaining the NGO channel of aid has been the supposed comparative advantage of NGO aid providers over the state. Since the early 1980s, if not earlier, it has been argued by both NGOs and their donor governments that NGOs are the epitome of what governments are not. They are not bureaucratic, not hierarchical, and not "stultifying of local initiative."[22] NGOs are supposedly more cost-effective, are better able to reach the poor and needy at the grassroots, and are more flexible and responsive. After a decade of NGO work and post–Cold War, freedoms had still not brought relief to the developing world, the NGOs' "shine" began to wear off and demands for empirical proof of the comparative advantages arose. It was found that exaggerated claims ignored the extent to which many NGOs were interdependent with governments and not autonomous, that many NGO projects had not been superior to state projects, and that indeed the New Policy Agenda and its bypassing of Third World states had in fact weakened those states further. In development circles, there has been a new call to "bring the state back in." It is now believed that channeling funding through NGOs has not been the great harbinger of civil society and democracy, but rather has at times served to weaken state institutions in the developing world.

The unsubstantiated claims about NGO relief and development work that are now being questioned offer lessons for examining current claims about NGO peacebuilding work. Claims surrounding NGO peacebuilding are not well proven, probably exaggerated, and if caution is not taken, could tarnish NGO reputations.

NGOs and Peacebuilding: Agents and Advocates

NGOs as the new conflict managers. Former UN Secretary General Boutros Boutros Ghali, after outlining the new challenges and strategies for UN responses to conflict in his 1992 *Agenda for Peace*, also prescribed increased cooperation between NGOs and the United Nations in peacebuilding activities. In a speech to NGOs in 1994, Boutros Boutros Ghali stated three areas in which NGOs can play a key role in building peace: in preventative diplomacy, because NGOs are familiar with the situation on the ground and are well placed to alert governments to nascent crises and emerging conflict; in peacemaking, where NGOs can give humanitarian and social aid under perilous and difficult conditions; and in post-conflict peacebuilding, where NGOs can help fragile governments and destitute populations to find the confidence and the resources to make peace last.[23]

Two alterations to Boutros Ghali's description seem appropriate. First, Boutros Ghali limited his use of the term "peacebuilding" to the post-conflict period, defining it as an "action to identify and support structures which will tend to strengthen and solidify peace in order to avoid a relapse into conflict."[24] The United Nations still views peacebuilding as largely a post-conflict activity designed to foster changes that will sustain peace in the long term.[25] Unlike Boutros Ghali, some theorists do not limit peacebuilding to post-conflict periods, that is, after peace agreements or cease-fires.[26] Lederach defines peacebuilding:

> as a comprehensive concept that encompasses, generates, and sustains the full array of processes, approaches, and stages needed to transform conflict toward more sustainable, peaceful relationships. The term thus involves a wide range of activities and functions that both precede and follow formal peace accords. Metaphorically, peace is seen not merely as a stage in time or a condition. It is a dynamic social construct.[27]

This more inclusive definition is adopted here since NGOs also do not limit themselves to post-conflict activities, though that may indeed represent the majority of their work.

The second problem with Boutros Boutros Ghali's description is that he failed to acknowledge that many NGOs and other unofficial actors have made specific contributions in mediation and conflict resolution. He saw the NGO role as chiefly one of humanitarian and social aid rather than specific engagement in the issues of conflict. He forecasted NGO contributions in preventative diplomacy before conflicts, humanitarian aid during conflicts, and reconstruction aid after conflicts.[28] This is not surprising given that most of the literature in conflict resolution has focused on third party intervention efforts by traditional, state actors or international state-based organizations like the United Nations while insufficient attention has been given to the role of "track-two diplomacy" by nontraditional third party intermediaries.[29]

There is a newer, though small, literature that does fo0cus on these track-two unofficial efforts, recognizing that NGOs directly involve themselves in processes of conflict resolution and peacebuilding including everything from mediation between disputants to establishment of peace training centers and efforts to build grassroots civil society and trust. This literature is expectant of the increased recognition and utilization of NGOs in today's conflict zones. Some of the literature focuses on relief and development NGOs;[30] some examines multiple types of NGOs, such as refugee or human rights, or does not distinguish between types of NGOs in the analysis.[31] Although the literature is still small, acclaim for the unofficial actor in peacebuilding, and in particular the NGO, has increased. Mawlawi exemplifies this general recognition of an evolving role for NGO actors:

> New governments and governmental institutions should recognize NGOs as effective and significant actors, and facilitate their input into systems of conflict prevention, early warning, mediation, and peace-building. The challenges and opportunities faced by the international community today should ensure that the numbers and significance of NGOs will continue to grow in the years ahead.[32]

Explanations for why there is this increased attention can draw from the vast literature on the proliferation of NGOs and debates about their importance in international affairs.[33] Most of the literature on peacebuilding NGOs follows the line of reasoning connected to the functionalist argument in which NGOs automatically develop to fill the gaps that cannot be met by state actors in our turbulent world. Much like the development literature, which expounds the comparative virtues of aid via NGOs, a literature has arisen that portends the coming age of NGO peacebuilders as having a comparative advantage over state actors in today's conflicts. In the quote above, Mawlawi points to two factors indicative of this type of explanation: he argues that NGOs possess qualities of an effective peaceworker and that the types of challenges and conflicts faced today are ones in which NGOs can be particularly useful.

Thus, one claim is that the nature of NGOs lends them qualities useful for peacebuilding work. Mawlawi provides the following breakdown of these attributes.[34] First, NGOs have an unofficial status. The NGO's lack of governmental affiliation allows it to engage in informal diplomacy that is nonthreatening to the disputing parties. There is less at stake in an NGO intervention than there is for official negotiations. Also, without official constraints and responsibilities, the NGO has more freedom than a governmental actor to suggest the unconventional and raise hypothetical questions that might bring breakthroughs in talks. Second, the role of NGOs in peacebuilding is facilitated by their impartiality. Impartiality is useful for helping disputants to reconceptualize the enemy and for eliminating misperceptions and misunderstandings so that objective issues can be addressed.[35] Impartiality lends trustworthiness to the NGO, allowing for discussion of core psychocultural and perceptual issues with the parties in dispute. This trustworthiness is also fostered by the NGO's long-term capability and commitment. Unlike official actors, many NGOs work in a given context for a long period prior to and after a conflict has come and gone. They have time to develop close relationships with disputants and familiarity with the issues at stake. This closeness is required to deal with the psychological issues that are part of conciliation. Governmental actors have high turnover rates and are less likely to be able to immerse themselves into a context with the energy required for long-term peacebuilding.[36] Finally, NGOs tend to have grassroots presence and connections. An NGO often enters a peacebuilding role after involvement in humanitarian work or development projects in the same situation. This local entrée uniquely positions NGOs to provide early warning and preventive actions to assess and abate conflict in its early stages. It also gives them in-depth site knowledge and contacts which can be used in the conflict resolution process at any stage of conflict.[37] Most NGOs work with local partnering organizations on the ground, giving them a high organizational capacity to implement programs.[38]

In addition to these attributes of NGOs which make them good peacebuilders, Mawlawi points to a second factor that has led to the need for NGO peacebuilding: conflict in today's world is particularly conducive to NGO intervention. As opposed to the great power wars of the past, nearly all modern conflicts are civil wars, fought within the boundaries of sovereign nations. Of 111 armed conflicts from 1989 to 2000, only 7 were interstate conflicts.[39] This reality has caused a necessary examination of new issues arising from these types of conflicts. Traditional concerns of the international system, including international anarchy, balance of power, nuclear deterrence, and arms races between superpowers, have for the most part been replaced by concerns over failed states, domestic resource division and governance, identity issues like ethnic nationalism and religious militancy, and humanitarian issues arising from war zones.[40] Today's internal and regional conflicts often involve deliberate and systematic attacks on civilians, generating tremendous numbers of refugees and internally displaced persons and spreading the conflict to neighboring countries. Thus, modern warfare raises environmental, refugee, humanitarian, and peacekeeping concerns.[41] NGOs, many would agree, are well positioned to address these concerns. The end of the Cold War also made it harder for states to define such interventions in terms of their national interest or in defense of ideology. The sticky issues of defining territorial sovereignty and governing powers in these conflicted states are ones that global powers have been shy to address, often hiding behind the uncertain legitimacy and legality of intervening in internal affairs of sovereign states. The reluctance of nation-states to intervene in many contemporary conflicts has opened a gap for NGOs to fill.

An explanation for why NGOs have entered peacebuilding work can follow this kind of functionalist logic that environmental factors have necessitated NGO work in peacebuilding. However, just as the growth in the numbers of development NGOs has been revealed as complex, this deterministic explanation for NGO adoption of peacebuilding mandates must also be reviewed in the light of at least two alternative or additional explanations. One is that for relief and development NGOs, which are the focus here, a peacebuilding mandate grew out of organizational change stemming from both organizational leadership committed to the values of peacebuilding and recognition by the organizations that much of their development work was useless unless they addressed issues of peacebuilding. In other words, relief and development NGOs chose to adopt peacebuilding mandates because they saw it as a natural outflow of the values that they represent in their relief work and in order to accomplish that primary task better. Another alternative explanation is that state actors have actively promoted NGOs as peacebuilders, not necessarily because they feel themselves incapable of fulfilling this function, but because it is less complicated or easier to have NGOs act as their peacebuilding agents and because they see support of NGO peacebuilding as a natural outgrowth of support of NGO development work. Government promotion and funding of peacebuilding programming has contributed to the adoption by NGOs of peacebuilding mandates. This explanation, where states encourage NGO peacebuilding as a purposeful strategy, raises many of the same questions as states using the NGO aid channel to further state interests. It blurs the line between state and private actor, in effect wiping away the very attributes for which the NGOs are praised. It also challenges the claims that NGOs are necessary for and particularly good at peacebuilding work. Maybe NGOs build peace because there is government funding for it.

The rest of this chapter will discuss the new peacebuilding mandate and the dilemmas it may pose for NGOs, particularly as it relates to the compatibility of their work with state agendas. In other NGO fields, such as human rights or development, understanding of NGO interaction with governmental actors is far more developed.[42] As in other fields, peacebuilding NGOs are not always working with governments or against governments; diverse kinds of NGOs play a role in peacebuilding and relate to governmental actors in distinct ways. In fact, many peacebuilding NGOs are currently debating and formulating their policies of interaction with the state, international organizations, and the military in complex humanitarian emergencies.[43] Thus, the generalizations made below may not apply to all NGOs in peacebuilding or to any given NGO at all times.

The following conclusions are based on research on U.S.-based, internationally operative peacebuilding NGOs. Most relevant for the research presented here were interviews conducted with seven different peacebuilding NGOs, three of which were humanitarian relief NGOs. The conclusions are also influenced by analysis of a larger set of data collected from organizational websites and documents of 54 peacebuilding NGOs, including 11 relief and development NGOs such as CARE, World Vision, Catholic Relief Services, and Mercy Corps.[44]

Motivations for adopting a peacebuilding mandate. Changing mandates are not a new thing in the relief and development world. Many organizations were founded in the aftermath of World War II to provide emergency relief. In the 1970s organizations began to add community development work to their agenda and then in the 1990s began exploring civil society building and peacebuilding as ways to cope with complex humanitarian emergencies or situations where populations are put at risk by war and violent conflict. Most NGOs have embarked on peacebuilding work chiefly as a result of a changing environment, exemplified by Rwanda,[45] where they realized that their aid giving would be futile unless long-term conflict issues were addressed, and agency leadership who were committed to peacebuilding values that then gained momentum in the entire organization. This is the story told by the NGOs, namely that the changing reality on the ground necessitated attention to peacebuilding and that their organizational values and the leadership representing them demanded it. Of the three explanations reviewed earlier, this argument fits a kind of functionalist and organizational agency path, but ignores the third possible explanation, which is that the availability of government funding for peacebuilding encouraged NGOs to engage in it. When pressed, some agency staff acknowledge that the impetus for their new mandate also arose from a changing NGO world, that is, other organizations are doing it, though they would deny that they are doing it only because there is funding for it.

Government agencies have begun to support peacebuilding work and to set up funding mechanisms for NGO work in peacebuilding. Several multilateral agencies and bilateral donors have created functional units or budget lines for aspects of post-conflict recovery.[46] In the early 1990s in Canada, peacebuilding as outlined in the 1992 *Agenda for Peace* captured a group of NGO and government policy-makers looking for a shared agenda between security, diplomacy, and development. The Canadian International Development Agency helped to convene a forum on peacebuilding issues. Eventually a Canadian "Peacebuilding Initiative" was launched, a peacebuilding fund was announced, and close working relationships were formed with Canadian NGOs as well as other government agencies, including USAID, the multilateral United Nations Development Programme (UNDP), and the World Bank. USAID launched an informal network of multilateral and bilateral agencies working in peacebuilding in late 1997.[47]

The time frame of government funding coincided with the adoption of peacebuilding by humanitarian NGOs. The work of peacebuilding does genuinely flow out of NGO work in relief and development, and governments have not artificially created this line of work for NGOs. There is cross-fertilization of ideas between the state and NGOs, and the evidence points to a group of factors that led to a consensus in the development community that strategies in conflict settings needed to be changed. At the same time, the fact that the peacebuilding mandate grows out of development work points to the probability that state and NGO relationships that exist in the development world will be reiterated in peacebuilding work.

Much of the peacebuilding work of humanitarian relief and development NGOs is integrated with their relief and development mandate in recognition of the power of their aid resources to do good or to do harm by exacerbating conflict. A 1999 study by development economist Mary Anderson, set out a framework for aid workers to evaluate the effects of their aid resources in a conflict setting.[48] Anderson's Local Capacities for Peace framework, which has proven useful for many NGOs, is about building indigenous capabilities, natural "connectors," such as market links or common interests, between feuding parties that mitigate or overcome conflict issues. The idea is that aid resources should attempt to reinforce and build on these connectors. For example, one of Catholic Relief Services' flagship projects is the Macedonia Parent School Partnership Project, which has since been replicated and adapted in other parts of Eastern Europe. The idea behind the project was to encourage ethnic Albanians, Turks, and Macedonians to work on a common project together—in this case improving school infrastructure. In the early 1990s, Catholic Relief Services entered Macedonia to help with the refugees spilling in from Bosnia. Catholic Relief Services became interested in preventing a similar crisis in Macedonia by initiating a project that combined reconciliation and conflict prevention with civil society building. This meshed with USAID's regional strategy of promoting democracy and market reforms as a means of giving people vested interests in maintaining peace. Catholic Relief Services received a three-year USAID grant, and after meetings with the Macedonian Ministry of Education and time spent learning the needs of grassroots communities, the school project began. U.S. government funding became an incentive for people to work together to repair their schools. For many participants, it was the first time they could recall meeting with other citizens in order to discuss community problems.

Given these natural connections with development work, it is hard to imagine that NGOs would cease their peacebuilding work if government funding dried up. NGOs have demonstrated that they are very committed to peacebuilding by institutionalizing peacebuilding concerns in staff training, project evaluations, and in their organizational structures with the creation of positions like "peacebuilding coordinator." They have, to varying degrees, attempted to educate their constituencies and private sources of funding on the merits of peacebuilding work so that they will not be reliant on government funding. Finally, for some organizations, peacebuilding is not only a practical, but a normative concern arising from, for example, faith commitments held by the organization and the teachings of religious traditions. The Mennonite Central Committee (MCC) is an example of an organization that has been working in peacebuilding, although it did not use the term, long before the recent trend. Nevertheless, the genuine commitment of these NGOs to the work does not mean that they will succeed at it nor does it diminish the possible problems with them adopting peacebuilding mandates, problems that may jeopardize the organizations themselves and their good relations with the state. The following section turns to these problems.

Peacebuilding and New Dilemmas of Cooperation

Moving toward advocacy roles. The work of Mary Anderson and others has challenged NGOs to think about the impact of their aid policies in conflict zones.[49] The exhortation mostly concerns NGOs carrying out relief and development work with a mindset toward peacebuilding, but the mandates of NGO work in peacebuilding do not necessarily stop there. Although most of these organizations would state that their primary goal is one of relief and development work, some of their peacebuilding work moves them into proactive engagement with the issues in the conflict. On the continuum from service provider to advocate, this may move the NGO closer to the advocate role and into the political realm of opinion shapers and pressure groups. Some designated peacebuilding NGOs, as distinct from relief and development NGOs, fall clearly into the advocacy camp, such as Witness for Peace or Christian Peacemaker Teams. They do not even claim neutrality in conflict zones, but rather choose to stand alongside an oppressed group. As explained below, much of the work of relief and development NGOs in peacebuilding is in education and mediation, which may be less contentious than the work of Witness for Peace or Christian Peacemaker Teams, but still involves greater risk than aid provision.

Many humanitarian NGOs seek to empower local institutions to work in peacebuilding through education and training programs. Catholic Relief Services implemented a three-year project in Rwanda, funded by the U.S. government, to develop educational curricula around peacebuilding for Rwanda's education sector. NGOs have also been involved in dialogue promotion and workshops for the purpose of encouraging talks between disputing parties. For example, World Vision's Ghana country director chaired meetings of a consortium of NGOs led by ActionAid to help resolve tribal conflict in northern Ghana. Involvement in direct conflict interventions or mediation work is more risky for relief and development organizations than integrating peacebuilding into development work. Engaging in politically contentious issues puts the relief mission, access to needy populations, relations with governments in the North and the South, and even the NGO's reputation in jeopardy. Even with the recognition that no aid is strictly neutral, that is, it has the ability to do good or harm, there is still a general consensus that the principle of nonpartisan aid should not be abandoned.[50] It is an aspiration if not always an achievement.

Nongovernmental organizations debate the degree to which peacebuilding work involves taking on a neutral role and to what degree it involves an advocacy role of standing on the side of justice for the sake of true peace. Most organizations that specialize in conflict resolution attempt to involve themselves in negotiation with neutrality. Yet, many relief and development organizations have written into their missions that they are concerned about justice, which may involve an adversarial approach in peace work. The MCC, that has actively been engaged in peace work and humanitarian relief work for decades, has had to ask more questions about the neutrality of peace work in recent years as Mennonites have moved toward more activist forms of peacemaking. The MCC, however, is careful about accepting government monies, particularly from the U.S. government, and as a pacifist organization does not work with military actors. Cooperating with the military in peacebuilding and using government funds are two more dilemmas faced by NGOs as they balance the need to maintain their integrity and trustworthiness and decide how much they will align with state actors.

Cooperating with militaries and international peacekeeping missions. In several complex emergencies like Bosnia and Somalia, aid workers have worked side by side with military personnel and private security companies.[51] There is concern about the effect of this on humanitarian operations of NGOs, but the concern may be magnified for an NGO involved in peacebuilding work.

Since relief and development organizations are often some of the first responders in times of emergency, they frequently need to establish a working relationship with militaries. Military force can guard refugee camps, protect relief supplies and workers, and distribute relief supplies.[52] Some view the military's increasing role as a relief provider as a positive development, arguing that there is a need for military scale operations, as with NATO in Kosovo, and that military actors are keen on improving their civilian relations and skills in rebuilding conflict areas. Indeed, an interviewed World Vision employee stated that they receive weekly calls from various factions of the U.S. military that would like to collaborate with or gain expertise from them. Others take a more negative view, arguing that the military is not truly interested in working in solidarity with the local population and international aid community, but is a hegemonic actor that only cooperates with civilian organizations in order to further its own military and political objectives. Military aid is ultimately not neutral, but conditional, used to gain compliance of local actors and to influence political processes.[53]

For ill or good, national and international armed forces are clearly not nonpartisan actors and in some cases have no pretences of being so.[54] If NGOs cooperate with them, the NGOs risk being tainted with the military's mistakes and goals. On the other hand, willingly or not, they can hardly avoid being tainted by the military operation if they operate in complex emergency, serving populations who are in protected areas.[55]

There are some pacifists within NGOs who are against military intervention in humanitarian work. Others see military intervention as essential for some protection purposes or for transport services. For example, after Hurricane Mitch, the military provided free transport of relief supplies via helicopters, which most NGOs do not possess.[56] Most NGOs agree on the principle that cooperation with military forces is only for activities that contribute to the protection and preservation of civilians and in most cases, only with militaries that are acting in accordance with humanitarian conventions such as the UN Declaration on Human Rights and the Geneva Convention and its protocols.[57] They see engagement with armed forces as an opportunity to influence military analysis and forums. In other words, since the military will be involved, there might as well be a deliberate effort to influence the character of military involvement and to help them to do a better job, advocating them to uphold international humanitarian conventions.

Using government funds for peacebuilding. Should NGOs accept government monies for their work in peacebuilding, like most do for their relief work? Regardless of how much of their budget derives from government grants, many NGOs are debating the appropriateness of using government monies for peacebuilding work. For example, a mediation project in the Middle East, funded by the U.S. government, might not be perceived as nonpartisan. There is also the concern that official funding preferences for peacebuilding do not match those of NGOs. World Vision is currently exploring options for peacebuilding funding from the United States, USAID in particular, Canadian, and U.K. governments, UN agencies such as the UN High Commission for Refugees, United Nations Children Fund (UNICEF), UNDP, and private sources. According to World Vision, most official funding tends to be limited to democracy and civil society building, elections, and governance. Indeed the UN definition of peacebuilding focuses on goals like establishing rule of law and human rights, demobilizing and reintegrating soldiers, and AIDS education.[58] World Vision would like to be more innovative and holistic in its peacebuilding programs, focusing on reconciliation, psychosocial work, and long-term transformation of conflicts.

State actors have tended to define the peacebuilding enterprise with a narrower scope and time frame. If the central purpose of U.S. foreign policy is to protect and promote U.S. interests, it is natural that certain conflicts will receive more attention than others and that the attention will seek to maximize marketable results. The United States has an interest in a public display of concern in the form of tangible relief commodities such as building houses and supplying food. These projects are immediately visible, and funds supporting them can be clearly accounted for. Peacebuilding "software" is more uncertain for governments. There is little in public funding coffers that is offered for "reconciliation" that donors see as an immeasurable goal. For the same reason, namely that it is hard to show tangible results, the U.S. government is generally not funding NGOs to host dialogues, though some European governments are more progressive in this.[59]

Despite this mismatch in funding goals, there is fierce competition for government funds. Humanitarian NGOs are now competing for big U.S. government grants with private development corporations. These so called "beltway bandits" are in the relief and development business, and will happily and quickly build housing in Albania without concern for the reconciliation and relationship issues that a Catholic Relief Services would take care to include as a component in the project.

For the most part each organization is striving to integrate peacebuilding projects into other programs in such a way that separate funding for peacebuilding is not required. When peacebuilding is a dimension added onto or integrated into relief and development programming, there is often enough undesignated money within the project that can be moved around for this purpose. Organizations might also combine private and public funding. For example, if Catholic Relief Services receives funding from a UN agency to build houses in Burundi and the United Nations is not interested in funding peacebuilding, Catholic Relief Services could use their own funding to add a reconciliation component to the project. These strategies are being pursued in part due to the limitations of NGO funding arrangements. Whether private or public, NGO funding tends to be for short-term, contractual work and not conducive to the long-term efforts of peacebuilding where results are not easily quantifiable. This leads to the final concern of accountability. Are NGOs chiefly accountable to those who hold the purse strings?

Accountability and evaluation of peacebuilding work. A final dilemma of NGO work in peacebuilding concerns the accountability structures of NGOs and the difficulties of evaluating work in peacebuilding. Whereas governments represent and are accountable to their citizens, the NGO world has an ill-defined constituency and tenable democratic status. NGOs are usually self-monitoring agencies whose performance evaluation is subject to their own reporting standards. The uncertainty surrounding whether NGOs are adequately accountable to their work is due in part to the difficulties in evaluating NGO performance.[60] Indeed the two issues of evaluation and accountability are very much conflated. Edwards and Hulme and others argue that incentives in the relief and development industry are set up such that NGOs are not very accountable to their beneficiaries, but rather to their donors.[61] In the interest of maintaining their funding, NGOs may be more prone to high profile relief operations where it can be demonstrated that 5,000 were fed and housed than to the long-term, hard to measure work of peacebuilding.

On a positive note, relief and development NGOs strive to demonstrate that their programs help to grow local capacity and ownership of peacebuilding practices, whether through targeted training or through discovery and utilization of latent capacities for peacebuilding within a community. Local relevance and ownership is a strong concern since experience has shown that unless programs have a broad base of support in their context, they cannot grow. So, instead of stating that they have accomplished a goal, agencies are attempting to measure things like whether their connections lead to increased local capacity and ownership for peacebuilding activity. In other words, is a strong local institution developing that can run workshops, mediation, etc.? This emphasis also encourages more participatory evaluation practices, ones that involve input from many stakeholders throughout the life of a project.

Evidence points to the donors pushing the NGOs to be more explicit in their evaluation of peacebuilding. This is laudable, though the objectives to be met are certainly ones that must coincide with the donor government agendas. At the same time, good evaluation methods and NGO knowledge about their own effectiveness will go a long way toward helping NGOs address some of the other operational dilemmas raised here. Evidence about what is effective and what is not in terms of neutrality or partisanship in peacebuilding, aligning with military actors or sanctioning the use of force, and cooperation with official actors for funds or logistical help, can help prevent worst-case scenarios from developing. One step in this direction is a new set of data on peacebuilding that has been compiled by Mary Anderson's organization, the Collaborative for Development Action in Cambridge, MA. Their "Reflecting on Peace Practice" project is an attempt to improve peacebuilding practice by gathering and evaluating experiences from a variety of recent conflict-focused programs. Reflecting on Peace Practice has identified several critical issues where lessons need to be drawn and applied to NGO practices. These issues include linkages of work between different levels, insider/outsider roles and relationships, trade-offs between working for the reduction of violence and social justice, how agencies deal with actions intended to disrupt peace processes, and indicators of impact and effectiveness criteria for peace work.[62]

Conclusion

One might question whether these are really new challenges for NGOs, raised by their new peacebuilding mandates or if they are merely the same dilemmas that NGOs face in their humanitarian work. The question is even more meaningful when it is recognized that much of the peacebuilding work of NGOs is integrated into their relief and development work. After all, Boutros Boutros Ghali was mostly right in forecasting NGO roles in peacebuilding as a post-conflict, aid-giving enterprise. It would be hard to argue that these dilemmas are fundamentally new for humanitarian NGOs. However, the peacebuilding mandates are, in the eyes of most NGOs, and in the eyes of those who analyze NGO work, something new. One can therefore argue that these operational dilemmas are being raised with new and greater intensity than ever before.[63]

This chapter has attempted to demonstrate that engagement in peacebuilding pushes NGOs into deeper territory than their aid work, and that the claims made about the NGO's comparative advantage in peacebuilding and its distinctiveness from state actors are not substantiated. In fact, NGO peacebuilding work has some firm ties with government initiatives and funding. The very strengths that NGOs are purported to have are compromised by these connections. Whether this is problematic depends on one's perspective on the necessity for NGOs to be free of government influence in order to be good peacemakers. Ties to state agencies may not be an issue if government support of post-conflict recovery and peacebuilding type initiatives are in line with good practices and if NGOs and governments agree on what these are. However, the evidence does not support this. Although programmatic strategies may often overlap, this chapter suggests that government actors operate with a different underlying peacebuilding framework than NGOs; their baseline interests and values clash. Governments prefer less risky interventions and would be cautious in supporting certain advocacy campaigns that challenge either Western or developing countries' interests. At the same time, when in their interests, governments will engage in non-neutral behavior, often involving use of force or other coercive measures. When making judgments about these interventions and the risks to be taken, priority is placed on the national interest and strategic concerns above the needs of the local population. Governments are interested in tangible results that show how foreign aid is being utilized in measurable ways in the short term; they operate on a funding and project cycle that is not conducive to the long-term work of building trust and peace after war.

In sum, the effectiveness of NGO work in peacebuilding is challenged by the fact that NGO agendas in peacebuilding are intertwined with state agendas and funding. NGOs are at risk of being used as agents of the state. At the same time, peacebuilding mandates may push NGOs into greater advocacy roles, thereby jeopardizing their good relations with state actors.

The answer is neither for NGOs to seek to work as completely independent or autonomous organizations nor for them to abandon peacebuilding altogether. Just as individual government agencies are constrained by the larger foreign policy agenda of which they are part, NGOs are inevitably both constrained and aided by a larger system. NGOs engaged in peacebuilding undoubtedly do important work and make important contributions, but how do we compare their impact with that of the billion dollar U.S. military operations in Somalia, NATO's operations in Bosnia, or diplomatic negotiations in Dayton? Certainly their impact is limited if compared to the capacity of official actors. While NGOs can arguably make significant contributions to peacebuilding at the levels of the grassroots and civil society, even if the NGOs directed all of their efforts to reconciliation work, they would probably not have the kind of resources that it would take to make a large impact on national-level conflict resolution processes.[64] Overly critical assessment of NGO work in peacebuilding fails to acknowledge the extreme difficulties of the tasks, and that no actor is doing them well. Storey argues that the biggest defense of NGOs in the Rwandan genocide is that "they were asked to perform impossible roles in vacuums left by those agencies—such as the UN and governments—which had the power to frame and enforce an appropriate political response."[65]

Peacebuilding cannot be the work of any one organization. No one organization will have all the funding, all of the skills, and all of the contacts necessary for the monumental and diverse tasks of peacebuilding in a given context. Different types of NGOs and NGO and government processes can complement one another.

There is a growing trend of cooperation between elite level conflict resolution organizations such as Conflict Management Group (CMG) in Cambridge, MA, and relief and development organizations. For example, CMG believes that peace talks with political actors in Colombia will ultimately be useless unless concrete changes are seen at the grassroots level of society, including reduction of poverty. Due to donor demands for concrete results of conflict resolution work, conflict organizations like CMG have begun to incorporate their negotiation work into a "development perspective." In this partnership, relief and development organizations gain expertise in conflict resolution techniques and skills. So, for example, CMG is working with Mercy Corps; and Washington-based expert organizations like the Center for Strategic and International Studies and Search for Common Ground are seeking collaboration with the likes of Catholic Relief Services and MCC. This is an intriguing development as it shares the mediation skills of the conflict resolution organizations with the operational capacity of the relief and development organizations.

Official actors especially have much to gain through cooperation with NGO peacebuilders. The military is increasingly being used for peacekeeping tasks that nongovernmental actors can perform with greater cost-effectiveness. Also, if NGOs can engage earlier and operate in a preventive mode, this too is a promising development. Governmental negotiations and peace work will be more successful when embedded in a larger political and social process. The work of NGOs can create new political space and expand the tools for resolving conflict, thereby increasing the capacity of governmental efforts. Many NGOs, especially the larger ones, see a need to better coordinate their peacebuilding work with official actors. Hopefully, they will draw lessons from the critiques of their development work and will be able to strike a balance between operating as mindless agents of the state and the worst hazards of advocacy work. As NGOs embark on peacebuilding, they will be making decisions that either more closely align them with state agencies or alienate them from state actors. Either path has its dangers. The challenge will be to replicate the best parts of the collaborative relationships with official actors while avoiding having their NGO agendas co-opted and directed by state interests.

Notes

1. Lester Salamon, *The Global Associational Revolution: The Rise of the Third Sector on the World Scene*, Occasional Paper 15 (Baltimore, MD: The Johns Hopkins University Institute for Policy Studies, 1993), 1. There were 176 international NGOs in 1909 and 28,900 by 1993. See Commission on Global Governance, *Our Common Neighborhood: The Report of the Commission on Global Governance* (Oxford: Oxford University Press, 1995). Statistics for growth of domestic NGOs can also be found in Thomas G. Weiss and Leon Gordenker, eds. *NGOs, the UN, and Global Governance* (Boulder, CO: Lynne Rienner, 1996).

2. For a discussion of these see Adil Najam, "Understanding the Third Sector: Revisiting the Prince, the Merchant, and the Citizen," *Organizational Management and Leadership* 7, no. 2 (1996): 203–19; Lester Salamon and Helmut Anheier, "In Search of the Non-Profit Sector. I: The Question of Definitions," *Voluntas* 3, no. 2 (1992): 125–51; Lester Salamon and Helmut Anheier, *The Emerging Sector: An Overview* (Baltimore, MD: The John Hopkins University Institute for Policy Studies, 1994); and Marilyn Taylor, "The Third Sector in International Perspective: Indianapolis, 1992," *Voluntas* 3, no. 3 (1992): 383–90.

3. Kriesberg includes growth of intergovernmental organizations as well as NGOs. See Louis Kriesberg, "Social Movements and Global Transformation," in *Transnational Social Movements and Global Politics: Solidarity Beyond the State*, ed. Jackie Smith, Charles Chatfield, and Ronald Pagnucco, 3–10 (Syracuse, NY: Syracuse University Press, 1997).

4. Jackie Smith, "Transnational Political Processes and the Human Rights Movement," *Research in Social Movements, Conflict and Change* 18 (1995): 185–219, 193.

5. James N. Rosenau, *Turbulence in World Politics: A Theory of Change and Continuity* (Princeton ND: Princeton University Press, 1990), 3–20.

6. Seyom Brown, *International Relations in a Changing Global System: Toward a Theory of the World Polity* (Boulder, CO: Westview Press, 1992), 115–27.

7. Weiss and Gordenker, *NGOs, the UN, and Global Governance*, 17.

8. Ibid., 209–10.

9. Ian Smillie, "Changing Partners: Northern NGOs, Northern Governments," *Voluntas* 5, no. 2 (1994): 155–92, 162.

10. Weiss and Gordenker, *NGOs, the UN, and Global Governance*; Peter Willetts, ed. *The Conscience of the World: The Influence of Non-governmental Organisations in the UN System* (Washington, DC: Brookings Institution, 1995); Anne Marie Clark, "Non-governmental Organizations and Their Influence on International Society," *Journal of International Affairs* 48, no. 2 (1995): 507–25; Thomas Risse-Kappen, ed., *Bringing Transnational Relations Back In: Non-state Actors, Domestic Structures, and International Institutions* (New York: Cambridge University Press, 1995).

11. Paul Ghils, "International Civil Society: International Non-governmental Organizations in the International System," *International Social Science Journal* 133, no. 3 (1992): 417–29, 429.

12. Michael Edwards and David Hulme, eds., *Beyond the Magic Bullet: NGO Performance Accountability in the Post-Cold War World* (West Hartford, CT: Kumarian Press, 1996).

13. UNDP (United Nations Development Program), *Human Development Report* (New York: Oxford University Press, 1993), 88.

14. Edwards and Hulme, *Beyond the Magic Bullet*, 2–3.

15. Smillie, "Changing Partners," 155.

16. Ian Smillie, "NGOs: Crisis and Opportunity in the New World Order" in *Transforming Development: Foreign Aid for a Changing World*, ed. Jim Freedman, 114–34 (Toronto: University of Toronto Press, 2000), 124–25.

17. Brian Smith, *More Than Altruism: the Politics of Private Foreign Aid* (Princeton: Princeton University Press, 1990), 19–20.

18. Ibid., chapters 2–3.

19. Terje Tvedt, *Angels of Mercy or Development Diplomats: NGOs and Foreign Aid* (Trenton, NJ: First Africa World Press, 1998), 4, 41–45. Tvedt provides a radical critique of NGO work along these lines.

20. Tvedt, *Angels of Mercy*, 45–46.

21. Ibid., 61.

22. Brown as quoted in Smillie "Changing Partners," 157. See also Tvedt, *Angels of Mercy* chapter 6.

23. John Sankey, "Conclusions," in *The Conscience of the World: the Influence of Non-governmental Organizations in the UN System*, ed. Peter Willetts (Washington, DC: The Brookings Institution, 1996), 275.

24. Boutros Boutros Ghali, *An Agenda for Peace* (New York: United Nations, 1992), 11.

25. United Nations General Assembly and Security Council, *Report of the Panel on United Nations Peace Operations*, A/55/305–S/2000/809 (New York: United Nations, 2000).

26. David Last, "From Peacekeeping to Peacebuilding: Conflict Resolution Theory and the Transition to Peace" (paper, International Studies Association, Minneapolis, March 17–21, 1998); John Paul Lederach, *Building Peace: Sustainable Reconciliation in Divided Societies* (Washington, DC: USIP Press, 1997); Elise Boulding and Jan Oberg, "United Nations Peacekeeping and NGO Peacebuilding: Towards Partnership," in *The*

Future of the United Nations System: Potential for the Twenty-first Century, ed. Chadwick F. Alger, 127–54 (New York: United Nations University Press, 1998).

27. Lederach, *Building Peace*, 20.

28. Kumar Rupesinghe, "Non-Governmental Organizations and the 'Agenda for Peace'," *Ecumenical Review* 47, no. 3 (1995): 324–28, 325.

29. Track-two diplomacy is described by Joseph Montville as "unofficial, informal consultation designed to develop concepts and ideas in the intellectual and moral basis for a movement towards settlement." Joseph Montville (speech, Annual DPI/NGO Conference, United Nations, New York, September 10, 1992). The term first appeared in Joseph Montville, "The Arrow and the Olive Branch: A Case for Track Two Diplomacy," in *Conflict Resolution: Track Two Diplomacy*, ed. J. McDonald, Jr. and D. Bendahmane, 5–20 (Washington, DC: US Government Printing Office, 1987).

30. See Pamela Aall, "Non-governmental Organizations and Peacemaking," in *Managing Global Chaos: Sources of and Responses to International Conflict*, ed. Chester A. Crocker, Fen Osler Hampson and Pamela Aall, 433–44 (Washington, DC: USIP Press, 1996), 443–4; Mary Anderson, "Humanitarian NGOs in Conflict Intervention," in *Managing Global Chaos* 343–54; John Prendergast, Frontline *Diplomacy: Humanitarian Aid and Conflict in Africa* (Boulder, CO: Lynne Rienner, 1996); Andrew Natsios, "An NGO Perspective," in *Peacemaking in International Conflict: Methods and Techniques,* ed. I William Zartman and J. Lewis Rasmussen, 337–64 (Washington, DC: USIP Press, 1997); Michael Edwards, David Hulme, and Tina Wallace, "Increasing Leverage for Development: Changes for NGOs in a Global Future," in *New Roles and Relevance: Development NGOs and Challenges for Change*, ed. David Lewis and Tina Wallace, 1–14 (Bloomfield, CT: Kumarian Press, 2000).

31. See Farouk Mawlawi, "New Conflicts, New Challenges: The Evolving Role for Non-governmental Actors," *Journal of International Affairs* 46, no. 2 (1993): 391–413, 413; Kumar Rupesingh, *The Role of Nongovernmental Organizations in Early Warning and Conflict Resolution* (London: International Alert, 1993); Mohmaed Sahnoun, "Managing Conflict After the Cold War," *Peace Review* 8, no. 4 (1996): 485–92; Paul Wehr, "The Citizen Intervenor," *Peace Review* 8, no. 4 (1996): 555–61; David Smock, ed., *Private Peacemaking: USIP-Assisted Peacemaking Projects of Nonprofit Organizations*, Peaceworks No. 20 (Washington, DC: United States Institute of Peace, May 1998).

32. Mawlawi, "New conflicts, New Challenges," 413.

33. See, e.g., Clark "Non-govermental Organizations," Willetts *Conscience of the World*; Risse-Kappen, *Bringing Trasnational Relations*; Weiss and Gordenker, *NGOs, the UN, and global governance*; Smith et al., *Transnational Social Movements.*

34. For lists of these attributes see Mawlawi, "New conflicts, New Challenges," 396–403 and Natsios, "An NGO Perspective," 343–45.

35. Mawlawi, "New conflicts, New Challenges," 398–99.

36. Mawlawi, "New conflicts, New Challenges," 400.

37. Mawlawi, "New conflicts, New Challenges," 410; Aall, "Non-governmental Organizations and Peacemaking," 439.

38. Natsios, "An NGO Perspective," 341–43.

39. Peter Wallensteen and Margareta Sollenberg, "Armed Conflict 1989–2000," *Journal of Peace Research* 38, no. 5 (2001): 629–44. Wallensteen and Sollenberg conclude that there were seven interstate wars, but there were also nine intrastate wars with foreign intervention.

40. See Chester Crocker, Fen Osler Hampson and Pamela Aall, "Introduction," in *Managing Global Chaos* xiii–xx, xvi–xvii; Lewis J. Rasmussen, "Peacemaking in the Twenty-First Century: New Rules, New Roles, New Actors," in *Peacemaking in*

International Conflict, 23–50; and Kumar Rupesinghe, ed. *Internal Conflict and Governance* (New York: St. Martin's, 1992), 12–13.

41. See, e.g., Adam Roberts, "The Crisis in UN Peacekeeping," in *Managing Global Chaos*, 297–320; Astri Suhrke, "Environmental Change, Migration, and Conflict: A Lethal Feedback Dynamic?" in *Managing Global Chaos*, 113–28.

42. See Smith, *More than Altruism*; Edwards and Hulme, *Beyond the Magic Bullet*. While cooperation among NGOs and the United Nations in relief development for complex emergencies is developed, such liaisons are not as far advanced among NGOs working in peacebuilding. See Natsios, "NGOs and the UN System."

43. Aall, "Non-governmental Organizations and Peacemaking," 436.

44. Since the peacebuilding work of these organizations continues to evolve, I should also note that my data only reflects their work through 2000.

45. Many relief and development NGOs to point to Rwanda as a pivotal moment for recognition of the need for peacebuilding. Interestingly, it is also a conflict in which states abdicated responsibilities of keeping the peace, sensing after Somalis that the stakes were too high.

46. Stewart Patrick, "The Donor Community and the Challenge of Postconflict Recovery," in *Good Intentions: Pledges of Aid for Postconflict Recovery*, ed. Shepard Forman and Stewart Patrick, 35–66 (Boulder, CO: Lynne Rienner, 2000), 42.

47. Michael Small, "Peacebuilding in Postconflict Societies" in *Human Security and the New Diplomacy*, ed. Rob McRae and Don Hubert, 75–80 (Montreal: McGill-Queen's University Press, 2001).

48. Mary Anderson, *Do No Harm: How Aid Can Support Peace—Or War* (Boulder, CO: Lynne Rienner, 1999).

49. See Larry Minear and Thomas G. Weiss, *Mercy Under Fire: War and the Global Humanitarian Community* (Boulder, CO: Westview Press, 1995); John Prendergast, *Frontline Diplomacy: Humanitarian Aid and Conflict in Africa* (Boulder, CO: Lynne Rienner, 1996); Andy Storey, "Non-Neutral Humanitarianism: NGOs and the Rwanda Crisis," *Development in Practice* 7, no. 4 (1997): 384–94.

50. Minear and Weiss, *Mercy under Fire*, 71.

51. See Spearin, Chapter 3, in this volume.

52. Prendergast, *Frontline Diplomacy*, 64.

53. For an excellent discussion of the debate, see Michael Pugh, "Civil–Military Relations in the Kosovo Crisis: An Emerging Hegemony?" *Security Dialogue* 31, no. 2 (2000): 229–42.

54. Pugh, "Civil–Military Relations," 230.

55. Pugh, "Civil–Military Relations," 235–36. For example, in Kosovo, as in Somalia, many NGOs called for military intervention to create "humanitarian zones or spaces" so that they could carry out their relief missions.

56. Cooperation here would of course be extremely limited since NGO and military operational styles are extremely different. The military is a hierarchical organization which likes to take charge and set up and run its own shop. For example, they set up their own camp, isolating them from the local population. UN agencies and NGOs are more disparate and have greater connections with locals, again exemplified in the fact that they set up shop in local offices and houses that they rent. See Thomas Weiss and Cindy Collins, *Humanitarian Challenges and Intervention* (Boulder, CO: Westview Press, 1996), 55.

57. For a list of some criteria of cooperation, as well other ethical and legal issues of humanitarian issues see "The Mohonk Criteria for Humanitarian Assistance in Complex Emergencies," *Human Rights Quarterly* 17, no. 1 (1995): 192–208.

58. United Nations General Assembly and Security Council, *Report of the Panel*, 3.

59. Andrew Natsios, "The Politics of Saving Lives," *Foreign Service Journal* 75, no. 12 (1998): 16–22.
60. Edwards and Hulme, *Beyond the Magic Bullet*.
61. See, e.g., Prendergast, *Frontline Diplomacy*, 13–15.
62. Collaborative for Development Action, "Reflecting on Peace Practice," http://www.cdainc.com/rpp.
63. In part, it was the intensification of some of these operational dilemmas (esp. staff ill-prepared to work in conflict zones and debates about "neutral" aid exacerbating conflict) that led NGOs to be more purposeful about their operations and impact in conflict zones. This, of course, does not mean that the dilemmas have gone away with the official intention to work at peacebuilding. Part of my argument is that they may be intensified if proactive peacebuilding is carried too far or not done well.
64. Prendergast, *Frontline Diplomacy*, 112.
65. Storey, "Non-neutral Humanitarianism," 393.

Chapter 3

Humanitarians and Mercenaries: Partners in Security Governance?

Christopher Spearin

P ost–Cold War security governance makes for strange bedfellows. This is because, increasingly, the obligation of providing security no longer rests predominantly with the state.[1] States are downloading responsibilities onto non-state actors and other opportunities are arising in which these actors can operate. Accordingly, how security is provided, by whom, in what combinations, and to what effect should be the foci of study. As such, this chapter provides a specific analysis of interaction between humanitarian nongovernmental organizations (NGOs) and a modern form of mercenaries: international private security companies (PSCs).[2]

While humanitarian NGOs are long-standing actors on the international landscape, PSCs, as will be explained below, are relatively new, post–Cold War actors. Though the notorious type of mercenaries, the soldier of fortune, still exists, this new type of mercenary activity is distinguishable as it is based on a corporate structure and it seeks a long-term presence. Hence, PSCs have collectively limited what they do and for what clients by following the general norms of international statecraft. Their client base is limited to states, NGOs, international organizations, and multinational corporations. Though they are profit oriented, they do not switch sides in search of higher reward. As for the services they offer, they range from advice to training to support to an operational presence that can consist of a hybrid, if not somewhat blurred concoction, of policing and military applications. Although the term "private military company" (PMC) is sometimes used in the literature, the acronym PSC is thus more appropriate in a cumulative sense because it takes into account these varied applications and, in the end, the goal in all cases is to make something or someone more secure.

With respect to specifically making humanitarian NGOs more secure, it is important to note that in the present context, these NGOs face substantial problems in the delivery of their assistance due to security concerns over the safety of personnel. PSCs, for their part, seek to be a legitimate actor in contemporary security governance. Because of the operational and political environments in which

NGOs find themselves and the need of PSCs to acquire clients, it is estimated that interaction between NGOs and PSCs will grow.[3] Overall then, the need for analysis of this emerging relationship is great given the fact that the fracturing and decentralization characteristic of contemporary security governance is likely to continue.

As such, this chapter is organized around achieving three linked objectives. One objective is to contextualize the political and operational milieu in which NGOs operate. This is needed to make plain the reasons why NGOs interact with PSCs, to indicate the limits of what PSCs can actually do for NGOs, and to identify the niche PSCs occupy. The second objective is to reveal potential operational problems for NGOs as a result of NGO–PSC interaction. This is required because while collaboration between NGOs and PSCs may ameliorate some of the problems noted in achieving the first objective, there are trade-offs and problems that the individual NGO may not have the necessary expertise and ability to remedy. For this objective, emphasis is placed on the managerial and operational constraints to which NGOs and PSCs are subject. The final objective is to provide an overview of the current capability and willingness of the NGO community, states, and the UN to respond to the kinds of issues made clear in achieving the second objective. This is essential to reveal the issues and motivations of the various actors involved in this particular aspect of contemporary security governance.

The achievement of these three objectives reveals the chapter's two primary arguments. First, interaction between NGOs and PSCs will not lead to a new humanitarian order through which all those in need of assistance will receive aid promptly and effectively. Although security governance may be fractured and decentralized, thus placing less attention on state activities, selectivity will still exist as NGOs and PSCs will not be able to escape the impact of statecraft. While both NGOs and PSCs may be autonomous actors with their own interests, they also have to respond to states and their activities will be influenced substantially by them. For NGOs, this is because of financial pressures, while for PSCs the dual pressures of the marketplace and normative concerns regarding the non-state use of force are at the fore. Second, attempts to handle problems resulting from the interaction between NGOs and PSCs will lack coherency and uniform direction into the foreseeable future. In other words, the general notion of governance meaning efforts among numerous actors, state and non-state, to bring about orderly activity and reliable responses, rather than just the result of numerous activities and relationships, will be a long-term task with an uncertain outcome.[4]

The Proliferation of PSCs and the Rise of NGO Need

The rise of the PSC phenomenon and the significant problems humanitarians face in the delivery of their assistance are both largely post–Cold War developments. With respect to PSCs, supply and demand factors stemming from the Cold War's end fueled the creation of PSCs and the marketplace they serve.[5] On the supply side, many countries downsized their armed forces in the hopes of capturing the peace dividend. Since 1989, the number of individuals in uniform fell by 7 million. While most of them simply retired or entered into the civilian marketplace, some former service personnel wished to apply their military skills in other endeavors, often in return for remuneration rates higher than what they earned in the public sector. On the demand side, and in the developed world, a combination of the gaps in force structures left by downsizing and the increased perceived utility of privatization in light of the rise of neoliberal thinking provided PSCs with opportunities in the seemingly sole preserve of the state: the provision of security. Again on the demand side, but in the developing world, the presence of PSCs made security services available to governments and other clients in weak states, thus filling a gap in security sectors made, in large part, by poor indigenous management and the end of superpower activism in and assistance to the developing world.

To date, no one has calculated the exact number of PSCs. Observations of general trends indicate that there are perhaps 200–300 firms that operate internationally. Ascertaining the exact number of firms and where they operate is difficult, however, given commercial dynamics that are evident in any industry. On a regular basis, new firms arrive on the scene, other firms close, firms merge or are bought out, and other firms add and drop services. What is more, calculation is made even more difficult because PSCs are often lumped into the larger group of military contractors. These companies provide logistical and maintenance services to armed forces and their overall numbers, somewhere in the low thousands, is equally unknown.

What is clear, however, is that collaboration between NGOs and PSCs serves as a way for PSCs to enhance their reputation, given the political and moral salience of humanitarian activities, and to differentiate themselves from soldiers-of-fortune. What is also evident is that humanitarianism presents a potentially lucrative marketplace for PSCs considering the problems that NGOs have faced in the post–Cold War era. Over the past decade, more than 200 humanitarian workers have been killed while carrying out their activities. These deaths have occurred regardless of the guiding principles or operating traditions of the particular NGO. The International Committee of the Red Cross, CARE U.S.A., Caritas, Save the Children, Norwegian Peoples Aid, German Agro Action, Médecins du Monde, and Médecins sans Frontièrs have all lost personnel. Although the large majority of these incidents have occurred in only 13 countries, their negative effects go beyond national borders.[6] When combined with the fact that many more NGO personnel have been taken hostage or threatened around the world, the wider overall impact has been to curtail the delivery of assistance due to security concerns. In the words of one NGO member, "[i]f aid workers are threatened, then so is aid."[7]

In order to provide further context to the interaction between NGOs and PSCs, it is necessary to consider the reasons why humanitarian workers are threatened in the post–Cold War environment and the dilemmas NGOs face in trying to ensure the safety of their personnel and the effective delivery of their assistance.

Dilemmas Faced by Humanitarian NGOs

On the surface, the matters of protecting humanitarians and facilitating their activities would seem to be relatively unproblematic. Dating back to nineteenth-century reasoning that noncombatants are to be protected from the scourge of war, states are bound to respect the importance and the necessity of humanitarian activity. This recognition is reinforced by international law. The delivery of assistance and the physical protection of those who provide the assistance are regulated by international legal provisions.[8] As for the providers of humanitarian assistance, a group in which NGOs have increasingly taken a prominent place, they self-regulate their activities by following the humanitarian norms of neutrality, impartiality, and independence. On one level, this approach preserves the understanding among states because, while assistance will have a political effect, the actual intention of the act is based on the sentiment of common humanity rather than in the political motivations of a particular state. As noted by Joanna Macrae and Nicholas Leader, these operational norms suggest "a shared understanding between humanitarian organizations, politicians and the military of the political function of aid in conflicting situations, and can be seen as part of the deal between these different actors."[9] On another level, such an approach is meant to ensure the safety of humanitarians in the field, thus allowing their operations to continue. Humanitarians are to be perceived by actors on the ground as weak, without a political agenda, and "armed" only with morally sound arguments.[10] Humanitarians themselves are to reinforce this perception by providing assistance to those in need without discrimination or hesitation. In total, states are to take a hands-off approach toward humanitarianism and humanitarians are not to give states or combatants on the ground cause for concern, a stance that they duly respect.

Post–Cold War humanitarian activity, however, confronts NGOs with numerous dilemmas and trade-offs that complicate the straightforward and universal provision of assistance. At the level of the international system, one concern is politicization from state agents that hampers the independence of NGOs and their ability to respond in all cases. Many NGOs now receive the bulk of their funding, often 80 percent or more, from state sources. This potentially creates a relationship of subservience and affects the universality of humanitarian assistance because funding may be contingent upon its utilization in a specific situation. NGOs, according to Leon Gordenker and Thomas Weiss, may not be willing to bite the hand that feeds them by striking out on an independent path.[11] Echoing this point is Mark Duffield, who contends that "[t]he growth of official funding channelled through NGOs, reinforced by the high cost of relief work has given donors a significant measure of influence."[12] A complicating factor for NGOs is that, because humanitarianism is increasingly seen as an industry that is dominated by a competitive contract culture, NGOs have to be cognizant of their image in the eyes of the donors. In addition, the proliferation of international humanitarian NGOs, now upward of 400 strong, increases the pressure on these organizations to compete for funding and respond to the interests and concerns of states.[13] In short, it is increasingly the provider or backer of assistance that determines where the resources are sent, not the fact that there are people in distress.[14]

One major effect of NGOs becoming *de facto*, if not *de jure*, foreign policy instruments of developed world states relates to conflict resolution. The post–Cold War increase in NGO operations reflects not only an upsurge in violence and the consequent increase in the numbers of those in need, but, as argued by Michael Bryans, Bruce Jones, and Janice Stein, it is also representative of NGOs filling a political security vacuum in the developing world.[15] Powerful states no longer have the ideological or geopolitical impetus to apply directly their resources and diplomatic clout, and to risk the lives of their military personnel in all parts of the world. Instead, NGOs are often contracted to fill the void in order for it to seem that states are at least "doing something." An NGO presence helps to form a "humanitarian alibi," action that avoids essential political measures made by states.[16] While state resources are obviously finite, such that their impact becomes minimal if they are spread too thinly, states have not yet reached this barrier in their international endeavors. NGOs, for their part, do not have the necessary expertise, mandate, or clout to fill the space left by states. Succinctly put by Diane Paul, "[r]elief organisations are increasingly being drawn into situations where assistance activities are not sufficiently supported by efforts to resolve the conflict."[17]

Second, many NGOs are concerned about the impact of the militarization of their work in theatre. This specifically concerns the benefits and drawbacks of NGOs working with militaries, frequently from the developed world, or with UN peacekeeping forces. In this case, the alibi has been eschewed and measures by states are being undertaken. On the one hand, military actors often have logistical assets that allow humanitarian assistance to reach those in need much more quickly than if NGOs provided the assistance alone. In fact, the geographical terrain and dangers may be such that NGOs cannot work alone. Military actors can both support and protect humanitarians, and provide the general regional stability so that humanitarians can conduct their operations unmolested. David Rieff writes of many humanitarians hoping for a "John Wayne and the Seventh Cavalry who will ride in to ensure that they can finally do their jobs."[18]

On the other hand, the paradox for NGOs is that the mere presence of intervening forces is interpreted as political action. In this regard, Eric Dachy of Médecin sans Frontières contends that "the right of intervention, peace-keeping operations invoking the use of force to guarantee the transport of relief aid, and wars fought for so-called humanitarian aims, these all constitute so many variations on a misleading theme: to accompany, or mask, a deliberate political choice with gestures of generosity and compassion."[19] In addition, if NGOs become too closely tied to state military actors, they might face the repercussions of military actions that may or may not have been designed to be, or perceived by combatants to have been impartial or neutral. This might lead to a loss of access or violence committed directly against humanitarian actors. As an example, Somali clansmen attacked the NGO World Vision in the early 1990s to reveal their anger toward American military activity in their country.[20] Moreover, these problems might not arise immediately. As state militaries and humanitarians often work on different timetables, NGOs might feel the brunt of the local actors' displeasure once the military presence is withdrawn.[21] In sum, NGO interaction with state militaries is a double-edged sword: necessity draws NGOs to military actors, while potentially negative consequences drive them away.[22]

Third, NGOs must deal with the ramifications of operational politicization on the ground. NGOs have been affected by the political implications of their humanitarian work in contemporary conflict. As noted by many analysts, post–Cold War conflict, which is largely taking place in the developing world intrastate context, has its own unique characteristics.[23] State authorities and resources are weak, black markets and other economic networks have taken the place of a state economy, human rights violations are considerable, and violence is often motivated by ethnic and religious cleavages. According to John Keegan, conflict is as a result changing in terms of rules, or the lack thereof, and the nature of the combatants: "The Clauswitzian analysis is breaking down . . . War is escaping from state control, into the hands of bandits and anarchists."[24]

In this type of conflict, governments are no longer willing or able to guarantee the continued safety of humanitarians. Similarly, the political impact of humanitarian activity is no longer ignored, and the values of neutrality and impartiality are no longer appreciated by many combatants. Accordingly, NGOs are targeted because the assistance they provide goes to civilians whose suffering is in many cases no longer the consequence of conflict, but a direct goal of it. Similarly, NGOs are targeted because the resources they bring with them are of use to the various warring parties. The invisible shield, as identified by the United Nations High Commissioner for Refugees (UNHCR), which once protected humanitarians and their activities, now would seem to be gone.[25]

Place and Limits of PSCs in Mitigating NGO Dilemmas

In order to respond to these dilemmas, NGOs have employed a variety of approaches. These approaches can overlap and they can differ from organization to organization and across time and space. But in all cases they deal solely with the matters of militarization and operational politicization. At one extreme, efforts have been redoubled to ensure the neutrality and impartiality of humanitarian assistance and to explain to those on the ground the reasons why these norms should be respected.[26] This approach follows what Koenraad Van Brabant refers to as an "acceptance strategy," one that will both protect NGO personnel and facilitate their continued operations.[27] At the other extreme, NGOs manipulate the delivery of assistance to the degree that NGOs pull out of a region in order to protest the human rights violations committed by the combating parties. Also toward this extreme are deterrence strategies that involve the close interaction with state military and political activities.[28] These more defensive choices are, according to David Rieff, the result of NGOs becoming "frustrated with the limits on what humanitarianism can accomplish on its own in a political vacuum."[29]

Between the two poles rests the "best practices" school of thought. This approach, which is espoused by Mary Anderson among others, looks at NGOs developing strategies to minimize the "harm" done by humanitarian operations in terms of contributing to and perpetuating the cycle of violence.[30] The "best practices" school sees NGOs embracing certain operational procedures to ensure that they leave a more benign footprint on the conflict's landscape. Van Brabant's idea of a protective strategy should also be put in this category because it requires NGOs to develop policies and procedures designed to reduce their vulnerability short of reliance upon the threat or use of force.[31] While the variety of options indicates the dynamism and flexibility of NGO activity, it also reveals that there is no sure way to handle the dilemmas NGOs face.

It is in this context and along this continuum that the interaction between NGOs and PSCs must be placed. As with other options, NGO reliance upon PSCs cannot overcome the dilemma of politicization from state agents. It does not change the nature of NGO funding nor does it provide NGOs with greater independence in decision making. NGO payments for PSC services would still come out of the same state-dominated coffers. In fact, collaboration between NGOs and PSCs may further perpetuate reliance upon the humanitarian alibi because states have increasingly pressured NGOs to purchase PSC services.[32] In this line of thinking, the alibi is valid only if the lives and operations of humanitarians are not overly in jeopardy. Moreover, assuming that an NGO did possess the appropriate level of non-state funding such that the dilemma of politicization was lessened, it would still not necessarily have the ability to dispense aid more freely through interaction with a PSC. While PSCs may not be sovereignty affirming as a result of their activities, a point to be discussed later, they recognize that they operate in a state-centric marketplace. In other words, PSCs work in a legal space provided by states. Their presence is agreed to by the state, and they respect the sovereignty of the state by either working alongside state security sector actors or with the permission of the government. Furthermore, in order to garner this permission, those firms that do provide offensive services, provide them only to state security sector clients. As a result, the possibility of a "Mad Max NGO" with a contracted military wing that establishes and maintains access to those in need is highly unlikely.[33]

Similarly, the capabilities of PSCs in comparison to those of state security sectors reveal both the limited abilities of PSCs and their resultant reduced potential in mitigating all of the issues emanating from the dilemma posed by militarization. On the one hand, the use of PSCs might be seen as a positive alternative to state security sector actors because firms seemingly do not have a political agenda of their own and, as they are employed by NGOs, can be more sensitive to humanitarian timetables. On the other hand, PSCs, despite the numbers of individuals they indicate are on call and their ability to purchase or rent equipment from the international marketplace, do not match the potential qualitative and quantitative resources of states.[34] PSCs do not maintain economies of scale similar to those of state security sectors because the costs associated with ensuring readiness and wide-ranging and substantial capabilities would be cost-prohibitive.[35] In addition, such a stance would be normatively and logistically problematic in the state system because of the concentration of resources and personnel that would be required. Even with the current fracturing and decentralization of security governance, states are currently only comfortable with the dispersed, on-call, and relatively small-scale organizational approach adopted by PSCs. As a result, many issues dealing with the militarization of humanitarian assistance will persist because large-scale "humanitarian" interventions will stay the sole preserve of states.

Instead, PSCs can occupy smaller scale and defensive niche roles that NGOs can rely upon in order to deal with dilemmas posed by some aspects of militarization and by operational politicization. With respect to protective measures, PSCs can provide training, risk assessment, advice, and security audits for NGOs. In this way, neutrality and impartiality might be preserved as appropriate procedures are devised and followed. With respect to deterrence, PSCs can provide defensive services such as guards to ensure the security of NGO personnel, facilities, and operations. PSC personnel can also provide logistical and security support for convoy operations and emergency evacuations.[36] In this way, while actors on the ground may nevertheless perceive NGO operations as one-sided and not neutral, NGOs can at least be physically protected. Furthermore, if they wish, NGOs can maintain their neutral and impartial stance in practice, as they will not be linked to the political mandates of foreign intervening forces.[37] Thus, CARE, Caritas, World Vision, and other NGOs have relied upon PSC services depending on the case at hand. Even the International Committee of the Red Cross, one of the staunchest followers of the humanitarian ethic, employs the services of the PSC ArmorGroup in its operations in the Democratic Republic of the Congo. At face value, the PSC is one option that humanitarian organizations might employ to help remedy some of the problems they face. But are there problems or potential implications with this non-state actor relationship?

NGO Dilemmas for Interaction with PSCs

Accountability. In most countries, state security sector actors are assumed to be made accountable through numerous methods meant to provide the checks and balances that deter illegal activity, the use of excessive force, and the abuse of authority. These are all sensitive matters given the implications they may have for order and stability. In all countries, these methods of accountability have evolved over time and are largely state specific in nature: public security sector actors are subject to both political and bureaucratic oversight and their personnel have sworn an oath and are subject to a legal code. These various methods allow the state to monitor and review the conduct of public security sector personnel in order either to deter inappropriate activities or to bring those to account should transgressions occur.

Private security companies too are subject to accountability measures, but in ways often different from those imposed upon state security sector actors. Just as contemporary security governance has evolved beyond the state to include many actors and issues, the resultant accountability mechanisms for PSCs are equally multifaceted. Home states in which PSCs are based can have legal structures governing the activities of firms, host states in which PSCs operate can subject firms to their legal direction, state and non-state clients can determine the limits of acceptable behavior for PSCs, and market forces can discipline PSCs to act in certain ways. The main matters, therefore, are the effectiveness and appropriateness of these avenues for accountability.

As clients, NGOs are often ill-prepared to be accountable for the PSCs they hire. A recent survey of 20 aid organizations, for instance, found that the NGOs generally lacked policies governing their use of PSCs.[38] This might be partially explained by the fact that NGOs are still coming to terms with the issues of security and the politicization of their post–Cold War operations. Only recently have some NGOs hired full-time security directors to ensure that security consciousness is integrated into NGO practices, procedures, and culture. The researchers of the aforementioned survey were disturbed, however, that aid agencies might be unaware that firms which supply unarmed guards may also have back-up support consisting of armored cars and rocket launchers.[39] Although these are defensive measures, such PSC activities could influence adversely conflict dynamics, lead to the loss of life, and impact negatively upon the delivery of future humanitarian assistance. Moreover, as the PSC's employer, the NGO might be legally responsible for the firm's actions. While these are all issues that a NGO should weigh if it chooses to hire a private deterrent, NGOs may nevertheless not be fully aware either of the implications or the nature of the services it has contracted.

The lack of consistent procedures and full understanding can also be attributed to internal divisions within NGOs. The PSC issue particularly reveals the different concerns and objectives of those at the field and executive levels of NGOs.[40] Personnel in the field tend to concentrate upon day-to-day operations, whereas those at the executive level concentrate their efforts upon institutional concerns such as fund-raising, promoting the NGO's image, and placating the NGO's donors. This divide also impacts upon the use of PSCs, a point recognized by PSCs and NGOs themselves.[41] Field personnel, who face directly the problems of militarization and operational politicization, have tended to be more pragmatic. In the words of one Canadian aid worker, "there are many times when I've wished we had a good quality mercenary group working with us."[42] Yet at the executive level, the issue of using private security services is troubling. Partially, this is because of the difficulty in reconciling humanitarian activity with the pursuit of profit.[43] But, more importantly, many officials do not wish to see the activities of their organizations reliant upon the use of "mercenaries." NGO officials tend to downplay their reliance upon PSCs to the point of denying that there has ever been any interaction between their particular organization and a PSC.[44]

This intra-NGO division coincides with the lack of harmony concerning contemporary security governance and the resulting contradictory pressures placed on NGOs. Elke Krahmann writes that there is a "fundamental mismatch between the current role of private security companies and existing political structures. The mismatch appears to be due to a variance between the norms of the public and politicians with regard to national and international security on the one hand and the distribution of political authority on the other."[45] In other words, many resist the idea of "mercenaries" having a prominent role in policy implementation. One can assume that NGO officials, representatives of non-state actors, may have similar misgivings about different actors like PSCs that contribute to contemporary security governance. This, however, may be a moot point because the key matter for concern is what the donors, such as states, think about the interaction between NGOs and PSCs. Therefore, NGOs must deal with the pressures of states, or some governmental elements within them, pushing for their use of PSC services while having at the same time to face the potential wrath of state and non-state donor organizations, which may not be pleased by NGOs employing PSCs.

PSCs, conflict dynamics, and the potential for operational politicization. The interaction between NGOs and PSCs may not necessarily lead to NGOs leaving a benign footprint in a particular environment. After a fleeting look, one might conclude that NGO reliance upon PSCs avoids the problems that arise from the reliance on indigenous actors. In Somalia in the early 1990s, for instance, many NGOs hired local clansmen in order to provide security. While many of these relationships were nothing more than protection rackets, they also revealed how NGOs became further implicated in the conflict. From one perspective, the funds NGOs distributed often went directly to supporting the various armed factions. As recognized by Mary Anderson and Stephen Kinloch, reliance on such actors leads to the indirect financing of factions in conflict and the further militarization of the citizenry.[46] From another perspective, because NGOs relied upon the security "services" of a certain clan, this seemingly linked the NGO with the political goals of the particular clan. From either perspective, an NGO's neutrality and impartiality, real or perceived, is compromised.

Problems such as these, however, cannot be escaped altogether through an NGO's reliance on a PSC. One of the general characteristics of contemporary security governance noted by Rhys Dogan and Michael Pugh is the trend toward transnational outsourcing and subcontracting, a trend that continues the fragmentation and decentralization. For them, firms "maintain their profit margins through the employment of local staff on local wages . . . [instead of employing] highly expensive expatriate experts."[47] PSCs are no different. In order to achieve savings and capitalize upon indigenous expertise, PSCs often rely upon local personnel. Affecting the ratio of foreign nationals to local employees are such factors as the level of risk, the size of the contract, the wishes of the client, and whether or not training of the local workforce is required.[48] Lifeguard, a PSC that operated in Sierra Leone, had managerial staff from South Africa, the United Kingdom, and the United States, but the bulk of its employees were from Sierra Leone. The ratio was anywhere from 3 to 15 local employees to every foreign national. Similar operations conducted by ArmorGroup in Central Asia and Africa also relied upon local manpower and expertise. While a PSC may be foreign in origin, it often does have very "indigenous" attributes.

There are two potential difficulties. First, as indigenous employees are used, NGO monies are being indirectly provided through PSCs to local actors who might possibly have problematic links to the conflict at hand. Given the nature of intrastate strife in which the divisions between military and civilian actors are increasingly arbitrary, it might prove to be a difficult, if not impossible, task for a PSC to ensure that its local personnel have no links to the different sides in any given hostility. Second, if these links did exist, this might attract a violent response to the NGO's presence, thus bringing about exactly what the NGO wished to avoid through reliance upon a PSC.

What is more, potentially problematic issues would remain even if a NGO elected to incur the extra expense and employ only foreigners. In order to achieve economies of scale, PSCs and their subsidiaries will often be employed by a variety of clients in a particular country. As was noted at a 2001 seminar on the interaction between NGOs and PSCs, "some apparently bonafide private security companies . . . may provide services of a more military nature to other clients whilst at the same time working for aid agencies."[49]

Consider the case of Sierra Leone where, as a result of its guarding of diamond mines, Lifeguard personnel became involved in fire-fights with the rebel movement, the Revolutionary United Front, while at the same time the firm was employed to assist NGOs.[50] In addition, PSCs can be inherently partial and linked to states in their activities, factors that might also impact negatively upon NGO activity. For instance in the past, in addition to its humanitarian clients, Lifeguard and later Southern Cross held contracts with the government of Sierra Leone for fisheries protection. Corporate links may also make this situation even more delicate. Some of Lifeguard's personnel became employees of the firm when Executive Outcomes, a PSC that fought the Revolutionary United Front on the behalf of the government, left Sierra Leone in 1997. Yves Sandoz, the Director of International Law and Communication of the International Committee of the Red Cross, recognizes that caution is in order: "It might be delicate to have a contractual relation with a company which is actively engaged on the side of a party to a conflict."[51] Although there have been no documented cases of these relationships leading to repercussions for humanitarians or their operations, it is clear that the potential exists.

Nongovernmental organizations may not have all the necessary information in order to make informed decisions regarding these trade-offs. As noted earlier, this may partly be because of the steep learning curve imposed by both the fracturing of security governance and the demands of post–Cold War humanitarianism. The level of urgency and the push of events may inhibit sober second thought.[52] But it is also the case that the PSC marketplace has not evolved to the point of allowing full disclosure; client confidentiality and a lack of transparency are the norm. NGO personnel might not be aware of a firm's other operations nor is the firm obliged to tell them. This could have an impact in terms of image and in-theater repercussions. In Uganda, for instance, the Federation of Red Cross and Red Crescent Societies ended their contract with a firm when they learned that it was linked to Saladin, a larger and better known "mercenary" company.[53] Similarly, because there is no centralized pool of information upon which NGOs can rely in order to inform their decisions, it may be difficult for them to keep up with the corporate world's myriad of subcontracting, purchasing, merging, and releasing of new "product lines."

State security sector capacity and reinforcing the effects of the alibi. Because PSCs often rely upon indigenous employees to facilitate their operations, one fear is that a shift in manpower might leave those in need even more vulnerable. One should ask, as Van Brabant does, "are you [the humanitarian organization] contributing to the privatization of security, whereby those who are able to pay can buy security while others have to live in fear, or are you contributing to increased wider, public security?"[54] One may agree with him that as the provision of security is normally the responsibility of the state and funded by taxes, paying for security services when the state is no longer making this provision and tax collection is minimal is appropriate.[55] But, as PSCs may draw people away from the public security sector to work as their indigenous employees, this reduces the capacity and the skill base, real and potential, of the state. Already in the developed world context, some have voiced concern that the fracturing and decentralization of contemporary security governance will lead to changes in career trajectories and incentives for currently serving security sector personnel.[56] In the developing world where security sector structures are often weak, the effects are likely to be more acute. Indeed, the need to turn to PSCs in the first place is representative of this weakness. Yet at the same point, the dynamics are such that the possibility of attempting to ensure the security of all might be replaced by ensuring the security of the few.

This problem cannot be easily overlooked because it may reinforce the negative effects of the humanitarian alibi. Without an intervening force present, civilians may not get the physical protection that they need. Adam Roberts suggests that "[p]rotection is properly seen not as an occasional add-on to humanitarian relief supplies, but as a key aspect of the international community's response to wars and crises."[57] The humanitarian alibi, however, prevents this integration. For Diane Paul, humanitarians may be able to provide comfort, but they cannot deal with their lack of physical security:

> While feeding the hungry and treating the wounded and displaced can be seen as a protection activity, attending to those needs when there is insufficient attention to the need for physical security from direct or indirect attack misses the mark. What in reality are protection failures are too often defined as humanitarian crises which, despite the fact that the term humanitarian includes the humane and dignified treatment of people, is often interpreted to mean assistance in the form of food, shelter, and healthcare. This shifts focus away from the real problem that which both causes the need for these services and cannot possibly be addressed through the distribution of relief supplies.[58]

Put more bluntly by David Bryer, a director of Oxfam: "[civilian] protection from violence is more vital than humanitarian relief."[59]

Collaboration between NGOs and PSCs, for its part, cannot provide the needed protection for civilians, however humane it might be. This is because PSCs only sell defensive services to NGOs given their state-centric orientation. But the fact that PSC operations may draw away security sector personnel, perhaps even the more competent and professional individuals, this further lessens the possibility that protection will be provided for those in need. The upshot is that not only may NGOs end up serving the cause of the humanitarian alibi; they may also augment its troublesome effects.[60]

Current Abilities and Approaches to Managing NGO–PSC Interaction

In recent years, those NGOs that are willing to contemplate the employment of PSCs have attempted to deal with the issue of standards and policies governing

NGO–PSC interaction. Increased communication through forums such as the InterAction Security Group and other NGO workshops over time might help to create a better profile of the different PSCs upon which NGOs might rely. Similarly, NGOs might be able to exchange information and reflect upon past practices. However, what still exists is the long-standing general desire of NGOs not to give up managerial autonomy for the sake of larger efficiency or greater coherence.[61] From one standpoint there is, according to International Alert, "a reluctance to develop and jointly agree [*sic*] standards, codes of conduct or guidelines as they are perceived as threatening to the flexibility and independence of aid agencies in situations that are unique."[62] Another standpoint, noted by R.C.D. Dangerfield and others, focuses not upon the maintenance of the humanitarian ethic, but instead upon the independence and uniqueness of each humanitarian organization: "NGOs are a fragmented area of the corporate world with different mandates and missions, which does not promote harmonization of approach or desire to self-regulate."[63] In both cases, long-standing and unique operational policies and mindsets might have to be sacrificed for the sake of standardization and coherent NGO-side input into contemporary security governance.

Due to these difficulties, NGOs have placed the onus instead upon states and the UN in order to help remedy their problems or at least to help them make informed decisions regarding trade-offs. Although the geopolitical environment has changed and the nature of post–Cold War humanitarianism is dramatically different, NGOs want to rely, as they did in the past, upon states and the UN to ensure their security when and where required.[64] Therefore, what are the capabilities and current policies of these actors to assist NGOs or to provide suitable information?

States. Admittedly, the development of state-based regulation of PSCs is in a nascent stage. While most states have neutrality and foreign enlistment regulations that reflect international legal norms dating back to at least the Hague Conventions at the turn of the twentieth century, these laws are generally anachronistic and not appropriate for managing the PSC phenomenon. Only South Africa and the United States have legislation that encompasses the PSCs based in their territory. In the near future, only the United Kingdom is likely to join these ranks; it produced a nonbinding green paper on regulation in 2002.

Nevertheless, even though the bulk of the world's states do not have PSC-specific regulations, analysis of these three states is still appropriate in the context of managing contemporary security governance. First, as the PSC is a relatively new phenomenon, the regulatory measures of these states might serve as a template for others. Second, in practical terms, given that these three states have a large number of the world's PSCs based within their respective territories, their potential impact in terms of input into the relations between NGOs and PSCs stands out.

What also stands out is the fact that existing regulations maintain the independence of humanitarian action. In the South African case, the Regulations of Foreign Military Assistance Act covers only instances of armed conflict, and even then, it exempts humanitarian activities from its purview. The act applies to "any action that has the result of furthering military interests of a party to the armed conflict, but not humanitarian or civilian activities aimed at relieving the plight of civilians in the area of armed conflict."[65] In the American case, NGO–PSC interaction seemingly falls under the purview of the International Traffic in Arms Regulations (ITAR) given that defense services refer to, "[t]he furnishing of assistance, including training, to foreign persons, whether in the United States or abroad, in the design, development, engineering, manufacture, production, assembly, testing, repair, maintenance, modification, operation, demilitarization, destruction, processing or use of defense articles."[66] However, although the ITAR does not deal specifically with humanitarian activities, in practice they have been exempt because of section 120.3 of the ITAR which states that, "[d]esignations of defense articles and defense services are based primarily on whether an article or service is deemed to be inherently military in character."[67] In the United Kingdom, while the investigation and debate following the release of the green paper has included how PSCs might better facilitate NGO operations, the actual proposals for regulation have not taken into account NGO activities.[68]

It would seemingly appear that the primary issue for these country's regulations is the preservation of the supposed sanctity and independence of the humanitarian activity.[69] The implications of collaboration between NGOs and PSCs or the actual effects of humanitarian activity on the ground are not concerns even though these are sensitive matters.[70] Hence, one reading of this situation is that official state approval would likely cut too deeply into the perceived independence of humanitarian activity. PSC activities, and implicitly the operations of the NGOs that they would support, would fall under state purview and likely cause great resentment in the humanitarian community. Alternatively, however, a cynical reading sees this independence as helping to maintain the humanitarian alibi, by design or outcome, as states would not be seen to sanction officially NGOs' use of PSCs. In effect then, state regulations do not deal specifically with the collaboration between NGOs and PSCs and the resulting sense of independence, albeit for substantially different reasons, may be of perceived benefit to both NGOs and states.

Moreover, the regulations that do exist do little to serve indirectly the needs of NGOs. This is because both the South African and American regulations deal predominantly with contract approval rather than with the licensing criteria and requirements for PSCs. While firms are obliged to register with their respective government in order to seek contracts, there are no mechanisms to ensure that firms can competently provide what they sell. Also, there are no provisions to assess that PSC personnel have the necessary expertise and do not have blemishes on their records for past service in state security sectors. This is left to the established internal policies of the firms that may not be transparent, appropriate, or even followed. This means that NGO concerns regarding accountability will not be mitigated through greater confidence in the quality of the service the PSC is contracted to do. Another matter is that state regulations do not require sufficient disclosure of a firm's past, its corporate structure and relationships, and its present contractual arrangements. Thus, in the American case, for instance, unless a PSC is willing to be forthcoming, it is only through freedom of information requests that NGOs and the public at large can learn what services a firm has exported and to whom.[71] The only guidance NGOs might find in the future rests in the British case. Both the green paper's options and the lobbying efforts by interested parties such as International Alert include measures to increase quality control and augment corporate transparency.[72] At present, however, there is little state-mandated oversight and control that would help to allay NGO concerns.

United Nations. Currently, the UN is not ready to contribute immediately to the overarching management of PSC operations that might allay NGO concerns about accountability and transparency. The world body's only regulatory device for mercenaries is its 1990 *International Convention against the Recruitment, Use, Financing and Training of Mercenaries*. The convention's approach toward the mercenary issue is largely anachronistic and not appropriate for PSCs, a point recognized by Sandoz: "I have the impression that the basic approach [of the convention] is not relevant today and that the problem of private security should not be essentially based on the mercenary issue as it was dealt with in the seventies."[73] Simply put, the convention was not designed to handle a type of mercenary activity that sought legitimacy through the sale of services to states and "respectable" organizations and non-state actors. Moreover, the changes required to make the United Nation's stance on the issue relevant are unlikely to be forthcoming soon nor helpful in countering NGO concerns. Indeed, for the UN, the mercenary issue is problematic given the embarrassments the organization has suffered at the hands of mercenaries and the hostility the developing world membership often directs toward the mercenary problem. Due to these tensions and the generally slow nature of the United Nation's decision-making processes, some estimates place the development of relevant PSC-centric regulation as not coming to fruition for 20 years.[74]

At the field level, however, UN operations are presently dealing with the PSC phenomenon in a sustained way. Despite the tensions within the world body, the UNHCR, the UN Children's Fund (UNICEF), and the World Food Program all have relied upon PSC services in their conduct of post–Cold War humanitarianism. This schizophrenic approach of the UN is representative both of the fiefdoms that make up the United Nation's "family" of organizations and the operational pressures and problems facing field organizations. The UN system, like NGOs, was obviously neither immune to nor ready for changes in contemporary humanitarianism. The UN Security Coordinator (UNSECOORD) was underfunded and designed for the more benign conditions of the Cold War and UN workers too have been killed.

Also, the organization's first choice, continuing reliance on legal measures such as the 1994 *Convention on the Safety of UN and Associated Personnel*, did not lead to the desired results. Though the convention did not come into force until 1999, it is clear that it was not setting behavioral norms. In 1998, for instance, the annual number of civilian worker deaths surpassed that of UN military casualties for the first time.[75] As a result, it is only over the past few years that greater attention has focused upon security measures and the improvement of UNSECOORD's capabilities, all long-term and challenging tasks involving changes in attitudes and procedures and a search for funding. Indeed, of the 13 aforementioned countries where many humanitarians have lost their lives, only 1 country has ratified the convention.[76] Similarly discouraging is that only 12 states have stepped forward to fund activities meant to increase UNSECOORD's capacity. Therefore, like NGOs, the UN faces similar problems and has similar motivations to turn to PSCs: they are responsive, they will follow their humanitarian mandates, and they can provide the required services to facilitate both protective and deterrence strategies.

Yet even with engagement of the PSC issue on this level, there are limitations on what inputs the UN can provide into guiding the relations between NGOs and PSCs. Certainly, the UN is relevant for NGO operations given the trend, as with states, to subcontract responsibilities to the NGO community. On the one hand, NGOs possess flexibility, capabilities, and a readiness to act that make them ideal to carry out activities authorized by the UN. On the other hand, there remains the concern that UN sanctioning affects the independence of NGOs and potentially taints them with a political mandate. However, the UN has not yet developed guidelines and practices on PSC usage that might seem to impinge further upon NGO freedom. PSCs are listed on the UN Supply Database for UN and UN-related organizations, but this service does not necessarily imply official endorsement. The only specific guidelines covering field operations support the sovereignty of member states and the state-centric nature of the PSC marketplace. This is explained by Martin Barber, the chief of Policy Development and Advocacy for the UN Office for the Coordination of Humanitarian Affairs: "The basic criteria for their use requires that PSCs are registered by the government of the country in which they are operating and that the government has authorized their use for a specific contract."[77] In sum, while current UN field arrangements prevent the further deterioration of NGO independence, they do not provide insight into managerial direction nor offer assurances of quality control.

Conclusion

In the post–Cold War environment, humanitarian NGOs find themselves in a dilemma. Sole reliance upon the attributes of the humanitarian ethic does not have the same currency as it did in the past, but moving away from this ethic, or at least taking steps to ameliorate the situation, is equally problematic. Fueling this dilemma are the facts that NGOs have been deprived of the assurances of security to which they had grown accustomed, their right to operate unmolested is no longer respected, and they are subject to the political machinations of states at a variety of levels. Hiring PSCs may alleviate some NGO concerns, but leaves others untouched and poses new ones that must be managed. NGOs, for their part, have so far placed operational and organizational independence ahead of developing standardized policies that would collectively allow NGOs to have input into the uniform structuring of contemporary security governance. Long-standing barriers to coordination will have to be overcome for a change to occur. As for states, they too are slow to come to terms with the nature of contemporary security governance. Hence, widespread state-based regulation of PSCs is not yet an international reality. Existing regulation does not solve NGO problems and may both preserve humanitarian independence and perpetuate the humanitarian alibi.

As for the UN, the little guidance it does offer serves only to ensure the sovereignty respecting qualities of the PSC marketplace. In the main, while one can argue that the development of structures to manage coherently state security sectors is an ongoing long-term task, it is clear that the interested parties concerning this element of security governance are divided in their interests and their capabilities. It would seem, therefore, that NGOs will continue to wrestle with the grayness and trade-offs of contemporary humanitarianism made all the more plain by NGO–PSC interaction.

With respect to the future, it will be interesting to observe and assess how NGOs will manage these gray areas. They may change such that donors become more familiarized with PSCs and accept the fractured nature of security governance. This would mitigate some NGO concerns about image. However, this evolution will also be influenced strongly by NGOs both educating themselves and their donors about the PSC industry, a process that may take upwards of a generation to bring about.[78] In this vein, the assertion by Robert Mandel is salient: "Policymakers and their publics need more discussion about acceptable types of private coercion, the occasions for its use, and the choice of who implements it."[79]

Coming to terms with contemporary security governance, however, will be no easy task in light of the divisions between and within NGOs. One step might be for NGOs to engage in greater dialogue with PSCs outside of crisis situations, although they have to be wary of current donor mindsets.[80] This might reveal NGO concerns to PSCs and perhaps structure individual PSCs toward better handling the sensitivities and needs of humanitarian clients. Indeed, the sense of urgency in engaging in such dialogue rests not just with determining how NGOs might best confront the dangers evident in post–Cold War humanitarian activity. There have been some cases in which humanitarian organizations have been sued by injured staff or the family members of deceased staff. Whereas an initial impetus behind NGOs turning to PSCs was to protect humanitarians so that assistance could be delivered, another issue now is willingness of personnel to join an NGO in the first place. In this regard, PSC services may be increasingly needed for the sake of insurance and maintaining the appeal of working for NGOs.[81] To reiterate, post–Cold War security governance, when taking into account operational pressures and the interests of many actors, makes, and will continue to make, for strange bedfellows.

Notes

1. See Elke Krahmann, "Private Firms and the New Security Governance," *Conflict, Security and Developments* 5, no. 2 (2005): forthcoming.
2. This chapter deals solely with contractual relations between NGOs and PSCs. For analysis that deals with the issue of NGOs relying upon, but not hiring, PSCs already in theater, see Christopher Spearin, "A Private Security Panacea? A Specific Response to Mean Times," *Canadian Foreign Policy* 7, no. 3 (2000): 67–80.
3. Antonio Donini, "Asserting Humanitarianism in Peace-Maintenance," in *The Politics of Peace Maintenance*, ed. Jarat Chopra, 81–96 (Boulder, CO: Lynne Rienner, 1998), 89.

4. See, for instance, Leon Gordenker and Thomas G. Weiss, "Pluralizing Global Governance: Analytical Approaches and Dimensions," in *NGOs, the UN, and Global Governance*, ed. Leon Gordenker and Thomas G. Weiss, 17–47 (Boulder, CO: Lynne Rienner, 1996), 17.
5. For additional background information on the causal ingredients, see David Isenberg, *Soldiers of Fortune Ltd.: A Profile of Today's Private Sector Corporate Mercenary Firms* (Washington, DC: Center for Defense Information, 1997); Robert Mandel, *Armies without States: The Privatization of Security* (Boulder, CO: Lynne Rienner, 2002); David Shearer, *Private Armies and Military Intervention*, Adelphi Paper 316 (Oxford: Oxford University Press for IISS, 1998); James Larry Taulbee, "Mercenaries, Private Armies and Security Companies in Contemporary Policy," *International Politics* 37, no. 4 (2000): 433–56; Peter W. Singer, *Corporate Warriors: The Rise of the Privatized Military Industry* (Ithaca, NY: Cornell University Press, 2003).
6. These countries are Angola, Afghanistan, Burundi, Cambodia, Ethiopia, Georgia, Iraq, Kenya, Kosovo, Rwanda, Somalia, Sudan, and Uganda. Roberta Cohen, "Safety for Those Who Bring Help," *Washington Post*, November 3, 2003.
7. Cited in Kathleen Kenna, "NGOs Forced to Rethink Strategy," *Toronto Star*, September 7, 2003.
8. Sven Chojnacki, "Humanitarian Actors, the International Humanitarian System and International Order" (paper, International Political Science Association, Quebec City, Canada, August 1–5, 2000), 9.
9. Cited in Sven Chojnacki, *The Times They Are A-changin': Prevention and Humanitarianism*, P01–308 (Berlin: Social Science Research Centre, October 2001), 10.
10. Daniel L. Byman, "Uncertain Partners: NGOs and the Military," *Survival* 43, no. 2 (2001): 97–114, 104.
11. Gordenker and Weiss, "Pluralizing Global Governance," 21.
12. Mark Duffield, "The Political Economy of Internal War: Asset Transfer, Complex Emergencies and International Aid," in *War & Hunger: Rethinking International Responses to Complex Emergencies*, ed. Joanna Macrae and Anthony Zwi, 50–69 (London: Zed Books, 1994), 59.
13. This number of humanitarian NGOs is noted in Chojnacki, "Humanitarian Actors, the international Humanitarian System and International Order," 12.
14. Ibid., 3.
15. Michael Bryans, Bruce D. Jones, and Janice Stein, "Mean Times: Humanitarian Action in Complex Political Emergencies—Stark Choices, Cruel Dilemmas," *Coming to Terms* 1 (1999), 2.
16. Larry Minear, "Humanitarian Action and Peacekeeping Operations," *Journal of Humanitarian Assistance*, February 1997, http://www.jha.ac/articles/a018.htm.
17. Diane Paul, *Protection in Practice: Field-Level Strategies for Protecting Civilians from Deliberate Harm*, Relief and Rehabilitation Paper No. 30 (London: Overseas Development Institute, July 1999), 30.
18. David Rieff, "Humanitarianism in Crisis," *Foreign Affairs* 81, no. 6 (2002): 111–21, 119.
19. Cited in ibid., 116–17.
20. Byman, "Uncertain Partners: NGOs and the Military," 104.
21. Ibid., 105. Beyond the inherent political difficulties, one must also note the different organizational and operational cultures between state security sector instruments and NGOs that pose some difficulties for coordination and execution. See Jane Barry, *A Bridge too far: Aid Agencies and the Military in Humanitarian Response*, Humanitarian Practice Network Paper No. 37 (London: Overseas Development Institute, January 2002).

22. There is also the ethical fear, noted by some, that relying on the use of arms to deliver assistance only serves to legitimize, mirror, and perpetuate the activities of war. See United Kingdom, House of Commons, Foreign Affairs Committee, *Private Military Companies*, Ninth Report of Session 2001–2002 (London: The Stationary Office, August 1, 2002), 26.

23. See Mary Kaldor, *New and Old Wars: Organized Violence in a Global Era* (Stanford: Stanford University Press, 1999); K.J. Holsti, *The State, War, and the State of War* (Cambridge: Cambridge University Press, 1996); Martin Van Creveld, *The Transformation of War* (New York: The Free Press, 1991).

24. Citation is taken from John Mueller, "Hatred, Violence, and Warfare: Thugs as Residual Combatants" (paper, American Political Science Association, San Francisco, August 30– September 2, 2001), 35.

25. Editor's Desk, "The 'Invisible Shield' of Protection Disappears," *Refugees* 4 (2000): 2.

26. Philippe Comtesse, "The New Vulnerability of Humanitarian Workers: What Is the Proper Response? An ICRC Delegate's View," *International Review of the Red Cross* 317 (1997): 143–51.

27. Koenraad Van Brabant, *Operational Security Management in Violent Environments: A Field Manual for Aid Agencies* (London: Overseas Development Institute, 2000), 58.

28. This may have obvious effects in terms of the neutrality, impartiality, and independence of humanitarian activity.

29. Rieff, "Humanitarianism in Crisis," 117.

30. See Mary B. Anderson, *Do No Harm: How Aid Can Support Peace—Or War* (Boulder, CO: Lynne Rienner, 1999).

31. Van Brabant, *Operational Security Management*, 58.

32. The contention that NGOs are pressured is made in Tony Vaux, Chris Sieple, Greg Nakano, and Koenraad Van Brabant, *Humanitarian Action and Private Security Companies: Opening the Debate* (London: International Alert, 2002), 10.

33. This term is found in Donini, "Asserting Humanitarianism in Peace-Maintenance," 89.

34. It is true that small numbers can make an impact. France's 1994 "Operation Turquoise" in Rwanda involved only 2,500 personnel. Similarly, the United Kingdom's 2000 "Operation PALLISER" in Sierra Leone featured the use of 800 paratroopers. However, one must note that these contingents could rely on considerable back-up support, a luxury for PSCs.

35. R.C.D. Dangerfield, B.D.A. Kite, D.J. Robinson, and A.J.I. Wilson, "Private Military Companies: Options for Regulation—A Response to the UK Government Green Paper" (paper submitted to the Foreign and Commonwealth office, United Kingdom, 2002), 33; Damian Lilly, *Green Paper Submission* (London: International Alert, 2002).

36. The identification of PSC services contributing to protection and deterrence approaches can be found in International Alert and the Feinstein International Famine Center, "The Politicisation of Humanitarian Action and Staff Security: The Use of Private Security Companies by Humanitarian Agencies" (international workshop summary report, Tufts University, Boston, MA, April 23–24, 2001), 2.

37. Admittedly, this approach does weaken the notion of humanitarian NGO solidarity with those in need.

38. Vaux et al., 6. *Humanitarian Action*, 6.

39. Ibid., 17. The report cites the example of ArmorGroup in Uganda and its use of quick response forces.

40. This general divide is documented in Byman, "Uncertain Partners," 102–03.

41. This point is dealt with in Christopher Spearin, "Private Security Companies and Humanitarians: A Corporate Solution to Securing Humanitarian Spaces?" *International Peacekeeping* 8, no. 1 (2001): 20–43.

42. Cited in James R. Davis, *Fortune's Warriors: Private Armies and the New World Order* (Vancouver: Douglas & McIntyre, 2000), 180.

43. An expanded notion of profit is documented in Henry Cummins, "Perception and Profit: Understanding Commercial Military and Security Service Provision" (discussion paper, Centre for Studies in Security and Diplomacy, University of Birmingham, 24 June 2002).

44. Vaux et al., 9. *Humanitarian Action*, 9.

45. Krahmann, "Private Firms and the New Security Governance."

46. Anderson, *Do No Harm*, 43, 138, 142; Stephen P. Kinloch, "Utopian or Pragmatic? A UN Permanent Volunteer Force," *International Peacekeeping* 3, no. 4 (1996): 179.

47. Rhys Dogan and Michael Pugh, *From Military to Market Imperatives: Peacekeeping and the New Public Policy*, Plymouth International Papers No. 8 (Plymouth University of Plymouth International Studies Centre, July 1997), 18.

48. Bernie McCabe (Lifeguard employee), in an interview with the author, April 10, 2000.

49. International Alert and the Feinstein International Famine Center, 4.

50. David Shearer, "Private Military Force and Challenges for the Future," *Cambridge Review of International Affairs* 13, no. 1 (1999): 80–94, 86.

51. Yves Sandoz, "The Privatisation of Security: Framing A Conflict Prevention and Peacebuilding Agenda" (paper, Wilton Park Conference, London, November 19–21, 1999), 1. See also Yves Sandoz, "Private Security and International Law," in *Peace, Profit or Plunder? The Privatisation of Security in War-Torn African Societies*, ed. Jakkie Cilliers and Peggy Mason, 201–26 (Pretoria: Institute for Security Studies, 1999).

52. Vaux et al., 15. *Humanitarian Action*, 15.

53. Ibid.

54. Van Brabant, *Operational Security Management*.

55. Ibid., 77, 79.

56. Deborah Avant, "Privatizing Military Training," *Foreign Policy In Focus* 7, no. 6 (2002), http://www.fpif.org/briefs/vol7/v7n06miltrain_body.html.

57. Adam Roberts, *Humanitarian Action in War: Aid, Protection and Impartiality in a Policy Vacuum*, Adelphi Paper 305 (Oxford: Oxford University Press for IISS, 1996), 86.

58. Paul, *Protection in practice*, 28.

59. Cited in Roberts, *Humanitarian Action in war,34*.

60. Some contend, therefore, that if money is to be spent on security, it is an open issue whether or not the security of all might be better ensured through the development of local capabilities. While such a development might hamper the perceptions of impartiality, neutrality, and independence, it might also better contribute to the long-term development of public capacity. One can wonder, however, if an NGO would be able to direct such a program given its probable lack of expertise in security matters and the potential openness of the program to manipulation. International Alert and the Feinstein International Famine Center, "The Politicisation of Humanitarian Action," 4; Van Brabant, *Operational Security Management* 347.

61. This general problem is noted in Andrew S. Natsios, "NGOs and the UN System in Complex Humanitarian Emergencies: Conflict or Cooperation?" in *NGOs, the UN, and Global Governance*, 67–81, 75.

62. International Alert and the Feinstein International Famine Center, "The Politicisation of Humanitarian Action," 5.

63. Dangerfield et al., "Private Military Companies," 45.

64. Ibid.

65. *Regulation of Foreign Military Assistance Bill*, B-54–97, May 20, 1998.

66. U.S. Department of State, Office for Defense Trade Controls, *Arms Export Control Act, International Traffic in Arms Regulation*, Title 22, United States Code, Section 120.9.

67. Ibid., Section 120.3.

68. U.K. House of Commons, 26. In this vein, the parliamentary committee examining the green paper has suggested that automatic licensing should exist for certain PSC clients. See page 33.

69. Certainly, this separation is at odds with other factors in this paper that see states intruding upon the independence of the humanitarian domain and framing the actions of NGOs.

70. David Rieff, for one, contends that "despite the best intentions of aid workers, and at times because of them, they become logisticians in the war efforts of warlords, fundamentalists, gangsters, and ethnic cleansers." David Rieff, "The Humanitarian Illusion," *The New Republic*, March 16, 1998, 30.

71. Leura Peterson, "Privatizing Combat, the New World Order," *The Center for Public Integrity*, October 28, 2002, 8. The author also notes that in May 2002, the Justice Department of the United States issued new guidelines that allow companies to challenge the release of information through freedom of information requests, thus further hindering public disclosure.

72. See U.K. Foreign and Commonwealth Office, *Private Military Companies: Options for Regulation 2001–02* (London: Stationery Office, February 12, 2002); Chaloka Beyani and Damian Lilly, *Regulating Private Military Companies: Options for the UK Government* (London: International Alert, 2001).

73. Sandoz, "The Privatization of Security," 3.

74. Dangerfield et al., "Private Military Companies," 71.

75. U.S. Department for International Development, "Conflict Reduction and Humanitarian Assistance" (policy statement, Washington, DC, February 1999), 5.

76. Cohen, "Safety for Those who Bring Help," A19.

77. Martin Barber, "Private Security Companies and Humanitarian Assistance," in *The Privatization of Security: Framing a Conflict Prevention and Peacebuilding Policy Agenda— the Report of the Wilton Park Conference* (London: International Alert, 2001), 35.

78. My thanks to Chris Seiple of the Institute for Global Engagement for raising this point regarding education and generational matters.

79. Robert Mandel, "The Privatization of Security," *Armed Forces and Society* 28, no. 1 (2001): 129–51, 147.

80. The general dearth of communication between PSCs, states, and NGOs is noted by many. Krahmann, "Private Firms and the New Security Governance." Cummins, "Perception and Profit," 2; Dangerfield et al., "Private Military Companies," 17.

81. For information on the suing of humanitarian organizations, see Koenraad Van Brabant, "Security Training: Where Are We Now?" *Forced Migration Review* 4 (1999): 7–10. Multinational corporations face similar legal pressures when their operations are in unstable areas. See *The Economist*, "Corporate Security: Risk Returns," November 20, 1999, 78.

Part III

Terrorism and Transnational Crime

Chapter 4

Drug Traffickers, Terrorist Networks, and Ill-Fated Government Strategies

Michael Kenney

On April 8, 1986, President Reagan signed National Security Decision Directive (NSDD) Number 221 in which he identified the "expanding scope of global narcotics trafficking" as a security threat to the United States and its democratic partners in the western hemisphere. Just three months earlier the president had signed another directive, NSDD Number 207, highlighting the growing threat to American security posed by terrorist groups intent on attacking "U.S. citizens and installations, especially abroad."[1] Both directives were issued in response to developments in transnational terrorism and drug trafficking and designed to prioritize foreign policy objectives, outline specific enforcement strategies, and clarify roles and responsibilities for federal agencies. Indeed, the 1980s were growth years for both illicit industries. According to U.S. government data, the number of international terrorist attacks against the United States and other countries increased for most of the decade, while transnational smuggling enterprises saturated U.S. drug markets with cocaine during the same period.[2] Dramatic incidents such as the Miami Dadeland Mall shootout in 1979, attributed by law enforcement officials to rival Colombian drug gangs, and the hijacking of TWA Flight 847 by Hezbollah militants in 1985, highlighted the danger to public security posed by these illicit non-state actors and the corresponding need for a more coordinated policy response from the United States and its allies.

To be sure, the 1980s were not the first decade in which private actors threatened the perceived security interests of the United States and other sovereign members of the Westphalian system. States have been battling transnational pirates, mercenaries, contraband smugglers, and religious extremists for centuries.[3] But while drug traffickers and terrorists enjoy lengthy, if nefarious, pedigrees, historically the international dimension of their activities has been limited by the transportation and communication technology available to them. The advent, improvement, and widespread diffusion of television broadcasting, commercial air travel, telephone and facsimile communications, computer-mediated information technology, and other technological developments of post industrial society has increased the speed and reliability of cross-border flows of people, ideas, capital, and commodities. The combination of sweeping technological change and government deregulation of trade and financial markets has shrunk geographic distances and reduced the relative costs of international exchange. The less-heralded side of globalization is that these technologies and policies benefit all willing and capable participants, whether they specialize in moving fresh-cut flowers, microprocessors, cocaine hydrochloride, or violent extremists across national boundaries.

The Reagan administration felt this sea change, as reflected in the rhetorical urgency of NSDDs 207 and 221. The broadening of traditional notions of security, often considered a post–Cold War phenomenon, began to take shape during the 1980s as the president and Congress increasingly defined national security in terms of protecting American citizens, territory, and values from unwanted depredations by thugs or drugs. Ironically, at the same time that many international relations scholars were clinging to established theoretical paradigms that privileged the centrality of states in world politics, the Reagan administration—credited rightly or wrongly with bringing about the collapse of America's lone superpower rival of four decades—found itself confronting a variety of security threats emanating not from sovereign competitors, but from presumably weaker non-state actors.

If transnational trafficking and terrorism underscore the challenges confronting contemporary states in protecting their citizens from psychoactive drugs and political violence, counterterrorism and counter-narcotics programs highlight the expansion of state power in attempting to bridge these growing gaps in governance. Over the past 25 years, U.S. drug control and counterterrorism budgets have grown steadily, as have the law enforcement agencies charged with protecting the nation from these transnational security threats. Between 1982 and 1999, the number of agents in the U.S. Drug Enforcement Administration (DEA), the lead federal agency for domestic and overseas counter-drug law enforcement, increased from 1,896 to 4,527. During the same period, the agency's annual budget increased from $244 million to $1,477 million.[4] Between 1993 and 1999, the number of Federal Bureau of Investigation (FBI) agents working on terrorism-related investigations increased from 550 to 1,383, while the agency's counterterrorism program grew from $78.5 million to $301.2 million.[5] Since the tragic events of September 11, 2001, the FBI has made counterterrorism the bureau's number one priority and assigned another 500 agents to work terrorism investigations.

The drug enforcement and counterterrorism programs of the United states have traditionally focused on reducing the "supply" of illicit drugs and terrorism. Since the early 1980s, U.S. drug control policies have privileged supply-reduction programs that eradicate illegal drug crops, destroy processing labs, interdict drug flows, apprehend suspected smugglers and dealers, and confiscate drug revenues. In Colombia, American law enforcers, intelligence analysts, and Special Forces soldiers have worked closely with their host country counterparts to implement such policies. This supply-reduction strategy has achieved notable results. During the 1990s, Colombian law enforcers arrested thousands of suspected drug traffickers, interdicted tons of drugs, and seized millions of dollars worth of illegal assets.

Moreover, between 1989 and 1996, police officials captured or killed almost all of the kingpins of the so-called Medellín and Cali cocaine "cartels." Eager to replicate these results in the campaign against terrorism, the U.S. government has prioritized similar headhunting strategies in its international counterterrorism strategy. Indeed, members of the intelligence community acknowledge that drug enforcement raids in Colombia during the 1990s serve as models for today's antiterrorism operations in Afghanistan, Pakistan, Yemen, and the Philippines.[6]

But if the Colombian drug war is to serve as the archetype for Washington's campaign against terrorism, policy makers should be clear on what lessons can properly be extrapolated from the model. The news from Colombia is not as encouraging as some policy outputs, and some high-level officials, suggest. Supply-reduction policies undertaken in Colombia over the last 25 years have not succeeded in eliminating the country's illegal drug trade. In fact, during the six years following the incarceration of the last original kingpin, the estimated potential production of cocaine in Colombia increased by 143 percent, from an estimated 300 metric tons in 1996 to 730 metric tons in 2001.[7] One explanation for these disappointing results can be found in the adaptability and organizational structures of Colombian trafficking enterprises. These fluid, loosely coupled networks bear numerous similarities to another set of non-state actors that has become central to policy makers since the Bush administration began its spirited crusade to "root out" terrorists from Buffalo to Baghdad over two years ago. Faced with persistent reminders from senior administration figures that the war on terror is for the long haul, a comparative analysis of drug trafficking and terrorist enterprises, along with government efforts to destroy them, is in order.

This chapter offers such an appraisal, highlighting the evolution of the Colombian drug trade and U.S. and Colombian drug enforcement efforts in the 1990s. The Colombian case is instructive due not only to the numerous similarities shared by Colombian trafficking enterprises and Islamic terrorist networks, including compartmentalized networks and an affinity for organizational adaptation, but also to the intensity of the U.S.–Colombian campaign to hunt down and dismantle leading trafficking groups. Few, if any, countries have cooperated more closely in Washington's war on drugs than Colombia. In spite of its strong antidrug efforts, or perhaps because of them, in recent years the illicit drug trade in Colombia has downsized and atomized, while producing greater quantities of cocaine and heroin for U.S. and European drug consumers. Developments in Colombia's post-cartel drug industry offer sobering lessons for those that wish to avoid repeating critical mistakes in the war on drugs.

Emergence of Colombian Cocaine Networks

The Colombian cocaine "cartels"[8] can be traced back to the 1970s, when numerous private entrepreneurs sought to exploit the demand for cocaine in U.S. drug markets by transporting small quantities of the drug from Ecuador, Bolivia, and Peru to Colombia, where it underwent further refinement in makeshift laboratories before final shipment northward. Over time and repeated exchange, these individuals developed transnational transportation and distribution networks capable of coordinating several multiton cocaine shipments a year. These wheel networks contained a core group that coordinated activities among different functional nodes, including cocaine base suppliers, processing labs, transportation rings, and distribution groups that delivered cocaine to independent retailers and funneled the profits to network leaders and investors.[9] While core groups were generally based in Colombia, support nodes were often located in different countries, including among others Bolivia, Peru, Guatemala, Mexico, the Dominican Republic, Spain, the Netherlands, and the United States. To reduce their exposure to law enforcement penetration, participants in cross-border transportation or wholesale distribution activities were often compartmentalized into small working groups or cells that maintained close communication with core groups and followed elaborate procedures for delivering large amounts of drugs to independent wholesalers and conducting other hazardous activities.

Core groups directed their respective networks by coordinating transactions, providing security, and securing resources from independent investors. They also gathered intelligence about government drug enforcement efforts and resolved disputes among different nodes. If something went wrong, informal relations of vertical accountability ensured that peripheral nodes answered to the core, protecting kingpins and investors from theft and other uncertainties. Decision-making authority flowed out and downward from the core, beginning with one or more kingpins that headed the transnational enterprise. Below the kingpins were "managers" responsible for line functions, such as transportation and wholesale distribution. Below managers were cell workers that carried out much of the daily work of the enterprise. Kingpins or trusted associates sought to maintain control over their operations through frequent communication with overseas managers, often mediated through brokers that provided an additional layer of insulation from law enforcers.

Colombian and U.S. law enforcers were slow to appreciate the size and sophistication of Colombian trafficking networks. Throughout the 1970s and the early 1980s, Colombian cocaine traffickers were able to conduct their affairs largely free from law enforcement pressure, as police agencies focused primarily on marijuana and heroin. While law enforcers targeted a number of cocaine traffickers through complex conspiracy investigations, such efforts were sporadic and failed to weaken Colombia's burgeoning cocaine industry. By the mid-1980s, U.S. and Colombian officials were fully attuned to the danger represented by a handful of wheel networks, particularly the notorious Medellín and Cali enterprises. With U.S. assistance, Colombian drug enforcers launched several crackdowns against the leaders of these transnational enterprises between 1984 and 1988, destroying processing labs, seizing cocaine shipments, arresting, and occasionally extraditing lower and middle-level traffickers. However, these offensives were short lived and did not significantly impact core group kingpins, whose security arrangements and skillful corruption of state officials allowed them to continue their illicit activities largely free from government interference.

During the 1980s, police officials discovered numerous multiton cocaine shipments in the United States, indicating the growing capacity of Colombian trafficking networks. When even the largest of these seizures failed to put a significant dent in drug availability, it became painfully apparent, as one former DEA official put it, that "the cartels' ability to produce cocaine far exceeded our capacity to seize it."[10] U.S. government data on cocaine prices confirmed this observation: throughout the 1980s the estimated average price of cocaine at the "dealer" level dropped from $201 per gram in 1981 to $68 per gram in 1989. During the same period, the estimated purity of cocaine at the same transaction level rose from 44 percent in 1981 to 71 percent in 1989.[11] Clearly, a change in counter-narcotics strategy was needed.

The Kingpin Strategy

In 1992 the DEA introduced a major supply-reduction initiative that quickly became the agency's signature counter-narcotics program. The kingpin strategy focused the DEA's investigative and intelligence strengths on dismantling major narcotics enterprises through the aggressive use of electronic surveillance technologies, including wiretaps, pen registers, and trap and trace devices. A kingpin was defined as the leader of an international trafficking enterprise that directed the production, transportation, and distribution of large quantities of cocaine or heroin, as well as the organization's financial operations. By neutralizing kingpins and dismantling their illegal operations, the DEA hoped to "significantly reduce the availability of drugs in the United States."[12]

Leaders from several Colombian wheel networks were the principal targets of the new strategy. Indeed, the initial kingpin list read like a who's who of Colombian traffickers, featuring such notorious criminals as Pablo Escobar, José Santacruz Londoño, Gilberto and Miguel Rodríguez Orejuela, Helmer Buitrago Herrera, and Iván and Jairo Urdinola Grajales. In close cooperation with the Colombian National Police (CNP), the DEA sought to disable the smuggling networks led by these traffickers by attacking their communications, transportation, and finance systems. Some initial results from the strategy were promising. After just a year and a half of operation, the DEA reported that kingpin investigations had led to the seizure of $210 million in drug proceeds, the confiscation of 144 aircraft and 91 boats, trucks, and cars, and the arrest of over 713 significant traffickers.[13] In Colombia, elite drug enforcement units destroyed hundreds of cocaine processing labs, seized thousands of kilograms of cocaine base and cocaine hydrochloride, eradicated hundreds of thousands of hectares of coca leaf plantings, and arrested hundreds of traffickers. Most remarkably, by 1996 all of the original kingpins were either dead or in jail, and their trafficking networks severely disrupted. Notwithstanding reports that some jailed kingpins were continuing their operations from behind bars, a number of government officials crowed that the days of the cocaine cartels were over. Some went even further. Following the arrest of Gilberto Rodríguez-Orejuela, the reputed *capo de tutti capi* of the Cali cartel, Colombian prosecutor general Alfonso Valdivieso exulted that "narco-trafficking is in the way of disappearing from Colombia."[14] In a war characterized by considerable frustration for law enforcers, the state appeared to have earned a major victory.

From Wheels to Chains: The Atomization of an Illicit Industry

Reports of the death of the Colombian cocaine trade turned out to be greatly exaggerated. Following a brief period of regeneration, hundreds of new and restructured trafficking enterprises emerged to produce greater amounts of cocaine than ever before. Rather than a handful of wheel networks that dominated cocaine production and exportation, the post-cartel drug industry was characterized by hundreds of small- and medium-sized concerns that stepped into the vacuum created by the disruption of the Medellín and Cali enterprises. Medium-sized groups included long-standing smuggling operations based in the Northern Cauca Valley and Atlantic Coast that largely avoided previous crackdowns. In addition, hundreds of family-based trafficking enterprises emerged, specializing in single phases of production, processing, and transportation activities. And following a period of recovery and rejuvenation, surviving nodes from several wheel networks reestablished their illicit operations, albeit on a smaller scale. New and reformed smuggling enterprises were not only smaller than their predecessors, but flatter, comprising no more than two layers of management and a dozen participants. Also during this period, leftwing guerrilla organizations, such as the Revolutionary Armed Forces of Colombia, and rightwing paramilitaries increased their participation in the drug trade.

A number of post-cartel narcotics enterprises were led by former midlevel managers of the Medellín and Cali networks. These private entrepreneurs drew on their experience, expertise, and contacts in redesigning their smuggling activities. Many apparently learned from the mistakes of their predecessors and deliberately downsized their operations to avoid law enforcement attention. They developed new transportation routes and reduced the size of their drug loads. Well-financed groups continued to exploit advances in transportation and telecommunications technologies, including the Internet. They also recruited professionals to assist their illicit activities, including financial consultants and computer systems engineers. Many groups pooled their resources and transacted through *ad hoc* support networks sometimes composed of members from past competitors.

Networks remain a basic organizing feature of the Colombian drug industry. While some wheels continue to function, recent years have witnessed the emergence of a number of chain networks. In these arrangements, international drug shipments proceed through a series of exchanges among independent groups that interact with suppliers and buyers. Chain networks are characterized by flat hierarchies, horizontal accountability, and loosely coupled nodes. Their signal accomplishment is to facilitate the movement of illicit drugs from Colombia to consumer markets without the controlled guidance, and political costs, of the former cartels.

Pursuing Profit or Jihad?

In 1989, the same year the CNP eliminated its first kingpin, a group of veteran resistance fighters from the Mujaheddin war against the Soviet Union in

Afghanistan built on the connections they made in this conflict to organize a multinational network of Islamic fighters to continue Jihad against other "infidel" states. Since then, this terrorist collective has carried out a number of well-coordinated attacks against the United States and other Western governments. Unlike a number of traditional terrorist groups in the greater Middle East and Europe, al Qaeda is a loosely coupled network of cells and associates spread over dozens of countries. While the devastating attacks on the World Trade Center and the Pentagon made Osama bin Laden a household name, the terrorist network he directed was implicated in several previous attacks against American citizens and soldiers, including the World Trade Center bombing in 1993, the attack on U.S. soldiers in Somalia in 1993, the simultaneous bombings of the U.S. embassies in Nairobi and Dar-es-Salaam in 1998, and the amphibious assault on the U.S.S. Cole in Yemen in 2000.[15]

While this chapter highlights the numerous organizational and operational parallels between terrorist networks and drug trafficking enterprises, there are important, if rather obvious, differences between al Qaeda and Colombian drug smuggling networks. For one thing, al Qaeda is a terrorist organization: it exists to carry out attacks of political violence and intimidation against a wide range of targets, including civilian noncombatants and combat soldiers, Western states and non-Western governments believed to support the West in al Qaeda's vision of the clash of civilizations. Drug trafficking enterprises are criminal organizations: they exist to smuggle illegal psychoactive substances that enjoy strong demand in many countries, Western and non-Western.

While individual members of terrorist groups may be influenced by financial considerations, the terrorist collective as a whole is motivated by a complex amalgam of religious, ideological, and political considerations. In the case of al Qaeda, these motivations include the establishment of a pan-Islamic caliphate, the removal of the U.S. military presence from Saudi Arabia, and the elimination of the state of Israel.[16] By contrast, while individual drug smugglers may have social and political ambitions that extend beyond criminal deviance, the organizations to which they belong are essentially economic. Trafficking organizations pursue satisfactory profits and reduction of unnecessary risks. Whereas the motivations of drug traffickers may wax or wane according to the pecuniary bottom line, al Qaeda members are true believers whose religious imperatives and political convictions may be largely unaffected by material considerations.

Beyond these basic motivational differences, al Qaeda parallels contemporary manifestations of organized crime in a number of ways. In particular, the terrorist group's complex structure bears a striking resemblance to the trafficking enterprises that have frustrated U.S. and Colombian law enforcers in recent years. Both contain transnational network structures characterized by relatively flat decision-making hierarchies. Both compartmentalize participants into separate semiautonomous cells that carry out many of the most dangerous activities of the enterprise. Both plan their illicit operations with meticulous care and place a premium on intelligence gathering and analysis. Both learn from experience, adapting their strategies and practices in response to information and feedback.

Similarities between Drug Traffickers and Terrorists

Networks. As discussed above, Colombian narcotics industry contains a host of wheel and chain networks that produce, process, transport, and distribute cocaine, heroin, marijuana, and other illicit commodities. Prior to September 11, 2001 and the ferocious counterterrorist response that followed, al Qaeda functioned largely as a wheel network. The "general emir," Osama bin Laden, provided ideological inspiration, strategic guidance, and managerial acumen to the enterprise, in close consultation with a senior advisory body known as the "Shura," or council. Experienced Shura members directed al Qaeda's training programs, military operations, and external affairs. Outside this core group stood four "committees" that specialized in different functions.

The military committee was responsible for recruiting, transporting, and training participants, conducting military operations, and manufacturing and acquiring weapons. The business and finance committee ran a number of profit-making enterprises, including construction, transportation, and agricultural firms, and managed al Qaeda's finances through investment companies, financial institutions, and privately funded charities. The "Fatwa" and Islamic study committee prepared the various religious pronouncements through which Osama bin Laden justified al Qaeda's operations. The media committee disseminated information about Jihad and al Qaeda through an Arabic language daily newspaper, *Nashrat al-Akhbar* or *Newscast*, and a weekly report. These four committees were linked with dozens of peripheral nodes, including training camps, warehouses, communications facilities, commercial businesses, and operations cells. State authorities have uncovered support nodes in a number of countries, including Sudan, Saudi Arabia, Afghanistan, Pakistan, Kenya, Tanzania, Germany, England, and the United States. Al Qaeda also served as an umbrella organization for nominally independent terrorist groups, such as Egyptian Islamic Jihad and the Algerian Armed Islamic Group (GIA), and entered into limited alliances with others.[17]

Paradoxically, decision-making authority throughout al Qaeda was hierarchical yet diffuse. Within the core group and peripheral nodes, social relations were based on vertical accountability. At the top stood Osama bin Laden and the Shura, which determined general policy for the network and considered major operations, such as the East African embassy bombings and the September 11 attacks. Bin Laden and the other leaders of the Shura Council issued general directives and even detailed instructions to different committees, which in turn supplied funding, logistical support, and guidance to peripheral nodes. However, some peripheral nodes, such as operations cells that gathered intelligence and conducted terrorist attacks, were loosely coupled from the core, and exercised considerable autonomy in carrying out their day-to-day activities. Still, these cells contained their own decision-making hierarchies with leaders that supervised other members of their group.[18] Under the management of bin Laden and his top associates, al Qaeda assumed a flat, linear network structure similar to many legal and illegal multinational business conglomerates.[19]

Compartmentalization. Traffickers and terrorists often loosely couple their operations to guard against penetration from law enforcers, and to limit such damage when it does occur. Leaders compartmentalize by organizing adherents into small working groups or cells that carry out many of the most dangerous activities of the network. Participants who face the greatest exposure to law enforcement efforts, such as traffickers who distribute drugs in wholesale markets and terrorists who carry out violent attacks in enemy territory, tend to be organized into the most rigidly compartmentalized cells. Cell size varies among organizations, but they are generally small, with more than three but fewer than a dozen participants. Within and between cells, information flows are circumscribed. Participants are told only what they need to know to carry out their immediate activities, and they are discouraged from asking questions about operations with which they are not directly involved. Cell activity is not constant, but tends to ebb and flow depending on ongoing activities and law enforcement pressure. Drug trafficking and terrorism tend to be part-time occupations.

Cells contain roles that define a division of labor among participants and rules that guide their behavior. Cells are organizationally flat, with one or two separate management levels. However, there is a hierarchy among members, with better-trained and more experienced personnel occupying senior positions that contain more responsibility. Some al Qaeda cell leaders have responsibility for choosing targets and planning operations. Logistics men are responsible for renting apartments, obtaining documents for cell members, and distributing money for activities. Soldiers act as lookouts and provide muscle during operations. A typical drug distribution cell in a Colombian trafficking network includes a leader that plans and coordinates the group's illicit activities, assistants that purchase motor vehicles and other equipment, deliver money, and punish errant employees, and lower-level workers that transport narcotics, manage stash houses, and run errands for their supervisors. In both trafficking and terrorist cells, members are subject to rules that require them to blend into their surrounding communities, avoid attracting unnecessary attention to the group, and protect their communications with the utmost secrecy. Participants in al Qaeda cells located in Western countries are instructed to shave their beards, avoid contact with neighbors, consolidate their daily prayers into fewer sessions, and implement various security measures when communicating by telephone. Members of trafficking cells are instructed to conduct their illicit activities during normal business hours, keep their lawns trimmed, avoid ostentatious spending, and implement various security measures when communicating by telephones.[20]

Planning operations. Drug trafficking and terrorism require research and planning. To evade interdiction by U.S. and Colombian authorities, Colombian traffickers research and design circuitous routes featuring multiple transshipment points, smuggling methods, and transportation vessels. A cocaine shipment may be smuggled out of Colombia hidden within a commercial fishing vessel, travel to Venezuela where it is repackaged inside a legitimate containerized cargo shipment, travel to Central America or Mexico where it is unloaded and repackaged inside a tractor trailer or other motor vehicle, and proceed to another transshipment point closer to the southwest border where it may be transferred to another vehicle and camouflaged in a different manner. Once in the United States, the drugs must be safely transported to one or more distribution points, temporarily stored in stash houses, and distributed to wholesalers. Finally, money must be collected from these transactions and repatriated to Colombian kingpins and investors, which may involve a complex series of financial transactions to lauder illicit drug proceeds. These activities must not only be coordinated among numerous participants, they must be executed quickly and smoothly, to avoid attracting unwanted attention from law enforcers.

Traffickers convene meetings to brainstorm different smuggling options, assign trusted participants to gather information about potential routes, discuss and amend transaction details with workers, and monitor shipments as they proceed through the route. To minimize exposure from law enforcers, they plan their transactions to account for potential contingencies. To minimize electronic intercepts of sensitive communications, they speak in code, change telephones frequently, clone cell phone numbers, use information technology, including email and online chat rooms, and camouflage their communications with off-the-shelf encryption technology.

Terrorist attacks on the devastating scale of September 11, 2001 also require considerable planning and preparation. Planners must choose potential targets and weapons, select and train participants, and arrange communication, transportation, financial, and other living arrangements for cell members. A hallmark of al Qaeda operations is the substantial amount of time and effort that goes into researching and planning attacks. Al Qaeda spent years preparing for the East African embassy bombings, conducting reconnaissance of potential targets, gathering bomb making and other materials, and identifying participants with the skills and commitment to execute the martyrdom operation. The coordinated attacks on the World Trade Center Towers and the Pentagon appear to have been the horrific culmination of months, even years of meticulous planning and coordination. According to FBI Director Robert Mueller, the operation was conceived by al Qaeda leaders in Afghanistan, while detailed planning and coordination was carried out by a cell located in Hamburg, Germany. The hijackers were selected to avoid notice from American officials, and entered the U.S. "easily and lawfully," over a period of 19 months, through eight different cities.[21] The pilots spent considerable time attending U.S. flight schools, using flight simulators to learn the controls of larger aircraft, and conducting surveillance on potential airports and flights. As the event drew closer, leaders and logistics men researched smaller airports, took cross-country practice flights, and held planning sessions in several locations around the United States. While sensitive operational details were most likely discussed in face-to-face meetings, the hijackers also communicated by telephone and the Internet, including email and online chat rooms.[22]

Responses to Government Strategies

Organizational adaptation.   Success for traffickers and terrorists depends on their ability to outmaneuver the law enforcement and military agencies. To do so, they gather and analyze intelligence about government enforcement activities and alter their practices in response to information and experience. Colombian trafficking networks change their practices in response to law enforcement efforts at virtually every stage of the production, transportation, and distribution of illicit drugs. When police and military authorities intercept precursor chemicals used to refine coca paste into cocaine hydrochloride, processing groups switch to alternative chemicals, develop filters to recycle used inputs, and construct facilities for storing and recycling chemical compounds. When law enforcement agents interdict shipments of fully refined narcotics, trafficking rings move their transportation routes and change their methods of conveyance, shifting among different types of sea-, air-, and land-based vessels and containerized cargo. When police officials apprehend members of distribution cells, other participants modify their operational signatures by changing telephone and fax numbers, purchasing new cell phones, calling cards, and automobiles, acquiring fresh warehouses, and forming new front companies. Cells that are compromised beyond repair are simply dissolved; their members transferred to other parts of the transnational network.[23]

Trafficking organizations alter their everyday practices as a result of acquiring knowledge and experience. They gather information about government counternarcotics efforts from a variety of sources, including their own associates, other smuggling groups, outside consultants, corrupt government officials, the news media, and public documents. Numerous enterprises have been known to manipulate the U.S. legal system to access indictments, search warrants, wiretap affidavits, criminal complaints, intelligence reports, and other sensitive documents that describe in detail how law enforcers conduct their criminal investigations. Lawyers send these documents back to Colombia, where they are analyzed by cartel leaders to identify confidential informants and prospective witnesses, learn about the latest law enforcement tactics, and change trafficking operations to avoid similar mistakes in the future.

Terrorist organizations also learn by acquiring, analyzing, and applying knowledge derived from their own experience or research. Similar to trafficking groups, terrorists learn in order to survive a hostile enforcement environment and to keep pace with changing counterterrorist tactics and technologies. As Bruce Hoffman, the director of the RAND Corporation's terrorism research unit, points out "the necessity for change in order to stay one step ahead of the counterterrorism curve compels terrorists to change—adjusting and adapting their tactics, modus operandi, and sometimes even their weapons systems as needed."[24] For example, over the last several decades, terrorists have adapted to increasingly stringent airline security precautions, including airport x-ray machines and metal detectors, background checks of ground crews, and matching bags to boarded passengers, allowing them to carry out devastating flight attacks irrespective of the new practices and technologies.[25] Hoffman refers to this phenomenon as the "technological treadmill," whereby fanatical groups develop increasingly sophisticated weapons and operations to counterterrorist enforcement programs.[26]

Terrorist networks gather information from a number of sources, including press reports, government documents, criminal proceedings, and physical surveillance. According to a recent unclassified Central Intelligence Agency (CIA) memorandum, al Qaeda operatives scour U.S. and foreign news sources for intelligence about U.S. counterterrorism activities and alter "their practices in response to what they have learned in the press about our capabilities."[27] Testifying before the United States Senate and House Select Committees on Intelligence, Deputy Secretary of Defense Paul Wolfowitz pointed out that unauthorized government leaks to newspaper reporters caused Osama bin Laden to stop using a satellite phone that U.S. intelligence agencies had been monitoring.[28] Once useful intelligence has been gathered, it spreads quickly through the terrorist network via telephonic, electronic, and human communication.

Similar to the more sophisticated Colombian trafficking enterprises, terrorist networks may also codify this knowledge in training manuals and other instruments that document organizational memories. During the 1990s, U.S. and Colombian law enforcers discovered manuals for one of the Cali wheel networks describing practices and procedures for conducting international drug flights and providing courtroom testimony. More recently, raids against suspected al Qaeda members have turned up a number of training manuals, computers, and documents that describe routines for a variety of activities, such as organizing cells, conducting reconnaissance of enemy targets, avoiding government surveillance, and constructing bombs and detonation devices. Al Qaeda occasionally updated these training manuals to incorporate lessons from experience, including previous terrorist attacks. Investigators have identified several similarities between the September 11 attacks and information contained in al Qaeda manuals to suggest that the hijackers drew extensively on these documents when planning and executing the operation.[29] U.S. officials also believe that al Qaeda modified its tactics for planning and executing terrorist operations after investigators determined that the network employed a traditional cell structure to carry out the East Africa embassy bombings in 1998 and the U.S.S. Cole Destroyer attack in 2000. "Every time we adopt or adapt some new ploy," states FBI Director Robert Mueller, al Qaeda attempts to "adopt a procedure to circumvent what we have done."[30] This affinity for organizational adaptation has helped al Qaeda carry out additional attacks even when under intense pressure from state authorities.[31]

When targeting kingpins is not enough. Similarities among traffickers and terrorists and lessons from two decades of war on drugs suggest a number of limitations in the joint military and law enforcement campaign to dismantle terrorist networks. In terrorist and trafficking enterprises, activities tend to be carefully researched, planned, and executed, reducing participants' exposure to government authorities. Terrorists and traffickers gather intelligence about law enforcement programs, and use this knowledge to change their own practices, helping them remain a step ahead of their multilayered, bureaucratic adversaries. They organize themselves into compartmentalized networks, complicating law enforcers' ability to trace and exploit linkages between cells and core groups. Compartmentalization also limits the damage of law enforcement penetration when it does occur. Multiple nodes on the network periphery provide leaders with a range of options in planning their illicit activities. If one cell is compromised, the resources and capabilities of other terrorist and trafficking nodes can be utilized. When cells are penetrated by law enforcers, they may lay low for extended periods or disband altogether, with prized participants transferred to other nodes in the network.

To be sure, all is not lost in the struggle between sovereignty-bound states and sovereignty-free terrorists and traffickers. For all their organizational sophistication, even the most well-funded illicit non-state actors cannot match the technological wizardry and military might of most Western states. When states cooperate effectively to confront these transnational security threats, the results can be impressive. Indeed, many cocaine cartels eventually fell prey to law enforcers in the 1990s. An important lesson of the kingpin strategy was that cartel leaders could be apprehended and their smuggling operations disrupted, at least temporarily, when U.S. law enforcement and intelligence agencies effectively coordinated their efforts with their Andean counterparts. Critical to bilateral cooperation was the generous provision of U.S. training, technology, and material resources to Colombian police, prosecutors, and military officials, some of which was used to create and maintain highly effective drug enforcement units. The kingpin strategy also confirmed the fundamental importance of tactical intelligence to counter-drug operations. U.S. and Colombian agents extracted valuable information from human and electronic sources, including confidential informants, telephone intercepts, and organizational memories captured in drug raids. Law enforcers skillfully used this knowledge to launch additional raids, capture more participants and organizational memories, add to existing intelligence databases, conduct further raids, capture more participants and documents, and so on, all in cascading fashion. Other essential tools included disinformation campaigns to confuse traffickers, handsome monetary rewards to encourage defections from high-ranking informants with access to the core group, and compartmentalized counter-drug operations to minimize leaks by corrupt officials.

A number of these tactics have been utilized in Afghanistan and Pakistan where U.S. Special Forces officers, FBI agents, and CIA operatives work closely with host country counterparts, such as Pakistan's Interservices Intelligence Directorate. With the help of U.S. intelligence, weaponry, and good old fashioned greenbacks, local police and intelligence officials have arrested hundreds of al Qaeda militants. Tools used in the hunt for al Qaeda are numerous and diverse, ranging from high-tech satellite surveillance systems, unmanned aerial drones, and data mining software to low-tech undercover operations, criminal informants, and tips from suspicious neighbors. Intelligence analysts sift through mountains of data provided by these electronic and human sources to identify al Qaeda's command and control structure and track down remaining participants. Law enforcers and military personnel carry out airstrikes and paramilitary raids against identified targets. During raids authorities arrest suspects and capture documents, computers, and other artifacts containing organizational memories that can be squeezed for additional intelligence about the whereabouts and impending activities of other network members. Government agents then use these data to conduct more raids and capture additional terrorists and organizational memories, which provide more data to be assessed, analyzed, and acted upon in the ongoing pursuit of Osama bin Laden and his top officials.

Similar to the war on drugs, supply-side strategies in the campaign against terror have disrupted al Qaeda's wheel topography and produced other noteworthy results. In Pakistan alone, officials have arrested over 450 suspected members of al Qaeda and the Taliban. Numerous al Qaeda leaders and managers have been apprehended or otherwise eliminated by Pakistani and other government authorities. One U.S. intelligence official claims that "some 40 percent of the top leadership is dead or in the pokey."[32] Widely reported kills include Mohammed Atef, the alleged military leader of the network, Ali Qaed Sinan al-Harethi, the suspected operations chief killed by a CIA Predator drone strike in Yemen, and Tariq Anwar al-Sayyid Ahmad, an alleged Egyptian operational planner for the network. More importantly, given that dead terrorists do not talk, several high ranking planners and coordinators, including Abu Zubaydah, Khalid Shaikh Mohammed, and Omar al-Farouq have been apprehended and turned over to U.S. authorities. Numerous prized catches, under compulsion from lengthy "stress and duress" interrogations, have provided the kind of timely, detailed tactical intelligence investigators need to identify additional nodes in the network, including names, addresses, and phone numbers. They have also provided greater insight into al Qaeda's operations, helping government authorities develop a better understanding of their illicit adversaries. Better intelligence has also improved military and law enforcement efforts to track down remaining leaders and, according to U.S. officials, foiled terrorist attacks in Bosnia–Herzegovina, France, Italy, Jordan, Macedonia, Singapore, Turkey, and Yemen.[33] Yet, the ultimate success of the campaign against terror depends on the ability of the U.S. government to deter future attacks against American interests at home and abroad. Here ongoing efforts to dismantle al Qaeda, and 20 years of war on drugs in Colombia, are less encouraging.

For all its accomplishments in capturing the leaders of the cocaine cartels, the kingpin strategy, and its successor programs, did not reduce the availability of Colombian drugs in U.S. markets. No sooner were such underworld luminaries as Pablo Escobar, Gonzalo Rodríguez Gacha, and the Rodríguez Orejuela brothers gunned down or imprisoned, than replacements emerged, eager to pick up where their predecessors left off. While individual enterprises may transact less frequently and in smaller quantities than before, on the whole the Colombian drug trade produces more cocaine and heroin today than it did during the so-called boom years of the 1980s and early 1990s. U.S. and Colombian law enforcement agencies continue to identify, investigate, and disrupt post-cartel trafficking enterprises. Ironically, today's efforts are hampered by yesterday's successes. Law enforcers have removed the largest, most notorious organizations from the Colombian drug trade only to confront hundreds of small, obscure, yet reasonably sophisticated groups about which they know reasonably little. Police officials and intelligence analysts have difficulty identifying many contemporary trafficking groups either because they are new to the trade or because their leaders rose from the murky ranks of midlevel cartel management. When DEA and CNP officials penetrate new groups, the damage is often limited to minor enterprises that specialize in single production or transportation activities. Meanwhile, illicit drugs produced in Colombia continue to flow across U.S. borders, driven by the appetites of American consumers.

Likewise, the campaign against terror has disrupted al Qaeda and weakened its ability to carry out large-scale attacks against the United States. To date, however, the transnational network appears to have been temporarily disrupted, as opposed to permanently dismantled. U.S., Afghan, and Pakistani officials acknowledge that hundreds, perhaps thousands, of al Qaeda operatives have eluded the international dragnet, including numerous middle management militants that helped plan the September 11 operation and provided logistical support to the hijackers. Small groups of al Qaeda operatives and supporters have spread across South Asia, Southeast Asia, and the Middle East, where they are believed to be targeting American interests.[34] Many of these nodes appear to be laying low for the time being, operating semiautonomously while maintaining links to network leaders through field commanders. Several attacks attributed to al Qaeda or its supporters during 2002 and 2003, including a nightclub bombing in Bali that slaughtered 180 people and a synagogue firebombing in Tunisia that killed 19, suggest that the network has not been completely immobilized.[35] And after more than two years of intense hunting for the network's top leaders, the U.S. and its allies have not managed to capture al Qaeda kingpins Osama bin Laden and Ayman al-Zawahiri, both of whom are believed to have be nursing their wounds in hiding, perhaps in the ethnic Pashtun tribal areas in northwest Pakistan. To the extent that kingpins, planners, and coordinators have managed to avoid capture or death, the terrorist network may be quicker to reemerge from the rubble of Operations Enduring Freedom and Anaconda and continue its Jihad against the United States and other "unjust, apostate" governments.

However, even if bin Laden, al-Zawahiri, and other leaders are captured or killed by the time this chapter sees the light of academic day, midlevel figures with sufficient expertise to continue terrorist attacks may rise within the network hierarchy. While removing the leaders of al Qaeda may have a greater short-term impact on the network's overall effectiveness than the capture of a drug kingpin will have on his cartel's business, it is unlikely that the capture of al Qaeda leaders alone will stop the terrorist network. Indeed, there have been reports that al Qaeda has already adapted to the loss of interdicted leaders by promoting from within and establishing ties with independent terrorist groups.[36] U.S. officials and independent observers suspect that the network may be transforming itself into "a more mobile, flexible and elusive force than ever before."[37] While it is still too early to know what form a "post-Osama" al Qaeda may take, nor the capacity of an entity to carry out terrorist attacks, one possibility would be similar to what transpired in the war on drugs when several wheel networks were replaced by chains that continued their illicit activities on smaller, but no less consequential, scales.

An al Qaeda chain network may be weaker than its predecessor and incapable of such ambitious, precisely calibrated attacks as those directed against the Twin Towers and the Pentagon. This development would undeniably constitute a victory of sorts for the United States in the "war on terror." It is also reasonable to suggest that a future version of al Qaeda may lack a single leader with the mythical stature and charismatic appeal of bin Laden, limiting the network's ability to appeal across a pan-Islamic base of Arabic supporters. Still, as the experience in Colombia indicates, illicit non-state actors are lead by all sorts of kingpins, some more charismatic than others. Indeed, charisma could represent an impediment for long-term survival, as magnetic extremists that inspire large numbers of followers may quickly find themselves under the counterterrorist microscope of the state. Assuming that bin Laden is eventually killed or captured by government forces, he may be replaced by lesser known, relatively uncharismatic leaders that organize their activities effectively enough to carry out small yet spectacular attacks on soft targets, while exploiting U.S. antipathy and their fallen hero's likely martyrdom status to recruit more followers.

It is also possible that al Qaeda may eventually be disassembled by government authorities. In this scenario it is likely that at least some surviving members will migrate to other groups, where they share their expertise and experience to help build small yet technologically adept networks that continue Jihad against the United States and other Western states. Something similar occurred when U.S. and Colombian authorities disrupted the Medellín and Cali wheel networks: numerous midlevel managers that eluded the drug enforcement dragnet joined other smuggling groups, or formed their own, drawing on existing resources, contacts, and expertise to continue their criminal careers. Post–al Qaeda groups may not possess the financial and organizational aptitude of bin Laden's enterprise prior to Operation Enduring Freedom, but they will have the defiant attitude, and it is conceivable that at least some of them will strive to carry out terrorist attacks against American interests.

New Strategies in the Fight Against Drug Trafficking and Terrorism

Combating the supply of terrorism. What, then, is to be done? Given the somber tone of the preceding pages, it may sound ironic, perhaps even cynical, to suggest that, in spite of the problems identified above, the United States should continue the counterterrorism crackdown. The source of this apparent contradiction lies in the imperative to demonstrate to political and religious extremists the world over that terrorism, to put it baldly, does not pay. In the past, Osama bin Laden reportedly suggested to his followers that terrorism is an effective political tool, particularly against the United States, which he and other Islamic extremists have seen as being averse to sustaining large numbers of American casualities, military or civilian. Bin Laden cited the withdrawal of U.S. Marines from Beirut following the 1983 barracks bombing, and the U.S. retreat from Somalia ten years later following the deadly attacks on eighteen Army Rangers in Mogadishu as examples of American leaders' unwillingness to tolerate even moderate casualty levels.[38] Additional accounts suggest that the terrorist kingpin interpreted tepid U.S. counterterrorist efforts in the 1990s, such as the retaliatory Cruise missile strikes ordered by the Clinton administration against al Qaeda training camps in Afghanistan following the East African embassy bombings, as indicating a lack of American resolve to dismantle his network.

The United States should prevent bin Laden and like-minded militants from entertaining such delusions by rigorously apprehending the perpetrators of terrorist attacks, destroying their weapons, freezing their assets, and prosecuting them in courts of law. In recognition that individual terrorists contain valuable repositories of knowledge and experience that can be exploited for intelligence purposes, whenever possible enemy combatants should be captured not killed, and interrogated with the utmost professionalism. Documents, computers, and other knowledge-based artifacts found in the possession of suspected terrorists should be carefully analyzed to develop intelligence for additional operations and evidence for subsequent prosecution. If top-level kingpins are captured they should not be made into martyrs through secret military tribunals concluding in foregone executions. Instead they should be prosecuted for their crimes, and discredited in the Islamic world through international diplomacy and public relations campaigns.

As in the war on drugs, international cooperation between the United States and its allies is critical to effective counterterrorism. The United States must work closely with its military, law enforcement, and intelligence counterparts in Pakistan, Afghanistan, Yemen, Saudi Arabia, the Philippines, and elsewhere given the transnational network structure of al Qaeda and other terrorist enterprises. The United States should provide communications and surveillance technologies, weaponry, and training in counterterrorist operations and investigative tactics. Where feasible, Washington should support the creation and maintenance of highly trained, super-equipped counterterrorist task forces. These elite units should draw on existing host country military, law enforcement, and intelligence strengths, while enjoying access to sophisticated U.S. technology, weaponry, and intelligence databases. Members should be carefully screened and vetted to reduce the potential for human rights violations and penetration by terrorist supporters. To match the short decision cycles of their illicit non-state adversaries, they should also be small, flat, and enjoy substantial autonomy when conducting field operations. To every extent possible, they should be free from cumbersome bureaucratic protocols, multilayered decision-making structures, and debilitating political pressures. While it may not be possible, or even desirable, to match all the features of illegal networks that operate outside the rule of law, the United States should strive to create network-hierarchy hybrids that blend existing strengths in counterterrorist technology and training with flatter, more fluid organizational structures.[39]

Addressing the demand-side of terrorism. However, if two decades of war on drugs demonstrate anything it is that illicit non-state actors are not likely to be defeated by law enforcement and military stratagems alone. If policy makers hope to achieve lasting victory in the campaign against terror we must move beyond a counterterror strategy based largely on supply-side initiatives. In the spirit of a long-standing, if often ignored, drug policy critique, the United States should devote greater diplomatic, political, and economic resources to addressing the "demand-side" of terrorism. Addressing the roots of Islamic terrorism will require substantial economic aid and educational programs for the Middle East and Central Asia, to address the poverty, social dislocation, and illiteracy that fuels political unrest. The United States should encourage governments in Pakistan, Bosnia, Indonesia, and Uzebekistan to reform extremist religious schools, so-called "Madrasas," that promote violence through the generous provision of educational assistance. Moreover, Washington should increase multilateral development assistance for global poverty reduction programs and conclude meaningful free-trade agreements with Morocco, Pakistan, and other counterterrorism allies that face systemic problems with unemployment and poverty.[40]

The United States must also encourage the formation of more open political systems in the Persian Gulf. However disagreeable and misguided the ongoing military campaign in Iraq has been to many, the United States should not squander the opportunity to help leave lasting democratic institutions in its wake that can serve as models for the rest of the region. Of course, any attempts at political reform confront strong authoritarian tendencies in Iraq, Saudi Arabia, and other Middle Eastern countries. The building of more inclusive and tolerant political climates that can serve as the cultural foundation for democratic institutions will require years of sustained efforts by Arab citizens. But to recognize the difficulties is not to accept the dubious proposition that the formation of stable electoral democracies in the Arab world is impossible. Naysayers would be wise to remember that not too long ago many observers asserted that Latin America and East Asia, with their Catholic and Confucian cultures respectively, were fundamentally incompatible with representative democracy. Since then numerous countries in both regions have experienced important progress toward democratic regimes based on the rule of law and the provision of civil liberties and political rights contained in the *Universal Declaration of Human Rights*.

New strategic thinking by policy makers is also in order, including a reconsideration of the large American military presence in the Middle East and a more balanced approach to the intractable Palestine dilemma. The recent announcement by Defense Secretary Donald Rumsfeld and Prince Sultan bin Abdul Aziz that the United States will withdraw all combat forces from Saudi Arabia is an encouraging step in the right direction.[41] The Conservative Likud Party's rejection of Prime Minister Ariel Sharon's plan to withdraw Israeli soldiers and settlers from the Gaza Strip is not. These issues contain far reaching implications for other actors in the region and deserve more careful consideration than offered here. But in reflecting on these questions, analysts and policy makers should avoid making terrorism profitable by appearing to acquiesce to their demands. After all, for years Osama bin Laden demanded a withdrawal of U.S. military forces from the Islamic holy lands of Mecca and Medina.

Clearly, none of these recommendations represent silver bullet solutions for dismantling illicit transnational networks, and Americans must brace themselves for future terrorist attacks and psychoactive drug flows. In wars on drugs and terrorism, states confront daunting adversaries: private transnational networks of criminals and terrorists compartmentalized into clandestine cells for the purpose of carrying out activities that states have declared illegal. Organizationally, these enterprises are smaller and flatter than their state competitors, allowing them to disperse information rapidly throughout their network structures. They adapt quickly to law enforcement and military efforts to disrupt their activities, using knowledge, technology, and experience to alter their operations. And they stand outside the rule of law, giving them the freedom to disregard the normative and legalistic barriers that constrain and inevitably slow down their sovereignty-bound competitors. States may set the rules of the game of international exchange, but non-state clandestine actors routinely flout them. While a supply-reduction counterterrorism strategy will continue to yield quantifiable policy outputs, the best we can ultimately expect from such policies are fleeting, symbolic victories as one network of extremists is replaced by another. In focusing overwhelming military, law enforcement, and intelligence efforts on a handful of terrorist groups and kingpins, while not sufficiently addressing the root causes of Islamic extremism, U.S. counterterrorism policies run the risk of merely weeding out the most notorious networks and providing opportunities for lesser known groups to materialize. As long as state strategies privilege the supply-side of drug trafficking and terrorism, transnational entrepreneurs and extremists will transact in their chosen commodities.

Notes

1. United States, The White House, "Narcotics and National Security," *National Security Decision Directive Number 221* (Washington, DC: The White House, April 8, 1986), http://www.fas.org/irp/offdocs/nsdd/nsdd-221.htm; United States, The White House, "The National Program for Combating Terrorism," *National Security Decision Directive Number 207* (Washington, DC: The White House, January 20, 1986), http://www.fas.org/irp/offdocs/nsdd/nsdd-207.htm.
2. While the U.S. government's data collection and analysis techniques for drug trafficking and terrorism have improved over time, the estimation of such "outputs" remains imprecise. My use of these approximations is to express agreement with broad trends rather than to suggest perfect knowledge of these illicit industries. See United States Department of State, *Patterns of Global Terrorism 2002* (April 2003), 161, http://www.state.gov/documents/organization/20177.pdf; and United States, The Office of National Drug Control Policy, *The National Drug Control Strategy: 2001 Annual Report* (Washington, DC: The White House, March 2001), 171.
3. See Michael C. Desch, Jorge I. Domínguez, and Andrés Serbin, eds., *From Pirates to Drug Lords: The Post-Cold War Caribbean Security Environment* (Albany, NY: SUNY Press, 1998).
4. Budget figures are expressed in nominal values. United States, Drug Enforcement Administration (DEA), "DEA Staffing and Budget," http://www.dea.gov/agency/staffing.htm.
5. Louis J. Freeh (Director, Federal Bureau of Investigation), "President's Fiscal Year 2000 Budget" (testimony, U.S. Senate Committee on Appropriations, Subcommittee for the Departments of Commerce, Justice, and State, the Judiciary, and Related Agencies, February 4, 1999), http://www.fbi.gov/congress99/freehct2.htm.
6. John F. Burns, "In Pakistan's Interior, A Troubling Victory in Hunt for Al Qaeda," *New York Times*, September 15, 2002; Dexter Filkins, "FBI and Military Unite in Pakistan to Hunt Al Qaeda," *New York Times*, July 14, 2002; Paul Kaihla, "Weapons of the Secret War," *Business 2.0*, November 1, 2001.
7. United States, DEA, "Changing Dynamics of Cocaine Production in Andean Region," *Drug Intelligence Brief*, June 2002. Of course, drug production and availability data are fraught with methodological peril and should be interpreted with caution. I use these figures to suggest broad, admittedly uncertain, trends rather than perfect knowledge of clandestine drug markets.

8. The term "cartel" is a conventional misnomer used by journalists, law enforcers, and scholars to refer to large, vertically integrated trafficking enterprises involved in several phases of drug production, transportation, and distribution. In reality, the Colombian drug industry was never dominated by one or two organizations that restricted production and set industry-wide prices, even during the heyday of the Medellín and Cali groups. In this chapter, I use the term for stylistic considerations rather than to suggest that the Colombian drug industry was cartelized.

9. A network refers to a series of nodes connected through repeated interaction. Nodes may be computers, individuals, groups, or formal organizations that interrelate, either directly with each other or indirectly through intermediaries. Peripheral nodes that interact with a central node serving as a communication and coordination center characterize wheel networks, also referred to as hub or star networks. Although some theorists juxtapose networks with other organizational forms, such as markets and hierarchies, in reality networks often contain elements of all three organizational forms, including hierarchies that structure relations among different nodes and markets that provide alternate suppliers and buyers. Some nodes are more equal than others, particularly in wheel networks where core nodes provide a steering mechanism to the enterprise. For general treatment of the network concept, see Albert-László Barabási, *Linked: The New Science of Networks* (Cambridge, MA: Perseus, 2002); Walter W. Powell, "Neither Market nor Hierarchy: Network Forms of Organization," *Research in Organizational Behavior* 12 (1990): 295–336; and Duncan J. Watts, *Six Degrees* (New York: W. W. Norton & Company, 2003). For a broad application of the network concept to transnational criminal organizations, see Phil Williams, "Organizing Transnational Crime: Networks, Markets and Hierarchies," *Transnational Organized Crime* 4, no. 3–4 (1998): 57–87. For discussion of wheel and chain networks and general application to criminals, terrorists, and social movements, see John Arquilla and David Ronfeldt, "The Advent of Netwar (Revisited)," in *Networks and Netwars: The Future of Terror, Crime, and Militancy*, ed. John Arquilla and David Ronfeldt, 1–25 (Santa Monica, CA: RAND, 2001).

10. Robert J. Nieves, *Colombian Cocaine Cartels: Lessons from the Front* (Washington, DC: National Strategy Information Center, 1997), 14.

11. U.S. Office of National Drug Control Policy, *The National Drug Control Strategy Report: 2001 Annual Report*, 171. "Dealer" level refers to cocaine purchases of between 10 and 100 grams. These data are compiled from the *System to Retrieve Information From Drug Evidence* maintained by the DEA.

12. United States, DEA, *U.S. Drug Threat Assessment: 1993* (Washington, DC: DEA Headquarters, September 1993), iii.

13. Nieves, *Colombian Cocaine Cartels*, 17.

14. Sam Vincent Meddis, "Colombia's Cocaine Chain," *USA Today*, July 24, 1995; R. Thomas Naylor, "Mafias, Myths, and Markets: On the Theory and Practice of Enterprise Crime," *Transnational Organized Crime* 3, no. 3 (1997): 1–45, 22.

15. *New York Times*, "Britain's Bill of Particulars: 'Planned and Carried Out the Atrocities'," October 5, 2001; U.S. Department of State, *Patterns of Global Terrorism, 2001* (Washington, DC: Department of State, May 2002), http://www.state.gov/s/ct/rls/pgtrpt/2001/html/; Michelle Zanini, "Middle Eastern Terrorism and Netwar," *Studies in Conflict & Terrorism* 22 (1999): 247–65; Michelle Zanini and Sean J.A. Edwards, "The Networking of Terror in the Information Age," in *Networks and Netwars*, 29–60

16. Magnus Ranstorp, "Interpreting the Broader Context and Meaning of Bin-Laden's *Fatwa*," *Studies in Conflict & Terrorism* 21 (1998): 321–30; U.S. Department of State; United States District Court, Southern District of New York, "Indictment," *United States of America v.*

Wadih El Hage, Fazul Abdullah Mohammed, Mohomed Sadeek Odeh, and Mohamed Rashed Daoud Al-'Owhali, Defendants, Case No. S(1) 98 Cr. 1023 (LBS), October 7, 1998.

17. Jamal Ahmed Al-Fadl, "Direct Testimony," *United States of America v. Usama Bin Laden, et al. Defendants,* Southern District of New York, February 6, 2001, http://crytome2.org/usa-v-ubl-02.htm; Rohan Gunaratna, *Inside Al Qaeda* (New York: Columbia University Press, 2002), 57–8, 77, 83–4; " 'Blowback,' " *Jane's Intelligence Review* July 26, 2001; Dana Priest and Douglas Farah, "Hezbollah, al-Qaida Team Up for Terrorism," *Washington Post,* reprinted in *The Ann Arbor News,* July 1, 2002; *New York Times,* "Britain's Bill of Particulars"; Jessica Stern, "Preparing for a War on Terrorism," *Current History* 100, no. 649 (2001): 355–57; United States District Court, Eastern District of Virginia, Alexandria Division, "Indictment," *United States v. Zacarias Moussaoui, Defendant* (December 2001), http://www.fas.org/irp/world/para/docs/mous_indict.html; Zanini and Edwards.

18. Peter L. Bergen, *Holy War, Inc.: Inside the Secret World of Osama bin Laden* (New York: The Free Press, 2001), 30; Gunaratna, *Inside Al Qaeda,* 82.

19. Bruce Hoffman, "Rethinking Terrorism and Counterterrorism Since 9/11," *Studies in Conflict and Terrorism* 25, no. 5 (2002): 303–16, 308.

20. Of course, these rules are sometimes broken, with potentially disastrous consequences for cells under investigation by state authorities.

21. Robert S. Mueller, III., Director, FBI, "Testimony of Robert S. Mueller," *Joint Investigation* (hearing, U.S. Senate Select Committee on Intelligence and the U.S. House Permanent Select Committee on Intelligence, 107th Congress, Second Session, October 17, 2002), 4, http://www.senate.gov/~intelligence.

22. Mueller, III. "Testimony of Robert S. Mueller"; Filkins, "FBI and Military Unite in Pakistan"; Judith Miller, Benjamin Weiser, and Ralph Blumenthal, "Holy Warriors Escalate an Old War on a New Front," *New York Times,* September 16, 2001; *New York Times,* "Britain's Bill of Particulars"; Don Van Natta Jr. and Kate Zernike, " 'Hijackers' Meticulous Strategy of Brains, Muscle and Practice," *New York Times,* November 4, 2001.

23. For more on trafficker adaptation, see Michael Kenney, "When Criminal Organizations Out-smart the State: Understanding the Learning Capacity of Colombian Drug Trafficking Organizations," *Transnational Organized Crime* 5, no. 1 (1999): 97–119.

24. Hoffman, "Rethinking Terrorism," 313.

25. Walter Enders and Todd Sandler, "The Effectiveness of Antiterrorism Policies: A Vector-Autoregression-Intervention Analysis," *American Political Science Review* 87, no. 4 (1993): 829–44, 843; Gregory A. Raymond, "The Evolving Strategies of Political Terrorism," in *The New Global Terrorism: Characteristics, Causes, Controls.,* ed. Charles W. Kegley (Upper Saddle River, NJ: Prentice Hall, 2003), 83; Jessica Stern, *The Ultimate Terrorists* (Cambridge, MA: Harvard University Press, 1999), 75.

26. Bruce Hoffman, *Inside Terrorism* (New York: Columbia University Press, 1998), 178–79, 180–1. For a systematic analysis of organizational learning by terrorists, see Brian A. Jackson, "Organizational Learning and Terrorist Groups" (unpublished paper, Washington, DC: RAND, 2002).

27. CIA, "Unclassified Memorandum," June 14, 2002.

28. Paul Wolfowitz (Deputy Secretary of Defense), "Prepared Testimony of Paul Wolfowitz," *Joint Investigation* (hearing, U.S. Senate Select Committee on Intelligence and the U.S. House Permanent Select Committee on Intelligence, 107th Congress, Second Session, September 19, 2002), http://www.senate.gov/~intelligence.

29. Judith Miller and Don Van Natta Jr., "In Years of Plots and Clues, Scope of Qaeda Eluded U.S.," *New York Times,* June 9, 2002; Van Natta Jr. and Zernike, " 'Hijackers' Meticulous Strategy."

30. Mueller, III., "Testimony of Robert S. Mueller," 4.

31. Josh Meyer, Eric Lichtblau, and Bob Drogin, "Gains and Gaps in Sept. 11 Inquiry," *Los Angeles Times*, March 10, 2002.

32. Kevin Whitelaw et al., "A Tightening Noose," *U.S. News and World Report*, March 17, 2003, 22.

33. Desmond Butler and Don Van Natta, Jr. "Qaeda Informant Helps Trace Group's Trail," *New York Times*, February 17, 2003; Filkins "FBI and Military Unite in Pakistan"; David Johnston and Douglas Frantz, "Arrests in Karachi Raising Hopes in Hunt for Al Qaeda," *New York Times*, September 15, 2002; Meyer, Lichtblau, and Drogin, "Gains and Gaps in Sept. 11 Inquiry."

34. U.S. Department of State, *Patterns of Global Terrorism 2002*, 119.

35. Whitelaw et al., "A Tightening Noose."

36. Bob Drogin, "No Leaders of Al Qaeda Found at Guantanamo," *Los Angeles Times*, August 18, 2002; Filkins "FBI and Military Unite in Pakistan"; David Johnston and Philip Shenon, "F.B.I. Issues Alert on Signs of New Terror," *New York Times*, October 12, 2001; Meyer, Lichtblau, and Drogin, "Gains and Gaps in Sept. 11 Inquiry."

37. James Risen and Dexter Filkins, "Qaeda Fighters Said to Return to Afghanistan," *New York Times*, September 10, 2002.

38. Hoffman, "Rethinking Terrorism," 313.

39. John Arquilla, David Ronfeldt, and Michele Zanini, "Networks, Netwar, and Information-Age Terrorism," in *Countering the New Terrorism*, ed. Ian O. Lesser, 39–68 (Santa Monica, CA: RAND Corportation, 1999).

40. Febe Armanios, "Islamic Religious Schools, *Madrasas*: Background," *Congressional Research Service Report for Congress*, October 29, 2003; Lael Brainard and Robert E. Litan, "No Stepping Back: America's International Economic Agenda for 2003–2005," *Brookings Review* 21, no. 1 (2003): 32–37; Keith B. Richburg, "Moroccans Paying a Price for Ties With U.S.: Many Citizens Say Loyalty Should Bring Greater Rewards for the Kingdom," *Washington Post*, May 22, 2003: A16.

41. Eric Schmitt, "U.S. to Withdraw All Combat Forces from Saudi Arabia," *New York Times*, April 29, 2003.

Chapter 5

Targeting Money Laundering: Global Approach or Diffusion of Authority?

Eleni Tsingou

"The goal of a large number of criminal acts is to generate profit for the individual or group that carries out the act. Money laundering is the processing of these criminal proceeds to disguise their illegal origin"—thus is money laundering defined in the official documentation of the Financial Action Task Force (FATF) on Money Laundering, an official body created in 1989 as international efforts to deal with this issue intensified. This definition goes to the heart of a dual problem: tackling money laundering is important in order to address organized crime such as drug trafficking, arms sales, and, most recently, terrorism. At the same time, detection is problematic because the financial transactions at stake mostly follow regular procedures; it is the way that funds are generated and the way in which they might be used that could be irregular.

The issue of money laundering became prominent in the 1980s, with the United States taking the lead in anti-money laundering legislation in 1986. The rise of concerns about "dirty money" was linked to concerns about narcotics[1] but also appears to coincide with the liberalization of financial markets. Efforts were further reinforced as fears about transnational organized crime followed the end of the Cold War and the establishment of post–communist states. But what makes money laundering important? In a narrow sense, money laundering practices affect the financial system, encouraging corrupt practice and bribery, and giving criminal groups influence in the way banking institutions operate. While this is a significant enough problem across the world, it is even more so in developing countries or states in transition where the financial and legal systems are still to mature. There are however, wider implications of the fight against money laundering, as in pursuing such activities, authorities are implicitly attacking organized crime. Whether it is drug trafficking, human trafficking and prostitution, or illegal arms sales, public officials often find it easier to address these problems through money laundering legislation and regulations than by targeting them directly.[2] Attending to these problems is of great importance to major countries in the international system but also goes a long way toward encouraging stability in the developing world.

This chapter examines cooperation among public authorities and between public and private institutions, and analyzes policies and practices that aim to curtail money laundering. The chapter argues that for such efforts to be effective, financial regulators and law enforcement agencies at the national and global levels need to reach an improved understanding of the goals and policies of combating money laundering and engage in closer cooperation. Most importantly, however, the analysis maintains that it is important for the private sector needs to accept strengthened self-policing functions. The perceived pattern of incentives has remained weak, however, and it is still unclear whether the events of September 11, 2001 have significantly changed that.

The chapter is organized in six parts. The first section provides a general overview of the subject of money laundering and highlights the reasons that put anti-money laundering initiatives in the policy agenda of public officials. The second section focuses on the principal dilemma in the fight against money laundering, namely the tension between the benefits and costs of pursuing such strategies. At the center of this problem is the wider challenge of reconciling public good and private interest and relying on the private sector to pursue public policy goals. The chapter proceeds to examine the plethora of official measures designed to deal with money laundering, stressing that aside from the most prominent high-level initiatives such as FATF, detection requirements have trickled down to almost every level of financial transaction. Section four shifts the focus to offshore and developing world financial centers and shows that money laundering matters in this context are actively addressed but that significant obstacles remain. This is followed by a review of private sector practices, which draws attention to the gaps between policy and practice. The final section examines the impact of September 11, 2001 on the fight against money laundering and evaluates the long-term effects of recently implemented policies and regulations.

What is Money Laundering?

Money laundering is the procedure whereby funds acquired through illegal activity are rendered legal by being processed in the financial system, thus disguising their origin. The type of illegal activity that generates the funds can vary but is often linked to corrupt practices, transnational organized crime networks, and increasingly, at least in the rhetoric and policies of the international community, terrorist groups. Targeting money laundering is thus a policy tool in the fight against such illegal activities. Money laundering methods used can be traced back 3,000 years, when Chinese merchants found ways to hide their profits from the ruling authorities for fear that these would be confiscated.[3] Money laundering generally entails three steps: placement, layering, and integration. In the placement stage, funds are divided into smaller amounts and are deposited in accounts or converted into monetary instruments and deposited in different locations. The layering stage consists of a series of conversions and other transactions that distance the funds from the original source. This is achieved through electronic transfers, the use of liquid monetary instruments such as traveler checks and the movement of funds toward jurisdictions with relatively lax reporting requirements. In the final stage, integration, the funds are reintroduced in the legitimate economy, through investments, spending, and other legal funding activities.[4]

Techniques vary but often consist of "starbust," where a deposit is divided into fragments and wired to hundreds of bank accounts everywhere in the world, or "boomerang," where funds are sent on a long journey through global financial markets before being returned to their origin.[5] In fact, such techniques are becoming increasingly sophisticated, and those engaging in money laundering are taking advantage of several jurisdictions as well as financial institutions and instruments to launder money. Financial liberalization and innovation have further assisted these individuals; the large volumes of transnational financial transactions can often disguise "dirty money" and the increasingly international character of many financial institutions means that funds can be moved within a banking entity to a branch in a national jurisdiction with less strict controls.[6] Similarly, financial innovation has provided launderers with an ever-expanding choice of financial instruments, some poorly regulated, and "cyberlaundering" is offering further possibilities to go undetected as it mostly ensures anonymity.

Because secrecy is an integral part of money laundering activities, it is impossible to provide an accurate figure of the amount of money that is annually laundered. Moreover, the figures that exist are often based on anecdotal evidence and are highly contentious.[7] The International Monetary Fund (IMF) has nevertheless estimated that the total could equal anything between 2 and 5 percent of the world's gross domestic product (GDP). This amounts to anything up to $2 trillion.[8]

Anti-money Laundering Measures: Tools in the Pursuit of Global Public Goods?

Public goods are "inclusive (public in consumption), based on participatory decision-making and design (public in provision) and just (public in benefits)."[9] Global public goods are not restricted to particular borders and can benefit multiple countries and generations.[10] They can be final, that is outcomes rather than goods in the standard sense. They may be tangible, such as the environment, or the common heritage of mankind, or intangible, such as peace or financial stability. They can also be intermediate "such as international regimes [which] contribute towards the provision of final public goods."[11] This chapter argues that the fight against money laundering has been defined in terms of the pursuit of such global public goods. To target money laundering activities is seen to be in the global public interest.

As outlined in the previous section, the first set of reasons for addressing money laundering are its effects on the economy and the financial system. Involvement in money laundering activities can affect public confidence in the financial system.[12] Moreover, money laundering practices are said to affect legitimate entities in the private sector. Launderers regularly use front operations such as shops and restaurants, which primarily rely on illegal activities for profit. In this context, legitimate businesses often find themselves undercut and find it difficult to compete. Another consequence is the distortion of financial market operations, as large sums of money may enter and leave the system suddenly, thus affecting the liquidity of financial institutions. A more drastic set of effects could lead to loss of control of economic policy, as in some developing countries; the sums laundered may correspond to a substantial part of national wealth. Money laundering activities can also alter investment patterns as funds are allocated to sectors where they do not risk detection and not necessarily to ones that are profitable or in need of investment. Developing countries may further see their privatization policies hampered should launderers become the main beneficiaries of such schemes and also, suffer reputation damage, if they are seen to tolerate such activities on their territory. Finally, states everywhere are affected through loss of tax revenue.[13] The second set of grounds focuses on corruption in the developing world, whereby criminal groups can use laundered money to consolidate their place in the political system and further contaminate the local private sector. In some cases, such criminal organizations can use their position to exercise coercive power and intimidate through violent activities and also, damage the institutions of the state by utilizing their wealth to corrupt public and private officials.[14] It is understood that the long-term development of such states is harmed by these corruptive elements.

The third set of incentives for targeting money laundering activities is defined in terms of social costs, from policing and health costs in the countries that deal with the effects of drug use, to the wider implications of the "pay-offs" of crime for corruption in the public and private spheres.[15] In these cases, the focus is on law enforcement and public policy, dealing with the consequences of money laundering and of the activities that generate the illicit funds.

The fourth set of motives in the fight against money laundering deal with the eradication of the activities that produce the funds in the first place. Organized crime[16] is most commonly manifested in drug trafficking, but illegal alien smuggling is also on the rise. At the same time, human trafficking, predominantly the trafficking of women and children for the purposes of the sex trade, is a source of substantial financial rewards for criminals, with most developed countries acting as recipients. Moreover, activities that can lead to money being laundered include illegal business deals on cars, antiques, endangered species, or arms.[17]

The final driving force for attacking money laundering practices is the extent to which the funds thus "cleaned" are used in ways that affect global stability. Until recently, such concerns concentrated on the political situation in countries in the developing world; drug trafficking centers such as Colombia and Afghanistan have also been politically unstable and violent, whereas "blood diamonds" in Angola and Sierra Leone have helped finance civil wars.[18] The events of September 11, 2001 have, however, shifted the focus to a much more global scale, rendering the fight against money laundering synonymous to the "economic war on terror."

All five sets of reasons for effectively dealing with money laundering are defined in terms of the pursuit of (global) public goods: assuring the integrity of the global economic and financial system, including in emerging markets and other countries in the developing world; eliminating corrupt practices in the public and private sectors of some developing nations; ensuring a more productive allocation of public resources; weakening organized crime, especially traffic in drugs, humans, and illegal arms; and promoting international stability by reducing the funds available for ethnic and civil conflicts and terrorist activities. It is understood that money laundering is global in scope at all relevant levels: organized crime is increasingly transnational, the financial mechanisms used to launder money transcend national boundaries and the use of the resulting funds can have global repercussions. As will be discussed in the subsequent section, such a global issue has generated an appropriately global institutional approach.

Certain questions remain, however. First, for a global good to be public, it needs to offer benefits while keeping costs to participants at a minimum. Is this also the opinion of emerging markets or offshore centers specifically targeted for their not so active fight against money laundering? In this context, it is important to establish whether an appropriate global approach is being constructed, and look at the "mixture between nation-specific and transnational public benefits."[19] Second, should not the largest beneficiaries of these public goods also take the lead in assuring their provision?[20] This is particularly pertinent considering the leading role of the United States at the various stages of the anti-money laundering efforts. The United States was instrumental in internationalizing the fight against money laundering in the 1980s and again, in linking money laundering and terrorist financing since 2001.[21] It is thus reasonable to expect the United States and other developed economies to be at the forefront of anti-money laundering initiatives, not only in theory but also in practice. Finally, what is the role of the private sector in this process? For global public policy goals to be achieved, a governance structure that includes both public and private actors is required, one that assigns roles and responsibilities.[22] In the absence of such a structure, can we rely on the private sector to self-police?

An additional question refers to the choice of promoted global public goods. While the cost of money laundering is linked to issues of economic and political development, especially with regards to states with weak institutional structures, there is little in the policy discourse about how money laundering and by extension, organized crime, affect democratic structures. Rees argues that liberal democracies exhibit twin weaknesses when faced with combating organized crime: the openness of their political and economic systems can be infiltrated by criminal elements while their compliance with the rule of law can constraint their ability to deal with these elements.[23] Recent concerns about civil liberties with respect to post–September 11, 2001 legislation can be viewed in this context.

Tackling Money Laundering: Official Measures and Global Policies

The global response to money laundering started taking shape in the 1980s, with an early initiative by the Council of Europe. The increasingly prominent Basel Committee on Banking Supervision also tackled the subject in 1988, urging the taking up by banks of a "general statement of ethical principles."[24] That a more concerted international effort was required was eventually recognized at the G-7 Summit of Paris in 1989, where the G-7 Heads of State, the European Commission and an additional eight countries convened the FATF on Money Laundering.[25] The FATF, based at the secretariat of the Organization for Economic Cooperation and Development (OECD) in Paris, embarked on the task of coordinating and harmonizing the global fight against money laundering as well as surveying practices and progress in different jurisdictions, and keeping up with the techniques and methods used by launderers. Its main task is to provide recommendations to countries and monitor their implementation and also, since 1999, to "blacklist" countries that are deemed noncooperative (Non-Cooperative Countries and Territories or NCCTs). This approach stems from the varied ways in which countries deal with money laundering; there is no single detailed definition and while all FATF members have enacted legislation on the subject, in most cases it has evolved from legislation on narcotics and sometimes does not adequately address other facets of money laundering. FATF definitions and standards have also been clear about keeping money laundering separate from fiscal fraud, counterfeiting and other white-collar crimes. These distinctions are not always carried through in the context of national efforts, where additionally, different public bodies have different degrees of authority and where in general, these issues are dealt with primarily in terms of law enforcement and not banking supervision. Members of the FATF have specialized divisions in their Treasury Departments, often assisted in their activities by narcotics units. The responsibilities of all these different bodies have become clearer, especially in recent legislation such as the U.S. Patriot Act or the U.K. Proceeds of Crime Bill, but there are serious doubts as to whether cooperation between them is satisfactory or efficient.

The FATF started with 16 members, had reached 28 by 1992 and its membership now stands at 33.[26] It has issued 40 recommendations, which are regularly updated. These are addressed to countries and deal with an extensive range of themes: the adoption of background policies that facilitate the fight against money laundering, such as implementing the Vienna Convention,[27] ensuring banking secrecy laws do not impede detection, and participating in multilateral initiatives and solutions; the criminalization of money laundering; the establishment of laws that allow for the seizure and confiscation of funds generating from criminal activity; the implementation of customer identification and record-keeping rules; the adoption of increased diligence of financial institutions, including the development of internal policies and controls; and the strengthening of international cooperation, including the exchange of information and the legal facilitation of mutual assistance.[28] These recommendations were reviewed and revised in 2003 to create a "comprehensive, consistent and substantially strengthened international framework for combating money laundering and terrorist financing." Changes include tougher provisions for high-risk customers, the extension of anti-money laundering measures to several nonfinancial businesses, the explicit extension to existing requirements to cover terrorist financing and the prohibition of shell banks.[29]

Monitoring of the implementation of the 40 recommendations takes two forms. All member countries carry out a self-assessment exercise and the FATF has a mutual evaluation procedure in place, whereby on-site visits by legal, financial, and law enforcement experts from other member governments are conducted. The FATF also has provisions for dealing with noncompliant members—although to this date, only Austria and Turkey have been in any way reprimanded.[30] Since 1999, the FATF has taken a further step, engaging in a "naming and shaming" campaign and identifying countries guilty of noncooperation. The first NCCTs report was made public in 2000 and is regularly reviewed.[31]

The FATF has been clearly at the forefront of anti-money laundering efforts, has raised the profile of the issue and, as explained below, been a useful framework within which to deal with terrorist financing at the international level. Nevertheless, the rather narrow membership, peer review procedures and, to this date, limited reprimands mean that its legitimacy can and has been questioned. It should also be noted that the FATF approach, in line with that of anti-money laundering regulations and legislation elsewhere, focuses on process and not on results.[32]

The FATF efforts are supplemented by a variety of groups and policies, ranging from regional task forces, the Egmont Group of Financial Intelligence Units, which annually brings together representatives of the relevant national agencies and currently counts 69 members,[33] and the United Nations Global Program against Money Laundering.[34] The IMF and the World Bank have also recently implemented a 12-months pilot program aimed at assessing anti-money laundering practices and providing technical assistance. This is in conjunction with the FATF and other relevant bodies.[35] Of course, national and EU-level policy-makers have adapted the recommendations and produced additional guidelines and legislation. The Financial Crimes Enforcement Network (FinCEN) of the U.S. Department of the Treasury actively monitors compliance to anti-money laundering measures and to the recent Patriot Act.[36] Similarly, the EU Directive on money laundering of 1991 was amended in 2001 and is now in place.[37] International banking, securities and insurance supervisors also provide regular information on their guidelines and initiatives.[38]

While this set of public bodies constitutes an impressive and increasingly coordinated institutional framework in the fight against money laundering, certain weaknesses remain. Anti-money laundering efforts are based on the cooperation between three distinct sets of actors: financial regulators and supervisors and international financial institutions; private sector institutions, mostly banks; and law enforcement agencies. While the first two sets of actors have a history and established patterns of cooperation and interaction both at the national and global levels, relations with the third are less well defined. The main international agency, Interpol, appears to have a marginal role in tackling money laundering, despite some important personnel links with the FATF and FinCEN.[39] Even at the domestic level, tensions can arise not only from lack of established procedures but also from different interpretations of the results of anti-money laundering efforts; while the financial sector assesses success in terms of lack of problematic instances, law enforcement bodies concentrate on quantifiable confiscated sums and convictions.[40] The strategies of regulators and law enforcement agents are indeed rather different; while the first group focuses on persuasion, cooperation, self-regulation, and sometimes, "private remedies," the second stresses prosecution, external regulation, and public justice and punishment.[41]

The Fight Against Money Laundering: The Case of Offshore and Emerging Markets

As the FATF focus on NCCTs has shown, an important part of the global strategy against money laundering revolves around improving practices and promoting transparency in offshore centers as well as in emerging markets and other developing countries. Offshore financial centers represent 1.2 percent of the world population and account for 3.1 percent of the world's GDP, yet handle a quarter of the world's financial assets.[42] Offshore centers are traditionally seen as having the following characteristics: "minimal or no personal or corporate taxation; effective bank secrecy laws; few, preferably no, restrictions or regulations concerning financial transactions; and protection of the secrecy of transactions."[43] Some analysts tend to view offshore centers and tax havens in general in terms of "parasitic state strategies," "where a state deliberately designs its policies to try to attract business and achieve self-enrichment in ways that are detrimental to global welfare and the rule of law."[44] Offshore centers are seen to be "abusing the system of sovereignty to advance parochial interests."[45] Developing nations may also be reluctant to adopt strict anti-money laundering rules as they might consider them damaging to their development strategy. As a result, some countries have few incentives to enthusiastically join the fight against money laundering and only strong leadership from other countries and the embarrassment of being black-listed may persuade them otherwise.[46]

Practices in developed world offshore centers are not particularly encouraging in this respect. The Swiss banking industry partly relies on secrecy laws as, for the most part, banks make money from private banking, that is, they manage the money of some very wealthy people who generally do not reside in the country.[47] This can lead to abuse of the banking system, as was shown in a high-profile case where UBS was reprimanded for dealing with funds that are suspected to have links to Sani Abacha, former Nigerian dictator.[48] Similarly, an information report produced by a committee of the French National Assembly, known as the "Montebourg Report," reviews practices in Luxembourg and highlights several issues for concern: the small number of instances of reporting of suspicion to the relevant public authorities and the associated practice of refusing clients instead, and the "privatization of the fight against money laundering," which is essentially in the hand of external auditors.[49]

Other groups of states pose additional problems in establishing a global anti-money laundering approach. Some states are "weak," such as countries in transition, where state structures, especially the legal and financial systems, are yet to fully develop. A different group of states is labeled "corrupt," and it has been argued that Mexico and Russia, now both members of the FATF, have in the past belonged in this category. Finally, some states are termed "criminal," the principal example being North Korea.[50]

With the potential exception of states falling in the "criminal" category, countries are officially on board when it comes to tackling money laundering and publicly espouse the pursuit of the global public goods that this entails. Yet privately, a large number of offshore and emerging markets may not quite come to the same conclusions. While not actively hampering anti-money laundering efforts, their analysis of the benefits and costs may show that the latter override the former.

Banking Sector Practices and the Legacy of Money Laundering Scandals in the United States

While public officials are taking an increasingly active stand against money laundering, for policies to work, the banking sector needs to follow the guidelines responsibly and not simply assume that the risk of irregularity is too small. Yet in some ways, the banks are part of the problem as much as they are part of the solution, as profit remains their primary aim. Are reasonable incentives in place for them to take on this task responsibly?

As Carse argues: "institutions should view anti-money laundering systems as an essential means of self-preservation—and not as a nuisance or an unnecessary expense imposed upon them."[51] Banks have some straightforward incentives to take anti-money laundering measures seriously, mainly to do with reputational and legal issues.[52] Indeed, they have adopted a series of procedures to combat money laundering and comply with regulatory requirements. These include special identification measures, the "know your customer" mantra applied to all financial services; monitoring processes based on internal systems and a comprehensive system of dealing with suspicious activity; up-to-date training programs; the implementation of auditing procedures and accountability measures such as signed attestations of knowledge of anti-money laundering measures, and evaluations; the setting-up of specialized anti-money laundering units; and the full participation and commitment of senior management.[53]

Major banks have gone further and taken the initiative to create appropriate standards by establishing the Wolfsberg Group of Banks.[54] The group was created in 2000 and issues global anti-money laundering guidelines for international private banks, focusing on correspondent banking relationships.[55] This extends the "know your customer" rule to correspondent banks, as well as the financial firms using the service.[56] The reasoning behind such a voluntary code of conduct was the harmonization of principles and the strengthening of private sector reputation and credibility.[57]

Despite those efforts, some real problems remain. "When the total costs to the banking system of the myriad anti-money laundering reporting requirements are correctly measured, few anti-money laundering efforts are cost effective."[58] This is indeed confirmed in a recent survey by the American Bankers Association, which places Bank Secrecy and Anti-Money Laundering requirements first in the ranking of compliance costs faced by banks.[59] The Patriot Act has further increased requirements but it is claimed that financial institutions have yet to implement centralized customer-identification systems—or even come to decisions as to how to go about it—and that training staff and building compliance expertise is a costly and lengthy process.[60] At the same time, the Act does not provide for additional funding for enforcement agencies; this questions the effectiveness of the current system of private sector incentives.

The existence of reliable incentives is further put in doubt when considering that legitimate elements of the financial system have been potentially engaging in money laundering. An account of a U.K. High Court judgment that found a small accountancy firm to have been involved in money laundering shows that the regulatory authorities were actually reluctant to investigate evidence and allegations that a more prominent and larger accountancy firm was also involved. This may be testament to an "institutionalized disinclination to undertake vigorous and open investigation of such cases."[61] The authors suggest that it may also be indicative of a particularly cozy relationship between regulators and the private sector. This could well have been an isolated incident, however, with only 2 percent of laundered funds eventually accessed,[62] further investigation is needed.

The U.K. financial system did not come unscathed from the Abacha affair either. Though most of the attention about the assets of the former Nigerian dictator focused on Switzerland, a portion of the funds were found to have come from, or subsequently gone to the United Kingdom. Reporting on this issue, the Financial Services Authority found in 2001 that 15 out of the 23 banks that had dealings with the Abacha family had "significant control weaknesses."[63]

The track record of U.S. authorities is similarly problematic. A review of the Bank of Credit and Commerce International (BCCI) case showed failure of the authorities to investigate allegations of irregularity, a blurred set of policy objectives as BCCI had dealings with Panamanian Dictator Manuel Noriega and played a part in the Iran–Contra affair, an undue private sector influence on the policy process, and legal constraints in the pursuit of transnational offenders.[64] More recently in 1996, Citibank was investigated in relation to the money laundering of illegal funds held by Raul Salinas, brother of former Mexican President Carlos Salinas. Little of essence had changed in the tackling of money laundering by the time the Bank of New York (BONY) scandal erupted in 2000. BONY had entered into several corresponding relations with Russian banks, after it had been documented in Congressional testimony that up to 40 percent of Russian banks were controlled by organized crime.[65] This may suggest that anti-money laundering requirements needed strengthening but it also implies that banks were prepared to overlook the measures in place.

The above analysis shows that the private sector is involved in the fight against money laundering and has taken some steps to implement measures that should deter such practices. Nevertheless, authorities, including U.S. authorities, have dealt with money laundering problems with some restraint and the cost of compliance for the private sector makes it unlikely that this is one area where it will take the lead. Authorities have been more active in promoting compliance by imposing fines on financial institutions whose controls are found lacking;[66] but are fines a cost-effective risk for the private sector? If anti-money laundering measures are to promote global public goods, the private sector needs to be more positively engaged and reconcile the tension between those public goods and its own private interests. As it stands, the private sector does not have the incentive to do so.

Has September 11, 2001 Changed Everything? Anything?

To what extent have the terrorist attacks on New York and Washington, DC altered public and private motivations to combat money laundering? They certainly have had a significant effect on the prominence of anti-money laundering initiatives, giving new impetus to official measures and the work of the FATF. Fighting terrorist financing was an "uncontroversial" early measure by the international community and brought about immediate effects with the freezing of assets.[67] The FATF responded by designing eight "Special Recommendations on Terrorist Financing." These include the criminalization of the financing of terrorism, the creation of provisions for freezing and confiscating assets, the requirement to report suspicious transactions with potential criminal links, the imposition of anti-money laundering requirements on alternative remittance systems, and the review of laws dealing with nonprofit organizations.[68] The FATF also produced a specific guidance document for the use of financial institutions.[69] Other public bodies provided additional reports and direction, including the Basle Committee, and the Wolfsberg Group of Banks issued a statement on the role of financial institutions.[70] These efforts were further consolidated through national regulation and legislation, most notably the U.S. Patriot Act.

In practice, however, these measures can only have limited effect and are not guaranteed to achieve the aim of reducing the financing of terrorism. When the U.S. Federal Bureau of Investigation attempted to design a profile of the way terrorists may use banks, it highlighted the practice of making a large deposit and withdrawing small amounts of cash at frequent intervals; yet practitioners say that this profile is consistent with that of approximately a quarter of a banks' customers.[71] An additional problem lies in that the funding of terrorism is often based on resources that are legitimate, requiring banks to essentially make value judgments about future use of money, as well the potential of a customer who has not to this day acted unlawfully to do so in the future; this is a subjective and time-consuming strategy that can also lead to discrimination on the basis of ethnic background and create biases linked to personal characteristics. Charities are also put into the spotlight and though many have been targeted with regards to their knowing or unknowing support of al Qaeda terrorists, other than encouraging charity verification field trips, standards remain vague and cannot produce a comprehensive approach.[72] Alternative remittance systems have also been targeted, most notably *hawala*,[73] which avoids wire transfers, paper trails and formal banking.[74] Finally, the sums involved in the financing of terrorism are very small, even in comparison to other activities that are related to money laundering. The attacks of September 11, 2001 may have cost less than $500,000 whereas there might be up to $500 billion worth of funds generated from drug trafficking annually.[75] This amount could be amassed with relative ease, as transactions not exceeding $10,000 do not require the same level of scrutiny: "if Mr. bin Laden [could] recruit thirty people willing to die on his behalf, he [would have had] no problem getting 100 to open bank accounts."[76]

It is still early to assess the impact of the terrorist attacks on long-term money laundering measures and practices. Nevertheless, a renewed impetus has put anti-money laundering firmly on policy and regulatory agendas, and public authorities in developed financial centers are taking the subject very seriously. The pattern of incentives for the private sector has also been adapted, and the shift reflects the "patriotic" element of the "economic war on terror." Significantly, early indications are that most of the measures taken since September 11, 2001 will have little impact on the financing of terrorism; in fact, its is argued that they have failed to "create positive economic incentives for compliance in order to counteract the existing disincentives for disclosure experienced by financial intermediaries and regulation jurisdictions."[77] They might, however, institutionalize the fight against money laundering in general and condition long-term private sector practices.

Conclusions

This chapter presented some observations on the policies and practices of the fight against money laundering. It showed that measures adopted and promoted in this process are often presented in the context of the promotion of a series of global public goods. The chapter argues that until recently, and despite the prolif-eration of official guidelines and the high-profile work of the FATF, talk was tougher than practice. Conventional explanations have focused on offshore cen-ters and developing countries as being the weakest links in the fight against money laundering. While the problems caused by lax regulations and banking secrecy laws are not disputed, other problems dominate. Official regulations need to be more consistent in terms of definitions and stricter with regards to applicability. Moreover, the three sets of actors-components of anti-money laundering measures—law enforcement bodies, financial regulators, and financial institu-tions—need to learn to cooperate on a national and global basis. This chapter fur-ther argues that the major tension lies in the gap between official policies and private practice in "developed" financial centers. The perceived pattern of incen-tives for the private sector to act decisively in the fight against money laundering is deemed inadequate, casting doubt on the possibility of the successful provision of the global public goods associated with the process. It also leads to questioning whether or not the implementation of measures would be too disruptive to global financial flows and hence, whether it is indeed in the interest of the global bank-ing system to push for such implementation. The chapter leaves open the possi-bility that the momentum created by the terrorist attacks of September 11, 2001 could have lasting effects on anti-money laundering measures and practices, but maintains that more evidence is required to confirm the trend.

Notes

1. Narcotics became a "national security" issue in the United States during the 1980s. For a comprehensive account see Eric Helleiner, "State Power and the Regulation of Illicit

Activity in Global Finance," in *The Illicit Global Economy and State Power*, eds. H. Richard Friman and Peter Andreas, 53–90 (Lanham, MD: Rowman and Littlefield, 1999).

2. Paul Bauer and Rhoda Ullmann, "Understanding the Wash Cycle," *Economic Perspectives* 6, no. 2 (2001), http://usinfo.state.gov/journals/ites/0501/ijee/clevelandfed.htm.

3. Sterling Seagrave, *Lords of the Rim: The Invisible Empire of the Overseas Chinese* (New York: Putnam, 1995).

4. Financial Action Task Force (FATF), "What is Money Laundering?", http://www1.oecd.org/fatf/MLaundering en.htm; Chris Odysseos, "Money Laundering: The Risky Business under International Attack," *PricewaterhouseCoopers* (March 2003), http://www.pwcglobal.com/cy/eng/about/press-rm/ArticlesCurrent/Money-Laund.html.

5. *The Economist*, "Getting to Them Through Their Money," September 29, 2001.

6. Nigel Morris-Cotterill, "Money Laundering," *Foreign Policy* 124, no. 3 (2001): 14–22, 16–22.

7. Jean Cartier-Bresson, "Comptes et mécomptes de la mondialisation du crime," *L'Economie Politique* 15, no. 3 (2002): 22–37.

8. *The Banker*, "Money Laundry Monitor," October 6, 2003.

9. Inge Kaul, "Public Goods: Taking the Concept into the Twenty-first Century," in *The Market or the Public Domain*, ed. Daniel Drache, 255–73 (London: Routledge, 2001), 264.

10. Inge Kaul, Isabelle Grunberg, and Marc A. Stern, "Defining Global Public Goods," in *Global Public Goods*, eds. Inge Kaul, Isabelle Grunberg, and Marc A. Stern, 2–19 (New York: Oxford University Press, 1999), 9–11.

11. Ibid., 13.

12. Helleiner, "State Power and the Regulation of Illicit Activity," 59.

13. John McDowell and Gary Novis, "The Consequences of Money Laundering and Financial Crime," *Economic Perspectives* 6, no. 2 (2001), http://usinfo.state.gov/journals/ites/0501/ijee/state1.htm.

14. Williams Phil, "Transnational Organized Crime and the State," in *The Emergence of Private Authority in Global Governance*, eds. Rodney Bruce Hall and Thomas Biersteker, 161–82 (Cambridge: Cambridge University Press, 2002), 165–8.

15. McDowell and Novis, "The Consequences of Money Laundering."

16. The concepts "organised crime" and "transnational organised crime" are widely contested. In the context of the international policy community, they refer to "a heterogeneous group of crimes carried out primarily for economic gain and involving some forms of organisation." See Monica Massari, "Transnational Organized Crime Between Myth and Reality," in *Organized Crime and the Challenge to Democracy*, eds. Felia Allum and Renate Siebert, 55–69 (London: Routledge, 2003), 57. A recent common definition of the *United Nations Convention against Transnational Organised Crime*, signed in 2000 has further determined what constitutes "transnational"—an offense has been committed in more than one state, has had effects in more than one state, has been committed in one state but prepared in a different state, or has been committed in one state by a group that is also active in another state. See ibid.

17. Phil Williams and Gregory Baudin-O'Hayon, "Organized Crime and Money Laundering," in *Governing Globalization*, eds. David Held and Andrew McGrew, 127–44 (Cambridge: Polity, 2002), 131.

18. Ibid., 133–4.

19. Todd Sandler, "Global and Regional Public Goods: A Prognosis for Collective Action," *Fiscal Studies* 19, no. 3 (1998): 221–47, 236.

20. Charles P. Kindleberger, "Dominance and Leadership in the International Economy," in *The International Economic Order—Essays on Financial Crisis and International Public Goods*, ed. Charles P. Kindleberger, 185–95 (Hemel Hempstead: Harvester Wheatsheaf, 1988), 189; Joseph S. Nye, Jr., "The American National Interest and Global Public Goods," *International Affairs* 78, no. 2 (2002): 233–44, 239.

21. Gilles Favarel-Garrigues, "Crime organisé transnational et lutte anti-blanchiment," in *Mondialisation et Gouvernance Mondiale*, ed. Josepha Laroche, 161–73 (Paris: Institut de Relations Internationales et Strategiques, Presses Universitaires de France, 2003); Gilles Favarel-Garrigues, "L'Evolution de la lutte anti-blanchiment depuis le 11 Septembre 2001," *Critique Internationale* 20 (2003): 37–46.

22. Wolfgang Reinicke, "Global Public Policy," *Foreign Affairs* 76, no. 6 (1997): 127–38.

23. Wyn Rees, "Transnational Organized Crime, Security and the European Union," in *Organized Crime and the Challenge to Democracy*, ed. Felia Allum and Renate Siebert, 112–25, 115.

24. Basel Committee on Banking Supervision, *Prevention of Criminal Use of the Banking System for the Purpose of Money Laundering* (Basel: Bank for International Settlements, 1988).

25. For general information on FATF, see the group's website http://www.oecd.org/fatf.

26. FATF member countries are: Argentina, Australia, Austria, Belgium, Brazil, Canada, Denmark, Finland, France, Germany, Greece, Hong Kong—China, Iceland, Ireland, Italy, Japan, Luxembourg, Mexico, Netherlands, New Zealand, Norway, Portugal, Russia, Singapore, South Africa, Spain, Sweden, Switzerland, Turkey, the United Kingdom, and the United States. Additionally, the European Commission and the Gulf Cooperation Council are counted as members.

27. The Vienna Convention is the 1988 *United Nations Convention against Illicit Trade in Narcotic Drugs and Psychotropic Substances*.

28. FATF, "The Forty Recommendations" (2003), http://www.oecd.org/dataoecd/12/26/2789371.pdf.

29. FATF, "New Anti-Money Laundering Standards Released," *Press Release*, June 20, 2003.

30. FATF, "More About the FATF and its Work" (2004), http://www1.oecd.org/fatf/AboutFATF_en.htm.

31. FATF, "Non-Cooperative Countries and Territories" (2004) http://www1.oecd.org/fatf/NCCT_en.htm. Countries currently on the NCCTs list are as follows: Cook Islands, Guatemala, Indonesia, Myanmar, Nauru, Nigeria, Philippines. Egypt and Ukraine were removed from the list in February 2004.

32. Daniel J. Mitchell, "US Government Agencies Conform That Low-tax Jurisdictions Are Not Money Laundering Havens," *Journal of Financial Crime* 11, no. 2 (2003): 127–33, 130.

33. Egmont Group, "Information Paper on Financial Intelligence Units and the Egmont Group" (2001), http://www.egmontgroup.org/info_paper_final_092003.pdf; Egmont Group, *Report of June 2002 Meeting*.

34. United Nations, "Global Program Against Money Laundering", http://unodc.org/unodc/money_laundering.html.

35. International Monetary Fund and World Bank, *Twelve-month Pilot Program of Anti-Money Laundering and Combating the Financing of Terrorism (AML/CFT) Assessments and Delivery of AML/CFT Technical Assistance* (Washington, DC: International Monetary Fund, 2003).

36. The Patriot Act, officially the *Uniting and Strengthening America by Providing Appropriate Tools Required to Intercept and Obstruct Terrorism (USA PATRIOT) Act of 2001*, has strengthened and increased reporting and "know your customer"

requirements for financial institutions. See also Department of the Treasury Financial Crimes Enforcement Netwok (FinCEN).

37. The amended Directive on the "prevention of the use of the financial system for the purpose of money laundering" extends coverage to all criminal activity—when it was previously concentrating on drug trafficking—and increases the types of businesses with requirement obligations to include lawyers, accountants, estate agents, luxury good dealers, and casino operators. See European Commission, *Proposal for a European Parliament and Council Directive Amending Council Directive 91/308/EEC of 10 June 2001 on Prevention of the Use of the Financial System for the Purpose of Money Laundering* (Brussels: Commission of the European Communities, 1999); European Commission, "Money Laundering: Commission Welcomes Council Adoption of New Directive" (2001), http://europa.eu.int/comm/internal_market/en/finances/banks/01-1608.htm.

38. The Joint Forum, *Initiatives by the BCBS, IAIS and IOSCO to Combat Money Laundering and the Financing of Terrorism* (Basle: Bank for International Settlements, 2003).

39. The Secretary General of Interpol Ronald Noble, served as president of the FATF while his director of cabinet was involved with FinCEN and cocreated the Egmont Group. See Ronald K. Noble, "Remarks at the Special Session of the Financial Action Task Force" (speech, Washington, DC, October 29, 2001), http://www.interpol.int/Public/ICPO/speeches/20011029.asp.

40. Favarel-Garrigues, "Crime," 168.

41. Hazel Croall, "Combating Financial Crime: Regulatory versus Crime Control Approaches," *Journal of Financial Crime* 11, no. 1 (2003): 44–55, 46.

42. Mattias Levin, *The Prospects for Offshore Financial Centers in Europe*, CEPS Research Reports No. 29 (Brussels: CEPS, 2002).

43. Ronen Palan, "Tax Havens and the Commercialization of State Sovereignty," *International Organization* 56, no. 1 (2002): 151–76, 155.

44. Bent Sofus Tranøy, *Offshore Finance and Money Laundering: The Politics of Combating Parasitic State Strategies*, The Globalization Project Report No. 11 (Norway: Ministry of Foreign Affairs, 2002), 5–6.

45. Palan moves away from conventional explanations of tax havens and disputes that parochial interest is their original *raison d'être*. He argues that tax havens could not be abolished without seriously challenging the Westphalian notions of sovereignty but does not reject that tax havens do actually take advantage of loopholes. See Palan, "TAX Havens and Commercialization," 157.

46. Beth A. Simmons, "The International Politics of Harmonization: The Case of Capital Market Regulation," *International Organization* 55, no. 3 (2002): 589–620, 605–7.

47. William Hall, "Number's Up for Secret Accounts," *Financial Times*, November 18, 2002.

48. Sarah Perrin, "Ironing Out Those Washday Wrinkles," *Financial Times*, November 18, 2002.

49. Montebourg Report, Assemblée Nationale, Rapport d'Information, "Volume 5—Le Grand Duché du Luxembourg" (2002).

50. Williams and Baudin-O'Hayon, "Organized Crime," 143–4.

51. David Carse, "Anti-money Laundering and the Role of Supervision," *BIS Review* 47 (2002), 1.

52. Basel Committee on Banking Supervision, "Customer Due Diligence by Banks" (Basel: Bank for International Settlements, 2001).

53. Anne T. Vitale, "US Banking: An Industry's View on Money Laundering," *Economic Perspectives* 6, no. 2 (2001), http://usinfo.state.gov/journals/ites/0501/ijee/vitale.htm.

54. The group consists of: ABN Amro, Banco Santander Central Hispano, Bank of Tokyo-Mitsubishi, Barclays, Citigroup, Credit Suisse Group, Deutsche Bank, Goldman Sachs, HSBC, J.P. Morgan Chase, Société Générale, and UBS. The anticorruption nongovernmental organization Transparency International was also instrumental in the initiative.

55. Correspondent banking refers to the relationship banks have with other banks in places where they do not have branches, and consists of providing an account and related services to the other institution for payments and other financial services.

56. The Wolfsberg Group, "The Wolfsberg Anti-Money Laundering Principles for Correspondent Banking," (2002), http://www.wolfsberg-principles.com/correspbanking.html.

57. Mark Pieth and Gemma Aiolfi, "The Private Sector Becomes Active: The Wolfsberg Process," *Journal of Financial Crime* 10, no. 4 (2003): 359–65.

58. Richard W. Rahn, "Follow the Money: Confusion at Treasury," *Washington Times*, January 23, 2003.

59. *ABA Banking Journal*, "Being Good Is Just the Beginning," June 2003, 35, 38.

60. *Business Week*, "Still Drowning in Dirty Money," December 1, 2003. Compliance expertise has been low in the agenda of some financial institutions: HSBC Bank, USA only hired its first full-time anti-money laundering compliance officer in September 2003 after being fined.

61. A. Mitchell, P. Sikka, and H. Willmott, "Sweeping It under the Carpet: The Role of Accountancy Firms in Money Laundering," *Accounting, Organizations and Society* 23, no. 5–6 (1998): 589–607, 591.

62. United Nations estimate, reported in *PricewaterhouseCoopers*, "One the Global Trails of Money Laundering," (2002), http://www.pwcglobal.com/extweb/indissue.nsf/DocID/18141E2C31AA040FCA256BD6001BAA59.

63. Michael Levi, "Money Laundering: Private Banking Becomes Less Private," in *Global Corruption Report 2001*, ed. Transparency International, 204–13 (Berlin: Transparency International, 2001), 205.

64. Nikos Passas and Richard B. Groskin, "Overseeing and Overlooking: The US Federal Authorities' Response to Money Laundering and Other Misconduct at BCCI," *Crime, Law and Social Change* 35 (2001): 141–75.

65. Phillip L. Robinson and Ethan S. Burger, "The Regulatory Framework and Potential Implications of the Bank of New York Money Laundering Scandal for Russia and the United States" (2000), http://www.american.edu/academic.dpts/acanst/transcrime/Publications/Burger_BoNY.

66. In the United Kingdom, Abbey received a record fine in 2003.

67. Martin Navias, "Finance Warfare and International Terrorism," in *Superterrorism: Policy Responses*, ed. Lawrence Freedman, 57–79 (Oxford: Blackwell, 2002), 58–9.

68. FATF, "Special Recommendations on Terrorist Financing" (2001), http://www.fatf-gafi.org/ pdf/SRecTF_en.pdf.

69. FATF, "Guidance for Financial Institutions in Detecting Terrorist Financing" (2001), http://www.fatf-gafi.org/pdf/GuidFITF01_en.pdf.

70. Basel Committee, "Prevention of Criminal use of the Banking System"; Wolfsberg Group, "The Wolfsberg Anti-Money Laundering Principles."

71. *The Economist*, "The Needle in the Haystack," December 14, 2002.

72. *The Economist*, "The Iceberg Beneath the Charity," March 15, 2003.

73. *Hawala* is the Arabic word for trust. The system consists of global money transfers based on a telephone call and the trust between *hawala* dealers. A customer in country A goes to the dealer with an amount of cash—the dealer telephones a counterpart in country B, who proceeds to give an equivalent amount of cash to the customer's

designated recipient. Money does not exchange hands and a "debit" system operates between dealers; the dealer in country A will in time operate an opposite deal. *Hawala* provides a "rapid, reliable and relatively cheap means for migrant workers to remit cash to poor and illiterate families." See Valpy FitzGerald, "Global Financial Information, Compliance Incentives and Terrorist Funding" (paper, University College, Oxford, January 30, 2004).

74. Thomas J. Biersteker, "Targeting Terrorist Finances: The New Challenges of Financial Market Globalization," in *Worlds in Collision*, eds. Ken Booth and Tim Dunne, 74–84 (Basingstoke: Palgrave, 2002), 76.

75. *The Economist*, "The Dirty Money that is Hardest to Clean Up," November 19, 2001.

76. Professor Charles Calomiris of Columbia University, quoted in *The Economist*, "Getting to Them Through Their Money," September 29, 2001.

77. FitzGerald, "Global Financial Information."

Part IV

HIV/AIDS

Chapter 6

HIV/AIDS: The International Security Dimensions

Stefan Elbe

Now in its third decade, HIV/AIDS is well poised to become the most devastating pandemic in modern human history. Throughout the world an estimated 42 million people are already living with HIV, while in some African countries national HIV prevalence rates are currently thought to be well in excess of one-third of the adult population. The immense scale of this pandemic means that almost three times as many persons die from AIDS-related illnesses every day, than died during the terrorist attacks on September 11, 2001. So great is the scale now reached by this pandemic that scholars and policy makers are beginning to recognize that in the worst affected countries the longer-term impact of HIV/AIDS will not be confined to the individual human tragedies suffered by those persons living with the virus and by their respective families. In these same countries HIV/AIDS will also have a plethora of wider economic, political, and social ramifications that will need to be carefully considered and addressed. Among these hitherto overlooked ramifications, this chapter suggests, are the emerging human, national, and international security dimensions of the illness. Scholars and policy makers will have to recognize these security dimensions in order to arrive at a more comprehensive understanding of the nature of the current pandemic and for the level of the international response to become commensurate with the extent of the humanitarian and global security challenge posed by the AIDS pandemic. The security sector, as a high-risk group and vector of the illness, can make a responsible contribution to international efforts to reduce the transmission of HIV in the years to come.[1]

The Global HIV/AIDS Pandemic

Even though the magnitude of the HIV/AIDS pandemic is clearly immense, determining its precise extent is fraught with complex difficulties. To date the most comprehensive data on the pandemic has been jointly compiled by the World Health Organization (WHO) and the Joint UN Program on HIV/AIDS

(UNAIDS). Even the figures provided by the WHO and UNAIDS are only estimates, however, and should not be taken as exact representations. They are subject to considerable political pressures and logistical difficulties, several of which remain beyond the control of UNAIDS. In many countries, for example, systematic HIV/AIDS surveillance remains mostly inadequate, making it hard to obtain reliable data and to detect hidden epidemics not captured by existing surveillance mechanisms. According to the WHO the number of reported AIDS cases ranges from less than 10 percent in some countries to almost 90 percent in others. The following figures are thus best seen as indicators of broad trends rather than exact representations, but this should initially suffice for the purposes of capturing and illustrating the broader security dimensions accompanying the AIDS pandemic.

The figures compiled by UNAIDS clearly illustrate the global scope of HIV/AIDS. This worldwide reach of the AIDS pandemic already emerged as early as 1985, by which time HIV cases had been reported from every region in the world. Since then there has been a steep and unexpectedly high rise in the number of infections worldwide. As of December 2003 UNAIDS estimates that around 40 million people are living with HIV or have AIDS. Conceptually, this number exceeds the entire population of a country like Spain or Argentina. Of these 40 million people, 37 million are thought to be adults aged 15–49, and 2.5 million are children under the age of 15. In 2003 alone an estimated 3 million people died of AIDS-related illnesses, and 5 million persons became newly infected with HIV.[2] To date, UNAIDS believes that around 25 million people have died from AIDS-related illnesses throughout the world.

Contrary to widespread belief, HIV/AIDS is not at all confined to sub-Saharan Africa. Every region of the world currently has a significant number of people living with HIV/AIDS, and the illness is thus best thought of as a pandemic rather than merely as an epidemic. Epidemiological indicators show that HIV is spreading quickly in Asia, the Indian subcontinent, the Caribbean, Russia, and in Eastern Europe. Table 6.1 lists the current UNAIDS estimates for the regional distribution of persons living with HIV at the end of 2003. Although these figures highlight the existence of important variations in the scale of the pandemic faced by the different regions of the world, they do not portray the differences that also exist within these regions.

The African continent, for example, has undoubtedly been affected particularly seriously by the pandemic. Yet it would be a mistake to generalize about the African continent in light of the important regional differences that also need to be acknowledged. In northern Africa there is only little information available on the scale of the epidemic, but it is the African region currently least affected by HIV/AIDS. In eastern Africa, by contrast, HIV prevalence rates continue to be very high, having now reached 15 percent of the adult population in Kenya. In western and central Africa, eight countries including Nigeria are close to or above the 5 percent prevalence mark, after which past experience indicates it becomes increasingly difficult to control the spread of the illness on a widespread basis in the general population. In southern Africa, where the situation is currently worst, four countries including Zimbabwe and Botswana are estimated to have prevalence rates in excess of one-third of the adult population, with several more ranging

Table 6.1   HIV/AIDS epidemic[1]

Region	Adults and children living with HIV/AIDS	Adults and children newly infected with HIV
Sub-Saharan Africa	25.0–28.2 million	3.0–3.4 million
North Africa and Middle East	470,000–730,000	43,000–67,000
South and Southeast Asia	4.6–8.2 million	610,000–1.1 million
East Asia and Pacific	700,000–1.3 million	150,000–270,000
Latin America	1.3–1.9 million	120,000–180,000
Caribbean	350,000–590,000	45,000–80,000
Eastern Europe and Central Asia	1.2–1.8 million	180,000–280,000
Western Europe	520,000–680,000	30,000–40,000
North America	790,000–1.2 million	36,000–54,000
Australia and New Zealand	12,000–18,000	700–1,000
World total	40 million (34–46 million)	5 million (4.2–5.8 million)

Note: [1] UNAIDS, *AIDS Epidemic Update*, 5.

between 10 and 20 percent. These regional variations notwithstanding, the African continent has definitely been hit hardest to date by the AIDS pandemic, and is the region most important to consider regarding the more immediate and emerging security dimensions of HIV/AIDS.

A further 5.3–9.5 million persons are thought to be living with HIV in the Asia and the Pacific region. Cambodia, Myanmar, and Thailand all have prevalence rates exceeding 1 percent among those between the age of 15 and 49. Of the national adult population, 1 percent may not initially seem like a very significant figure, but it is worth recalling that in South Africa as recently as 1990 less than 1 percent of pregnant women attending antenatal clinics tested HIV-positive. Only a decade later, South Africa has an adult prevalence rate of close to 20 percent, and is officially the country with the largest number of people living with HIV/AIDS in the world. Yet 10 years ago scholars would have been very unlikely to predict such high prevalence rates among the general population. If not adequately addressed on the basis of responsible public policies, more serious epidemics could emerge in Asia over the course of the next decade, especially in populous countries such as China and India. China has already registered HIV cases in all of its 31 provinces with an estimated one-half to one million of its population currently living with HIV,[3] and the Chinese Ministry of Health projects that there could be as many as 10 million Chinese living with HIV by the year 2010 if effective precautions are not taken.[4] India, in turn, rivals South Africa in having the highest number of HIV-positive persons living in any one country given its large population of around 4 million persons.

It will be necessary to consider the evidence that is emerging both from Africa and Asia not only in order to arrive at a better understanding of future security implications there, but also with an eye to the possibility that similar scenarios might emerge in other areas of the world. Epidemiological indicators show that the illness is currently spreading in the Caribbean, Russia, and Eastern Europe as well. In terms of growth rates, in fact, the area most seriously affected by HIV/AIDS is Eastern Europe and Russia, where there were an estimated 250,000 new infections in 2001, bringing the regional total to an estimated 1 million people living with HIV. At the end of 2001 Ukraine alone had an estimated 250,000 such persons, making Ukraine's the worst epidemic in the European region, with 1 percent of adults between the ages of 15 and 49 being HIV-positive.[5] Significant increases in HIV prevalence have similarly been observed in the Russian Federation, the Baltic States, and several Central Asian republics.

When using national HIV prevalence rates as an indicator, by contrast, the second most seriously affected region in the world after Africa is Latin America and the Caribbean. In this region there are now 12 countries that have an estimated adult prevalence rate of more than 1 percent, and an estimated 1,650,000–2,490,000 persons living with HIV. Haiti and the Bahamas are among the worst affected countries in this region, with an estimated adult prevalence rate of 6 percent and 3.5 percent, respectively. In the high-income countries of North America and Europe, by contrast, there are less than 2 million persons living with HIV, with an estimated 66,000–94,000 new infections occurring in 2003. AIDS-mortality in these countries has declined due to the availability of expensive antiretroviral therapies, but this has not been accompanied by a commensurate decrease in HIV transmission rates. What is more, this unique medical advantage has allowed many Western analysts to hitherto underestimate the true nature and extent of the HIV/AIDS pandemic currently affecting other regions of the world.

Putting these figures into historical perspective would reveal the AIDS pandemic to be, at least in numerical terms, among the worst pandemics to have confronted mankind. In the first decade of the twenty-first century alone it may well claim more victims than the Spanish influenza epidemic of 1918–1919, which is thought to have caused between 25 and 40 million deaths worldwide.[6] It will, in all likelihood, also exceed the number of victims of the bubonic plague in Europe given that UNAIDS estimates an additional 45 million persons will become infected with HIV by 2010 unless stronger and successful efforts are made to curb transmission rates. It is precisely this immense and unanticipated scale of the AIDS pandemic that raises important questions as to whether it might have implications that go beyond the health sector, and extend into the security sector. Perhaps nothing symbolizes the recent addition of HIV/AIDS to the security agenda more dramatically than the landmark Security Council meeting devoted specifically to the negative impact of AIDS on international peace and security in Africa. This meeting, held on January 10, 2000, was the first time that the Security Council explicitly found a health issue to be of a serious enough magnitude to be considered a threat to international peace and security. In his function as President of the World Bank James Wolfensohn argued unequivocally before the Council that "[m]any of us used to think of AIDS as a health issue. We were wrong. . . . Nothing we have seen is a greater challenge to the peace and stability of African societies than the epidemic of AIDS . . . We face a major development crisis, and more than that, a security crisis."[7] The reasoning, however, as to exactly why HIV/AIDS also represents an international security issue still remains ambiguous. Indeed, the Security Council itself asked governmental and nongovernmental agencies to further analyze and reflect on the security implications of HIV/AIDS. The remainder of this chapter will thus outline three trajectories along which the AIDS pandemic, if not addressed comprehensively, is likely to evolve important security dimensions in the years ahead.

HIV/AIDS as a Human Security Issue

One way in which HIV/AIDS is already having important security ramifications, and will continue to do so for many years to come, is within the broader framework of "human security."[8] This notion, advanced by the UN Development Program in its 1994 Human Development Report, seeks to redress the perceived imbalance in security thinking that has predominated over past decades, and wishes to refocus its attention on the needs and welfare of individuals, rather than just that of states and territories. In the course of the twentieth century the social importance of addressing widespread illnesses was gradually superseded by the even greater threat posed by large-scale industrial wars and the specter of a global nuclear confrontation. During this same period of human history important medical advances in treating widespread illnesses were also achieved. Concomitantly security thinking became increasingly focused on avoiding the outbreak of armed conflict, and became closely associated with the activities of states. Within this understanding of security, the greatest threats to security tended to emanate from the military capabilities of other states.

In the post–Cold War human security framework, by contrast, security is understood to encompass more than just the absence of armed conflict. It additionally incorporates the ability of persons to live safe, healthy, and productive lives. Freedom from fear and freedom from want are just as important within this conception of security. Its sphere of legitimate security concerns consequently includes a variety of nonmilitary threats to the survival and welfare of individuals and societies, such as disease, hunger, unemployment, crime, social conflict, political repression, and environmental hazards.[9] To some extent, of course, the divergence between the state and individuals is artificial, as the two cannot always be completely divorced. Threats to the state will also often impact on the lives of individuals, and a state depends on individuals, families, and communities to function. Nevertheless, in those countries where the state has largely abandoned, or become sufficiently removed from, the wider needs of its population, the human security approach allows for a useful shift of emphasis.

Much in this vein the Human Development Report went on to define human security as "safety from constant threats of hunger, disease, crime and repression. It also means protection from sudden and hurtful disruptions in the patterns of our daily lives—wither in our homes, our jobs, in our communities or in our environments."[10] Specifically, the report identified seven components of human security: economic, food, health, environmental, personal, community, and political.[11] Although this particular way of thinking about security has provoked considerable debate in post–Cold War security studies, especially regarding its breadth as an analytical concept, it is important to bear in mind that such thinking about the notion of security is not as novel as it might initially appear in the context of the contemporary debate. Emma Rothschild has shown how many of these ideas have evident Enlightenment roots that can be traced back at least to the eighteenth and nineteenth century, if not earlier.[12] From this perspective, the narrowing of security thinking in the course of the twentieth century represents a historical anomaly—one linked, perhaps, to the extraordinary violent nature of the twentieth century. In either case, the idea of human security has not only been embraced by the UN Security Council, but has also attracted a wider coalition of national governments, including Canada, Norway, and Japan.[13]

If the human security approach is intimately concerned with securing not only the survival of the state, but also the survival and welfare of individual human beings, then HIV/AIDS clearly amounts to an important security issue within this framework. Quantitatively, HIV/AIDS is already among the five most frequent causes of death worldwide. In Africa the illness even vies for the unenviable position of posing the greatest human security threat. In Africa HIV/AIDS is not only the leading cause of death, it is also estimated to cause more than ten times as many deaths as armed conflict. AIDS thus already poses a numerically greater risk to the survival and welfare of individuals in Africa than armed conflict. Qualitatively, moreover, HIV/AIDS also directly and indirectly affects most of the components of human security identified by the UN Development Program. At the most basic level, HIV/AIDS is a lethal illness that threatens the life of those who develop AIDS and who do not enjoy access to life-saving medicines. As a result, the average life expectancy in some African countries is likely to drop by as much as 20 to 30 years over the next decades. By 2010 the life expectancy in many countries could even be lower than at the beginning of the twentieth century, to no small extent due to the impact of HIV/AIDS, thus further undermining virtually an entire century of modest developmental gains.[14]

Beyond these individual tragedies, HIV/AIDS also has a plethora of direct and indirect human security ramifications for those families and communities affected by the illness. Unlike many other illnesses associated with old age—like heart disease, cerebrovascular disease, and lower respiratory infections—AIDS-related illnesses affect persons at a much younger and more productive age. Consequently there is an important relationship, for example, between high HIV prevalence rates and levels of food security. As persons become too ill they may become unable to provide or acquire nourishment for their families or be unable to tend to the fields in order to secure adequate levels of food. They may even have to sell off their possessions or livestock in order to compensate for this lack of income. The same holds true for their more general ability to generate income, as individuals become too ill to maintain steady employment. What is more, many urban dwellers decide to return to their villages once they become ill, thus further perpetuating this cycle.

High rates of HIV/AIDS also have human security implications in terms of the level of education individuals may benefit from. If one or both parents become ill, children may be kept away from school in order to help in the domestic household or to generate income themselves. Eventually, many of these children will become orphans. In Sierra Leone it is estimated that the number of children orphaned due to HIV/AIDS is around five times as high as the number of children who were orphaned during the recent conflict.[15] To this must be added the immense impact of HIV/AIDS on the education sector as a whole, as scores of teachers succumb to the illness. It is thought that in some regions in southern Africa around a fifth of secondary school teachers are currently HIV-positive, with the result that some schools are already being forced to close. In 1999 it was estimated that 860,000 primary school children in sub-Saharan Africa had lost teachers due to AIDS-related illnesses.[16]

The human security of individuals may also be affected more intangibly, through social stigma and exclusion, which may, in turn, manifest itself in violent attacks on persons known to be living with HIV or being closely associated with such persons. One particularly tragic case occurred in South Africa where Gugu Dlamini died at the age of 36 as the result of a beating she received by her neighbors in the outskirts of Durban in December of 1998 after she revealed—on World AIDS Day—that she was HIV-positive. When viewed from the perspective of human security, therefore, HIV/AIDS is undoubtedly a security issue of overwhelming proportions, and this represents one of the important ways in which HIV/AIDS is already evolving a significant security dimension. Indeed, the immense individual and social impact of HIV/AIDS is precisely the kind of issue that human security advocates would like to draw attention to beyond the specter of armed conflict. This does not mean, however, that one has to adopt a human security framework in order to recognize the emerging security dimensions of HIV/AIDS; these dimensions also extend into the state-centric framework of national security.

HIV/AIDS and National Security

In those countries currently experiencing very high HIV prevalence rates, HIV/AIDS is also beginning to have ramifications that will be of interest to scholars and analysts working within a more conventional national security framework. Within a state-centric security perspective the impact of HIV/AIDS on the armed forces and on the political stability of the worst affected countries are particular causes for concern. The armed forces, for one, are not a marginal group within the global AIDS pandemic, but occupy a central position within it. Prevalence rates of sexually transmitted diseases among military populations in peacetime are widely believed to exceed those of the comparative civilian population. Although data currently remains inadequate and patchy, intelligence assessments indicate that in many African militaries this also holds true in the case of HIV.[17] There are a variety of factors that can expose military populations to higher levels of HIV prevalence, including that soldiers are of a sexually active age, that they are mobile and stationed away from home for long periods of time, that they often valorize violent and risky behavior, that they have opportunities for casual sexual relations, that they seek to relieve themselves from the stress of combat, and because other sexually transmitted diseases increase the chance of HIV transmission during unprotected sexual intercourse.

As a result of these factors several defense ministries in sub-Saharan Africa are now documenting HIV prevalence rates among the armed forces between 10 and 20 percent. This is only the average figure, however, with some countries where the AIDS virus has been present for more than ten years, reaching rates as high as 50–60 percent.[18] The U.S. National Intelligence Council believes HIV prevalence in selected military populations in sub-Saharan Africa to be: Angola 40–60 percent, Congo-Brazzaville 10–25 percent, Ivory Coast 10–20 percent, Democratic Republic of Congo 40–60 percent, Eritrea 10 percent, Nigeria 10–20 percent, and Tanzania 15–30 percent.[19] These figures are compatible with a recent defense intelligence assessment carried out by South Africa, which provided the following figures: Angola 50 percent, Botswana 33 percent, Democratic Republic of Congo 50 percent, Lesotho 40 percent, Malawi 50 percent, Namibia 16 percent, South Africa 15– 20 percent, Swaziland 48 percent, Zambia 60 percent, and Zimbabwe 55 percent.[20]

Nor is the impact of these prevalence rates only of marginal relevance for the armed forces in question. According to Maj. Gen. Matshwenyego Fisher, chief of staff of the Botswana defense force, "AIDS in the military as well as in the national environment, is no longer an academic issue; it is a reality that has to be tackled with all the vigor and effort that is commensurate with its ramifications."[21] Indeed, these prevalence rates are having an impact in at least four areas that are important to the efficient operation of the armed forces. First, they are generating a need for additional resources to train and recruit new soldiers to replace sick ones, ones who have died, or ones who are expected to die in the near future. More resources will also be needed for looking after those members of the armed forces who are ill or in the process of dying. Second, these high prevalence rates are also affecting staffing issues in the armed forces. High HIV prevalence rates eventually lead to a decrease in the available civilian conscription pool to draw upon for new recruits, lead to deaths among the more senior and experienced officers at higher levels of the chain of command, and can lead to a loss of highly specialized and technically trained staff that can be replaced neither easily nor quickly. Third, although persons living with HIV can usually carry out normal duties, AIDS has implications for the ability of daily military tasks to be carried out efficiently by leading to an increased absenteeism and to lower levels of morale as healthy soldiers have to deal with increased work loads until sick ones are replaced, and have to watch fellow soldiers die a painful death. Fears of attending to injured soldiers in light of the possibility of becoming infected with the lethal illness, and the question of how to secure the blood supply during military operations, are similarly becoming concerns for the efficient execution of deployments. Finally, HIV/AIDS generates new political and legal challenges for civil–military relations in terms of how to deal with the issue of HIV/AIDS in the ranks and how to treat persons living with HIV.[22] The Namibian armed forces, for example, recently lost a lengthy court case as to whether its decision to exclude HIV-positive persons from joining the armed forces is constitutional.

Beyond this direct impact on the armed forces of countries in which prevalence rates are highest, the growing AIDS pandemic also has security implications in terms of political stability within these states. This link is more difficult to assess, but there are already four countries in sub-Saharan Africa where HIV prevalence is estimated to exceed 30 percent: Botswana with 38.8 percent, Lesotho with 31 percent, Swaziland with 33.4 percent, and Zimbabwe with 33.7 percent, raising important questions about the longer-term impact of such prevalence rates on their political stability. When states become unstable or fail, it is often because the central monopoly on the use of armed force is disputed, and because the government's popular legitimacy has been severely eroded. Such processes of state collapse do not necessarily occur instantaneously but can, as William Zartmann has argued, be likened to "a long-term degenerative disease"[23]—a bitterly ironic designation when applied to the question of HIV/AIDS. Moreover, state collapse is normally a multifaceted phenomenon involving at least three interrelated processes: the transformation or destruction of the economy, the weakening or dissolution of political institutions at local and national levels, and the damaging of a wide array of social institutions such as the family, the education system, and the health care sector.[24] Although HIV/AIDS is unlikely to generate state collapse independently of other factors, high rates of HIV/AIDS nevertheless contribute to all three of these processes, thus giving rise to significant concern about the long-term impact of HIV/AIDS on the worst affected states if life-saving medicines are not made widely available.

HIV/AIDS contributes to the first trajectory involved in processes of state collapse in that it exacerbates the resource burden faced by countries and can thus play a role in the intensification of resource competition between different social groups. The armed forces, for example, are likely to attempt to secure a greater share of public expenditure in order to offset some of their emerging resource demands. In southern Africa, the Namibian Deputy Minister of Defense Victor Simunja has already expressed serious concern about the resource burden that HIV/AIDS poses for the Namibian military, arguing that "[n]ot only is the readiness of soldiers for deployment and active duty likely to be severely impaired, but the cost of health and social care of the military personnel affected and infected with the HIV/AIDS related diseases is likely to increase significantly in the coming years."[25] The civilian sector will simultaneously be facing a similar increase in resource demands, thus fueling resource competition between these two groups. According to one study, in 1997 more than 2 percent of gross domestic product (GDP) was already being used for public health spending toward HIV/AIDS in 7 of 16 African countries sampled. These are countries where traditionally total health spending accounts for around 3–5 percent of GDP.[26] In the mid-1990s it was estimated that "66 per cent of Rwanda's health budget and over a quarter of the health budget of Zimbabwe were spent on treatment for people with HIV."[27] In Malawi, the public health system is already inundated by the pandemic with up to 70 percent of hospital bed occupancy taken up by patients suffering from AIDS-related illnesses.

Such competition over scarce resources between the military and civilian sector will be exacerbated further still because even though the most severe impact is probably going to occur at the level of individual households and particular industries, AIDS is predicted to have a long-term macroeconomic impact in those states worst affected by the illness, although the extent of this impact is still a matter of considerable debate among economists. According to a report published by the National Intelligence Council (NIC) the worst affected countries will suffer from a reduction in economic growth of up to 1 percent of GDP per annum due to AIDS, and the latter could consume more than half of the health budgets of those countries.[28] A report by the secretary general of the UN, in turn, finds that in the next twenty years the worst affected countries could well lose up to a quarter of their projected economic growth.[29] In a sub-Saharan African country with a prevalence rate of around 20 percent, the annual growth of GDP would be 2.6 percent lower.[30] A recent WHO report conservatively estimates that AIDS will account for 17 percent of the lost earning potential of sub-Saharan Africa's total 1999 GDP.[31] While these kinds of losses could be absorbed for a year or two, they pose larger problems when they become cumulative, occurring year after year as they are likely to do. Given that HIV/AIDS does affect the economically most productive demographic group, that HIV/AIDS undermines the belief in the long-term sustainability of the economy, that it could discourage private as well as foreign investment, and given that AIDS affects the middle management of many companies as well as their highly trained workers that are in smaller supply, these figures could well be indicative of broad trends. In future, both military and civilian sectors will thus have to compete with each other in order to try to secure a higher proportion of public resources to meet their higher costs, and they may well have to do so at the same time that overall public revenue is declining.

HIV/AIDS also contributes to the second trajectory usually involved in processes of state collapse by generating at least four additional challenges to the political sphere in countries where prevalence rates are very high. First, HIV/AIDS could further undermine the ability of state officials to govern effectively in the long run. Crucial resources are already being reportedly diverted from running state services to treating people with HIV/AIDS. Basic government services will thus become more difficult to deliver as mortality rates among those working for the state increase. In many countries with high prevalence rates the effectiveness of the police forces, too, is coming under increasing pressure from the illness. The police forces of the fourteen SADC countries are now taking HIV/AIDS very seriously, and are trying to find ways to cope with the reduction in personnel as well as bracing themselves for things to become much worse in the years to come.[32] In Kenya, AIDS was believed to be the cause of 75 percent of deaths in the police force between 1999 and 2000,[33] and the Zambian police force is similarly reported to have felt the severe impact of HIV/AIDS.[34] The judicial system, too, is affected, with staff serving in justice institutions, such as judges, prosecutors, court clerks, and lawyers facing similar levels of mortality as other sectors of society.[35] All other things held equal, this means that in future it will become more difficult to fight crime and fewer arrests will probably be made. It will also become more difficult to handle internal rebels or domestic challenges to power.

Second, HIV/AIDS could also facilitate political tensions over decisions about who will have access to life-saving medicines. Diseases have ravaged many countries for decades without necessarily fueling political instability. Yet, unlike other diseases that are strongly linked with poverty, HIV/AIDS additionally afflicts the educated and moderately wealthy middle classes. Given the current availability of antiretroviral treatments for HIV/AIDS, many elites with access to resources will be able to substantially relieve their predicament by purchasing expensive medicines. The plight of other social groups, however, is less certain. If the elites are not seen to be working in their interests and securing the availability of medications for them as well, this could contribute to further social polarization. Randy Cheek argues that the "[u]neven distribution of essential HIV treatment based on social, ethnic, or political criteria could well put unmanageable pressures on social and political structures, threatening the stability of regimes throughout Southern Africa."[36] Indeed, those living with HIV might become increasingly susceptible to populist leaders promising radical solutions, rather than relying on more democratic ones. According to an opinion poll carried out by the Institute for Democracy in South Africa in October 2000, one of the primary reasons for Mbeki's decline in popularity was his stance on HIV, which provoked friction in the governing coalition in 2003.[37]

HIV/AIDS also contributes to the third trajectory frequently involved in processes of state collapse, namely the undermining of a wide array of social institutions such as the family, the education system, and the health care sector. These dimensions were already outlined when considering the human security implications of HIV/AIDS, and include not only the decrease in average life expectancy, but also the potential generation of up to 40 million orphans in the years to come.[38] Many of these children will be exposed to the stigma of the illness and will be more vulnerable to malnutrition, illness, abuse, and sexual exploitation.[39] Often, children are also left to exchange sexual services in return for other vital goods, such as shelter, food, physical protection, and money.[40] This development is not of concern for human security theorists alone. Martin Schönteich, of the Institute for Security Studies in South Africa, links this rise in the number of orphans due to HIV/AIDS with an exponentially increasing crime rate for the next 5 to 20 years.[41] He argues that these orphans will be susceptible to exploitation and radicalization, and might well turn toward crime and militias in order to maintain their existence as they receive inadequate support from their families and communities.[42] Crime bands and militias, after all, not only have the potential to address the material needs of youths, they can also perform important psychological functions such as providing them with surrogate father figures and role models.[43]

In these ways, HIV/AIDS can potentially exacerbate a variety of economic, political, and social tensions within the worst affected countries. In so doing HIV/AIDS also contributes to all three trajectories usually associated with processes of political instability and state collapse, and it is currently pushing developments further in this direction. Beyond seriously affecting the armed forces, therefore, in the worst affected countries AIDS also generates longer-term concerns about social stability, both for those countries directly affected as well as for those with interests in these regions. The significance of this dimension is likely to grow considerably in the years to come as mortality rates increase further. If, moreover, high prevalence rates also emerge in China, India, and Russia in the years ahead, this could have wider security implications beyond the African continent. All of these countries are still in the early phase of their epidemics and are important international security actors who have yet to respond adequate to the challenge posed by HIV/AIDS.

At the same time, there is also an important source of hope with regards to the question of the long-term political stability of the worst affected states. Given the relatively long cycle of the progression from HIV to AIDS, there is still a window of opportunity for concerted efforts to make medicines available to people living with HIV/AIDS. Indeed, there is an important difference between prevalence rates and morality rates. In the case of HIV/AIDS, staggering prevalence rates of 30 percent or more of the adult population translate into a significantly smaller annual mortality rate, given the long cycle of the illness. Mortality rates in any given year will not amount to 30 percent or more, but rather to a lower figure, especially when measured as percentage of the total population, rather than just the adult population. In South Africa, for example, the combined number of projected adult AIDS cases and deaths to occur each year over the next decade is between 1.5 percent and 4 percent of the adult population.[44] These figures are clearly very serious and represent an immense humanitarian tragedy, especially because they will occur year after year. Yet they also point to a crisis that is potentially still manageable with sufficient local, national, and international will. The most prudent strategy, therefore, in terms of addressing these emerging national security dimensions of the pandemic would be to act in the present before mortality rates increase even further. Such efforts would also help to address the international security dimensions of the global AIDS pandemic.

HIV/AIDS and International Security

The significance of the impact of HIV/AIDS on the armed forces goes beyond the domestic considerations of those countries affected. It also gives rise to an important international security dimension because many of these same armed forces regularly contribute to international peacekeeping operations aimed at mitigating and containing armed conflicts. HIV/AIDS poses additional logistical and political problems for these peacekeeping operations, as it becomes increasingly well known that peacekeepers are at a special risk both of contracting and spreading HIV when and where they are deployed. There are three important ways in which HIV/AIDS has already begun to affect peacekeeping operations over the course of the past years.

First, it has become increasingly well known that peacekeepers can contribute to the spread of HIV where and when they are deployed. "Here," Richard Holbrooke has argued, "we get into one of the ugliest secret truths . . . about AIDS: it is spread by UN peacekeepers."[45] In his view this creates "almost the greatest irony of all: in the cause of peacekeeping to spread a disease which is killing ten times as many people as war."[46] In Sierra Leone, for example, the civil war seems to have escalated the number of infections partially due to peacekeepers who were, among other places, from Zambia, Kenya, and Nigeria—all countries with high prevalence rates in the military.[47] Although accurate data is again lacking, one recent report notes that "32 percent of peacekeepers [in Sierra Leone] originate from countries with HIV prevalence rates greater than five percent."[48] Given such circumstances, the HIV/AIDS Coordinator Hirut Befecadu has insisted that "the population should be protected from the soldiers as well, because most of the troops come from places where AIDS is a problem."[49]

The recognition that peacekeepers can be sources of HIV transmission has begun to create political problems for international peacekeeping operations, as countries cite this problem as a ground for refusing to host such missions. In Eastern Africa, for example, Eritrean officials initially wanted a guarantee that no HIV-positive soldiers would be deployed there. They wrote to the Security Council in March of 2001 explicitly requesting that countries contributing troops should screen them for HIV. The letter contained an "appeal to troop contributing countries to understand our concern. Eritrea is at the moment engaged in a very rigorous national campaign to prevent the spread of AIDS."[50] This political problem was further exacerbated by the subsequent emergence of accusations of sexual abuse against one peacekeeper. The Eritrean government has demanded that the peacekeeper accused of sexually abusing an under-age girl is brought to justice and used the opportunity to add its concern that it had asked peacekeepers to be tested for HIV/AIDS, but that this had not yet been properly implemented.[51]

In Asia, political problems have also been emerging over the past decade regarding the transition authority in Cambodia. As the UN arrived in Cambodia between the spring of 1992 and September 1993 in order to implement the peace agreement and in order to organize democratic elections, the HIV rate appears to have increased dramatically.[52] By the end of 1999 there were an estimated 220,000 people living with HIV. Although there is insufficient data to discern what proportion of this increase was due to the presence of international peacekeepers, some officials in Phnom Penh place considerable blame for the spread of the epidemic in Cambodia on the UN Transition Authority in Cambodia (UNTAC).[53] The UNTAC mission was unique at the time and brought more than 20,000 foreign people into Cambodia. This influx of people, many of whom were civilian officials and not just peacekeepers, also infused a fair amount of money into a country otherwise struggling with poverty for many years. On average, sex workers, who are coming in some cases from as far away as Eastern Europe, reportedly doubled the number of their clients per night from five to ten during the time of the UN mission. Subsequent testing on UNTAC soldiers from the United States and from Uruguay shows that they were infected with the HIV subtype E, which had previously only been found in Southeast Asian and in Central Africa.[54] Realizing the potential problem with the Cambodia mission, the Indonesian military decided to screen 3,627 soldiers that participated in UNTAC. Twelve of these tested HIV positive, at least seven infections of which are likely to have been acquired while in Cambodia. This figure exceeded the only other two deaths among Indonesian peacekeepers that resulted from non-AIDS related causes.[55] Nor is this a problem confined to Asia and Africa. During the Balkans conflict, Zagreb officials, too, made a vocal attempt to ensure that African peacekeepers do not serve in Croatia in light of the risk of HIV transmission.[56] In the long run, therefore, the impact of HIV/AIDS may well influence the willingness of countries to host such operations.

A second way in which the impact of HIV/AIDS on armed forces could pose a future challenge for international peacekeeping operations is that it may also make such missions increasingly unpopular among those countries that contribute peacekeepers to them. After all, many of the factors that render national military populations a high-risk group in terms of HIV/AIDS apply just as well to international peacekeepers. Peacekeepers, too, can be posted away from home for long periods of time. In one case, Nigerian peacekeepers were on field duty, without rotation, for up to three years.[57] In this particular case the incidence rate was actually correlated to the duration of the deployment, increasing to 7 percent in the first year, to 10 percent after two years, and even 15 percent after three.[58] Peacekeeping missions additionally tend to attract large numbers of sex workers, thus linking two high-risk groups.[59] Countries may consequently become reluctant to contribute to peacekeeping operations if they realize that some of those who are deployed will return HIV-positive. Of the 10,000 troops that Nigeria sent to Sierra Leone in 1997, 11 percent of the returning ones tested HIV-positive.[60] The Nigerian government admitted in December of 1999 that there was an extremely high prevalence rate among its troops participating in the ECOWAS Monitoring Group (ECOMOG) peacekeeping operations in neighboring West African states.[61] Although specific figures were not given, Vice President Abubakar Atiku described the situation as "grave." This is actually part of a larger trend whereby more peacekeepers have succumbed to AIDS-related illnesses since the 1980s than to battle injuries.[62] These losses are not only regrettable from the point of view of the individual soldiers and the armed forces, but also for peacekeeping operations in general as soldiers with valuable prior experience die prematurely from AIDS-related illnesses.

This problem affects soldiers deployed from Western countries as well. One report indicates that soldiers from Finland who had been on a tour of duty in Namibia also became infected with HIV in the early 1990s and brought the virus back home with them.[63] Other soldiers from such diverse areas as Europe, Asia, and North America similarly became infected with HIV during their mission in Cambodia in 1993, while another 45 Indian soldiers similarly tested positive for HIV after returning from Cambodia in 1993.[64] Moreover, two Bangladeshi peacekeepers became infected with HIV in Cambodia in 1993 and one more in Mozambique in 1994, while ten Uruguayan peacekeepers similarly became HIV-positive while in Cambodia.[65] Some Western troops serving in Bosnia, too, are reported to have contracted the illness.[66] Given that peacekeepers are often stationed far away from their domestic environments, they have the potential not only to bring, or bring back, HIV with them, but they may also introduce new and different strands of HIV into the populations where they are deployed, or upon returning from these deployments.

Third, the high rate of HIV in the African armed forces also makes it more difficult to staff international peacekeeping operations. Depending on the mission involved, peacekeeping operations can be notoriously difficult to staff and it is not always easy for the UN to find sufficient peacekeepers to meet its operational demands. This problem is further exacerbated by HIV/AIDS, which could lead to a decrease in the personnel that states can contribute to such operations.[67] Greg Mills, director of the South African Institute of International Affairs, has studied this problem in relation to SADC and found that during the SADC Blue Crane peacekeeping exercise, which was held in South Africa in April 1999, nearly 50 percent of the 4,500 participating troops reportedly turned out to be HIV-positive. Moreover, 30 percent of the South African contingent was not medically fit for deployment, raising particular questions about the ability of South Africa to contribute to international peacekeeping operations in the years ahead, and more general questions regarding the Western strategy of devolving peacekeeping operations to the subregional level in Africa.[68] Indeed, the Deputy Defense Minister of South Africa Nozizwe Madlala-Routledge echoes, "South Africa must be able to fulfill its obligations toward its people as well as the international community," and this, "is only possible through healthy and motivated soldiers."[69] In future, HIV/AIDS could thus also add to the increasing strain on the number of soldiers that armies can contribute for peacekeeping operations.

The Security Council has now begun to take this issue seriously enough to address it formally through passing Resolution 1,308 that urges member states to screen their soldiers voluntarily. It also calls upon the secretary general to provide predeployment orientation on the prevention of the spread of HIV for peace-keepers. The Bangladeshi armed forces, as one of the largest contributors to peacekeeping operations, are also beginning to take the issue seriously. Of some 90,000 soldiers screened so far after deployment, only three are reported to have tested positive, which means their prevalence rates are still low by Asian standards.[70] In 2001, moreover, peacekeepers from the UN mission in Eritrea and Ethiopia have completed the first two-week AIDS prevention course to be offered to peacekeepers, along with 50 soldiers from the Eritrean Defense Force. The course trainer Steve Talugende points out that "[t]his is just the beginning. UNAIDS intends to deploy officers in other peacekeeping missions to coordinate HIV and AIDS control activities."[71] Furthermore, the UN has already purchased over 1.5 million condoms for its peacekeepers in Sierra Leone and East Timor—rationed on the basis of one condom per peacekeeper per day,[72] and distributed 15,000 AIDS awareness cards for peacekeepers.[73] Despite these important efforts, the impact of HIV/AIDS on the peacekeeping operations adds an important international security dimension to the pandemic as well, especially as it will prove very difficult in practical terms for the UN to deploy only HIV-negative soldiers in light of the important human rights considerations involved and the need to rely on certain armed forces to meet their operational requirements.

Conclusion

This chapter has drawn attention to the important human, national, and international security dimensions that the global AIDS pandemic is giving rise to. It is important that scholars and international policy-makers begin to acknowledge these dimensions more widely. First, awareness of these security dimensions of

HIV/AIDS is a necessary step in order to arrive at a more comprehensive understanding of the nature and extent of the contemporary pandemic. While the economic and social implications are now being considered more widely and seriously by scholars and policy makers on a country-by-country basis, this is not yet occurring with reference to the security dimensions of HIV/AIDS. Second, it is also necessary to acknowledge these emerging security dimensions in order for the level of the international response to become commensurate with the extent of the global challenge posed by the AIDS pandemic. International efforts will have to be intensified and better resources in order to address these emerging security dimensions, as well as the immense humanitarian catastrophe this pandemic signifies. Finally, these security dimensions must also be taken seriously because the security sector, as a high-risk group and vector of the virus, must also make a responsible contribution to international efforts to reduce the transmission of HIV.

Indeed, armed forces around the world should be encouraged to implement responsible HIV/AIDS education programs that discuss the illness in an open and serious manner, and that simultaneously work to reduce the stigma attached to the illness. The military has a rigid and hierarchical organizational structure, and thus also a captive audience, that lends itself to implementing such measures and that would allow it to perform an important role in the quest to reduce the scale of the pandemic in the years to come. Armed forces should thus strive to make voluntary and fully confidential testing available on a widespread basis, including counseling both before and after the test, and should reevaluate what military practices expose soldiers to particularly high risk with regard to HIV transmission, making amendments where possible. Crucially, however, the armed forces will have to address the issue of HIV/AIDS with due consideration of the important human rights issues involved. Human beings living with the virus are not the enemy in the quest to address the illness, but the most important source for making viable improvements in future. Consequently, they must also be included rather than excluded from these processes. Finally, those armed forces possessing advanced medical infrastructure should continue research for a viable and affordable AIDS vaccine. After all, it would be in the evident interest of Western militaries to engage in research on those strands that predominate in the various regions of Africa to which they might be deployed at some point in the future.

In addition to these very specific measures that international agencies and the armed forces can adopt in addressing the global AIDS pandemic, an effective strategy for the security sector with regard to HIV/AIDS would also incorporate, second, a greater appreciation and support for the wider efforts currently being made to combat the pandemic, such as making cheaper drugs available internationally and contributing to the Global Fund to Fight AIDS, Tuberculosis, and Malaria. Such wider efforts are necessary because the root causes of the AIDS pandemic are located in a much broader set of economic, political, and structural conditions that will have to be reevaluated and alleviated if any attempt to turn back the spread of the pandemic is to be successful in the future. The security sector would do well to recognize the convergence of interest with regards to addressing the global AIDS pandemic and to broadly support this wider endeavor. It would certainly be prudent to do so because the armed forces constitute a high-risk group with regards to HIV, and because of the overwhelming humanitarian dimension of the illness. All of the new security challenges that HIV/AIDS is currently giving rise to are likely to lessen if there is a significant decrease in the AIDS pandemic. Such wider international efforts to reduce the transmission of HIV, in turn, will only be successful in the long run if they also take into account the multiple security dimensions of the AIDS pandemic outlined above.

Notes

1. This chapter draws on research carried out for the International Institute for Strategic Studies, some aspects of which are presented in more extensive form in Stefan Elbe, *Strategic Implications of HIV/AIDS*, Adelphi Paper 357 (Oxford: Oxford University Press for IISS, 2003).
2. UNAIDS, *AIDS Epidemic Update* (Geneva: UNAIDS, 2003), 3.
3. Ann Hwang, "AIDS over Asia: AIDS Has Arrived in India and China," *Guardian* (Manchester), January 16, 2001.
4. John Gittings, "War on Prejudice as China Awakes to HIV Nightmare," *Guardian* (Manchester) November 3, 2000.
5. UNAIDS, *Report on the Global HIV/AIDS Epidemic* (Geneva: UNAIDS, 2002), 33.
6. Lester Brown et al., *Beyond Malthus: Nineteen Dimensions of the Population Challenge* (New York: W. W. Norton, 1999), 122.
7. James Wolfensohn (speech, UN Security Council, New York, January 10, 2000).
8. For the notion of "human security" see UN Development Program (UNDP), *Human Development Report, 1994: New Dimensions of Human Security* (New York: Oxford University Press, 1994). With specific reference to HIV/AIDS, see also Ulf Kristoffersson, "HIV/AIDS as a Human Security Issue: A Gender Perspective" (paper, Expert Group Meeting, Windhoek, Namibia, November 13–17, 2000); Deepika Grover, "Local Responses to AIDS in South Africa: Gender/Human Insecurity and Social Organising in the Context of Dwindling Social Resources" (paper, International Studies Association, Chicago, February 21–24, 2001); and Pieter Fourie and Martin Schönteich, "Africa's New Security Threat: HIV/AIDS and Human Security in Southern Africa," *African Security Review* 10, no. 4 (2001): 29–57.
9. UNDP, *Human Development Report*, 22.
10. Ibid., 3.
11. Ibid., 24–25.
12. Emma Rothschild, "What is Security?," *Daedalus* 124, no. 3 (1995): 53–98.
13. Members of the Human Security Network include Austria, Canada, Chile, Greece, Ireland, Jordan, Mali, The Netherlands, Norway, Slovenia, South Africa (as an observer), Switzerland, and Thailand.
14. David Gordon (remarks, United States Institute for Peace Current Issues Briefing Panel "Plague Upon Plague: AIDS and Violent Conflict in Africa," Washington, DC, May 8, 2001).
15. Peter Piot, "AIDS and Human Security" (speech, UN University, Tokyo, Japan, October 2, 2001), 7, http://www.unaids.org/whatsnew/speeches/eng/ piot021001tokyo.html.
16. International Crisis Group, *HIV/AIDS as a Security Issue* (Washington, DC and Brussels: June 19, 2001), 16.

17. UNAIDS, *AIDS and the Military* (Geneva: UNAIDS, 1998), 2.
18. Lindy Heinecken, "AIDS: The New Security Frontier," *Conflict Trends* 3, no. 4 (2000): 12–15.
19. National Intelligence Council, *National Intelligence Estimate: The Global Infectious Disease Threat and Its Implications for the United States* (Washington, DC: 2000), 34.
20. Lindy Heinecken, "Living in Terror: The Looming Security Threat to Southern Africa," *African Security Review* 10, no. 4 (2001): 11.
21. Quoted in UNAIDS, *AIDS and the Military*, 7.
22. For an elaboration of these points, see Elbe, *Strategic Implication*, chapter 2.
23. I. William Zartman, "Introduction: Posing the Problem of State Collapse," in *Collapsed States: The Disintegration and Restoration of Legitimate Authority*, ed. William Zartman, 1–14 (Boulder, CO: Lynne Rienner, 1995), 2.
24. Chris Allen, "Ending Endemic Violence," *Review of African Political Economy* 81 (1999): 317–22, 318–19.
25. *Panafrican News Agency* (Daka), "HIV/AIDS Hitting the Armed Forces in Africa," July 9, 2001, http://www.panapress.com.
26. Kofi Anna, Secretary General of the UN, *Review of the Problem of Human Immunodeficiency Virus/Acquired Immunodeficiency Syndrome in All its Aspects*, A/55/779 (New York: UN, February 16, 2001), 8.
27. United Kingdom, House of Commons, Select Committee on International Development, *HIV/AIDS: the Impact on Social and Economic Development*, Third Report of Session 2001–02 (London: The Stationary Office, March 29, 2001), Section 2, Paragraph 113, http://www.parliament.the-stationery-office.co.uk/pa/cm200102/cmselect/cmintdev/519/51901.htm.
28. United States (U.S.) National Intelligence Council, *Global Trends 2015: A Dialogue About the Future With Nongovernment Experts* (Washington, DC: December 2000), 17.
29. Annan, *Review of the Problem*, 5.
30. Ibid., 9.
31. World Health Organization, *Macroeconomics and Health: Investing in Health for Economic Development*, Report of the Commission on Macroeconomics and Health (Geneva: WHO, 2001), 31.
32. Raphael Tenthani, "SADC Police Chiefs Warned to Regard AIDS As Security Issue," *Panafrican News Agency* (Dakar), July 31, 2000, http://www.africast.com.
33. Mark Schneider and Michael Moodie, *The Destabilizing Impacts of HIV/AIDS*, (Washington, DC: Center for Strategic and International Studies, 2002), 6.
34. *BBC News*, "Sex-workers 'Raped' by Zambian Police," April 23, 2002.
35. UNAIDS, *AIDS as a Security Issue* (Geneva: UNAIDS, 2002).
36. Randy Cheek, "Playing God with HIV: Rationing HIV Treatment in Southern Africa", *African Security Review* 10, no. 4 (2001): 20.
37. Cheek, "Playing God with HIV," 25–26.
38. U.S. National Intelligence Council, "Global Trends 2015," 17.
39. Annan, *Review of the Problem*, 9.
40. Kristoffersson, "HIV/AIDS as a Human Security Issue," http://www.unaids.org.
41. Martin Schönteich, "Age and AIDS: South Africa's Crime Time Bomb?," *African Security Review* 8, no. 4 (1999), http://www.iss.co.za.
42. Jordan S. Kassalow, "Why Health Is Important to U.S. Foreign Policy" (paper, Council on Foreign Relations, New York and Washington, DC, April 2001), http://www.cfr.org.
43. Judith Large, "Disintegration Conflicts and the Restructuring of Masculinity," *Gender and Development* 5, no. 2 (1997): 23–30.

44. See Alan Whiteside and Clem Sunter, *AIDS: The Challenge for South Africa* (Cape Town: Human & Rousseau and Tafelberg, 2000), 68–89.

45. Richard Holbrooke (comments on Voice of America, June 8, 2000), http://www.fas.org/man/dod-101/ops/war/2000/06/000608-aids1.htm.

46. Mark Schoofs, "A New Kind of Crisis: The Security Council Declares AIDS in Africa a Threat to World Stability," *The Village Voice*, January 12–18, 2000, http://www.villagevoice.com.

47. James Astill, "War Injects AIDS into Sierra Leone," *Guardian* (Manchester), May 21, 2001.

48. U.S. General Accounting Office, *UN Peacekeeping: UN Faces Challenges in Responding to the Impact of HIV/AIDS on Peacekeeping Operations* (Washington, DC, December 2001), 8.

49. Simon Robinson, "Battle Ahead," *Time*, July 16, 2001, 31.

50. Roxanne Bazergan, "UN Peacekeepers and HIV/AIDS," *World Today* 57, no. 5 (2001): 6–8, 6.

51. UN Integrated Regional Information Network "Official Concern Over Sex Case And HIV/AIDS," September 1, 2001, http://www.irinnews.org.

52. Erich Follath, "Robin Hood und die Multis," *Der Spiegel* 14 (2001), 158.

53. Bazergan, "UN Peacekeepers and HIV/AIDS," 7.

54. Chris Beyrer, *War in the Blood: Sex, Politics and AIDS in Southeast Asia* (London: Zed Books, 1998), 64–65.

55. *The Lancet*, "HIV and peacekeeping operations in Cambodia," November 11, 1995, 1304–5.

56. Johanna Mendelson Forman and Manuel Carballo, "A Policy Critique of HIV/AIDS and Demobilisation," *Conflict, Security & Development* 1, no. 2 (2001): 73–92, 77.

57. Manuel Carballo, Carolyn Mansfield, and Michaela Prokop, *Demobilization and Its Implications for HIV/AIDS* (Géneva: International Centre for Migration and Health, 2000), 39.

58. A. Adefolalu, "HIV/AIDS as an Occupational Hazard to Soldiers—ECOMOG Experience" (paper, 3rd All African Congress of Armed Forces and Police Medical Services, Pretoria, South Africa, October 24–28, 1999), 4–11.

59. Maggie Farley, "U.N. Seeks to Curb Role in Spread of AIDS Health: World Organization Wages Campaign to Curtail International Peacekeepers' Involvement in Transmission of the Disease," *Los Angeles Times*, January 7, 2000.

60. *Agence France-Presse*, "Obasanjo Warns Soldiers Against Unprotected Sex," May 19, 2000.

61. Omololu Falobi, "Nigerian Government Admits HIV Infection Among ECOMOG Soldiers," *AF-AIDS*, January 4, 2000.

62. Heinecken, "AIDS", 12–15.

63. Farley, "UN Seeks to Curb Role."

64. *United Press International*, "Indian Soldiers Returning From U.N. Duty in Cambodia Test HIV Positive," September 5, 1993.

65. U.S. General Accounting Office, *Un Peacekeeping*, 10.

66. See Marie-France Guimond, Noah S. Philip, and Usman Sheikh, "Health Concerns of Peacekeeping: A Survey of the Current Situation," *Journal of Humanitarian Assistance* (July 2001), http://www.jha.ac/articles/a067.htm.

67. United Kingdom, Ministry of Defence, *The Future Strategic Context for Defence* (London: Ministry of Defence, 2001), Paragraph 19, http://www.mod.uk/issues/strategic_context.

68. Greg Mills, "AIDS and the South African Military: Timeworn Cliché or Timebomb?" in *HIV/AIDS: A Threat to the African Renaissance?*, ed. Michael Lange (Johannesburg, South Africa: Konrad Adenauer Foundation, 2000), 70.

69. *South African Press Association*, "Sexual Behavior of Soldiers Must Change: SANDF," August 2, 2001, http://www.sapa.org.za.
70. Waliur Rahman, "AIDS warning for Bangladesh army," *BBC News*, December 6, 2001.
71. *Agence France-Presse*, "Eritrean Troops, UN Peacekeepers End AIDS Prevention Training," July 29, 2001.
72. Thalif Deen, "UN Focuses on Links Between AIDS and Peacekeeping", *Inter Press Service*, July 17, 2000.
73. U.S. General Accounting Office, *UN Peacekeeping*, 11.

Chapter 7

NGOs as Security Actors in the Fight against HIV/AIDS?

Carrie Sheehan

In the post–Cold War era there is increasing attention by scholars and policy makers to changing definitions of security, and explorations of the linkages between health and security. It is argued that security no longer only involves the defense of the state from outside military attacks; security is greater than that. Within the concept of human security,[1] individual human life is deemed more important than merely maintaining the viability of a given state and ensuring the absence of armed conflict; it is the freedom from want and freedom from fear for individuals. It is with this backdrop of contested notions of security that a health issue like HIV/AIDS can be understood as a security issue. Furthermore, the increasing attention toward the nonmilitary aspects of security has brought new actors into the security realm. One such actor, the nongovernmental organization (NGO), in general, and the development or health NGO specifically, can be understood as a security actor when and if HIV/AIDS is understood as a security threat.

HIV/AIDS has been called a security threat by the U.S. government as well as other state governments and international organizations, most notably the Joint United Nations Programme on HIV/AIDS (UNAIDS). At different points in time, or concurrently, the U.S. government has employed a traditional security framework, which focuses mostly on the destabilizing effects of high HIV prevalence rates in foreign militaries, and a human security framework, which focuses on the myriad negative impacts caused by HIV/AIDS to individuals in the developing world. Meanwhile, NGOs are increasingly prominent in enacting programs in the developing world to deal with both the underlying issues and manifestations of extreme poverty. NGOs are quite active in the health arena, broadly defined, and have often been at the forefront of the fight against HIV/AIDS. NGOs were often the first major player working to fight and treat the disease, especially where governments denied or ignored the issue.[2] Thus while prominent actors in treating and halting the spread of the disease, are NGOs working in the area of HIV/AIDS addressing the virus and the disease—both in words and action—as a security threat? If HIV/AIDS is a new security issue, NGOs, by their active participation in fighting HIV/AIDS, especially in the developing world, may have no choice but to be a security actor. However, this does not mean that NGOs will necessarily recognize or promote their status as new security actors.

The security studies literature and the literature on the role of NGOs in international development policies and practice have begun to examine some of these issues. There is a long-standing debate about the definition of national security and whether specific issues or problems constitute threats to the nation.[3] Starting in the 1970s and 1980s, theorists and practitioners of international security debated whether military security needed to be expanded to include economic issues impacting the state.[4] The end of the Cold War generated more attention to whether "traditional" notions of security that are state-centered and militarily focused had become anachronistic.[5] The so-called "new"[6] notions of security discuss not only disease epidemics, but also mass migrations, drug trafficking, and global warming, among other issues, as threats to international security generally, and U.S. national security, more specifically.[7] Following the release of the UNDP's 1994 *Human Development Report* that coined the term human security, studies began to employ this concept that locates the object of security at the level of the individual rather than the state. According to the concept of human security, security is more than the absence of armed conflict and maintenance of state survival; security is the quality of life for the average person. Within the new security studies literature a subset has looked at the nexus of health and security[8] and the security implications of the HIV/AIDS pandemic specifically.[9] The health and security literature focuses on whether health issues are threats to security and if so why they are threats to security, but it has not incorporated the NGO as a security actor into their analyses.

Another approach to security studies by Barry Buzan, Ole Wæver, and others focuses on processes of securitization, that is, how problems become defined and labeled as security threats. For theorists of securitization " '[s]ecurity' is thus a self-referential practice, because it is in this practice that the issue becomes a security issue—not necessarily because a real existential threat exists but because the issue is presented as such a threat."[10] While the securitization literature has focused on how issues such as the environment may become securitized, it has not focused on health security.

Another relevant set of literature looks at the increasing importance and rise of NGOs internationally, within the UN system and beyond.[11] Scholars and practitioners have noted the increasing role that NGOs play within the UN system and as implementers of state policies by programming international aid granted by state governments. These actors that were once seen as outside the purview of traditional studies of security are now increasingly brought within the security domain albeit through the lens of human security. NGOs work mostly with civilians, and especially during times of conflict and disaster to ensure that individuals' human security concerns are addressed.[12] There are numerous studies documenting the role that NGOs play internationally and some specifically addressing HIV/AIDS.[13] Nevertheless, in the security studies literature and the international development and NGO literature there are few studies that examine the NGOs role in promoting security through their work addressing the effects of the HIV/AIDS pandemic. This chapter seeks to address the gap in the research.

   This chapter begins by looking at the emergence and history of the securitization of HIV/AIDS in the U.S. government. It shows how increasingly U.S. policy-makers began to view the HIV/AIDS pandemic as a security threat, sometimes using a traditional security rationale and other times using a human security rationale. While evaluating the development of U.S. policy toward the security dimensions of HIV/AIDS, this chapter also reports on levels and sources of U.S. government funding for international HIV/AIDS programs to demonstrate the increasing attention given to the HIV/AIDS pandemic. Second, this chapter analyzes some U.S.-based development and health NGOs that the U.S. funds to conduct HIV/AIDS projects overseas, mostly in Africa and Asia. It examines what these NGOs are saying about HIV/AIDS and security and what they are doing about HIV/AIDS and security by using both a traditional and human security framework. Using insights from securitization theory this chapter examines whether NGOs are securitizing HIV/AIDS in order to bring the issue to the top of the policy agenda. The conclusion evaluates to what extent U.S. government and NGO strategies match their rhetoric concerning the security implications of the HIV/AIDS pandemic and what the implications of this are.

Development of U.S. Government Policy on HIV/AIDS and Security

It was not until the year 2000 that HIV/AIDS was declared a security threat by the U.S. government. However, as early as 1987 U.S. intelligence officers were trying to get permission to study HIV/AIDS and its impact on U.S. national interests, but were unable to do so until 1990. This eventually resulted in a classified report titled *The Global AIDS Disaster*, that projected 45 million infections by 2000, the majority in Africa.[14] In 1992 the Central Intelligence Agency (CIA) allowed the U.S. State Department to publish unclassified portions as a white paper. The CIA conducted two more major studies in 1995 and 1999: *National Intelligence Estimate 95–5* and *National Intelligence Estimate 99–17*. In addition to providing valuable information about the impact of HIV/AIDS around the world, these U.S. intelligence studies were crucial for other U.S. policy makers to eventually make the linkage between HIV and security.
   In July 1995, the Department of State released the report *U.S. Strategy on HIV/AIDS* for both U.S. government programs and activities affecting international HIV/AIDS efforts.[15] The report discusses the multifarious effects of HIV/AIDS on U.S. foreign policy including, international development, security, and key U.S. national interests. The report presents an action strategy for U.S. international AIDS policy in three parts, including the prevention of new HIV infections, the reduction of personal and social impact, and the mobilization and unification of national and international efforts. The report also included five appendices, one of which, appendix D: *The Impact of AIDS: U.S. Security Interests/Concerns*, was authored by the National Intelligence Council and based largely on *National Intelligence Estimate 95–5*. The report is the first public U.S. document that draws linkages between HIV and security. Importantly, the report uses a traditional security framework to draw these linkages by focusing on protecting "politico-military structures."

Thus the most important section for linking HIV/AIDS to a traditional definition of national security is found in appendix D which states: "In terms of military significance, HIV/AIDS is not a 'war-stopper'; it will not immediately render large numbers of field troops unfit for combat. However, as the HIV/AIDS pandemic erodes economic and security bases of affected countries, it may be a potential 'war-starter' or 'war-outcome-determinant'. "[16] This finding is significant and is found repeatedly in later government, think tank, and newspaper accounts because it provides a strong though indirect link in traditional strategic military terms of why HIV/AIDS in the developing world is considered a threat to the United States. Also in this section of the report is a recommendation that "[a]ll appropriate support should be given to DOD's [the Department of Defense] military-to-military educational programs on HIV/AIDS that are geared to improving prevention strategies in foreign militaries."[17] In addition, under the action plan the Secretary of State and the Secretary of the Department of Health and Human Services agree to send a joint letter to Congress on the impact of HIV/AIDS "including the implications for U.S. foreign policy and national security interests."[18] Thus, they draw an explicit link between military readiness and HIV. The report resulted in institutional collaboration of health and foreign policy institutions within the U.S. government on HIV/AIDS for the first time. Thus in 1995, one finds some of the important groundwork laid for a future policy of HIV/AIDS as a U.S. national security threat.

In August 1998, Dr. Kenneth Bernard became the first person on the U.S. National Security Council to be appointed as the special assistant to the president for International Health Affairs, a position he himself proposed.[19] This is significant because it was the first time an international health expert was included on the U.S. National Security Council, thus working to legitimize the health and security nexus. He also included HIV/AIDS on his agenda. According to Jonathan B. Tucker, "Bernard was convinced, for example, that the infection of a quarter of Africa's population with the HIV/AIDS virus would lead to widespread political instability and conflict on that continent, with inevitable security ramifications for the United States."[20] During his time on the National Security Council, Dr. Bernard focused on a wide range of issues that bridge international health and U.S. national security, including tuberculosis, HIV/AIDS in the developing world, bioterrorism, and immunization campaigns to enforce truces in war.[21] Tucker further argues: "Bernard also had ambitious personal objectives: His primary goal was to institutionalize the emerging perception of public health as a national security issue."[22] This is a key example of the institutionalization of the link between health and security by the Clinton administration, which helped to legitimize the health and security nexus in general, and the HIV/AIDS and security nexus specifically.

The first and arguably most influential policy statement regarding HIV/AIDS as a security threat occurred at a special session of the U.N. Security Council (UNSC) on HIV/AIDS to mark the U.S. presidency of the Security Council. At the UNSC meeting on January 10, 2000, Vice President Al Gore announced: "Today, in sight of all the world, we are putting the AIDS crisis at the top of the world's security agenda. We must talk about AIDS not in whispers, in private meetings, in tones of secrecy and shame. We must face the threat as we are facing it right here, in one of the great forums of the earth—openly and boldly, with urgency and compassion."[23] This was significant for several reasons. First, it was the first time that the UNSC dealt with an international health issue as a security threat. Second, by placing HIV/AIDS on the agenda of the UNSC, the United States was showing a commitment to the linkage between health and security. Third, it placed Africa as a continent of strategic importance to the United States.

Concurrently with the meeting of the UNSC, a declassified version of National Intelligence Estimate 99–17D—*The Global Infectious Disease Threat and its Implications for the United States*—was published. The report examines how infectious diseases, including HIV/AIDS, would affect United States and global security in the coming years. It focuses on the migratory potential of diseases to affect U.S. citizens, its threat to U.S. armed forces overseas, and how diseases can magnify social and political instability in countries and regions of strategic interest to the United States. The report employs both traditional and human security frameworks to discuss the impact of HIV/AIDS internationally on U.S. interests. In the preface, John C. Gannon, chairman of the National Intelligence Council wrote: "This report represents an important initiative on the part of the Intelligence Community to consider the national security dimension of a nontraditional threat. It responds to a growing concern by senior U.S. leaders about the implications—in terms of health, economics, and national security—of the growing global infectious disease threat."[24] Thus, the report looks at the "non-traditional" threat of HIV/AIDS, but in both traditional security and human security terms.

Only three months later, at the end of April 2000, the Clinton administration formally announced that AIDS was a threat to U.S. national security. According to Dr. Kenneth Bernard,[25] the Clinton administration was debating whether to make a formal declaration of AIDS as a U.S. national security threat when Barton Gellman made the announcement in *The Washington Post* on April 30, 2000 in a front page article entitled: "AIDS Is Declared Threat to Security; White House Fears Epidemic Could Destabilize World."[26] The article suggested that "[c]onvinced that the global spread of AIDS is reaching catastrophic dimensions, the Clinton administration has formally designated the disease for the first time as a threat to U.S. national security that could topple foreign governments, touch off ethnic wars and undo decades of work in building free-market democracies abroad."[27] In addition, the article outlines the new role of the National Security Council in infectious diseases and the creation on February 8, 2000 of a White House interagency working group instructed to "develop a series of expanded initiatives to drive the international efforts" to combat the disease.[28]

Soon after President Bush came to office, his administration also declared HIV/AIDS a threat to U.S. national security. Secretary of State Colin Powell has been at the forefront of linking HIV/AIDS in Africa and U.S. national security in the Bush administration. During a week-long tour of Africa in May 2001, Secretary Powell announced outside a Nairobi health clinic: "There is no war causing more death and destruction, there is no war on the face of the earth right now that is more serious, that is more grave, than the war we see here in sub-Saharan Africa against HIV/AIDS."[29] Secretary Powell's visit to Africa closely preceded the UN General Assembly Special Session on HIV/AIDS in New York in June 2001, thus signaling continued U.S. support for combating HIV/AIDS globally.

President Bush released *The National Security Strategy of the United States* in September 2002 and HIV/AIDS and international health feature prominently. In the document, the U.S. promises to continue "to lead the world in efforts to reduce the terrible toll of HIV/AIDS and other infectious diseases."[30] Also in September 2002, the National Intelligence Council released a report *The Next Wave of HIV/AIDS: Nigeria, Ethiopia, Russia, India and China*. The report finds that in these five populous countries the number of infected people will grow from around 14 to 23 million to an estimated 50 to 75 million by 2010, with significant economic, social, political, and military implications.[31] In discussing the report, George Tenet, Director, CIA, told the Senate Intelligence Committee in February 2002: "The national security dimensions of the virus are plain: It can undermine economic growth, exacerbate social tensions, diminish military preparedness, create huge social-welfare costs and further weaken already beleaguered states."[32] He thus echoed the National Intelligence Council report's emphasis on both the traditional security and human security implications of HIV/AIDS. On December 1, 2003, World AIDS Day, Colin Powell spoke of the national security implications of HIV/AIDS for the nations of sub-Saharan Africa.

U.S. Government Bilateral Funding for HIV/AIDS Globally[33]

The first year that the U.S. Agency for International Development (USAID) became engaged in combating the HIV/AIDS pandemic in the developing world was 1986, spending $1.1 million. From 1986 to 1993 there was a steady increase in U.S. government funding for HIV/AIDS internationally until it leveled off at approximately $125 million in 1993, where it stayed flat for seven years. It was not until the link between AIDS and security was addressed in 2000 that international funding for HIV/AIDS substantially increased. In fact, prior to January 2000, USAID was the only agency to receive targeted HIV/AIDS funding for international programs. This changed in late 1999 when then Vice President Al Gore announced the creation of the Leadership and Investment in Fighting an Epidemic (LIFE)[34] initiative and requested a $100 million appropriation for 2000, increasing the total international HIV/AIDS U.S. government funding to $347 million. Funds from the LIFE Initiative were divided between the Centers for Disease Control and Prevention that received $35 million and USAID that was awarded $65 million. Some of the funding was dispersed to nonprofit organizations registered with the U.S. government known as "Private Voluntary Organizations" (PVOs).[35]

The real shift in priorities for HIV/AIDS funding occurred in 2001 when U.S. government spending for HIV/AIDS internationally increased by more than 100 percent to $740 million. In 2001, the government agencies receiving targeted funding now included the Department of Defense with $10 million, Department of Labor with $10 million, and the Department of Agriculture with $25 million,

Table 7.1   U.S. spending on global HIV/AIDS in 2002 and 2003 (in US$ millions)[1]

	2002	2003
USAID	435	626
State Department	0	2
Global Fund	175	348
Centers for Disease Control—GAP	144	183
Centers for Disease Control—International Research	11	11
Department of Defense	14	7
Department of Labor	9	10
Department of Agriculture	25	25
National Institutes of Health	218	252
Total	$1,031	$1,463

Note: [1] The Henry J. Kaiser Family Foundation, "US Government Funding for HIV/AIDS in Resource Poor Settings," HIV/AIDS Policy Fact Sheet (Washington, DC: Kaiser Family Foundation, January 2004).

in addition to USAID with $340 million and the Centers for Disease Control and Prevention with $104.5 million. Thus in 2001, the total U.S. bilateral international assistance for HIV/AIDS totaled nearly $466 million, including $100 for the Global Fund to Fight HIV/AIDS, Tuberculosis, and Malaria. Of USAID's $340 million, some money went to a World Bank Program, leaving approximately $284 million for USAID programming decisions, of which nearly 70 percent was programmed by NGOs who are registered PVOs. The years 2002 and 2003 continued to see huge increases in U.S. government funding for HIV/AIDS globally topping the $1 billion mark (see Table 7.1).

Each of these agencies has different types of HIV/AIDS programs. In general, USAID funding is spent on six categories of programs: prevention; policy analysis and systems development; care and treatment; surveillance; children infected and affected by AIDS; and mother-to-child transmission reduction efforts. National Institutes of Health spending is on international research on HIV/AIDS, including antiretroviral therapy and vaccine development. The Centers for Disease Control and Prevention through its Global AIDS Program focuses on reducing HIV transmission through prevention of sexual, mother-to-child, and blood transmission, community and home-based care and treatment, and surveillance. The Department of Defense program focuses on training and prevention activities for foreign military and uniformed services within selected African countries where the U.S. has defense ties. The program, which is managed by the Naval Health Research Center in San Diego, has taken place in 19 countries in Africa. The Labor Global HIV/AIDS Workplace Initiative works to reduce HIV infection rates through workplace based prevention and education programs and to improve the workplace environment for people living with HIV/AIDS. The Department of Agriculture program donates food aid through the section 416(b) program. In 2000 one begins to see substantial increases for U.S. government

HIV/AIDS funding globally and by 2001 many U.S. government agencies with varying foci received funding. Funds go to security agencies like the Department of Defense, in addition to health agencies like the Department of Health and Human Sciences and the Centers for Disease Control and Prevention, and development agencies like USAID.

Since the UN Security Council meeting in January 2000, there is a continuing emphasis by the U.S. policy of naming HIV/AIDS a U.S. national security threat. While it is inconclusive whether the "securitization" of HIV/AIDS bears responsibility, one does see substantially increased funding for HIV/AIDS internationally and a diversification of agencies through which that funding is programmed beginning in 2000. However, policy discussions on the multi-sectoral impact of HIV/AIDS, including security, could be responsible for this diversification of programming agencies and funding. The Department of Defense funding for an international health initiative is path breaking in this regard and clearly makes a statement about the link between HIV/AIDS and security. However, what about the NGOs that the U.S. government funds to implement many of its HIV/AIDS programs overseas? By examining U.S.-based NGOs one can see the role these organizations have as security actors and compare their understandings of the problem HIV/AIDS poses with that of the U.S. government.

U.S.-based International NGOs and HIV/AIDS

Nongovernmental organizations are an important group of organizations to look at how well policies regarding HIV/AIDS and security as put forth by U.S. government are being implemented. Furthermore, NGOs are important in their own right. As mentioned earlier, NGOs were often the first organizations in the developing world to mount a concerted effort to combat the virus. Over time their numbers have expanded and there is a proliferation of NGOs working in developing countries to address the HIV/AIDS pandemic, many of which are U.S.-based organizations registered as PVOs with the U.S. government. These organizations have expertise in a variety of areas including, but not limited to, education and training, public health, women's rights and empowerment, food security, and microfinance. The U.S. government has been addressing HIV/AIDS as more than just a health or a development issue, but also as a security issue. Do NGOs who are mainly involved in relief, development, and health programs have the same view?

This section draws on public documents from over 50 U.S.-based NGOs that have projects in the developing world designed to address the HIV/AIDS pandemic. There are a large number of NGOs that have projects in the developing world designed to address the HIV/AIDS pandemic, including both international NGOs and indigenous NGOs. However, this chapter focuses on a subset of U.S.-based NGOs that are registered as PVOs[36] with the USAID or are members of InterAction, which is "a coalition of 160 U.S.-based private relief, development and refugee assistance agencies."[37] Together these two factors account for nearly all of the prominent NGOs with headquarters in the United States.[38]

In the United States, NGOs that are registered as PVOs are an important group for implementing U.S. foreign assistance. According to a recent USAID publication,

PVOs receive about one-third of USAID's development assistance budget.[39] Furthermore, three of the top five international NGOs in the United States, namely CARE, Catholic Relief Services (CRS), and Save the Children, receive around half of their overall funding from the U.S. government.[40] In comparing the U.S. government policy to NGO policies, it adds an interesting dimension to look at those organizations that are partially funded by the U.S. government. In many respects these PVOs comprise one component of the U.S. government response to the HIV/AIDS pandemic, even while the same organizations assert their autonomy and independence from the government.[41]

In 2000, 436 organizations were registered as PVOs with USAID and worked in 159 countries in nearly every area of development, including health and nutrition. The PVO registry lists 150 NGOs with projects on "HIV/AIDS and infectious diseases."[42] Some of these organizations focus on infectious diseases other than HIV/AIDS or focus on HIV/AIDS domestically. Even so nearly one-third of all registered PVOs in 2000 had at least one project involving HIV/AIDS. While this may sound impressive, many of these organizations are extremely small with total funding for their organization below $1 million annually and many of them focusing on a single country.

The following explores what PVOs are saying about HIV/AIDS and security by examining the 49 U.S.-based PVOs that are members of InterAction and are currently implementing HIV/AIDS projects in the developing world.[43] In addition, it discusses HIV/AIDS programming by PVOs and how it impacts traditional security concerns and broader human security concerns of the HIV/AIDS pandemic in two parts. The part on traditional security examines those PVOs that, while not members of InterAction, have specific HIV/AIDS projects that work with foreign militaries and thus clearly have an impact on traditional security through their programs. The part on human security discusses the programs of the three largest U.S.-based PVOs, CARE, CRS, and World Vision, to explain the wide range of HIV/AIDS projects that impact human security.

NGOs' Mention of HIV/AIDS as a Security Issue

In keyword searches for "HIV," "AIDS," "security," and "military" of the 49 InterAction members that are engaged in HIV/AIDS work internationally, only eight of them mention anything having to do with "HIV/AIDS and security" on their website. These organizations are Africare, American Jewish World Service, CARE, CRS, Church World Service, United Methodist Committee on Relief, U.S. Fund for UNICEF, and World Vision. A ninth organization, Lutheran World Relief, makes a mention of the connection between "the world's problems and U.S. security at home," but does not discuss HIV/AIDS specifically. Even among these eight, HIV and security is mentioned very few times on their sites. Furthermore, most often the websites provide links to news articles, the UN website or other places on the Internet where the link between HIV/AIDS and security is discussed. Only four organizations have original material on the subject.

Africare mentions the UN Security Council resolution on HIV/AIDS but does not use the phrase "HIV/AIDS and security" in its discussion of the resolution. On

CARE's website, in a question and answer session with their director of HIV/AIDS, Kristin Kalla refers to the U.S. calling HIV/AIDS a security threat as a "positive development," though does not specifically refer to it as one herself. CRS merely reprints a news story from *The Catholic Herald* that has one mention of HIV and security in the article.[44] Church World Service has links to news stories about the UN Security Council meeting in January 2000, but never refers to HIV as a security threat.

There are really only four organizations whose websites refer in original content to HIV as a security issue and even in these sites there is scant mention of it. The American Jewish World Service wrote an editorial in the *New York Times*, which said that HIV is a threat to global stability, but emphasizes the humanitarian impact of the pandemic: "The AIDS epidemic is a humanitarian catastrophe. But as the virus spreads insidiously around the world, it is becoming something else, a threat to global and regional stability, because of its potential to disrupt the economic, political and military structures of key countries."[45] The United Methodist Committee on Relief has links to UNAIDS and journalist accounts discussing the link between HIV/AIDS and security. It also has its own statement regarding HIV/AIDS and security in its role as a member of the Ecumenical Advocacy Alliance. The Alliance issued a communiqué that identified the HIV/AIDS pandemic as one of the gravest challenges to health and also "to prospects of social and economic development and global security."[46] The U.S. Fund for UNICEF has several mentions and hyperlinks to the UNAIDS site discussing HIV/AIDS and security which can be explained by the fact that it is an organization designed to help fund UNICEF, part of the UN system.

The most extensive mentions of the link between HIV/AIDS and security occur on the World Vision website. An article in the *Seattle Post Intelligencer* by Joseph Riverson, an advisor on AIDS for World Vision, discusses the security implications of AIDS: "The AIDS epidemic already has devastated my continent, Africa. Of the 42 million people worldwide with AIDS, more than 29 million live there. But the pandemic's center of gravity is shifting to Europe and Asia, where sheer population size—let alone military and economic power—threaten global security."[47] Also posted on their website is an advocacy letter they developed for individuals to lobby their Congressman in favor of the *Debt Relief Enhancement Act, H.R. 4524*. The text of the letter includes the following: "Complete debt cancellation is needed for the fight against HIV/AIDS and to ensure global security through poverty reduction."[48] On April 17, 2002, Ken Casey, senior vice president for World Vision gave a statement before a hearing of the House International Relations Committee of the U.S. Congress titled *AIDS Orphans and Vulnerable Children in Africa: Identifying the Best Practices for Care, Treatment and Prevention*. While the majority of his statement concerns the role of faith-based organizations, of which World Vision is one, in HIV/AIDS care, treatment, and prevention and lessons learned from World Vision's over a decade of experience with HIV/AIDS programming, the concluding section discusses security in his plea to the Congress. In the concluding comments he states:

> The HIV/AIDS pandemic in Africa has left in its wake at least 13 million orphans and 2–3 times the number of vulnerable children. The massive and growing number

of orphans and other vulnerable children in HIV/AIDS-affected areas constitute a humanitarian and development crisis of unprecedented proportions. If the international community does not respond immediately and at a large scale to this crisis, the potential threats to national, regional, and global security and stability will be severe. A generation of marginalized young people who grow up without guidance and support are highly susceptible to recruitment by terrorist networks, warlords and guerilla groups, criminal gangs, and other forces who can tear societies apart.[49]

It follows that U.S.-based NGOs are for the most part not promoting the link between HIV/AIDS and security in the public documents they post on their websites. Even the few that do promote this link mention it not more than once or twice. It is not a focus of the extensive information presented on their response to the HIV/AIDS pandemic on their public websites. While websites are but one available information source, they show what information the organizations are trying to advertise to the general public and more importantly, to their donors. Especially the larger NGOs have a wealth of information on their websites about their projects on HIV/AIDS and use the web as part of their communications strategy to reach their computer literate audiences, and attract financial and other support. However, unlike U.S. government agencies in their material on the web, these NGOs are by and large not "securitizing" the HIV/AIDS pandemic.

One venue where one finds a discussion of HIV/AIDS as a U.S. national security issue is at meetings of the Advisory Committee on Voluntary Foreign Aid (ACVFA). The ACVFA is a committee organized by the U.S. government that brings together U.S. government development assistance organizations and members of the PVO community that are active in international development and humanitarian assistance to discuss key issues.[50] An examination of the public transcripts from the ACVFA meetings in the years 2000–2002 showed several opportunities for members of U.S. development assistance organizations and U.S.-based NGOs to discuss HIV/AIDS internationally. Some of this discussion involved a debate about the security implications of HIV/AIDS.

The focus of September 14, 2000 meeting was exclusively on "Combating the HIV/AIDS Pandemic in Developing Countries." Publicly available notes from the meeting show PVOs as proponents of the "securitization" of HIV/AIDS. For example: "An audience member noted that there had been countless references to this battle against AIDS as a war. She agreed that it is a vital national security issue. Given this, she pointed out, resources need to come from the military budget. This would be a bold step that would help ensure that funds from HIV/AIDS are not siphoned from development projects, and would also avoid the phenomenon of 'development agencies fighting each other over crumbs'. "[51] Mr. Louis Mitchell, ACVFA member, opened the panel on NGO strategies and successes "recalling that during the morning sessions the fight against HIV/AIDS has been described as a war . . . . The purpose of this meeting is to get out the word that this is a war."[52] Of the ten recommendations and lessons from the meeting, the first one was that "[t]he challenges posed by the global HIV/AIDS pandemic extend well beyond medical/health issues and affect all development sectors. The response must be comprehensive and cross-sectoral."[53]

Thus, in this forum for relief and development assistance, the need to link HIV/AIDS to national security was an object of discussion. One sees NGOs making strategic decisions to link HIV/AIDS to national security in order to secure additional funding rather than taking away funds for HIV/AIDS from the monies already allocated to development assistance. In other words, linking HIV/AIDS and security is presented as a way to increase the overall pie of development assistance and to use funds allocated to traditional security through the Department of Defense and other budgets.

Two meetings of the ACVFA during 2001 included the HIV/AIDS pandemic on its agenda. The meeting on January 10, 2001 focus was "A New Agenda for Foreign Aid." The ACVFA gave seven recommendations for U.S. foreign assistance priorities, the last of which was to "[l]aunch a more comprehensive and better funded assault on the HIV/AIDS pandemic."[54] While not directly discussing the security dimension, the group further reported that "[t]he HIV/AIDS pandemic is not solely a health issue, but rather, a crosscutting theme that affects all sectors and threatens economic and political stability."[55] However, in the discussion period "one participant pointed out that new messages, such as American security interests might be needed. He reminded the audience that President Eisenhower had sold the interstate highway system as the 'National Defense Highway System'. Several others agreed that linking development assistance to U.S. national interests is critical."[56] Here once again the NGO community appears to consider the idea of "selling" HIV/AIDS as a security issue in order to gain attention and funds for addressing the pandemic.

The October 17, 2001 meeting of the ACVFA also included HIV/AIDS as one of its agenda topics, but had no mention of HIV/AIDS as a security issue.[57] However, a finding of the meeting was a recommendation to the NGO community to "[d]evelop a strategy to educate the Congress and PVO/NGO constituencies about development and the link to national and global security."[58] In the weeks following September 11 there was concern that funding would turn away from global concerns to focus on security at home.

The next meeting to discuss HIV/AIDS was the October 9, 2002 meeting which included on its agenda *Update on the Global Fund to Fight HIV/AIDS, Tuberculosis and Malaria*. During the session on the Global Fund there was no discussion on the linkages between HIV and security, though there was discussion about the need for multisectoral approaches to HIV/AIDS and the importance of not separating HIV/AIDS from other issues such as health, food security, and education.[59] In sum, during the ACVFA meetings, there was less discussion on HIV/AIDS and security over time with the most emphasis occurring during the September 2000 meeting, which was the first meeting focusing on HIV/AIDS to follow the January 2000 UNSC meeting.

Newspaper analysis of the 49 InterAction members discussing HIV and security was unable to reveal any newspaper accounts other than those reported in earlier. However, early debates in February 2002 on the Bush administration budget for 2003 brought the linking of security to international assistance, of which international HIV/AIDS funding is one component, to the forefront. These debates, as documented in U.S. newspapers, are another place where one sees NGOs making linkages between their work and international security, even though they do not discuss HIV/AIDS specifically. Some U.S.-based international NGOs positioned their projects as a way to enhance U.S. national security and the war on terrorism. According to one newspaper account, "[s]ome Americans involved in grass-roots international assistance say that if the focus on national security gives foreign aid more urgency, they are for it."[60] According to another account, Mary McClymont, President of InterAction, in discussing the foreign aid budget employed "the rationale advanced by the administration for its war on terror" by contending "that increases in foreign aid will 'enhance our own state security'."[61] Thus, some in the NGO community are at least contemplating "securitizing" international assistance in order to gain more support for the work they do. In a world of competition for funding, PVOs have been debating whether to link development assistance, of which HIV/AIDS assistance is one component, to the needs of U.S. national security, especially post–September 11. In the words of one email from a development list server: "A lot of organizations have been thinking hard about whether (or how) to connect their issue to the public's deep concerns about security. Many groups are already moving in that direction."

Nevertheless, there has not been an official move in that direction. Apart from statements by InterAction on behalf of its members and personnel as opposed to organizational commentaries, there is not much evidence that NGOs are engaging with HIV/AIDS and security as official policy. There is scant mention of the links between HIV/AIDS and security on the NGO websites, nor other statements of support for this policy. When there are statements of support in the ACVFA meetings, Congressional hearings and newspaper accounts, it appears that NGOs are trying to sell the security implications of their work to government officials in an attempt to gain greater funding sources for their work.

Turning to the work of NGOs and their role in reducing the insecurity caused by HIV/AIDS, the following sections discuss NGOs as security actors in the sense of a traditional security issue and a human security issue. It specifically examines NGOs that have projects with foreign militaries in order to decrease HIV prevalence in these "risk groups" that have the responsibility to defend their nations. Questions of military readiness clearly fall under a notion of a traditional security concern. It then examines the three largest U.S.-based international NGOs in terms of budget and scope and their work with civilians in addressing the human security issue HIV/AIDS represents. While providing only examples of their work, this section demonstrates the breadth of programs that NGOs implement in the HIV/AIDS arena to help reduce human insecurity.

HIV/AIDS as a Traditional Security Issue: NGO Projects with Foreign Militaries

For those who emphasize a traditional view of security issues, NGOs who work with militaries in HIV/AIDS prevention and awareness projects have the most direct link between their work and security. For those who conceptualize HIV/AIDS and security by narrowly focusing on the HIV/AIDS pandemic's impact on military readiness and defense, this is the work of NGOs that most clearly contributes to an increase in security. However, an analysis of U.S.-based international NGOs shows very little activity in this area. Moreover, research commissioned by UNAIDS suggests that this is the case for European-based NGOs as well as U.S.-based NGOs.[62] According to a study conducted for UNAIDS on HIV/AIDS and the Uniformed Services in Kenya, Tanzania, and Uganda, there is inadequate attention placed on bilateral initiatives with the uniformed services regarding HIV/AIDS awareness and prevention. According to their analysis: "The reluctance of NGOs and the bilateral agencies to become involved is difficult to comprehend. They need education on the key position these services have in relations to the stability of the state, the role these services play in HIV transmission and their need for assistance. To date the involvement has been patchy and has not been sustained over time."[63]

Specifically two U.S.-based NGOs work with foreign militaries on HIV/AIDS prevention and awareness: Family Health International (FHI) and Population Services International (PSI). While both of these organizations are registered PVOs, neither is a member of InterAction and in comparison to more traditional development NGOs, which tend to work in wide range of sectors, FHI and PSI focus exclusively on health. FHI and PSI were among the top 20 NGOs for receiving U.S. government funding in 2000.[64]

Family Health International heads a Uniformed Services Task Force on HIV/AIDS in conjunction with UNAIDS as part of their "Initiative on HIV/AIDS and Security." FHI began working on HIV/AIDS awareness and prevention programs with foreign militaries in Africa and Asia in the early 1990s. Their "AIDS Control and Prevention Project" (AIDSCAP) that began on August 12, 1991 and concluded on December 31, 1997 was at the time the largest international HIV program ever undertaken and many of its projects specifically targeted militaries.[65] The military was one of the target populations in AIDSCAP and they focused some of their activities at military bases. One example is FHIs work with the Zimbabwe military from 1995 to 1997 with the goal of stabilizing or reducing sexually transmitted infections prevalence among the armed forces, with a special emphasis on HIV. The purpose of the project was to reduce high-risk sexual behavior through behavior-change interventions with the Zimbabwe National Army and the Air Force of Zimbabwe. According to FHI's final report for the AIDSCAP, one of the lessons learned was that "[d]ue to issues of national security, it is difficult to design and monitor effectiveness of projects with the armed forces, even though they are much needed and appreciated. Even when constraints are outlined and understood at the onset, implementation can be frustrating for both parties and requires commitment and understanding of limitations on both sides." Another example is FHI's three-year project from 1993 to 1996 with the Cameroon armed forces, which focused its prevention and awareness activities at 11 military bases in Cameroon. FHI has a lot of experience implementing HIV/AIDS projects with militaries though the period of 1991–1997 was the height of their activity. Nevertheless, FHI remains committed to this area and are sharing "lessons learned" through chairing of the Uniformed Services Task Force on HIV/AIDS.

Population Services International is working with a number of militaries in Africa, Asia, and Latin America on HIV/AIDS prevention and awareness. PSI includes the military and police as one of its target groups in many of its programs and has been actively engaged in projects with foreign militaries beginning in 2001. PSI has received funding from the Department of Defense for programs with the Togolese Armed Forces[66] and the Eritrean military. With the participation of the Armed Forces of Togo, PSI began implementing "Operation Full Protection-Armed Forces of Togo" in four Togolese military bases in October 2001. Their activities include peer education of soldiers by soldiers, behavior-change campaigns, the diagnosis and treatment of sexually transmitted infections, and the establishment of voluntary counseling and testing for the armed forces. Through PSI's Eritrean Social Marketing Group, the Department of Defense awarded a one-year grant for interpersonal communications activities for HIV/AIDS prevention among the military in Eritrea starting in September of 2001.[67] In activities not funded by the U.S. Department of Defense, PSI partnered with the Cambodian military to implement an HIV/AIDS prevention initiative.[68] In Bolivia, PSI uses mobile video units funded by AIDSMark in military camps, truck stops, brothels, and other locations frequented by target groups to put on shows that mix entertainment, AIDS prevention communications, and Pantera condom advertising and samples.[69]

While FHI and PSI are both very active in HIV/AIDS programming with foreign militaries, it is a small percentage of their HIV/AIDS projects. They are also only two of over 100 U.S.-based international NGOs active in HIV/AIDS projects worldwide. Thus, while there is some activity in this area, it is small in comparison to HIV/AIDS work by NGOs with civilian populations.

HIV/AIDS as a Human Security Issue: NGO Projects for Civilians

For those who conceptualize HIV/AIDS as a human security threat any work being conducted by the NGO community, if effective and efficient, should contribute to the overall goal of decreasing situations of insecurity that HIV/AIDS creates. The 49 InterAction members discussed previously, conduct a variety of HIV/AIDS projects in Asia, Africa, Eastern Europe, and Latin America. As mentioned earlier, their projects include HIV/AIDS education, prevention, care, counseling, support to AIDS orphans, supplementary feeding, and microfinance projects for those living with HIV/AIDS. Rather than discussing all 49 organizations in detail, the following focuses on the three largest U.S.-based NGOs who have an HIV/AIDS program: CARE, CRS, and World Vision. Because of the size of these organizations and the breadth of their programming on HIV/AIDS, examining their programs demonstrates the various ways the work of NGOs impact the human security dimensions of HIV/AIDS.

CARE has approximately 60 projects on three continents that are either completely HIV/AIDS focused or have an HIV/AIDS component.[70] Their geographic scope is quite large with projects in 3 countries in Latin America, 4 countries in Asia, and 14 countries in Africa. Many of these projects focus on HIV/AIDS control and prevention and then have a specific target area such as child health, reproductive health, education, and youth education. There are also projects that focus on supplementary feeding for those with HIV/AIDS as well as other care and support projects. In addition, there are several multisectoral projects, which include HIV/AIDS interventions within larger projects. Thus, CARE's projects span the continuum from emergency relief to rehabilitation to development.

In all of CARE's projects there is an emphasis on integrating HIV/AIDS interventions into other emergency relief and development interventions. The emphasis is therefore on incorporating an HIV/AIDS component into ongoing programs rather than separating HIV/AIDS as a distinct issue. A look at some of CARE's projects in Ethiopia demonstrates this strategy. For example, in the "South Gondor Relief and Rehabilitation" project the HIV/AIDS portion of the project, which involves providing food and medicines to clinics caring for people living with HIV/AIDS, is one small component of a much larger project. Also, in the project "Strengthening Communities Through Partnerships for Education" (SCOPE) the goal is to achieve universal primary education in Ethiopia. However, SCOPE incorporates HIV/AIDS education for school children into its interventions. There are some CARE projects that focus almost exclusively on HIV/AIDS, such as the "Urban HIV/AIDS Control and Prevention Project." In this project, CARE proposes to reduce the incidence of mother-to-child transmission of HIV/AIDS in one district of urban Addis Ababa through a three-pronged intervention that includes comprehensive communication for behavior change to increase the practice of risk-reduction behaviors by women of reproductive age and their partners; implementation, monitoring, and evaluation of innovative and effective pilot voluntary counseling and testing services; and technical, management, and financial support to local community-based organizations and NGOs to reduce the socioeconomic effects of HIV/AIDS on affected families.

According to its website, CRS promotes community-based programs that help those infected with HIV/AIDS, while addressing the underlying causes of AIDS and reducing the spread of HIV.[71] They also address AIDS related stigma, poverty, and the special vulnerabilities and burdens faced by women. At the conclusion of 2002, their AIDS projects were serving approximately 2 million people affected by HIV/AIDS in 31 countries. Project activity is concentrated in Africa, but the agency also works in Asia and Latin America. As one example, a CRS project in Zimbabwe works through a network of ten parish mission hospitals to establish AIDS committees where groups of community volunteers visit and care for the sick, perform AIDS preventive education dramas, and engage individuals in income-generating activities. Overall, CRS has projects in home-based care for individuals and families living with HIV/AIDS, support to orphans and vulnerable children affected by AIDS, behavior change and life skills education, voluntary counseling and testing, and income-generating projects for people living with HIV/AIDS and their families. Most CRS projects concentrate on training community volunteer educators to provide home-based care to those affected by HIV/AIDS. In addition, CRS is involved in looking at the linkages between food security and HIV/AIDS and the different nutritional needs for people living with HIV/AIDS.

At the conclusion of 2002, World Vision had more than 80 projects in 25 countries that addressed HIV/AIDS is some way.[72] The majority of World Vision's projects are in sub-Saharan Africa, but World Vision also has HIV projects in Asian countries such as Myanmar, Cambodia, Thailand, and India. World Vision's first significant project on HIV/AIDS started in Uganda in 1990 for assistance to AIDS orphans. This project combines direct support to orphans along with income-generating activities for those who care for them. Another area of programming is its youth program, which focuses on awareness of HIV transmission and prevention. World Vision's largest HIV/AIDS program is its HOPE Initiative, which includes 12 countries in sub-Saharan Africa.[73] The HOPE Initiative involves three key areas: care for orphans and vulnerable children; home-based care for people living with HIV/AIDS; and prevention activities among youth and the general public, including voluntary counseling and testing, and the prevention of mother-to-child transmission.[74]

World Vision's niche compared to the other two NGOs is its focus on AIDS orphans. It addresses what they believe are the seven core needs of orphans and vulnerable children: education support; emergency nutritional support; referrals and transportation to health outreach and social workers; protection from abuse and neglect; spiritual and psychosocial counseling and support; succession planning to prepare for parental death; and HIV prevention and awareness. However, World Vision projects cover the gamut of HIV/AIDS interventions, including links to food security as well as microenterprise development support in addition to the areas mentioned above.

Even by examining just these three NGOs in brief—CARE, CRS, and World Vision—one can see the depth and breadth of NGO work on HIV/AIDS in the developing world. Since their work is focused on civilians, when effective they play an important part in promoting human security. Of these three organizations, only World Vision promoted the link between HIV/AIDS and security on their websites for their donors and supporters. Still, if one looks at the human security dimensions of HIV/AIDS that focuses on the quality of life for individuals, HIV/AIDS projects are part of the human security effort.

Conclusion

The preceding discussion has shown that the U.S. government, especially since the beginning of 2000 has been at the forefront of the "securitization" of HIV/AIDS. Furthermore from 2000, the U.S. government has substantially increased its funding for HIV/AIDS globally and has begun to disperse funds through a variety of government agencies, including USAID and the Centers for Disease Control and Prevention, but also most notably the Department of Defense. In 2002 and 2003, the U.S. government allocated $14 million and $7 million respectively to the Department of Defense for its military-to-military HIV/AIDS awareness and education programs. This is a small percentage of the total assistance for HIV/AIDS funding overseas and an infinitesimal percent of the U.S. military budget. Thus while the U.S. government has rhetorically supported HIV/AIDS as a traditional security threat, especially in sub-Saharan Africa where it is undermining military readiness, the funding amounts demonstrate that this is a minor emphasis in the U.S. governments funding priorities. U.S. government funding through USAID and Centers for Disease Control and Prevention's Global AIDS Program which focuses on human security concerns such as care for people living with HIV/AIDS and HIV/AIDS prevention is significantly higher with 2002 and 2003 funding at $435 million and $626 million, respectively for USAID and $144 million and $183 million, respectively for the Global AIDS Program.

Examining what NGOs, which the U.S. government funds, are saying about the HIV virus and its possible security implications showed some evidence that NGOs engage in "securitizing" the HIV/AIDS pandemic when meeting with U.S. government officials in the ACVFA forums and in Congressional hearings as a strategic move to get more funding. However, these same NGOs do not make these arguments when advertising their HIV/AIDS programs with donors and the public and tend to focus on more traditional health and development rationales. In terms of NGO programming, most NGOs researched for this chapter do not focus their HIV/AIDS prevention, awareness, treatment, and care programs on a traditional security emphasis of working with militaries and prefer to focus on human security, that is, their work with civilians. It can be explained by the fact that these organizations traditionally focus on the most vulnerable civilian populations in both times of conflict and peace. While FHI and PSI both have experience with HIV/AIDS projects for the military, it is only a small percentage of the work these two organizations do to combat HIV/AIDS globally. In addition, some of this may be a problem of funding, since USAID funding cannot be used for projects with militaries, NGOs would need to compete for the small sums from the Department of Defense or find money from nongovernment donors. In addition, if people believe that NGOs are tools of militaries they are less likely to gain access to the people they hope to help.

As for the human security aspects of HIV/AIDS, NGOs work in innovative ways to address the multifarious effects that HIV/AIDS has on populations, especially in high prevalence areas in the developing world. Thus, while NGOs are not at the forefront for discussing the linkages of HIV/AIDS and security, it probably does not matter. The work of NGOs helps contribute to overall human security and according to their individual missions and mandates are focused on the humanitarian aspects of the disease. In conclusion, they do not need to use the language of human security in order to continue to do so, though they may choose to as a strategy to increase funding and attention to the HIV/AIDS pandemic that is a humanitarian tragedy deserving of continued attention.

Notes

1. The term human security was first coined by the UNDP in 1994. See UNDP, *Human Development Report* (New York: Oxford University Press, 1994).
2. See Leon Gordenker, Roger A. Coate, Christer Jönsson, and Peter Söderholm, *International Cooperation in Response to AIDS* (London: Pinter, 1995).

3. For an early example see Arnold Wolfers, "National Security as an Ambiguous Symbol," in *Discord and Collaboration*, ed. Arnold Wolfers, 147–65 (Baltimore, MD: Johns Hopkins University Press, 1992).

4. Jessica T. Mathews, "Redefining Security," *Foreign Affairs* 68, no. 2 (1989): 162–76.

5. For example see Peter J. Katzenstein, ed., *The Culture of National Security: Norms and Identity in World Politics* (New York: Columbia University Press, 1996).

6. These threats to security are really not "new." Disease epidemics, mass migrations, and other events were seen as threatening to state stability, however, the language of security was not used until recently. One example in the health arena is William McNeill, *Plagues and People* (New York: Doubleday, 1976).

7. A few examples on migration and security include Myron Weiner, ed., *International Migration and Security* (Boulder, CO: Westview Press, 1993); Nana Poku and David T. Graham, eds., *Redefining Security: Population Movements and National Security* (Westport, CT: Praeger, 1998). Some examples on the environment and security include Thomas Homer-Dixon, "Environmental Scarcities and Violent Conflict," *International Security* 19, no. 1 (1994): 5–40; Norman Myers, "Environment and Security," *Foreign Affairs* 70, no. 3 (1991): 115–31.

8. See Jack Chow, "Health and International Security," *The Washington Quarterly* 19, no. 2 (1996): 63–77; Christopher F. Chyba, *Biological Terrorism, Emerging Diseases, and National Security: Project on World Security Rockefeller Brothers Fund* (New York: Rockefeller Brothers Fund, 1998), http://www.rbf.org/pdf/Chyb_Bioterrorism.pdf; Paul Farmer, "Social Inequalities and Emerging Infectious Diseases," *Emerging Infectious Diseases* 2, no. 4 (1996): 259–69; David P. Fidler, "The Globalization of Public Health: Emerging Infectious Diseases and International Relations," *Indiana Journal of Global Legal Studies* 5, no. 1 (1997): 11–52; Laurie Garrett, "The Return of Infectious Disease," *Foreign Affairs* 75, no. 1 (1996): 66–79; Dennis Pirages, "Microsecurity: Disease Organisms and Human Well Being," *The Washington Quarterly* 18, no. 4 (1995): 5–17; Andrew T. Price-Smith, "Infectious Disease and Global Stability at the Turn of the Century," *International Journal* 54, no. 3 (1999): 426–42; Andrew T. Price-Smith, *The Health of Nations: Infectious Disease, Environmental Change, and their Effects on National Security* (Cambridge, MA: MIT Press, 2001).

9. See Stefan Elbe, Chapter 6, this volume; Price-Smith, *The Health of Nations: Infectious Disease, Environmental Change, and Their Effects on National Security and Development* (Cambridge: MIT Press, 2001); Stefan Elbe, "HIV/AIDS and the Changing Landscape of War in Africa," *International Security* 27, no. 2 (2002): 159–77; Robert L. Ostergard, Jr. "Politics in the Hot Zone: AIDS and National Security in Africa," *Third World Quarterly* 23, no. 2 (2002): 333–50.

10. Barry Buzan, Ole Wæver and Jaap de Wilde. *Security: A New Framework for Analysis* (Boulder, CO: Lynne Rienner, 1998), 24.

11. For example see Lester Salomon, "The Rise of the Nonprofit Sector," *Foreign Affairs* 73, no. 4 (1994): 109–22; Jessica T. Mathews, "Power Shift: The Age of Nonstate Actors," *Foreign Affairs* 76, no. 1 (1997): 50–66; Peter Willetts, ed., *The Conscience of the World: The Influence of Nongovernmental Organizations in the UN System* (Washington, DC: Brookings, 1996); Maryann K. Cusimano, Mark Hensman, and Leslie Rodrigues, "Private-Sector Transsovereign Actors—MNCs and NGOs," in *Beyond Sovereignty: Issues for a Global Agenda*, ed. Maryann K. Cusimano, 253–82 (Belmont, CA: Wadsworth, 2000).

12. Some analyses discuss the controversial role that NGOs can play. For example see David Rieff, "Humanitarianism in Crisis," *Foreign Affairs* 81, no. 6 (2002): 111–22.

13. See Christer Jönsson and Peter Söderholm, "IGO-NGO Relations and HIV/AIDS," in *NGOs, the UN, and Global Governance*, eds. Thomas Weiss and Leon Gordenker, 121–38 (Boulder, CO: Lynne Rienner, 1996); Ezekiel Kalipeni, Susan Craddock, Joseph R. Oppong, and Jayati Ghosh, eds., *HIV&AIDS in Africa: Beyond Epidemiology* (Malden, MA: Blackwell, 2004); Leon Gordenker, Roger A. Coate, Christer Jönsson, and Peter Söderholm, *International Cooperation in Response to AIDS* (London: Pinter, 1995).

14. Barton Gellman, "World Shunned Signs of Coming Plague," *Washington Post*, July 5, 2000.

15. United States Department of State, *US Strategy on HIV/AIDS*, Publication No. 10296 (July 1995), http://dosfan.lib.uic.edu/ERC/environment/releases/9507.html.

16. Ibid.

17. Ibid.

18. Ibid.

19. Jonathan B. Tucker, *Scourge: The Once and Future Threat of Smallpox* (New York: Atlantic Monthly Press, 2001).

20. Ibid., 196.

21. Ibid., 197.

22. Ibid., 197.

23. The White House, Office of the Vice President, "Remarks as Prepared for Delivery by Vice President Al Gore, UN Security Council Session on AIDS in Africa," January 20, 2000, http://www.un.int/usa/00_002.htm.

24. David F. Gordon, *National Intelligence Estimate: The Global Infectious Disease Threat and Its Implications for the United States*, NIE 99–17D (Washington, DC: National Intelligence Council, January 2000).

25. Dr. Bernard was special assistant to the National Security Council on International Health during the Clinton administration. He then became special advisor on National Security to the Department of Health and Human Services.

26. Kenneth Bernard, "Health and Security" (statement, United States Institute of Peace, Washington, DC, March 14, 2002).

27. Barton Gellman, "AIDS is Declared Threat to Security; White House Fears Epidemic Could Destabilize World," *Washington Post*, April 30, 2000.

28. Ibid.

29. United States Institute of Peace, *AIDS and Violent Conflict in Africa*, Special Report of the United States Institute of Peace (Washington, DC: United States Institute of Peace, October 2001).

30. *The National Security Strategy of the United States of America* (Washington, DC: The Office of the President of the United States, September 2002).

31. David F. Gordon, *National Intelligence Estimate: The Next Wave of HIV/AIDS: Nigeria, Ethiopia, Russia, India and China*, ICA 2002–04D (Washington, DC: National Intelligence Council, September 2002).

32. *Kaiser Daily HIV/AIDS Report*, "CIA Director Tenet Declares AIDS is Security Threat to United States," February 12, 2003, http://www.kaisernetwork.org/daily_reports/rep_index.cfm?hint =1&DR_ID = 16030.

33. See Priya Alagiri, Todd Summers, and Jennifer Kates, *Spending on the HIV/AIDS Epidemic: A Three Part Series* (Boston, MA: Henry J. Kaiser Family Foundation, 2002).

34. The LIFE Initiative focused on nine countries in Africa, plus India.

35. "A PVO is a registered nonprofit organization that receives part of its annual revenue from the private sector, received voluntary contributions of money, time, or in-kind support from the general public, works or wants to work overseas, is financially viable with overhead accounting for no more than 40 percent of expenses, has a board of

directors, fits within USAID priorities, and does not have alleged terrorist ties," USAID, *Foreign Aid in the National Interest: Promoting Freedom, Security, and Opportunity* (Washington, DC: USAID, 2002), 140.

36. The terms PVOs and NGOs are used interchangeably throughout this chapter.

37. Not all, but most InterAction members are registered as PVOs with USAID. One notable exception is Oxfam, which does not accept U.S. government funding.

38. Specifically, data was compiled from the USAID's PVO registry, NGO Websites, and transcripts of meetings of USAID's Advisory Committee on Voluntary Foreign Aid (ACVFA).

39. USAID, *Foreign Aid in the National Interest*, 141.

40. Ibid., 117.

41. For a recent discussion of some of the dilemmas NGOs face in providing humanitarian aid and maintaining independence from their governments see Rieff, "Humanitarianism in Crisis."

42. See http://www.pvo.net/usaid/.

43. A list of InterAction members with HIV/AIDS projects can be viewed at http://www.interaction.org/aids. Sources used for the analysis included written summaries for the meetings of the ACVFA and Lexis-Nexis for newspaper accounts of statements by InterAction representatives and these 49 PVOs.

44. Linda Busetti, "Catholic Relief Services Launches 'Africa Rising' Campaign," *Catholic Herald*, June 28, 2001.

45. *New York Times*, "AIDS as a Threat to Global Stability," October 4, 2002.

46. "Global Trade and HIV/AIDS First Priorities for New Ecumenical Alliance," December 11, 2000, http://gbgm-umc.org/mission/news2000–2/ncaids121100.html.

47. Joseph Riverson, "AIDS a Century from Now," *Seattle Post Intelligencer*, December 1, 2002.

48. World Vision, "Letter to Congress for Debt Relief Enhancement Act," http://www.worldvision.org/worldvision/wvususfo.nsf/stable/globalissues_debtrelief.

49. Ken Casey (Senior Vice President, World Vision International), "AIDS Orphans and Vulnerable Children in Africa: Identifying the Best Practices for Care, Treatment and Prevention" (statement, House International Relations Committee, April 17, 2002), http://www.worldvision.org/worldvision/wvususfo.nsf/stable/globalissues_aids_testimony.

50. For more information on the ACVFA see USAID, "ACVFA," http://www.usaid.gov/about_usaid/acvfa.

51. ACVFA, *Combating the HIV/AIDS Pandemic in Developing Countries* (Washington, DC: USAID, September 14, 2000), 26, http://www.usaid.gov/about_usaid/acvfa/acvfafullreptsept2000.pdf.

52. Ibid., 12.

53. Ibid., 27.

54. ACVFA, *A New Agenda for Foreign Aid* (Washington, DC: USAID, January 10, 2001), 2, http://www.usaid.gov/about_usaid/acvfa/acvfafullreptjanuary2001.pdf.

55. Ibid., 4.

56. Ibid., 6.

57. This is probably because of the meeting's close proximity to the September 11, 2001 attacks on the World Trade Center and the Pentagon. The U.S. government less than one month after attacks was focused on traditional security concerns and on terrorism.

58. ACVFA, *USAID's Strategies for Conflict Prevention, Procurement Reform, the Global Development Alliance, and HIV/AIDS* (Washington, DC: USAID, October 17, 2001), 10–11, http://www.usaid.gov/about_usaid/acvfa/acvfafullreptoct2001.pdf.

59. ACVFA, *Monterrey to Johannesburg to Beyond: What the Administration's New Development Initiatives Mean for US Foreign Assistance Policy and Programs*

(Washington, DC: USAID, October 2002) 4–5, http://www.usaid.gov/about_usaid/acvfa/acvfafullreptoct2002.pdf.

60. Howard LaFranchi, "Foreign Aid Recast as Tool to Stymie Terrorism: Looking to Fight Root Causes of Attacks, Some Call for Doubling International Aid," *The Christian Science Monitor*, February 26, 2002.

61. Peter Slevin, "US Urged to Double Overseas Aid: Assistance Groups Link Funding to the War Against Terrorism," *Washington Post*, February 12, 2002.

62. Lee Curran and Michael Munywoki, *HIV/AIDS and the Uniformed Services: Stocktaking of Activities in Kenya, Tanzania and Uganda* (Washington, DC: USAID, August 2002).

63. Ibid.

64. USAID, *Foreign Aid in the National Interest: Promoting Freedom, Security, and Opportunity* (Washington, DC: USAID: 2002).

65. For information on the AIDSCAP Program see: Family Health International, *AIDSCAP Final Report* 1, August 21, 1991–December 31, 1997, http:/www.fhi.org/en/aids/aidscap/aidspubs/special/final/capfn1.html.

66. PSI, "News: Protecting Togo Military from AIDS," http://www.psi.org/news/051002d.html.

67. PSI, "Eritrea Social Marketing Program," http://www.psi.org/where_we_work/eritrea.html.

68. PSI, "Social Marketing and Communication for Birth Spacing and AIDS Prevention in Cambodia," http://www.psi.org/where_we_work/cambodia.html.

69. PSI, "Bolivia Social Marketing Program," http://www.psi.org/where_we_work/bolivia.html.

70. CARE Project Search, http://www.careusa.org/careswork/searchwork.asp.

71. CRS, "HIV/AIDS Programming," http://www.catholicrelief.org/what_we_do_overseas/aids/index.cfm.

72. World Vision, "HIV/AIDS Summary Page," http://www.worldvision.org/WorldVision/wvususfo.nsf.

73. The World Vision HOPE Initiative countries are: Burundi, Ethiopia, Kenya, Lesotho, Malawi, Mozambique, Rwanda, South Africa, Swaziland, Tanzania, Uganda, Zambia, and Zimbabwe.

74. World Vision, "Hope Initiative," http://www.worldvision.org/worldvision/appeals.nsf/hope_projects.html.

Part V

Small Arms and Light Weapons

Chapter 8

The Proliferation of Small Arms and Light Weapons

Mike Bourne

The use and misuse of Small Arms and Light Weapons (SALW) are estimated to result in over 500,000 deaths per year, and countless injuries.[1] For example, one often cited statistic indicates that in 90 percent of conflicts since 1990, SALW have been the only weapons used in fighting, and have contributed to between 30 and 90 percent of civilian deaths in those conflicts.[2] SALW were used extensively in the organization and conduct of the Rwandan Genocide; are the primary weapons of narco-insurgents and paramilitaries in Colombia; and are the dominant tools of ongoing insurgency in Iraq, to name but a few examples. Their widespread availability and misuse contributes to transnational organized crime and conflicts of all types, and is closely related to current concerns such as weak and collapsed states, human rights abuses, and the pantheon of both traditional and nontraditional security issues. They are the tools of the trade for terrorists, rebels, and criminals and their spread has gone largely unchecked for many decades.

Concern about the spread and use of SALW has developed rapidly since the mid-1990s. Initially stemming from increasing international involvement in peacekeeping operations in intrastate conflicts,[3] various concerned groups have raised issues related to SALW in a variety of situations and for a variety of purposes ranging from major armed conflict to criminality. Due to the wide-ranging implications of the misuse of SALW, constituencies of concern include those that are primarily concerned with: conflict prevention and resolution, conflict management and peacebuilding, security sector reform, development, humanitarian assistance, law and order, and a range of other issues.

Definitions of SALW have proved contentious throughout the development of the issue and international responses. The UN Panel of Governmental Experts on Small Arms disaggregated the two terms by making the distinction that: "Broadly speaking, small arms are those weapons designed for personal use, and light weapons are those designed for use by several persons serving as a crew."[4] This primarily includes revolvers, pistols, rifles, assault rifles, and various types of machine guns. Additionally it also includes some larger weapons such as portable antitank and antiaircraft weapons, and the shoulder fired missiles and rockets that cause great concern for the potential for terrorist attacks on passenger aircraft—everything from the ubiquitous AK-47 to Stinger missiles. These weapons are possessed and used by most military forces, some police forces, and civilians. They are also the primary weapons of many non-state actors with which this volume is concerned: rebel groups, militia, criminals, and some terrorist organizations.

This chapter outlines and examines the nature of the proliferation of SALW, with a particular emphasis on the roles of non-state actors. Non-state actors of various types populate the processes of SALW proliferation as suppliers, facilitators, and recipients. However, they do not do so autonomously or in isolation from states. While the spread of SALW is considerably less state-centric than the proliferation of other types of weapons, the dominant framework within which SALW spread occurs remains the legal trade involving or authorized by states.

Section one outlines the concerns about SALW and some of the key characteristics of their proliferation. Sections two and three then add to these understandings by focusing on the spread of SALW to conflicts on the supplier and recipient sides of the processes, respectively. In so doing this chapter demonstrates that SALW proliferation is an area of national and international security concern that operates in system populated by both state and non-state actors. Indeed, the illicit flow of SALW to conflicts is not a threat outside of the reach of states. Rather, it is a phenomenon that relies on the cooperation between states and those non-state actors that are suppliers, facilitators, and recipients of illicit SALW. It is because of this that the fight against SALW proliferation requires cooperation among states and other non-state actors: civil society groups at the international and national levels.

Concerns about SALW and the Characteristics of their Proliferation

Small arms and light weapons represent a new type of proliferation concern, but a long-standing proliferation problem. While the potential for weapons of mass destruction to spread into the hands of terrorist organizations has generated considerable concern in the post–Cold War era, it is SALW that routinely spread to non-state actors engaged in violence. SALW have long been the primary instruments of civil wars, armed crime, government repression and human rights abuses, and genocide.

Concern about SALW stems from the wide implications of the excessive availability and misuse of these weapons in a variety of contexts. The *Small Arms Survey* has usefully distinguished between the direct and indirect effects of small arms availability and misuse. The direct effects relate to the use and misuse of SALW in all settings including conflict, crime, and social violence. The availability of SALW in conflict-prone contexts is a key factor in the scale and destructiveness of conflicts. Likewise, for crime and social violence, the presence and use of SALW makes violence more destructive. It also contributes to fear and insecurity, sometimes stimulating intrastate security dilemmas and arms races that can intensify violence and destruction. Indirect effects relate primarily to the environment of insecurity and the broader implications of use such as increasing burdens on health care, criminality, and the privatization of security; humanitarian impacts on respect for human rights, on the delivery of aid, and on humanitarian agency staff; and development impacts at both micro and macroeconomic levels.[5] Widespread armed violence can strain health care systems and create insecure environments in which public services such as education can be overwhelmed. Armed violence, facilitated by the availability of arms that SALW proliferation provides, can deter investment and tourism, destroy infrastructure, and hinder or reverse sustainable development. A resultant environment of pervasive insecurity can contribute to the growth of "cultures of violence" and destroy social capital. The presence of well-armed criminal groups that are often better equipped than police forces can undermine governance, creating government no-go areas. While all of these potential impacts are highly context specific and are shaped and driven by a range of other factors, such as poverty and unemployment, the proliferation of SALW is often a critical element in their exacerbation and key challenge to their management and reversal.

Many of these impacts relate to the misuse of SALW. The misuse of SALW and all associated direct and indirect effects draw on the availability of those arms to the wide range of actors that engage in violent activity. However, the availability of SALW does not cause the outbreak of violence, in the sense that their presence does not inevitably lead to their use. Thus, Edward Laurance contends that while it is not possible to claim a causal relationship between SALW and violence, there is "an undeniable critical mass of 'correlational' evidence."[6] This correlation is partially explained by the potential catalytic effects of SALW availability on potentially or already violent environments. These effects, while highly contentious, were noted by the UN Panel of Governmental Experts on Small Arms which claimed succinctly that:[7]

> Accumulation[s] of small arms and light weapons by themselves do not cause the conflicts in which they are used. However, the availability of these weapons contributes towards exacerbating conflicts by increasing the lethality and duration of violence, by encouraging a violent rather than peaceful resolution of differences and by generating a vicious circle of greater sense of insecurity leading to greater demand and use of such weapons.[8]

Many uses and most acquisitions of SALW are legal and legitimate. Thus, the production, acquisition, accumulation, and use of SALW can be legal or illicit. However, the broad range of misuses and associated constituencies of concern has created a degree of fragmentation in the framing of the problem.[9] In spite of this fragmentation, according to the *Small Arms Survey*, "[s]mall arms proliferation is dominated by the chaos and destruction caused by the weapons of petty criminals and organized crime, insurgents and rebels, as well as repressive governments."[10]

The key role of proliferation. The UN Disarmament Commission claimed in 1994: "wherever there is violence, terrorism, subversion, drug trafficking, common and organized crime and other criminal actions, their link to the illegal acquisition of arms has been demonstrated."[11] The emphasis on acquisition is pervasive throughout the SALW literature, with most academic and policy literature focusing on the supply side of the phenomenon. The nature of SALW proliferation is inadequately understood. There are, in fact, only a handful of explicit attempts to thematically outline and analyze the nature of the spread of these weapons. Much of the rest of the burgeoning literature on SALW focuses on building reliable data and case studies of particular aspects of the trade in SALW, or particular responses to their flow, accumulation, and misuse, thereby providing useful data for thematic analysis that has yet to be drawn together.

Proliferation of SALW occurs at all levels of the international system, ranging from large government-to-government transfers to domestic retail markets and small-scale cross-border trafficking. Processes at all levels may feed into SALW acquisitions by rebels, terrorists, criminals, militia, and other illicit recipients. The nature of these processes, their relative significance, and the construction of the capacity of recipient non-state actors to acquire arms through different channels are key aspects of the nature of SALW proliferation that are in need of further examination and analysis.

The notion that the misuse of SALW is facilitated by their illicit acquisition is commonly criticized: legally acquired weapons are often misused, and most illicit weapons originate in the legal sphere. Nevertheless, distinctions between legal and illicit SALW transfers remain central to understanding the nature of their proliferation.

Distinctions between legal and illicit. The dividing line between legal and illicit transfers of SALW is extremely blurred.[12] This is, in part, due to the vagueness of legal reference points used in such definitions. These reference points were outlined by the 1997 UN Panel of Governmental Experts on Small Arms that defined illicit weapons trafficking as "that international trade in conventional weapons which is contrary to the laws of states and/or international law."[13] Thus, the sources of law through which legal and illicit arms transfers are delineated are fragmented—relying on the supplier and recipient's specific legal structures, with no universally applicable criteria for illegality save the circumvention of UN arms embargoes—the application of which has been increasing but inconsistent.[14]

Most analyses of SALW apply three rather than two categories of legality: legal; gray market, where the legality is unclear; and black market, that is, purely illegal trade conducted without the involvement of the state. This has led to an analytic framework that emphasizes the lack of clarity by outlining a spectrum of legality ranging from legal transfers to the black market, and defined primarily with reference to the degree of state involvement and authorization.

Since many laws are unclear and are applied inconsistently and without transparency, and since states may break their own laws in the pursuit of other goals a further distinction is required within the category of illicit transfers. Thus, most analysts distinguish between black and gray market transfers: Black market refers to wholly illicit transfers of weapons primarily by private actors. Gray market arms transfers fall in between the purely illicit black market and legal arms transfers. Within this commonly made distinction it is useful to distinguish categories according to the types state involvement that represent distinct dynamics and motivations within the gray area. Thus grayness can reflect one of two types of involvement: the covert supply of arms to conflict protagonists, particularly insurgent groups, by governments and/or state security agencies; and grayness caused by a lack of clarity on whether arms exported from a state are approved by competent authorities through due process defined by law. In practice this may include a deliberate failure to follow due process because of the connivance of corrupt officials bribed by black market dealers.

The first represents a deliberate use of the illicit arms transfers by states, while the latter often represents the opposite, the failure, manipulation or circumvention of government regulatory structures by illicit arms traders, facilitated by state officials or legally authorized agents. Therefore this chapter uses four categories of legality in arms transfers: legal transfers, covert aid, gray market, and black market.

SALW proliferation processes. The traditional image of the conventional arms trade is a state-centric model that envisages spread through state-to-state transfers of different types. This image relates primarily to the trade in major conventional arms. The spread of SALW is significantly broader based, with multiple channels, processes, and actors. This leads many analysts to refer to SALW spread as "diffusion" rather than "proliferation".[15] The structures of spread for SALW are more broadly based and diffused than for other types of weapons. There is a significantly greater number of producers of SALW than for other types of arms. The most up to date published estimate is that of the second edition of the *Small Arms Survey*, which puts the figure of manufacturers of SALW and ammunition at 1,042 companies in 98 states.[16] Additionally, as almost all states possess SALW, most of these have the potential to transfer weapons from their own stocks. The spread of SALW is less state-centric, with non-state actors playing key roles as both suppliers and recipients in both the legal and illicit trades.

Numerous activities occur within transfer processes. Illicit transfers of all types tend to involve particularly convoluted combinations of these transfer processes taking circuitous routes and passing through many countries and many actors' hands in order to reach their destination. These activities may include production; stockpiling; licensing of exports; brokering; transportation; transit, that is, moving through the territory, ports, and airports of other states en-route to their destination; payment and the provision of financial conduits, including money laundering; and the provision of official or forged documentation, especially end-user certificates, that is, official documents providing an assurance that the recipient is or has authorized the end user of the weapons.

The distinctions between legal, gray, covert, and black market transfers relate significantly to the level of government authorization and involvement. Yet given the number of different activities that form stages in SALW flow processes, these distinctions may apply more clearly to a particular stage in the flow than as aggregate categories of channels.[17] Thus as SALW find their way from suppliers to illicit recipients they may cross back and forth across the spectrum of legality.

Overall, therefore, there is a picture of SALW diffusion that emphasizes its distinctive complexity when compared with that of other arms. Further, key characteristics of SALW spread have been raised by analysts in both academic and policy arenas as particular focal points. Many of these reflect the predominant concern about the flow of arms to conflicts. Thus, a dominant image of arms flows to conflict parties, particularly to rebel groups, has been superimposed on top of this picture of distinctive complexity. The core aspects of this dominant image reflect the blurred boundaries and complex construction of SALW spread and correlate with the primary centers of distinctiveness. These key aspects are: a vast global stock of SALW, a vibrant globalized illicit trade, and a central role for nefarious arms brokers.

A vast global stock of SALW. The *Small Arms Survey* estimates that there are approximately 639 million firearms, which includes most small arms, but not light weapons, in global circulation.[18] The *Small Arms Survey* then breaks down this estimate into the main sectors of accumulation. Of these the greatest proportion, 59.2 percent, are believed to be privately and legally owned by civilians.[19] The world's military forces are believed to be in possession of 242.6 million firearms, that is, 37.8 percent of global stocks; and police forces, which are of a similar number to the world's military, but require fewer weapons, account for 18 million or 2.8 percent of global stocks.[20] Somewhat surprisingly, given the great concern attached to their acquisition of arms, insurgent forces are estimated to account for only 1 million firearms, or 0.2 percent of the estimate.[21] However, for the purposes of this chapter, it suffices to say that there are a vast number of weapons diffused and circulating among unregulated non-state actors, and beyond the reach of policy structures.

Implicit within the SALW literature that uses such estimates, is the assumption that vast global accumulations of new and surplus SALW, combined with poor legal controls, leads inevitably to broad and substantial availability through diverse channels. References to vast global stockpiles of SALW, open to all who can pay, are pervasive in the handling of arms transfers in the "new wars" literature.

A core aspect of this premise is that global accumulation leads inevitably to availability at all levels. This reflects the logic of globalization implicit in so much of the literature: "Though only tentative conclusions can be drawn, their accessibility is linked to the liberalization of markets and the emergence of new brokering activities."[22] This does not mean that local or regional aspects of the availability of SALW have been ignored, but nor have they been systematically analyzed. The phrase "awash with arms" has been applied to many states and regions. Renner claimed in 1997 that "[s]mall arms are so ubiquitous that many regions of the world find themselves awash in them . . . acquiring them is 'as easy as buying fish in the market'."[23] Nevertheless, explanations of accumulation, availability, and flow have tended to jump between levels without reference to the existence of structures and dynamics at each level of analysis. Likewise, much emphasis has been made of the intrastate character of the majority of violence perpetuated with these weapons. However, even this is referred to as a global phenomenon: "That the outbreak of internal arms races in many countries around the world has stimulated the expansion of global arms-trafficking networks . . . "[24]

By emphasizing difference, particularly the breadth of the structures of spread beyond the reach of states into the realm of non-state actors, most analyses have emphasized the global aspects of flow, thereby implying that a lack of state centricity in spread structures generates a world without barriers between local armed actors and international arms markets. This globalization logic implies a lack of boundaries, a transnational fluidity in circulation where anything is possible. The leap from the local to the global, and the flow back down again, is portrayed as a world of globalized illicit, or less-than-legal, trade populated by a new race of private profiteers: arms brokers and transport agents.

Vibrant globalized illicit trade. In terms of its dollar value, the illicit trade in SALW accounts for only a small proportion of the global trade of these weapons: an estimated 10 percent or less.[25] Illicit flows of SALW, however defined, have been dominant on the agendas related to SALW. This is largely because they are seen as disproportionately contributing to the primary sectors of concern: crime and, particularly, conflict. While there are substantial definitional problems associated with the boundaries between legal and illicit transfers it is generally agreed that "illicit arms flows follow a very different pattern from legal ones."[26] However, as noted by Krause:

> One of the greatest difficulties in constraining the proliferation of small arms and light weapons is the fact that several proliferation pathways can be both licit and illicit in nature. One clear policy goal of the international community (or at least some elements of it) has thus been to widen the divide between licit and illicit transfers . . .[27]

Many early analyses of SALW began their explanations of the significance of illicit transfers, or more particularly, of black-market transfers with reference to the physical characteristics of SALW: their small size and low weight creates a propensity for illicit transfer since they are easily concealed.[28] In combination with the globalization of all forms of trade and the ever increasing volume of goods flowing around the world, this creates an environment of impunity for those engaged in arms trafficking that places greater strain on customs services.

As demonstrated by the machinations in the preparatory stages of the UN Conference on the Illicit Trade in Small Arms and Light Weapons in All Its Aspects there is a view, particularly among certain governments, that the problems of illicit trade lie in the purely black markets rather than those aspects of illicit trade that have some link with states or their officials. This emphasis, however, has not been repeated among NGOs and academics. These concerned groups and individuals take an opposing view that emphasizes the blurred boundaries among the legal trade, the black market, and the various shades of gray in between. Within this more nuanced view it is generally assumed that the gray market is of significantly greater size than the black market, due largely to the improbability of a complete lack of knowledge and collusion by governments or their officials. Thus, while illicit transfers take place, they do not occur in an entirely anarchic transnational system generating a large global black market, but rather reflect "weak law-makers" or enforcement combined with corruption, rather than "powerful law-breakers." Nevertheless, the rise of transnational criminal organizations has been noted with great concern in this regard.

Concern about illicit transfers has also been largely framed at the global level. Even at this level, claims are seldom made about which types of actors can access which types of channel. The *Small Arms Survey* did make such a claim, though its basis remains unclear:

> While it is difficult to distinguish between grey and black-market transfers, research has provided sound evidence that each market has its own unique characteristics. The grey market is generally much larger, both in terms of value and volume; its covert transfers tend to supply small arms to non-state actors (e.g. rebel groups) in countries or regions in war or conflict. The black market is usually much smaller than the grey market; its illegal transfers tend to supply arms to individuals and criminal organisations. Of course, there are exceptions to these rules. More research is needed to understand the characteristics and ever changing dynamics of such markets.[29]

Many analysts have claimed that the gray market is probably far larger than the black market.[30] However, when one takes the threefold disaggregation of illicit transfers—black, gray, and covert—into account, this appears questionable or at least lacking in specificity. While the *Small Arms Survey* also noted that "[a] further distinction must be made between international and internal illicit arms transfers...,"[31] there has been no systematic analysis of the structures and dynamics of the various types of illicit arms transfer at each level, or across the levels. Conversely, a study by Sislin et al. claimed that non-state actors engaged in conflict obtained arms in three main ways, two of which operate largely at the local level: domestic procurement, such as theft and capture; indigenous production, though this was limited; and importation. Importation was, however, also seen as occurring largely by accessing a global black market through arms brokers.[32] Indeed, within the dominant image of flows to conflicts through illicit channels, a central aspect that has been emphasized is the role of private arms brokers and dealers.

A central role for nefarious arms brokers. The role of private brokers and transport agents in various aspects of the flow of SALW has been recognized as a core aspect of illicit trafficking.[33] While brokers are active within the legal trade, much of the concern about their activities has centered on the illicit transfer of weapons to insurgent groups and embargoed governments. Inadequate controls over these brokers are a commonly lamented feature of the post–Cold War era SALW trade and, although progress is being made, only 18 states have controls over brokers in place.[34] The primary role of these actors is in facilitating access to global markets for actors that would not otherwise have that access. As such they form the link between illicit recipients and global accumulations.

Taking advantage of "globalizing" illicit exports of conflict commodities such as illicit drugs and diamonds, brokers and some poorly regulated private air and sea freight companies navigate legal loopholes and acquire SALW on behalf of illicit recipients in the world's hotspots. Their realm is the illicit market. While it is not known how much of the illicit trade, or more specifically the flows of arms that fuel conflict, are attributable to these brokers, their role is believed to be highly significant. The prominence of brokers on the agendas of those concerned with SALW is high.

This image is largely implicit, coming to the fore largely through emphasis rather than explicit articulation, with the exception of the *Small Arms Survey's* claim that "[t]hough only tentative conclusions can be drawn, their accessibility is linked to the liberalization of markets and the emergence of new brokering activities."[35] While this picture is complicated by the role of governments as arms brokers and covert illicit suppliers, this channel remains uppermost in the dominant image of SALW proliferation. Superimposed upon the diffusion image of distinctive complexity this prevailing understanding points to a transnational global network—a distinct global illicit arms market system of transnational structures and processes. Thus, these unscrupulous privateers complete the prevailing image of SALW spread and flows to conflict. A massive and unregulated global stock of arms open to all through an illicit market populated by these shadowy figures.

Non-State Actors and the Supply of SALW to Conflicts

The supply of SALW to conflicts is more complex and varied than the prevailing image implies. It commonly involves a combination of legal, gray, covert, and black market activities. This section outlines key features of such transfers and the role of brokers therein. In so doing it clarifies the nexus between the legal and illicit transfers, and between states and non-state actors as suppliers and facilitators of supply. These nexus have evolved significantly throughout the Cold War and post–Cold War eras.

Legal trade. In addition to their production in 98 states, SALW and ammunition are held in the stockpiles of every military and many police forces around the world. These stockpiles, particularly of surplus weapons, are a common source for both legal and illicit arms transfers. Indeed, the huge stockpiles of arms and ammunition built up during the Cold War in the former-Soviet Union are commonly seen as a major source of arms for international illicit transfers—particularly to rebel groups and embargoed governments. Certainly, the collapse of export controls in many Eastern European countries combined with the presence of large stockpiles and cash-strapped arms industries gave many of these countries a deserved reputation as the source of many illicit arms in the early post–Cold War period. However, since then many improvements in export controls have been achieved. Rather, the greatest significance of the vast global stocks of arms is that almost any state can be a source of arms for illicit transfers.

The legal arms trade has undergone significant changes in the post–Cold War era. According to David Mussington in the shift from the Cold War to the post–Cold War era the structure of the international MCA market shifted from duopolistic to oligopolistic; stable supplier–recipient pairs transformed into fragmented supply networks; and the dominant export incentive had shifted from the political to the economic.[36] The same processes have occurred in the legal

SALW market, though its structure was always a significantly looser oligopoly than for other weapons. The legal market for SALW has become more fragmented and competitive, with medium suppliers eroding the dominance of the major and large suppliers and competing with each other and surplus suppliers for shrunken markets.[37]

Broadly speaking, as a result of the same dynamics that have transformed the global legal SALW trade into a competitive buyers-market, the extraregional aspects of SALW flows to conflicts have undergone concomitant decoupling from global political rivalries and an associated commercialization of motive and shift into the legal side of the arms transfer spectrum.

Covert aid. Covert aid has long been a feature of SALW flows to conflict. It was particularly significant during the Cold War, but has remained a key element of arms flows to rebel groups. The provision of covert aid is a major nexus between the legal trade and illicit flows. During the Cold War, superpowers and their bloc allies engaged in considerable illicit or covert arming of insurgent groups. For instance, U.S. supplies to insurgent forces increased dramatically in the 1970s as the experiences of their involvement in the Vietnam War left the U.S. government more reluctant to directly involve itself in conflicts around the globe. The supply of SALW was therefore used as a major tool for intervention without risks to U.S. personnel.[38] The scale of such covert aid was particularly large during the 1980s as the Reagan doctrine increased the utilization of arms transfers as a foreign policy tool against the perceived vanguards of the "evil empire".[39]

The United States operated constructed pipelines to supply arms, predominantly SALW, to insurgent groups such as the Unión Nacional para la Independencia Total de Angola (UNITA) in Angola, the Contras in Nicaragua, and the Mujahideen in Afghanistan. The scale of this assistance varied hugely with relatively openly conducted aid to the Mujahideen, running at approximately $670 million worth of arms and equipment per year, dwarfing the more covert aid to other insurgent groups such as the $70 million of arms provided annually to the Contras in Nicaragua, and the $30 million of arms transferred to UNITA in Angola each year.[40] Irrespective of the scale of aid, however, the channels through which SALW were transferred at the extraregional level stages of the pipelines were strikingly similar.

Arms and ammunition were sourced through arms brokers and purchased from former Soviet clients and others. Thus the arms provided through the U.S. pipeline to the Mujahideen in Afghanistan were chosen on the basis of being only Soviet-made or Soviet-designed weapons, at least until 1985. These were purchased from a variety of countries, including East Germany, Egypt, Israel, India, Turkey, but predominantly from China.[41] Likewise, the pipeline that supplied the Contras in Nicaragua included Soviet-type weapons obtained from Israel, in this case from stocks captured from the Palestine Liberation Organization (PLO) in Lebanon.[42] In a few cases new U.S. weapons and more sophisticated light weapons from Western-bloc allies were supplied, thereby undermining the deniability of transfers. For example, U.S.-made Stinger missiles were provided to the Mujahideen in Afghanistan after 1986.[43] Nevertheless, Soviet-type weapons were the dominant source of SALW in Central Intelligence Agency (CIA) pipelines.

Most arms pipelines in the Cold War era used a regional client state as the primary conduit for transfers of SALW to insurgent groups. These client states received the supplies of SALW from the CIA supply lines and channeled them to the insurgent group. These regional states were Pakistan, for the Afghan Mujahideen; Zaire, for UNITA in Angola; Honduras, for the Contras in Nicaragua; and Thailand for Cambodian groups. In addition to these primary conduit states, secondary conduits were also cultivated within the region in order to enhance cover and provide flexibility within the pipeline. These included South Africa, for UNITA, and El Salvador, for the Contras.

The SALW provided by the CIA arrived at the regional stage of the pipeline by two primary routes. The first, and dominant, route was supply through or in parallel with legal military aid to the regional governments. In this mechanism, additional arms, often far in excess of the actual aid to the governments, were earmarked for the insurgents.[44] For example, when supplying the Contras in Nicaragua Honduras and El Salvador were provided with greater levels of military aid on the understanding that the rebels would be supplied.[45] Likewise, the CIA supplied arms to Zaire on aircraft it had chartered either privately or from the U.S. Air Force. In the latter case a token amount of aid to the Zairian military was included to make the transfer appear to be one of the U.S. government's regular deliveries of legal military aid to Kinshasa.[46] Similar mechanisms were used in Soviet covert aid to the Farabundo Marti National Liberation (FMLN), the PLO, and others; and in Chinese aid to African liberation movements.

In the post–Cold War era, covert aid from these states has virtually disappeared. It has not, however, vanished from the range of supply channels feeding arms to today's insurgents. Covert aid is now predominantly a regional affair, with neighboring governments arming rebels with arms both from their own stockpiles and imported from the global legal market for this purpose.

Regional covert aid has long been a feature of insurgent arming. During the Cold War, much of this activity was overshadowed by the large extraregionally organized arms pipelines. Indeed, in many cases, regional covert aid ran alongside or fed into these pipelines. For example, in Latin America the Contras were provided with ammunition by Honduras when supplies in the CIA sponsored pipeline ran low.[47] Nevertheless, in many cases during the Cold War the predominant role in arms supplies played by many states was as a channel for other state's covert aid. Conversely, while covert transshipment continues to occur frequently in the post–Cold War era, it seems overshadowed by the incidence of covert aid that is predominantly conducted by regional states. In the post–Cold War era regional covert aid has been a particular feature of conflicts in sub-Saharan Africa, the Middle East, and Central and South Asia. This has included Ugandan aid to Rwandan and Sudanese rebels, and Sudanese aid to Ugandan rebels; Liberian aid to the Revolutionary United Front (RUF) in Sierra Leone; Uzbek aid to rebels in Tajikistan; Iranian and Russian aid to the Northern Alliance in Afghanistan; Syrian and Iranian aid to the Kurdish Workers' Party (PKK) in Turkey.[48]

Arms brokers and post–Cold War SALW flows to rebel groups. In the post–Cold War era, arms brokers and regional state and non-state actors form a link between the global SALW market and warring factions. Such actors have supplied and facilitated the supply of the tools of war and genocide to Rwanda in 1994, vicious warlords in the civil wars in Liberia, Sierra Leone, and the Democratic Republic of Congo; the Revolutionary Armed Forces of Columbia (FARC) "narco-insurgents"; and the repressive Taleban in Afghanistan.

For much of the Cold War era the roles played by these types of actors, including sourcing, transporting, financing, and providing a veil of legality through forged documents, were predominantly subsumed into extraregionally organized arms pipelines. Indeed, some of the global and regional infrastructure of the current mechanisms of SALW flows to insurgents stem directly from these pipelines. In many cases the networks of arms brokers that were key to the sourcing patterns of such pipelines have simply moved from supplying extraregional patrons to supplying regional patrons and insurgent forces.[49]

The growing numbers of arms brokers in the post–Cold War era have increased the opportunities of conflict protagonists to access extraregional sources of SALW. While it is not currently possible to estimate precisely what proportion of arms flows to conflict are facilitated by brokers as this changes throughout conflict as arming patterns of recipients evolve, it is clear that they have played a significant role in facilitating and arranging the flow of arms to conflict protagonists.[50]

Broadly speaking, brokers are contracted by regional patrons or conflict-protagonists to facilitate the purchase of arms on their behalf from the global market. The sources accessed by these brokers tend to be the legal exports from states with poor enforcement of export regulations or low capacity to authenticate the end-user documentation provided fraudulently by the brokers. This practice has increased significantly in the post–Cold War period as war economies have replaced the aid of major power patrons as the dominant financing mechanism of SALW flows to conflict.[51] Brokers are also a link between those factions and global markets for commodities extracted from the conflict area by those factions. Indeed, the structure of these war economies and transnational networks is a primary determinant of nature of SALW acquisitions by conflict factions.

Even at the height of the Cold War when warring factions often enjoyed the benefits of extraregional covert aid, many insurgent groups cultivated independent illicit commercial alliances in order to purchase supplementary arms and also to provide alternatives to foreign patronage, which was vulnerable to the vicissitudes of the patron's global agendas. For example, the diamond trading networks that fuelled UNITA's war against the Movimento Popular da Libertacao de Angola (MPLA) government of Angola from the early 1990s predate the official cessation of covert assistance from the United States and South Africa.[52] Indeed, some arms brokers, such as Victor Bout and Leonid Minin, appear to specialize in the niche market of supplies to conflict. It should be noted that such channels are not only constructed by specialist arms brokers. Other actors, such as oil and diamond mining corporations, have also facilitated or taken part directly in illicit arms supplies. For example, the French oil company, Elf Acquitaine allegedly brokered and financed arms transfers to Sassou-Nguesso's forces in Congo-Brazzaville in 1997.[53]

Leonid Efimovich Minin was a typical nefarious arms broker. Developing and drawing on close relationships with illicit recipients, such as the former warlord and president of Liberia Charles Taylor, Minin's unscrupulous activities demonstrate the requirements and roles of arms brokers. Minin facilitated and arranged numerous UN embargo busting arms transfers to Liberia between 1998 and 2000. These included supplies of surplus SALW from Niger in December 1998; and 68 tons of SALW from the Ukraine in March 1999 that initially went to Burkina Faso and were then ferried on Minin's private plane to Liberia.

One key aspect of the *modus operandi* of illicit arms brokers is the forging of end-user certificates. For instance, in July 2000 Liberia's neighbor, Ivory Coast, imported 5 million rounds of Ukrainian 7.62 mm ammunition as part of a deal arranged by Minin using an apparently authentic end-user certificate signed by General Robert Gueï, the then president of Ivory Coast.[54] This ammunition was subsequently ferried on to Liberia. Additionally, Leonid Minin apparently also made numerous illicit copies of the end-user certificate of Ivory Coast issued to him for the legal ammunition deal that were to be used in subsequent transfers to provide the appearance of legality to the source countries.[55]

Leonid Minin was arrested in Italy on August 5, 2000, revealing the importance of close links with illicit recipients. An arms deal arranged by Minin was incomplete at the time of his arrest. In this case Valery Cherny, a former Russian test-pilot, ran a Moscow-based arms brokering and transport company Aviatrend that arranged the deal, in connection with Leonid Minin.[56] After Minin's arrest, Valery Cherny was unable to continue with the planned further deliveries of arms and ammunition to Liberia since it was Minin and not Cherny that had the necessary contacts with Taylor.[57]

Revealing the links between the export of natural resources from conflict zones and the influx of arms, Minin's timber company Exotic Tropical Timber Enterprise (ETTE), with extensive timber concessions in Liberia, Taylor's government owed approximately US$2 million to Minin's company, largely for arms deals. The government therefore issued a number of tax exemptions of Minin's timber exports as payment. The Liberian government was under a UN arms embargo primarily because it was believed to be channeling arms to the RUF rebels in Sierra Leone. In addition to procuring these arms on Charles Taylor's behalf, Minin also played a role in the subsequent transfers to the RUF. For instance, the ETTE also transported weapons to rebel-held areas of Sierra Leone.[58] ETTE was also reported to have been exploiting forest resources inside Sierra Leone and to have ferried shipments of RUF diamonds on the return journey.[59]

Supply channels of SALW to illicit recipients in conflict also involve numerous front companies established by specialist illicit traffickers in order to hide the illicit nature of transfers through the provision of legal documentation or to launder money or other commodities exchanged for the weapons. While these companies are often legally established, their prime role is to facilitate illicit trafficking and therefore they are clearly illicit specialists in spite of their legal status.[60] However, the range of facilitating roles is complete and tends to move fluidly between legal, gray, and black markets. This is demonstrated in the aforementioned Liberian cases by the complex combination of ostensibly legal arms exports. These are facilitated by both genuine end-user certificates, issued as a form of covert aid or market–market commodity, and forged certificates, and are diverted by private actors and transporters.

Arming Patterns of Non-State Actors: Money Matters, But Not Alone

Given the predominant emphasis on the role of arms brokers as a link between rebel groups and the global SALW market, one could be forgiven for assuming that such channels provide the bulk of rebel arms. However, this is not the case. The accessing of supplies of arms and ammunition depends upon a range of factors and multiple types of channels. In addition to the channels discussed above, non-state actors may also purchase arms on local small-scale black markets or, in some regions, large and relatively organized black markets, such as those in Latin America and South and Central Asia. They may also rely on what weapons can be stolen and captured from government forces. Thus, the arming patterns of non-state actors, such as rebel and pro-government militia, in areas of conflict are complexly constructed and depend in part on the accessibility of arms from these other sources.[61] Nevertheless, for the purposes of this chapter, the key question is whether the features of SALW proliferation examined above mean that any actor with sufficient funds can obtain whatever arms it wishes, and whether they are all able to do so in a broadly comparable manner.

Some analysts point to the growth of a global illicit economy in parallel with the globalization of legal trade.[62] Improved transport and communications infrastructure has facilitated the growth of commercial interactions across the globe regardless of their legality.[63] However, while a warring faction's economic interactions may have a global reach, in terms of the markets of developed states in which illicit commodities such as drugs and conflict diamonds are sold, they tend to be organized around regionally constructed illicit networks that spread outward from the conflict zones.[64] Direct links between insurgent forces and international markets are rare. The same is true of SALW flows from the extra-regional level that tend to originate in legal markets that can only be accessed by intermediaries such as brokers or states.

Mark Duffield claims that "[p]olitical actors have been able to control local economies and realize their worth through the ability to forge new and flexible relations with liberalized global markets."[65] However, for the SALW trade at the extraregional level, these relations with liberalized global market remain predicated upon the ability of warring factions to contract brokers or gain the assistance of regional states in order to dupe the legal SALW trade.

Regional actors provide insurgent groups and their business allies with access to international markets on which to sell the natural resources or other illicit commodities that generate hard currency for arms purchases from international sources. For example, some Ugandan army officials have been alleged to have illicitly engaged in a range of "informal cooperation" activities with the Sudan People's Liberation Army (SPLA), including some involvement in the illicit gold trade.[66] On a larger scale, the Ivory Coast port of San Pedro was particularly important for the Front National Patriotique du Liberia's (NPFL) exports of natural resources such as timber; and Thailand was crucial to the export of timber by the Khmer Rouge in Cambodia.[67] Likewise, the regional dimensions of the trade in conflict diamonds and illicit drug trafficking have a strong link with arms flows. For example, exports of conflict diamonds from UNITA in Angola and the RUF in Sierra Leone were highly regionalized, often involving illicit trafficking of diamonds to neighboring states and entering the channels of legal diamond exports from those states. Thus, regional transnational networks and neighboring governments form the key link between warlords and the international diamond market.[68]

Significantly, this regional facilitation provides not only the financial resources with which to make SALW purchases, but also generates or maintains the networks through which those weapons flow. SALW often flow through these same networks with the same traffickers exchanging arms for these other commodities. In the case of conflict diamonds, for example, UNITA is believed to have actively sought out arms dealers willing to take diamonds in exchange for weapons.[69] Likewise, the flow of arms to rebel groups in Liberia and Sierra Leone was facilitated by the networks generated and entrenched by the export of diamonds, gold, timber, and other resources through regional states. In other regions the war economies of insurgent groups are an integrated part of regional black markets in various commodities. For example, the drug trade and SALW trafficking are intimately related to insurgent groups in Myanmar, Afghanistan, and Colombia. R.T. Naylor has claimed that while

> [i]t is no longer the operation of this or that individual black market . . . This does not add up to a monolithic criminal conspiracy. Modern black markets are complex, but they are not integrated into neat monopolies or cartels. If they were, they would be easier to control. Instead of an organizational hierarchy one finds a series of arms-length commercial relationships . . . The result is that a modern covert arms deal is likely to take place within a matrix of black market transactions.[70]

In fact, in most cases, SALW flows to illicit recipients in conflict take place in a matrix of legal, covert, gray, and black-market transactions and facilitating roles. The construction of this matrix is largely dependent upon the political economy of conflict at the regional and local levels.

In many cases the networks for the export of natural resources also act as the financial conduits for the payment for arms deals with brokers or regional governments facilitating the sale of illicitly acquired commodities and using the proceeds to acquire arms on the legal global market. In other cases financial conduits may also be constructed independently of extractive war economies. This is particularly the case for embargoed government forces. For example, a Bahrain bank was the conduit for a deal between the National Islamic Front (NIF) government of Sudan and some arms dealers for French helicopters.[71] Likewise, sanctions busting arms imports by the government of Serbia during the war in the former Yugoslavia were financed with assets that had been transferred by the government to front companies' bank accounts in Cyprus whose strict secrecy laws enabled the flow of finance for arms deals.[72] Indeed, the provision of financial conduits is primarily a means of laundering the origin of money in arms purchases by governments under an arms embargo.

Some conflict commodities, such as diamonds, can be exported to legal markets, provided that regional actors and brokers are able to launder them. Others, such as illicit drugs remain within the illicit market. Thus the nature of the commodities being traded, and the associated requirements for market access, is an important distinction in relation the types of actors that are incorporated into an insurgent group's commercial alliances especially with respect to the character of relationships and the necessity for facilitation in the return trade in SALW.

To some extent, therefore, the structures and determinants of access to SALW by illicit recipients are a function of the interaction and nexus of legal and illicit markets. Arms brokers are of critical importance in forming these nexus and navigating the various thresholds between legal and illicit realms. However, regional states may play similar roles. Thus, while enhancing regulation of arms brokers will contribute to a contraction of the space in which illicit arms transactions occur, it will not prevent arms flows to illicit and abusive recipients.

In addition to these networks and nexuses, the character and ability of a rebel group to access different sources of arms depend upon their regional, political, and economic support from neighboring states, the presence or lack of a large regional black market, and numerous other factors. Rebel groups with similarly lucrative war economies, but selling different commodities or operating in different regions, will have different arming patterns as a function of these variables. Given these intervening structures between rebels and the global arms market, it is clear that money matters, but not alone.

Even the most efficient globalizers among rebel and terrorist groups remain constrained by these realities. The LTTE in Sri Lanka, for example, are a well-organized military force "reminiscent of many professional armies" and have accessed directly extraregional sources, including the global legal market.[73] Their arms procurement wing, known as the "KP Department" and headed by Kumaran Pathmanathan, is also highly professionalized and its members are trained in the arts of gunrunning such as document forgery and international shipping and investments. Through the use of front companies based in Europe and Africa, forged end-user certificates, and so forth, the LTTE is able to play all the roles usually associated with regional facilitators and has accessed sources in the former Soviet Union and the Middle East.[74] Significantly, they have their own merchant-shipping network, the Sea Pigeons, which has, in combination with their sophisticated procurement networks, allowed the LTTE to obtain arms from international sources without the direct collusion of regional actors.[75] What distinguishes the LTTE from other similarly large and sophisticated insurgent forces is not the revenue of its war economy or its territorial control—Jaffna has been controlled at some periods, but not continuously—but rather its structure: a transnational network with global reach as well as a terrorist organization and insurgent force.

Similarly, al Qaeda has also been able to acquire some weapons and support equipment in a similar pattern. According to Gunaratna:

Al Qaeda also had a worldwide network of procurement officers, such as US citizen Essam Al-Ridi, Osama's personal pilot, who obtained communication equipment from Japan; scuba gear and range finders from Britain; satellite phones from Germany; and night vision goggles and scope, video equipment, Barrett 50 caliber sniping rifles and a T-389 plane from America.[76]

Thus, the cell structure of al Qaeda provides it with ostensibly legal representatives capable of purchasing weapons and equipment in extraregional states. This global access was reportedly used in 2000–2001 to build links with Russian and Ukrainian mafias to purchase SALW and equipment. However, much of the arming of its forces occurs through mechanisms more closely associated with other, non-global, insurgent forces. In Afghanistan, al Qaeda's guerrilla army, the 055 Brigade, was integrated into the Taleban's Army of the Islamic Emirate of Afghanistan from 1997 to 2001, were well armed. Many, and possibly most, arms acquisitions have been procured in other ways, most notably from the South Asian black market and from weapons provided by the Taleban in Afghanistan. The latter was reportedly covert aid composed of weapons provided to the Taleban by the Pakistani intelligence service.[77] Significantly, such autonomous supply operations continued in 2001 and 2002 when the U.S.-led forces were engaged in campaigns against al Qaeda and the Taleban in Afghanistan. While apparently possessing SALW in abundance, hi-tech support equipment continued to be imported.[78]

Conclusion

Understandings of the spread of SALW have evolved rapidly as concern has grown since the mid-1990s, generating a prevailing framework that centers on distinctions between legal and illicit flows. This focus on "illicit" SALW spread has been reflected in most multilateral policy responses. For instance the two global policy responses to the problems of SALW spread are a "Firearms Protocol":[79] an additional protocol to the *UN Convention against Transnational Organised Crime* that was adopted by the UN General Assembly in May 2001, but is not yet in force;[80] and the *Programme of Action.* Agreed at the July 2001 UN Conference on the Illicit Trade in Small Arms and Light Weapons in All its Aspects.[81] Some significant regional agreements have also been reached such as the *Inter-American Convention Against the Illicit Manufacturing of and Trafficking in Firearms, Ammunition, Explosives, and Other Related Materials;*[82] the *EU Programme for Preventing and Combating Illicit Trafficking in Conventional Arms;*[83] the *ECOWAS Moratorium,*[84] and many others.[85]

However, supply channels to rebel groups and embargoed governments are not illicit all the way down, but rather move fluidly between the legal, covert, gray, and black-market realms. While nefarious arms brokers are important conduits and facilitators of these damaging arms flows, they are not the sole perpetrators of illicit arming. Thus, the illicit spread of SALW is a function not only of unscrupulous non-state actors, but also of a range of structures and processes that occur and persist in the legal realm through both the actions and inactions of states. Both states and non-state actors are part of the problem of proliferation. Recent experience in beginning to tackle the problem, such as in the development of national action plans, regional agreements, and the UN *Programme of Action*, indicate that cooperation between states and civil society is a key ingredient in the formulation and implementation of responses. Nevertheless, significantly more work remains to be done. The role of NGOs in spurring these developments and maintaining a degree of momentum within will remain crucial to the prospects for controlling these pernicious weapons and ameliorating the destruction of their proliferation and misuse.

Notes

1. Small Arms Survey, *Small Arms Survey 2001: Profiling the Problem* (Oxford: Oxford University Press and Small Arms Survey, 2001), 1.
2. International Committee of the Red Cross (ICRC), *Arms Availability and the Situation of Civilians in Armed Conflict* (Geneva: ICRC, 1999).
3. Rana Swadesh, *Small Arms and Intra-State Conflicts*, UNIDIR Research Papers No. 34 (Geneva: UNIDIR, 1995).
4. United Nations, *Report of the Group of Governmental Experts on Small Arms*, A/54/258 (New York: United Nations, 1999).
5. Small Arms Survey, *Small Arms Survey 2001*, 197–249.
6. Edward Laurance, *Light Weapons and Intrastate Conflict; Early Warning Factors and Preventive Action: A Report to the Carnegie Commission on Preventing Deadly Conflict* (New York: Carnegie Corporation of New York, 1998), 12, 20–2.
7. See Small Arms Survey, *Small Arms Survey 2001*, 200–8, for an outline of the hotly debated relationship between small arms and violence. See also Ian Anthony, "Causation and the Arms Trade, with Reference to Small Arms," in *Small Arms Control: Old Weapons, New Issues*, ed. Jayantha Dhanapala, 59–75 (Geneva: UNIDIR, 1999).
8. UN, *Report of the Panel of Governmental Experts on Small Arms* (New York: United Nations, 1997), 9, paragraph 17.
9. Keith Krause, *Small Arms and Light Weapons: Proliferation Processes and Policy Options* (paper, International Security Research and Outreach Programme, International Security Bureau, July 2000), at http://www.smallarmssurvey.org, 2.
10. Small Arms Survey, *Small Arms Survey* 2001, 68.
11. UN General Assembly, *Report of the Disarmament Commission*, A/49/42 (New York: United Nations, 1994), 13, quoted in Michael T. Klare and David Anderson, *A Scourge of Guns: The Diffusion of Small Arms and Light Weapons in Latin America* (Washington, DC: FAS Arms Sales Monitoring Project, 1996), 57.
12. Limited transparency on legal SALW transfers makes it difficult to determine whether a transfer is legal, gray, or black. A good review of the current level of transparency can be found in Maria Haug et al., *Shining a Light on Small Arms Exports: The Record of State Transparency*, Small Arms Survey Occasional Papers No. 4 (Geneva: Small Arms Survey, 2002).
13. UN, *Report of the Group of Governmental Experts on Small Arms*, A/54/258, 24, paragraph 56.
14. While a range of bodies of international law have some implications for arms transfers, including international humanitarian law and human rights law, UN arms embargoes are the only explicit and globally applicable legal restrictions. For a discussion of these different bodies of international law see Emmanuela Gillard, "What's Legal? What's Illegal?" in *Running Guns: The Global Black Market in Small Arms*, ed. Lora Lumpe, 27–52 (London: Zed Books, 2000).

15. Michael T. Klare, "Light Weapons Diffusion and Global Violence in the Post-Cold War Era," in *Light Weapons and International Security*, ed. Jashit Singh, 1–40 (London: BASIC, 1995).

16. Small Arms Survey, *Small Arms Survey 2002: Counting the Human Cost* (Oxford: Oxford University Press, 2002), 59, notes 1 and 2. In the previous year in the *Small Arms Survey*, this estimate was over 600 companies in 95 countries producing, or having previously produced, small arms, light weapons, and ammunition. Small Arms Survey, *Small Arms Survey 2001*, 10–11. Thus, in recent years the primary improvement in data has been in relation to the number of manufacturers, with only few extra states being added to the list of producers.

17. While such a reorientation of the application of these terms is potentially too convoluted for directly feeding into policy discourse, it creates the potential for an analytic rigor to assess the accuracy of characterizations of SALW spread in a global and varied regional and local contexts. It also allows more accurate reflection of the linkages and construction of different structures and processes of SALW spread. This chapter draws on some of the results of a more comprehensive development, application, and analysis of such a framework. Michael Bourne, *An Examination of Small Arms Proliferation and Areas of Conflict: Developing Frameworks and Analysing Processes* (Ph.D. dissertation, University of Bradford, U.K., 2004).

18. Small Arms Survey, *Small Arms Survey 2003: Development Denied* (Oxford: Oxford University Press, 2003), 57.

19. Small Arms Survey, *Small Arms Survey 2002*, 103.

20. Ibid., 104.

21. Ibid., 103–4.

22. Small Arms Survey, *Small Arms Survey 2001*, 197.

23. Michael Renner, *Small Arms, Big Impact: The Next Challenge of Disarmament*, Worldwatch Paper No. 137 (Washington, D.C.: World watch Institute, 1997), 19.

24. Michael T. Klare, "The International Trade in Light Weapons: What Have We Learned?" in *Light Weapons and Civil Conflict: Controlling the Tools of Violence*, ed. Jeffrey Boutwell and Michael T. Klare (New York: Carnegie Commission on Preventing Deadly Conflict, 1999), 15.

25. Small Arms Survey, *Small Arms Survey 2001*, 141.

26. Ibid., 168.

27. Krause, *Small Arms and Light Weapons*, 21.

28. See for a discussion Aaron Karp, "Small Arms—The New Major Weapons," in *Lethal Commerce: The Global Trade in Small Arms and Light Weapons*, ed. Jeffrey Boutwell et al., 17–30 (Cambridge, MA: American Academy of Arts and Sciences, 1995); and Klare, "International Trade," 14.

29. Small Arms Survey, *Small Arms Survey 2001*, 190.

30. Aaron Karp, "The Rise of Black and Gray Markets," *The Annals of The American Academy of Political and Social Science* 535 (1994): 175–89; and Jasjit Singh, "Illicit Trafficking in Small Arms: Some Issues and Aspects," in *Curbing Illicit Trafficking in Small Arms and Sensitive Technologies: An Action-Oriented Agenda*, ed. Péricles Gasparani Alves and Daiana Belinda Cipollone, 9–18 (Geneva: UNIDIR, 1998).

31. Small Arms Survey, *Small Arms Survey 2001*, 167.

32. John Sislin et al., "Patterns in Arms Acquisitions by Ethnic Groups in Conflict," *Security Dialogue* 29, no. 4 (1998): 393–408.

33. See Brian Wood and Johan Peleman, *The Arms Fixers-Controlling the Brokers and Shipping Agents* (Oslo: PRIO, NISAT, AND BASIC, 1999). and Brian Wood and Elizabeth Clegg, *Controlling the Gun-Runners: Proposals for EU Action to Regulate Arms Brokering and Shipping Agents* (London: Saferworld, NISAT, and BASIC, 1999).

34. Biting the Bullet, *Implementing the Programme of Action on Small Arms: 2003: Action by States and Civil Society* (London: IANSA, 2003), 156. For example, Slovakia, a notorious center of broker activity, introduced a new arms bill in April 2002 cutting number of companies licensed to trade in arms by two-thirds, which according to police was over 600 before the law was introduced. See "Arms Traders Face New Hurdle to Doing Business," *The Slovak Spectator*, May 13, 2002.

35. Small Arms Survey, *Small Arms Survey 2001*, 197.

36. See David Mussington, *Understanding Contemporary Arms Transfers: An Analysis of the Post-Cold War Arms Trade and Supplier Strategies for Limiting Conventional Weapons Proliferation*, Adelphi Paper 291 (London: Brassey's for IISS, 1994), 58.

37. Small Arms Survey, *Small Arms Survey 2001*, 15.

38. Ibid., 57.

39. Ibid., 319–20. For example, the change from the Carter to the Reagan regime in the United States in 1981 resulted in an increase in U.S. involvement in Central American conflicts, including the provision of arms aid to the Contras in Nicaragua.

40. S.D. Muni, "Arms and Conflicts in the Post-Cold War Developing World," in *Between Development and Destruction: An Enquiry into the Causes of Conflict in Post-Colonial State*, ed. Luc Van de Goor et al. (London: Macmillan, 1996), 201.

41. These included surplus Israeli-made mines bought from Egypt, 100,000 rifles from India, tens of thousands of rifles, mortars, and ammunition from Turkey, and Soviet small arms from East Germany, reportedly purchased by the CIA with the assistance of British MI6. See Bobo Pirseyedi, *The Small Arms Problem in Central Asia: Features and Implications* (Geneva: United Nations Institute for Disarmament Research, 2000); Olivier Roy, *The Lessons of the Soviet/Afghan War*, Adelphi Paper 259 (London: Brassey's for IISS, 1991), 35–6; Chris Smith, "Light Weapons and Ethnic Conflict in South Asia" in *Lethal Commerce*, 62.

42. The CIA pipeline to the Contras in Nicaragua included weapons obtained from Israel, which supplied arms captured from the PLO in the 1982 invasion of Lebanon. These were obtained by retired Air Force Major General Richard Secord acting on behalf of the CIA. See Klare and Andersen, *A Scourge of Guns*, 77, and R.T. Naylor, "Loose Cannons: Covert Commerce and Underground Finance in the Modern Arms Black Market," *Crime, Law & Social Change* 22, no. 1 (1995): 49.

43. Although these weapons were more sophisticated than Soviet SA-7, the supply of Western weapons was largely a result of congressional pressure on the CIA to abandon its previous principles of ensuring deniability, which in turn was spurred by the beleaguered position of the Mujahideen forces, rather than an absence of Soviet-type alternatives. According to Olivier Roy: "It was under Congressional pressure that the CIA changed . . . in 1985, providing American-made arms, including Stinger missiles, for the first time." See Roy, *The Lessons of the Soviet/Afghan War*, 35–6. According to Jane's Infantry Weapons for the years 1984–1985, the Stinger missiles were the relatively new successor to the US Redeye missile. Ian V. Hogg, *Jane's Infantry Weapons: 1984–1985* (Coulsdon: Jane's Information Group Limited, 1985), 678.

44. For example, prior to the provision of covert aid for the Contras through military aid packages to Central American states, El Salvador received $33.5 million in military aid in 1983 and Honduras received $27.5 million. In the next year, when covert aid was being provided, these figures jumped to $176.8 million and $76.5 million, respectively. See Klare and Andersen, *A Scourge and Guns*, 79.

45. Ibid., 77–8.

46. John Stockwell, *In Search of Enemies: A CIA Story* (London: André Deutsch, 1978), 59.

47. Klare and Andersen, *A Scourge of guns*, 78.

48. For detailed examination of the regionalization of covert aid see Bourne, *An Examination of Small Arms Proliferation*.
49. Wood and Peleman, 7–17.
50. Small Arms Survey, *Small Arms Survey 2001*, 95–139, and Wood and Peleman *The Arms Fixers*.
51. David Keen, *The Economic Functions of Violence in Civil Wars*, Adelphi Paper 320 (London: International Institute for Strategic Studies, 1998). William Reno, "Privatizing War in Sierra Leone," *Current History* 96, no. 610 (1997): 227–30; William Reno, "The Business of War in Liberia," *Current History* 95, no. 601 (1996): 211–15; William Reno, "War, Markets, and the Reconfiguration of West Africa's Weak States," *Comparative Politics* 29, no. 4 (1997): 493–510; Mats Berdal and David Malone, eds., *Greed and Grievance: Economic Agendas in Civil Wars* (London: Lynne Rienner, 2000).
52. R.T. Naylor, "The Insurgent Economy: Black Market Operations of Guerrilla Organizations," *Crime, Law and Social Change* 20, no. 1 (1993): 41.
53. Wood and Peleman, *The Arms Fixers*, 13; and Al Venter, "Arms Pour into Africa," *New African*, January 1999, 12.
54. UN, *Report of the Panel of Experts pursuant to Security Council Resolution 1343 (2001), paragraph 19, concerning Liberia* (New York: UN, October 2001), 47.
55. Ibid., 47.
56. Ibid., 47.
57. Ibid., 49.
58. "Minimal Contracts," *Africa Confidential* 42, no. 13 (June 2001), 3.
59. Small Arms Survey, *Small Arms Survey 2001*, 133, fn. 45.
60. See Silvia Cucovaz, "Interrelationship between Illicit Trafficking in Small Arms, Drug Trafficking, and Terrorist Groups in South America," in *Curbing Illicit Trafficking in Small Arms and Sensitive Technologies: An Action-Oriented Agenda*, ed. Péricles Gasparani Alves and Daiana Belinda Cipollone (Geneva: UNIDIR, 1998), 40.
61. The construction and evolution of arming patterns, regional black-markets, and other structures and processes of SALW spread to conflicts are examined in greater depth in Bourne, *An Examination of Small Arms Proliferation*.
62. See e.g., Carolyn Nordström, *Shadow Sovereigns*, Joan B. Kroc Institute for International Peace Studies Occasional Paper 17: OP2 (Indiana: University of Notre Dame, 1999).
63. See in relation to arms trafficking Ian Anthony, "Current Trends and Developments in the Arms Trade," *The Annals of the American Academy of Political and Social Science* 535 (1994): 34. For example, these improvements have also facilitated the maintenance of links with members of the same ethnic group living abroad. Many identity-based factions, such as the LTTE in Sri Lanka or the IRA among numerous others, rely on finances sent by sympathetic or coerced members of a Diaspora for a significant proportion of their finances. See Peter Chalk, "The Tamil Tiger Insurgency in Sri Lanka," in *Over a Barrel: Light Weapons & Human Rights in the Commonwealth*, ed. Abdel-Fatau Musah and Niobe Thompson (New Delhi: Commonwealth Human Rights Initiative, 1999), 82–4.
64. These regional networks center around key source areas such as the "Golden Triangle" and the "Golden Crescent" in the case of drugs trafficking.
65. Mark Duffield, "Globalization, Transborder Trade, and War Economies," in *Greed and Grievance: Economic Agendas in Civil Wars*, ed. Mats Berdal and David Malone, 69–89 (London: Lynne Rienner, 2000), 72.
66. "UGANDA/SUDAN: Bordering on war," *Africa Confidential* 36, no. 15, (1995), 3.

67. Global Witness, *Thai-Khmer Rouge Links, and the Illegal Trade in Cambodia's Timber—Evidence Collected January–May 1995*, http://www.globalwitness.org/reports/show.php/en.00036.html.

68. See, e.g., Robert Fowler, *Report of the Panel of Experts on Violations of Security Council Sanctions Against UNITA* (New York: United Nations, 2000), paragraphs 83–8; Global Witness, *A Rough Trade: The Role of Companies and Governments in the Angolan Conflict* (London: Global Witness, December 1998), 12; Ian Smillie, Lansana Gberie, and Ralph Hazleton, *The Heart of the Matter: Sierra Leone, Diamonds and Human Security* (Ottawa: Partnership Africa Canada, 2000).

69. Fowler, *Report of the Panel of Experts*, paragraph 81.

70. Naylor, "Loose Cannons", 20.

71. "SUDAN: Secret Weapons," *Africa Confidential* 36, no. 10 (1995), 8.

72. Naylor, "Loose Cannons", 37.

73. Chalk, "The Tamil Tiger Insurgency," 75–7.

74. Ibid., 80.

75. They have also operated with a significant degree of autonomy in the regional black-market, with operations in Afghanistan, Myanmar, and Singapore, as well as further afar such as South Africa. Ibid., 79–82; and Tara Kartha, *Tools of Terror: Light Weapons and India's Security* (New Delhi: Knowledge World, 1999), 150.

76. Rohan Gunaratna, *Inside Al Qaida* (London: Hurst and Company, 2002), 59–60.

77. Ibid., 58–9.

78. Small Arms Survey, *Small Arms Survey 2003*, 73.

79. Full title: The Protocol against the Illicit Manufacturing of and Trafficking in Firearms, Ammunition and Other Related Material.

80. See discussion of the protocol in Sarah Meek, "Combating Arms Trafficking: Progress and Prospects," in *Running Guns*, 183–207. See also UN Press Release *GA/9866*, May 31, 2001.

81. UN, *Report of the United Nations Conference on the Illicit Trade in Small Arms and Light Weapons in All Its Aspects* (New York: UN, 2001).

82. William Benson, *Light Weapons Controls and Security Assistance: A Review of Current Practice* (London: Saferworld and International Alert, 1998), 30. This convention promotes information exchange and interstate cooperation on eradicating the illicit production and trade of light weapons. It was negotiated through the OAS, and is hoped to provide a model for other regional initiatives. It also provided a model for the UN ECOSOC Firearms Protocol.

83. Ibid., 28.

84. The text of the moratorium and other resources on its implementation can be found at http://www.nisat.org.

85. For an overview of these regional measures and their implementation see Biting the Bullet, *Implementing the Programme*.

Chapter 9

NGOs and the Shaping of the European Controls on Small Arms Exports

Holger Anders

The power to decide on foreign policy traditionally rests with governments. This is particularly so if policy decisions affect matters of national security such as the manufacture and trade of conventional weapons. During the Cold War, governments were largely autonomous from nongovernmental actors such as arms control campaigners and advocates in their policy formulation and making on arms control. Since the end of the Cold War, however, nongovernmental policy advocates have become prominent actors in policy debates on conventional weapons controls. This at least is suggested by the emergence of prominent policy coalitions between certain governmental and nongovernmental actors jointly pursuing shared aims such as the international ban of anti-personnel landmines or greater controls on the international trade in military small arms. Indeed, this increased role of nongovernmental participation in policy making on conventional arms control opens the question of whether we are witnessing a shift toward the governance of arms control. That is, is there a shift in policy-making authority on conventional arms control away from governments and to nongovernmental policy actors?

This chapter seeks to answer this question with regard to the role of nongovernmental advocacy networks in the creation of the current regime on small arms control in the European Union. The creation of the regime has included the active participation of nongovernmental policy experts and advocacy networks on both national and transnational levels. The first section of this chapter provides an introduction to the new role of nongovernmental actors in small arms control. The second section looks at the development of the present European control regime. The third section investigates the part played by nongovernmental advocacy and policy coalitions between governments and nongovernmental actors in creating the regime. The fourth section then looks at the impact and limits of nongovernmental advocacy. The chapter argues that nongovernmental campaigners and advocates have attained an unprecedented level of access to policy making on arms control in the European Union. This has enabled them to significantly shape and bring forward the EU control regime. At the same time, governments have retained their authority in decision making on arms control. Thus, even as important drivers of developments in arms control and as partners of policy coalitions with governments, nongovernmental actors regularly fail to see their policy aims fully realized.

New Policy Actors and Security Issues

New security actors in arms control. The participation of nongovernmental advocates in governmental debates on arms control is not a new phenomenon. For example, a network of humanitarian campaigners successfully lobbied governments to abolish dum-dum bullets for causing unnecessary suffering to combatants at The Hague Peace Conference in 1899.[1] During the Cold War, it was especially issues of nuclear weapons control and disarmament around which advocacy networks of scientists and activists formed. Such networks have become known as epistemic communities, that is, networks "of professionals with recognized expertise and competence in a particular domain and an authoritative claim to policy-relevant knowledge within [their] domain or issue-area."[2] In the 1950s and early 1960s, for example, European and U.S. scientists and policy advocates sought to jointly influence the U.S. administration's view regarding the *Nuclear Test Ban Treaty* that was eventually signed by the United States, the Soviet Union, and the United Kingdom in 1963.[3] Similar epistemic communities lobbied the U.S. administration to adopt the *Anti-Ballistic Missile Treaty* in 1972,[4] as well as the Soviet government regarding its nuclear policies.[5]

What has changed since the end of the Cold War is the frequency with which prominent nongovernmental advocacy networks on arms control are emerging and their focus on conventional weapons. This is partly related to a renewed governmental interest in conventional weapons control, an area that was largely ignored during the Cold War. Also, the focus of security agendas has shifted toward the many violent intrastate conflicts that are ravaging the developing world. Through cooperation between nongovernmental organizations (NGOs) working in areas directly affected by this violence and organizations in the developed world, nongovernmental networks have been able to successfully draw governmental attention to the devastating human costs of the lack of controls on conventional weapons. What is also new is that these networks on arms control are less frequently composed of scientific policy experts than of nongovernmental campaigners and activists ranging from arms control, human rights, humanitarian law, and development organizations to faith-based and peace groups. Such advocacy networks tend to not only focus on identifying and working together with governments sympathetic to their aims, but they also engage in public activities to raise awareness for their aims among and mobilize support from the general public.

A good example for a "transnational advocacy network"[6] within the field of conventional weapons control is the International Action Network on Small Arms

(IANSA). Founded in 1998, it brings together over 500 NGOs from nearly 100 countries working to end the proliferation and misuse of Small Arms and Light Weapons (SALW). This weapons category includes shoulder-fired missiles and grenades, mortars, light machine guns, assault rifles and pistols, that is, weapons that can be carried by one to three people. Central to the advocacy campaign on SALW control is to lobby governments to introduce strict controls on the international trade in this subcategory of conventional weapons at national, regional, and international levels. Apart from information gathering and dissemination on the human costs associated with SALW proliferation and misuse, IANSA has become an important partner for governments sympathetic to the aim of greater controls on SALW. This was evidenced at the UN Conference on Small Arms in 2001. There, IANSA members were allowed to present their views and aims during the official discussions on the *Programme of Action on Small Arms* that was negotiated at this conference.[7] In short, what is "new" about nongovernmental advocacy on arms control since the end of the Cold War is the greater importance attached to conventional weapons control and that governments are increasingly willing to discuss controls on the trade in such weapons with the active participation of not scientific experts, but of NGO coalitions.

Small arms control as a new security issue. The emergence of nongovernmental advocacy networks as new security actors is of course also closely related to the emergence of new threats on security agendas. As mentioned, with the end of the Cold War, violent intrastate conflict has received considerably more international attention than has previously been the case. It has also become more accepted that uncontrolled arms transfers and the trade in natural resources often fuel such conflicts. In particular the widespread and cheap availability of SALW was identified as a significant contributing factor to such violent conflicts. This availability was a result of decades of unrestricted SALW exports by the superpowers and their allies to allied Third World regimes and the increasing number of countries in the developing world that began producing SALW domestically.

Easy to use, requiring little maintenance, and readily available on licit as well as illicit arms markets, SALW have been identified as the weapons of choice for armed groups who have been accused of committing gross violations of international humanitarian law. SALW have thereby become associated with many of the civil wars that have claimed the lives of predominantly civilians, most of them women and children. Further, SALW have also been identified as a threat to reconstruction in post-conflict situations, where SALW often contribute to armed banditry and seriously hamper sustainable development. Misuse of these weapons by armed forces under governmental authority also undermines respect for human rights and humanitarian law. In addition, the use of SALW in organized crime and domestic violence has direct effects on populations in the developed world.[8]

Based on these realizations, several NGOs and policy experts began in the early 1990s to call for greater governmental efforts to counter and end SALW proliferation. Their voice received substantial support when, in 1995, the UN secretary general made explicit references to the devastating effects of light weapons that "are actually killing people in hundreds of thousands" in the armed conflicts the

UN were dealing with. He consequently urged the international community to counter the threat of SALW proliferation to international peace and security.[9] Following this emergence of SALW as a security issue, the Organization of American States adopted in 1997 the *Inter-American Convention on Illicit Firearms* and the European Union adopted the *Programme for Combating Illicit Arms Trafficking*. In 1998, there were also efforts for the first time to address SALW control not only in the context of the combat against illicit trafficking or organized crime, but also as requiring controls on the legal trade in these weapons. The Economic Community of West African States, for example, adopted the *Moratorium on the Importation, Exportation and Manufacture of Small Arms in West Africa*. The European Union adopted the *Code of Conduct on Arms Exports* as a means to achieve high common export standards and restrictive export criteria. The same year, the Southern African Development Community adopted a *Programme to Tackle Small Arms Proliferation and Trafficking*.[10]

In 2001, governments also reached agreement on a *Protocol against Illicit Firearms* that was negotiated within the framework of the 2001 *UN Convention against Transnational Organized Crime*. Acknowledging threats to the "security of each state, region and the world as a whole, endangering the well-being of peoples, their social and economic development and their right to live in peace," the Firearms Protocol seeks to "promote, facilitate, and strengthen cooperation" against illicit trafficking and manufacturing of firearms.[11] Governments also gathered in the same year at the UN Conference on Small Arms to negotiate the consensus-based, politically binding *UN Programme of Action on Small Arms*. This program addresses SALW trafficking and excessive accumulations as a "serious threat to security, stability and sustainable development" and as causing human suffering, exacerbating violence, undermining respect for international humanitarian law, and fueling crime and terrorism.[12]

In sum, the issue of SALW only emerged on security agendas in the mid-1990s, and it was not until 1997 that governments began to agree on joint measures to combat the uncontrolled trade and proliferation of SALW. Nongovernmental policy groups and experts have, since then, been closely involved with the formulation of governmental initiatives to combat SALW proliferation. This points to the often direct link between the emergence of new security threats and new actors in the formulation of security policy since the end of the Cold War.

The European Small Arms Regime

The threats posed by SALW proliferation are perceived and responded to differently in each region of the world.[13] In Europe, responses to SALW proliferation focus particularly on export controls. The reason for this is that France, Germany, the United Kingdom, Italy, the Netherlands, and Sweden are among the top 12 exporters of major conventional weapons.[14] While not all of these countries have significant small arms industries, Germany, France, Belgium, Austria, Italy, and Spain are among the top 13 SALW producers and exporters in the world.[15] Accepting a special responsibility as major arms exporters, many European governments have reviewed their national arms export controls and have jointly agreed to prevent the export of weapons "which might be used for internal repression or international aggression or contribute to regional instability."[16] Military small arms are, in this context, subjected to the same export controls as other conventional weapons such as tanks or fighter jets. Apart from addressing SALW control as an export issue, European governments have further engaged in measures to counter illicit trafficking in conventional weapons, as well as to provide technical assistance to governments requesting such assistance in combating destabilizing accumulations and spreads of SALW.[17]

Important to note here is that over the last decade or so, European countries, and particularly the members of the European Union, have achieved an unprecedented level of cooperation on arms export controls. This section will review this development and demonstrate how European governments have moved from coordination of arms control policies toward the convergence of these policies.

From coordination on arms control policies . . . The origins of arms control cooperation between EU member states can be traced back to 1969 and the creation of the European Political Cooperation (EPC). Regular meetings of the foreign ministries of European Community (EC) members offered a forum in which to coordinate national policies so as to enhance the collective voice of Western European interests. At times, such coordination extended to security policies and arms export controls as evidenced by EC arms embargoes on, for example, Libya and Syria in 1985, and South Africa in 1986. However, the EPC remained largely limited in its use by member states, which kept exclusive national control over their arms trade.[18] A change in this approach occurred with the first Gulf War and the end of the Cold War. Having contributed to arming Iraq during the 1980s, several European countries were confronted with having inadvertently contributed to regional instability in the Gulf. The conflict also demonstrated the shortcomings of a common control system relying on exclusively national policies. For instance, "the denial of exports to Iraq by some Community members, for reasons of international security, had little practical effect given the export practices of other Community members."[19]

Responding to this shortcoming, the EC members convened in 1991 an *ad hoc* working group, known as COARM, to negotiate a list of common arms export criteria. These criteria were adopted by the EC Councils of Luxembourg and Lisbon in 1991 and 1992, and served as the basis for strengthened cooperation on conventional arms control. The end of the Cold War also acted as a catalyst for developments at national levels. Italy, for example, engaged in an overhaul of its national arms export law and adopted new legislation to enhance controls on the export, import, and transit of military equipment in 1990.[20] Similarly, Belgium adopted new arms control legislation in 1991,[21] as did Sweden in 1992.[22] However, European governments continued to undermine each other's export policies. For example, the Luxembourg and Lisbon criteria were often interpreted differently in European capitals, and while Portugal and Italy were observing a self-imposed arms embargo on Indonesia in the early 1990s, Germany, the United Kingdom, and the Netherlands continued their exports. Likewise, some member states exported to sub-Saharan Africa, while others denied licenses on the grounds of undesirable effects of arms exports in the region.[23] To counter such conflicting national policies, the mandate of COARM was extended in 1994 to explore possible steps toward a harmonization of national arms export policies.[24] In 1997 then, the U.K. government adopted new national guidelines to govern British arms exports that became the basis for a British–Franco EU initiative to work toward a strengthening of common arms export controls.

. . . To cooperation on arms control policies. After several months of governmental negotiations on this joint British–Franco initiative, EU member states adopted in June 1998 the cornerstone of the EU arms control regime: the *EU Code of Conduct on Arms Exports*. The Code provides for common arms export criteria against which member states will, on a case-by-case basis, consider the granting or denial of arms export licenses. In order to improve common understandings on the interpretation of these criteria, the Code also includes operative provisions for denial notification and consultation mechanisms on arms export licenses among member states. In addition, the EU Code obliges member states to submit annual reports on their arms exports to the EU Council, which form the basis of an annual consolidated report. Participating governments, therefore, agreed to considerably more transparency and accountability among each other on their arms exports than had previously been the case. In 1999, public transparency on European arms exports improved substantially through the publication by the EU Council of the consolidated report on arms exports under the EU Code of Conduct.

Given the positive experiences in the implementation of the EU Code, EU governments have also become more willing to address a broader scope of conventional and SALW control issues. This is evidenced by the issue of arms brokering controls, that is, controls on the middlemen in arms transfers who bring together buyers and sellers, negotiate arms transfer, or otherwise facilitate arms transfers. Against the background of emerging evidence that unscrupulous brokers play a key role in illicit arms trafficking,[25] an increasing number of EU member states started joining those, who had already enacted specific regulations to control arms brokering activities conducted on their territory. This development was complemented by the adoption of the *EU Guidelines on the Control of Arms Brokering* in 2001, which were reinforced by the *EU Common Position on Arms Brokering* in 2003. Under this Common Position, EU member states committed themselves to license arms brokering taking place on their territory and to decide on granting or denying a brokering license, on a case-by-case basis, according to the criteria stipulated in the *EU Code on Arms Exports*.[26]

The current EU control regime on conventional arms, which includes military SALW, is thus based on the controls governments have adopted on national levels as well as a variety of policy instruments that governments jointly agreed on over the last decade. This regime provides for considerably more cooperation among EU member states than was the case during the Cold War. However, it would be a fundamental mistake to assume that the steady development of greater governmental cooperation on arms control was self-explanatory or inevitable. Rather, the current EU control regime is the outcome of sometimes intense political negotiations between governments and between governments and nongovernmental advocacy groups. These issues are explored in the following section of this chapter.

Policy Coalitions and Nongovernmental Advocacy

As argued in the previous sections, the European arms control regime emerged against the background of changing security interests after the fall of the Berlin Wall, of lessons learned regarding arms export controls in the wake of the first Gulf War, and the proliferation of violent conflicts involving tremendous human suffering in the developing world. At the same time, European governments, while agreeing that greater cooperation on arms export policies was desirable, held very different interests as to how far such cooperation should go. As argued in a report by a nongovernmental research center in 1992:

> On the EC level, concepts vary largely and make it difficult to agree on a single policy. At one extreme, France expounds a defense philosophy based on national autonomy and independent nuclear capability. This implies self-sufficiency in weapons production and foreign sales to sustain an industry of the required size. The U.K. has always seen positive political utility in arms transfers as a means of enhancing the security of non-EC allies of overseas possessions. Belgium, Denmark, Germany, Italy and the Netherlands have distanced themselves from using arms exports as an instrument of foreign policy, and/or taken public positions in favor of restraint. At the far end of the scale come Ireland and Luxembourg, with no evident interest in production or export.[27]

This meant that, although governments could agree on the Luxembourg and Lisbon criteria as a basis of greater cooperation, there was no immediate consensus on further promoting such cooperation. Particularly France and the United Kingdom opposed measures for greater multilateral arms control, especially if these were to entail limitations to their national flexibility in deciding on arms exports. An example of this protection was given during the negotiations on the COARM mandate in 1994, where France was adamant to have a reference included that "no mention in the mandate should be construed as curtailing national decision-making capability."[28] In contrast, states such as Germany, the Netherlands, and Ireland pointed out that the Luxembourg and Lisbon criteria and the lack of common interpretations left the European arms regime with significant weaknesses. Underlying support for greater cooperation by Germany was the fact that the German national arms export regulations were already more restrictive than those agreed on at a multilateral level. Thus, German authorities are obliged under national law to deny licenses for war weapons exports if there is a risk that these weapons will be used in a peace-disturbing action, particularly military aggression, or there is reason to believe that the licensing of an arms export would contradict Germany's obligations under international law.[29] The stipulation of such legally binding export criteria, complemented by national political guidelines on arms exports, went further than in many other European states. It was therefore easier for Germany and governments with similarly restrictive national export policies to argue for the adoption of high common standards on a multilateral level than for other member states.[30]

Calls for greater multilateral cooperation on arms exports also fell within the scope of interests of those European countries that had only small- to medium-sized defense industries, such as the Netherlands and Sweden, and which sought to foster their image as proponents of peaceful international relations. The states that advocated stricter controls consequently began to support each other's positions in intergovernmental negotiations. However, given the unanimous decision-making structure on arms export policies within the EU Council and opposition by several states to greater cooperation on arms control, it was clear by the mid-1990s that European governments found themselves at an impasse. It was within this context that nongovernmental advocacy emerged as an important catalyst for policy change from 1995 onwards.

The campaign for the EU code of conduct. If changes in the post–Cold War era sparked governmental interest in enhancing conventional weapons control, it also led to a refocusing by several nongovernmental advocacy groups on this issue. Particularly in the United Kingdom, a small number of nongovernmental arms control groups and advocates developed an early commitment to work toward greater transparency and accountability regarding European arms exports. A focal point for their activities was the idea of an EU code of conduct on arms exports that arose out of discussions among nongovernmental policy experts in 1991 and 1992.[31] The code of conduct was to build on the Luxembourg and Lisbon criteria, but, apart from seeking to strengthen the formulation of the criteria, the model code went further in two important respects. The first was that this code would include enhanced information exchanges among member states on the exports they granted or denied. This meant that a state denying an arms export would inform all other member states about this denial. States would agree to not use such information for their own commercial advantage, but would consult the state that previously denied the license should they wish to grant an essentially identical transaction. This would foster continuous debate and consensus among member states on how they interpreted common export criteria.

The second element was the obligation of member states to submit national annual reports on their arms exports to the EU Council, which would draw up an annual consolidated report in turn. As explained by one of the nongovernmental experts behind the idea of an EU code, one of the main weaknesses in European arms control was the lack of transparency. The envisioned reporting mechanism under the proposed code would challenge the secrecy surrounding the arms trade. Once adopted, nongovernmental advocacy could first be directed at making the annual consolidated report of the EU publicly available. Moreover, as states would be committed to drawing up annual national reports, advocacy could then be directed toward the publication of these national reports. This would allow domestic political constituencies to measure the export record of their governments against their commitment under the code. In other words, the consolidated report would establish an important dynamic element toward greater transparency.[32]

A key nongovernmental player behind this idea of an EU code was the London-based, independent foreign affairs think tank Saferworld, which together with partner organizations and international lawyers drew up a model for such a code. The model code was officially launched in May 1995. Saferworld and its partners subsequently engaged in a series of advocacy efforts that included awareness raising measures such as press conferences in several European countries and the collection of signatures among the public. Advocacy efforts also led to growing support for the idea of a code among key members of national parliaments and the European Parliament that passed several resolutions calling on EU member states to strengthen common arms export controls.[33]

There were also an increasing number of NGOs that began to join the call for an EU code in the United Kingdom and in other European countries. Within several months of the launch of the initiative, a network of over 600 European NGOs had emerged that endorsed the campaign.[34] This growth of the advocacy network was greatly facilitated by the circumstance that the adverse consequences of arms proliferation mobilized organizations and constituencies that had no previous history in arms control advocacy. The broad thematic and geographic spread of network members further meant a considerable increase in specialized knowledge about specific aspects of the arms trade, of the various national regulations and practices on arms control policies, as well as the political environment in which these policies are formulated.[35] The support for the code initiative by large organizations such as OXFAM, Amnesty International, or Save the Children was of particular benefit because these organizations have national offices in various European countries, and could therefore mobilize constituencies to which the British NGOs that originally proposed the code had no access. By joining resources, NGOs could consequently significantly enhance the spread and potential impact of their advocacy work.

Importantly, Saferworld and partner organizations also approached governments directly on the need for greater European arms control regulations. The aim was to identify sympathetic and potentially sympathetic governments and to foster consensus among them so as to enhance their position on joint policy objectives. Thus, by building consensus, these governments would be on stronger grounds from which to rally other governments around their cause. The key advocacy tool in this regard was the organization of seminars to bring together senior civil servants and other key policy makers from sympathetic countries to discuss the need for a common European policy on arms export controls. These seminars included the COARM representatives of Germany, the Netherlands, Sweden, Belgium, and Ireland, that is, countries that had all expressed their sympathy for restrictive common arms export policies.

These seminars certainly did not lead to an immediate support by these governments for the idea of a code. Indeed, the code was often greeted with skepticism because even certain sympathetic governments initially judged its objectives as too ambitious. However, the seminars provided for the first time an open space for informal discussions between not only governments and nongovernmental advocacy actors, but also between governments that shared common interests regarding arms export controls. In the view of one participating nongovernmental expert, the importance of these informal meetings was that "it allowed for 'open' thinking—rather than trotting out government positions."[36] Ideas and arguments could, therefore, be developed much more easily than was the case within the consensus-bound forum of COARM itself, where policy initiatives were easily blocked by governments that did not wish to change the status quo.[37]

Direct contact with government officials also allowed policy advocates to gain a better picture of governmental thinking and positions on arms export controls, and to voice the interests of their constituencies. In turn, government officials could benefit through the provision by policy advocates of technical knowledge and in-depth understanding of aspects of the policy issue under discussion.[38] In addition, cooperation with nongovernmental actors allowed sympathetic governments to enlist transnational support for their own positions. This was evidenced in 1996, when the Dutch government, in preparation for its upcoming EU presidency, informally launched the idea of an EU program to address light weapons trafficking. Being well connected with arms control and peace groups, the Dutch government could thereby affirm that it would have domestic and transnational support for its proposal.[39] This strengthened the position of the government in its claim that its proposal enjoyed broad public support throughout Europe. However, despite this emerging policy coalition between certain governments and between these and nongovernmental advocates as well as the resultant momentum toward an EU *Code on Arms Exports*, it was far from certain that the opposition of particularly the French and British governments to greater cooperation could be overcome. It was only in 1997 that several developments took place that opened the way for progress toward the envisioned code.

As mentioned, since the mid-1990s, there was growing international awareness about the serious problems caused by illicit arms trafficking and SALW proliferation. Drawing on this momentum, the Dutch government tabled a proposal for a joint program to address the issue of SALW proliferation during its presidency of the European Union in early 1997. Initially, there was considerable political opposition stemming from the fact that addressing SALW proliferation requires greater restraint and controls of the legal trade in these weapons. In turn, this would require limitations on national flexibility regarding arms export decisions. As one observer argued, several states were "reluctant to agree to a programme which explicitly focused on restraining legal as well as illicit arms accumulations and transfers."[40] As a compromise solution the Dutch government focused on a program for preventing only illicit arms flows. While having a restricted focus, the proposed program would initiate a process of regular practical cooperation of law enforcement agencies, governments, and EU bodies. Moreover, it would regularly bring up the issue of conventional arms control on the agenda of the EU Council. It would thereby promote political momentum toward greater cooperative efforts to combat arms trafficking.[41] The adoption of the *EU Programme for Combating Illicit Arms Trafficking* in 1997 was therefore an important step toward strengthened multilateral arms control.

A second major development occurred with the British general elections in May 1997 that brought to power the Labour Party. While in opposition, key members of the Labour Party, including shadow foreign minister Robin Cook, had become vocal supporters of greater arms control on both national and multilateral levels. Of particular relevance here had been the recent publication of the findings of the Scott Inquiry that had been set up in 1992 after the collapse of trials of a British company for alleged illegal exports to Iraq during the 1980s. The *Scott Report* had the effect of "sharply focus[ing] the attention of politicians and the public alike on the urgent need to reform British arms export controls."[42]

Once in power, the new Labour government announced an "ethical foreign policy" as the basis of British foreign affairs that included the adoption of new political guidelines for British arms exports. These guidelines took on board several, but certainly not all, of the recommendations by British nongovernmental advocates.[43] Importantly, the new "ethical foreign policy" also included a commitment to work toward an EU code of conduct on arms exports. This represented a significant shift from the position of the previous Conservative government and its opposition to a strengthening of multilateral cooperation on arms policies. This shift also meant a decisive change in the constellation of national interests at the European level because France was becoming isolated among the three largest member states in its opposition to tighter controls. Specifically, the previously existing tacit consensus between France and the United Kingdom to keep legal arms transfers largely off the EU agenda was undermined.[44]

It was against this background that the United Kingdom took over the EU presidency in January 1998. This presented a valuable opportunity for the U.K. government to take on a leadership role on multilateral arms control by promoting a common code on arms exports. Moreover, the chances for the success of a policy initiative seemed favorable. The U.K. government could be certain to have the support of the coalition of like-minded governments that already for years had called for a strengthening of existing common arms control policies. Strategically, the U.K. presidency approached France at an early stage so as to ensure at least the tacit consent of the state that could be expected to be most important source of opposition. It led to the tabling of a joint British–French draft of a code of conduct that was negotiated during COARM meetings in the followings months.[45] While these negotiations took place behind closed doors, drafts of the text drawn up by COARM were regularly leaked to nongovernmental policy advocates. This allowed advocates to closely follow the discussions as well as to submit to and lobby their national governments for specific policy elements that should be included. Indeed, public criticism of Saferworld of the text proposed by the U.K. government led to the complaint of the British Foreign and Commonwealth Office that Saferworld was undermining the government's position both at home and on the EU level.[46]

More importantly though, the adoption of an EU code depended on the emergence of consensus between governments as to which specific policy elements should be included. Differences of views existed in particular between states such as Sweden, Belgium, Ireland, and the Netherlands on the one hand, and France on the other. Among others, views differed on the formulation of the human rights criterion that would be part of the code. While the former governments favored general restraint in exports to serious human rights violators, France argued for a formulation that left greater room for national interpretation. France also opposed a publicly accessible EU consolidated report on arms exports, and therefore greater public transparency. In the end, consensus could only be reached through several compromises. As explained by a Dutch official: "[a]s consensus was required from all 15 member states, France was in a very strong position. It was felt that it was important to get a code agreed even if it meant watering it down."[47] When the *EU Code of Conduct on Arms Exports* was eventually adopted in June 1998, several of the criteria fell short of what certain governments and nongovernmental advocates had hoped for. Significantly, however, the EU Code did include a mechanism for information exchanges between governments and an obligation of member states to submit annual national reports to the EU Council. Two of the main objectives of nongovernmental advocates thereby became an integral part of the new EU arms control regime.

Nongovernmental advocacy on arms brokering controls. If the adoption of the EU Code represented a victory for nongovernmental advocacy, several specific policy aims remained unfulfilled. One of these was the stipulation of controls on arms brokers, who are the middlemen who arrange for or otherwise facilitate arms transfers between buyers and sellers. As transferred weapons in brokered deals do not necessarily originate from the country in which the broker operates, national arms export laws usually do not apply. This weakness has been ruthlessly exploited by unscrupulous brokers for the illicit transfer of particularly SALW to embargoed governments and armed forces without the risk of legal punishment in the country where they operate.[48] Nongovernmental policy advocates consequently argued for the inclusion of brokering controls in the EU Code. However, by 1998, only Germany, Sweden, and the Netherlands had relevant national regulations in place. In contrast, the remaining 12 EU member states considered arms brokering as a peripheral problem and opposed the adoption of controls.

This situation only began to change from 1999 onwards with the publication of several investigative research reports both by nongovernmental policy experts and groups of governmental experts that had been convened within the UN to investigate violations of arms embargoes in relation to, for example, the armed conflict in Angola.[49] These reports provided credible evidence that the combat against illicit arms trafficking urgently required the establishment of national and multilateral controls on arms brokers. Against this background emerged a growing willingness among certain governments to close the loopholes of lacking controls on arms brokering in their national legislation. By 2001 relevant amendments in national regulations had been undertaken in Austria. France, Finland, and Belgium followed suit in 2002 and 2003, while several other EU member states were in the process of formulating relevant amendments to their national regulations.[50] These developments on national levels were complemented by the emergence of certain governments as champions of brokering controls on a multilateral level. This led to the adoption of the already mentioned *EU Guidelines on Arms Brokering* under the Swedish EU presidency in 2001. The guidelines, however, merely recommended to

EU member states to adopt brokering controls and left it up to national governments to decide whether they to do so or not.[51]

While nongovernmental policy advocates welcomed the adoption of the EU guidelines as a useful first step, they strongly argued that brokering controls had to be agreed on high common standards in all EU member states in order to be efficient. This argument was also increasingly promoted by those EU member states that already had brokering controls in place or were in the process of formulating national brokering controls. Significantly, it led to a growing momentum among EU member states to work toward the establishment of common controls in all EU member states so as to avoid that a lack of controls in one country would undermine existing controls in other countries. Governments sympathetic to the aim of common controls on brokering subsequently informed nongovernmental policy advocates in 2002 that COARM would negotiate a relevant instrument over the following months. Based on the information thus provided, a network of European NGOs[52] engaged in two coordinated letter-writing campaigns to their respective COARM representatives. These letters urged governments to adopt comprehensive brokering controls and were sent to coincide with the COARM meetings in February and May 2003.[53] Interesting to note here is that, in contrast to negotiations on the *EU Code on Arms Exports*, governments did not leak draft texts of the negotiated *Common Position on Arms Brokering*. Nevertheless, COARM representatives were willing to answer questions by nongovernmental policy advocates about the feasibility of having certain specific policy elements included in the Common Position.[54]

Negotiations within COARM again showed considerable differences among EU member states regarding their preferred policy choices. While there was agreement that cooperation on brokering controls was desirable, governments disagreed on several of the specific policy elements that should be included in the Common Position. One issue was the adoption of controls on activities of European arms brokers operating from abroad. Such extraterritorial controls were favored among others by Belgium, Sweden, and Finland, all countries that already had or planned to have extraterritorial controls in their national legislation. Other countries, however, opposed such controls. This was partly based on concerns that such controls would lead to unjustifiable administrative burdens for national licensing bodies and the defense industry, and that the enforcement of such controls is notoriously difficult.[55] Another issue of disagreement was that of imposing a registration obligation for arms brokers. This was favored by France and Belgium, for instance, both of which require that everyone wishing to engage in the trade in military materials, including brokers, require a prior authorization by the state. Many other governments, however, opposed such a requirement, again partly based on concern about administrative burdens and partly because it contradicted national practices.[56]

Despite such disagreements, governments eventually succeeded in finding a compromise for the adoption of the *EU Common Position on Arms Brokering* in June 2003. All EU member states are now obliged to license brokering activities taking place on their territory and to assess license applications against the criteria of the *EU Code of Conduct on Arms Exports*. In contrast, extraterritorial controls on arms brokering and a registration requirement for brokers are only recommended. Governments are, therefore, free to choose whether to adopt such controls or not. Insofar as nongovernmental advocacy on brokering controls is concerned, the adoption of this Common Position certainly represents a further victory. Thus, nongovernmental policy advocates had argued for more than five years that controls on arms brokering are an essential element in the combat against illicit arms trafficking. While it would be wrong to assume that nongovernmental advocacy forced governments into adopting brokering controls, it certainly ensured that governments took note of the issue. It would also seem that nongovernmental advocacy encouraged certain governments that might otherwise not have done so to speak out in favor of brokering controls on high common standards at the EU level.[57]

Impact and Limits of Nongovernmental Advocacy

As demonstrated above, nongovernmental advocacy groups have gained an unprecedented level of access to governmental policy-making on conventional arms control in Europe over the last decade. This is evidenced by the now regularly organized seminars between government representatives and nongovernmental groups to discuss ways of enhancing the effectiveness of the European arms control regime or the frequent willingness in many EU member states to consult nongovernmental policy advocates on policy changes on a national level. Such increased participation by nongovernmental advocates in governmental policy debates on arms control clearly testifies to a change in governmental perception. By now, it would seem that governments are not only willing to listen to concerns and ideas of nongovernmental policy advocates, but are considering such advocacy as a valuable contribution to defining feasible ways of strengthening arms control measures. If this shows that there has been a change in relations between governments and nongovernmental advocates in the field of conventional arms control, what has been the impact of nongovernmental advocacy on the development of the European arms regime?

Impact of nongovernmental advocacy. One particular nongovernmental contribution to this regime has certainly been in the field of awareness raising among governments and the public on the need for greater governmental cooperation on arms control, but also on specific issues such as SALW proliferation, illicit arms trafficking, and arms brokering controls. By finding allies in governments sympathetic to the aims of nongovernmental advocacy, this advocacy could significantly contribute to setting governmental policy agendas on both national and multilateral levels. Such developments were not necessarily straightforward. For example, nongovernmental advocacy had failed to generate sufficient governmental support to address arms brokering in 1998 under the *EU Code of Conduct on Arms Exports*. Rather, it took several more years before a critical mass of governmental support emerged for the aim to establish common controls on the level of the European Union. Nevertheless, it would seem justified to say that without the continuous lobbying efforts of nongovernmental groups, governments that supported the aim of adopting enhanced controls on the EU level would have faced considerably more opposition by those governments that viewed such controls as unnecessary.

Apart from this often-acknowledged role of nongovernmental groups in agenda setting, these groups had an important role as catalysts for the emergence of governmental policy coalitions. The seminars and round tables that nongovernmental policy experts organized with sympathetic governments from the mid-1990s onward would seem to have made a substantial contribution to facilitating the identification of shared aims between these governments and their subsequent willingness to jointly pursue these aims at the EU level. Moreover, with respect to the campaign on a European code of conduct, NGOs were critical in preparing the ground for the initiative of the new Labour government during its presidency of the European Union in 1998. By finding allies among front bench opposition members, the liaising of NGOs and Labour officials allowed for the establishment of a developed policy project on a code if Labour were to win the U.K. general elections. One involved nongovernmental expert thus argued that the work that had already been done in formulating a policy project "meant that when the new government came to power, it was in a position to move quickly with a clear agenda. If the plan hadn't existed, I don't think it would have tabled the Code during the British EU presidency."[58]

In addition, the early involvement of nongovernmental policy advocates in the project to establish an EU code on arms exports allowed these advocates to successfully convince governments that further governmental cooperation needed to be based on dynamic processes. This strategic vision has found its expression in the mechanism for information exchanges under the EU Code, as well as the obligation to draw up annual national reports on arms exports to be submitted to the EU Council. Further, the aim of advocates to use the reporting requirement as a first step to dismantle the secrecy surrounding arms exports is increasingly realized. Following an initiative of the Finnish government during its presidency of the European Union in 1999, the consolidated report on arms exports under the *EU Code of Conduct* has been made publicly available. This has sent an important signal to those EU member states that had never published data on national arms exports. By 2003, 12 out of the 15 EU member states were publishing their national reports. In turn, this has led to the regular debates nongovernmental advocates had hoped for in national parliaments and the European Parliament on the arms export policies of EU member states.

In sum, the European regime on conventional weapons control would not seem likely to have emerged in its present form in the absence of nongovernmental advocacy efforts. However, does this assertion qualify the claim that there has been a shift in policy authority in arms control toward nongovernmental policy advocacy and, therefore, toward a governance of European arms control policies? To answer this question, a closer look at the limits of nongovernmental advocacy is necessary.

Limits to nongovernmental advocacy. If nongovernmental advocacy has succeeded in contributing to the shaping of the current European regime on arms control, nongovernmental arms control advocates and campaigners have failed to generate sufficient political momentum on several specific policy aspects. One issue already mentioned is the adoption of a stringent and restrictive human rights criterion in the *EU Code of Conduct on Arms Exports* that was favored by certain governments and nongovernmental policy advocates. Nongovernmental advocates and sympathetic governments are also strongly arguing, albeit unsuccessfully, for the establishment of multilateral information exchanges under the Code. This would entail that, if an EU member state wishes to authorize an arms export that has previously been denied by another member state, the state wishing to export would not only consult with the one state that denied the export, but with all member states. Such a change from the currently existing bilateral consultation mechanism to a multilateral mechanism would considerably further the emergence of common interpretations and application of the EU export criteria. It would regularly lead to discussions among all EU member states regarding the destinations to which arms exports should not be authorized. However, despite support for such multilateral consultation by the Netherlands,[59] for instance, there is an evident lack of interest among other EU member states to change the present consultation mechanisms.

A further issue on which nongovernmental advocacy has failed so far is the change of the status of the EU Code from its present form as a political declaration into a legally binding document that would oblige EU member states to integrate the Code export criteria as minimal standards into their national laws. Such a change is supported among others by Germany, which argues that its national arms export laws already are more restrictive than the criteria stipulated in the EU Code.[60] However, there is clear opposition to such a move by various other governments. Likewise, there is very scant support among European governments for the calls of nongovernmental advocates for greater parliamentary scrutiny on arms exports. This would entail that national parliaments receive a notification by their government prior to the authorization of arms exports to sensitive destinations with a request to parliament for an advisory opinion on the expediency of the proposed export. Apart from Sweden, which is the only EU member state to operate such a system, there are no governments that are willing to establish such prior parliamentary notification.

These failures to achieve change of specific policy elements demonstrate that, even when nongovernmental advocates find allies in sympathetic governments for policy changes, this is far from saying that this will lead to the envisioned changes. In addition, there are many issues on which nongovernmental advocacy has failed to even find allies among governments. One of these is the establishment of strict controls or a ban on authorizations to produce European weapons systems under license in foreign countries. Another is strict controls on reexportations of weapons originally exported by an EU member state.[61] While certain EU member states have adopted relevant national regulations, there has not emerged any government as a champion for promoting policy change on these issues on the EU level so far. Another issue is the control of brokering-related activities. Nongovernmental advocates are adamant that if illicit arms trafficking is to be effectively prevented, governments must not only establish controls on those who bring together buyers and sellers in arms transfers, but also on those who organize related activities such as transportation and financing these transfers.[62] However, nongovernmental advocacy not only failed to mobilize a governmental coalition to push for such policy change on the EU level, but also to convince individual EU member states to adopt comprehensive controls on brokering-related activities on a national level.

In short, the existence of nongovernmental advocacy by itself or even if coupled with support by sympathetic governments, is clearly not sufficient to achieve policy change. This is particularly so where specific policy elements are concerned rather that the general acceptance of the need for controls in certain areas of the arms trade.

Conclusion

This chapter sought to critically assess the role of nongovernmental advocacy in the emergence of the current European arms control regime and to investigate whether this role provides evidence for the claim of a move toward a governance of arms control policies. After highlighting the increasing prominence of nongovernmental advocacy on arms control and the emergence of "new" security issues such as SALW control, the chapter traced the evolution in Europe from governmental coordination on arms control toward greater cooperation. It argued that this development was essentially driven by the efforts of policy coalitions between certain governments. The emergence of such coalitions was significantly facilitated and fostered by nongovernmental advocates. Moreover, nongovernmental advocacy was critical to mobilizing political support for the adoption of the *EU Code of Conduct on Arms Exports*. The close cooperation with sympathetic governments also allowed nongovernmental advocates to make important contributions to the shaping of the regime by convincing governments of the desirability of having information exchanges and annual reporting mechanisms included in the EU Code. Further, nongovernmental advocacy successfully encouraged governments to address such arms control issues as brokering controls and to establish common controls on the EU level. Nongovernmental advocacy, therefore, certainly made a substantial contribution to the emergence of the European arms regime.

However, the failure of nongovernmental advocates in coalition with sympathetic governments to achieve policy changes on specific policy elements, or to even foster the emergence of governmental policy coalitions on certain other policy elements, clearly demonstrates that there are limits to nongovernmental advocacy. In short, albeit nongovernmental advocacy played a significant role as a driving motor for policy change and made important contributions to shaping new policies, it did not achieve changes on specific policies in the absence of governmental support. It is on these grounds that arguments concerning a shift in policy-making authority toward nongovernmental advocates and, therewith, toward a governance of arms control policies find their limits.

Notes

1. Don Hubert, *The Landmine Ban: A Case Study in Humanitarian Advocacy*, Occasional Paper 42 (Providence, RI Thomas J. Watson Jr. Institute for International Studies, 2000), 1–3.

2. Peter Haas, "Introduction: Epistemic Communities and International Policy Coordination," *International Organization* 46, no. 1 (1992): 1–35, 3.

3. Thomas Risse-Kappen, *Cooperation among Democracies: The European Influence on U.S. Foreign Policy* (Princeton, NJ: Princeton University Press, 1995).

4. Emanuel Adler, "The Emergence of Cooperation: National Epistemic Communities and the International Evolution of the Idea of Nuclear Arms Control," *International Organization* 46, no. 1 (1992): 101–45.

5. Matthew Evangelista, *Unarmed Forces: The Transnational Movement to End the Cold War* (Ithaca, NY: Cornell University Press, 1999); Jeffrey Checkel, *Ideas and International Political Change: Soviet/Russian Behavior and the End of the Cold War* (New Haven, CT: Yale University Press, 1997).

6. Margaret Keck and Kathryn Sikkink, *Activists beyond Borders—Advocacy Networks in International Politics* (Ithaca, NY: Cornell University Press, 1998).

7. Ilhan Berkol, *La Conférence des Nations Unies de Juillet 2001 sur les Armes Légères: Analyse du Processus et de ses Résultats*, Rapport 2001/4 (Brussels: Groupe de Recherche et Information sur la Paix et la Sécurité, 2001). For further information on IANSA and its role in the field of SALW control see http://www.iansa.org.

8. For further information on the small arms issue see, e.g., IANSA and Small Arms Survey, http://www.smallarmssurvey.org.

9. UN, *Supplement to an Agenda for Peace: Position Paper of the Secretary-General on the Occasion of the Fiftieth Anniversary of the UN*, A/50/60 (New York: UN, 1995).

10. See Small Arms Survey for copies of these documents.

11. UN, *Protocol against the Illicit Manufacturing of and Trafficking in Firearms, Their Parts and Components and Ammunition, supplementing the UN Convention against Transnational Organized Crime*, A/RES/55/255 (New York: UN, 2001).

12. UN, *Programme of Action to Prevent, Combat and Eradicate the Illicit Trade in Small Arms and Light Weapons in All Its Aspects*, A/CONF.192/15 (New York: UN, 2001).

13. Owen Greene, "Examining International Responses to Illicit Arms Trafficking," *Crime, Law & Social Change* 33, no. 2 (2000): 151–90.

14. Björn Hagelin, Pieter Wezeman, Siemon Wezeman, and Nicholas Chipperfield, "The Volume of Transfers of Major Conventional Weapons: By Recipients and Suppliers, 1998–2002," in *SIPRI Yearbook 2002: Armaments, Disarmament and International Security* (Oxford: Oxford University Press, 2003), 470.

15. Small Arms Survey, *Small Arms Survey 2002: Counting the Human Cost* (Oxford: Oxford University Press, 2002), 20.

16. European Union Council, *European Union Code of Conduct on Arms Exports*, 8675/2/98 (Brussels: European Communities, 1998).

17. European Union Council, *Third Annual Report According to Operative Provision 8 of the European Union Code of Conduct on Arms Exports*, 13657/01 (Brussels: European Communities, 2001).

18. Ian Davis, *The Regulation of Arms and Dual-Use Exports by EU Member States: A Comparative Analysis of Germany, Sweden and the UK* (Ph.D. dissertation, University of Bradford, U.K., 1999).

19. Saferworld, *Regulating Arms Exports: A Programme for the European Community* (London: Saferworld, 1991), 12.

20. Legge 09/07/1990 n° 185 Nuove norme sul controllo dell'esportazione, importazione e transito dei materiali di armamento. [Law 09/07/1990 n° 185 New norms for the control of the export, import, and transit of armaments.]

21. Loi du 5 août 1991 relative à l'importation, à l'exportation et au transit et à la lutte contre le trafic d'armes, de munitions et de matériel devant servir spécialement à un usage militaire et de la technologie y afférente. [Law of August 5, 1991 concerning the

import, export, and transit and the fight against trafficking of arms, munitions, and materials intended specially for military use and of related technology.]

22. Military Equipment Act of 1992.

23. BASIC, Saferworld, and World Development Movement, *A European Code of Conduct on the Arms Trade*, Pamphlet (London: BASIC, Saferworld, and WDM, undated), 1.

24. Davis, *The Regulation of Arms and Dual-Use Exports by EU Member States*, 156.

25. Brian Wood and Johan Peleman, *The Arms Fixers: Controlling the Brokers and Shipping Agents*, Report 3/99 (Oslo: International Peace Research Institute, 1999).

26. European Communities, "Council Common Position 2003/468/CFSP of 23 June 2003 on the Control of Arms Brokering," *Official Journal of the European Union* L 156 (2003): 79–80.

27. Saferworld, *Arms and Dual-Use Exports from the EC* (London: Saferworld, 1992), 5.

28. Bernard Adam, *Union européenne et exportations d'armes* (Brussels: Groupe de Recherche et Information sur la Paix et la Sécurité, 1995), 87.

29. Kriegswaffenkontrollgesetz vom 20. April 1961.

30. This was not merely for altruistic reasons related to concerns about negative consequences of irresponsible arms transfers, but also to ensure a "level playing ground" for domestic defense companies. These rightly argued that they lost out on export contracts that were simply snatched up by defense companies in other European countries with less stringent national arms export criteria (Undisclosed interviewee, 2004).

31. Davis, *The Regulation of Arms and Dual-Use Exports by EU Member States*, 98.

32. Paul Eavis, Saferworld (interview, London, December 5, 2002).

33. For example, European Communities, "Resolution on the Need for European Controls on the Export or Transfer of Arms," *Official Journal of the European Communities* C 043 (1995): 89–90; European Communities, "Resolution on a European Code of Conduct on the Export of Arms," *Official Journal of the European Communities* C 34 (1998): 163–64.

34. Saferworld, *Update*, Autumn 1995 (London: Saferworld, 1995), 3.

35. Eavis, interview.

36. Ibid.

37. Alberto Estévez, Arias Foundation—Europe (interview, Paris, February 12, 2003).

38. Eavis, interview; Owen Greene, University of Bradford (interview, Bradford, U.K., December 2, 2002).

39. Greene, interview.

40. Greene, "Examining International Responses to Illicit Arms Trafficking," 171.

41. Ibid.

42. Saferworld, *Update*, Spring 1996 (London: Saferworld, 1996), 7.

43. Saferworld, *Update*, Autumn 1997 (London: Saferworld, 1997), 1.

44. The French general elections had brought to power the Socialist party in June 1997 and the new French prime minister indicated his interest in working together with the United Kingdom to bring about an improvement of European common arms export controls. See Saferworld, *Update*, Autumn 1997, 2. Nevertheless, until late 1997, other members of the French government seemed to remain hostile to the idea of an EU code. See Ian Davis, *The Regulation of Arms and Dual-Use Exports: Germany, Sweden and the UK* (Oxford: Oxford University Press, 2002), 101.

45. Davis, *The Regulation of Arms and Dual-Use Exports by EU Member States*, 170.

46. Eavis, interview.

47. Quoted in Geraldine O'Callaghan, *EU Pays High Price for French Support on Code of Conduct*, Report No. 64 (London: British American Security Information Council, 1998).

48. Wood and Peleman, *The Arms Fixers*.
49. For example, ibid.; UN. *Report of the Panel of Experts on Violations of Security Council Sanctions Against UNITA*, S/2000/203 (New York: UN, 2000).
50. Holger Anders, *Controlling Arms Brokering: Next Steps for EU Member States*, Rapport Hors-série 2004/1 (Brussels: Groupe de Recherche et Information sur la Paix et la Sécurité, 2004), 21–23.
51. European Union Council, *Third Annual Report According to Operative Provision 8 of the European Union Code of Conduct on Arms Exports*, 13657/01 (Brussels: European Communities, 2001), 6–7.
52. This network emerged within the framework of the European Arms Campaign. This campaign ran from late 2002 until mid-2003 and brought together NGOs and NGO networks from some seven EU member states in a joint advocacy effort for strengthened EU arms export controls. See Agir Ici, *Surveillons les ventes d'armes, sauvons des vies!* (Paris: Agir Ici, 2003).
53. Henry Smith, Saferworld (interview, Dublin, December 13, 2003).
54. Undisclosed interviewee 2003.
55. Holger Anders, "Braking Arms Brokering: New EU Rules Agreed," *European Security Review*, no. 19 (Brussels: International Security Information Service-Europe, 2003), 7–8.
56. Ibid.
57. Smith, interview.
58. Eavis, interview.
59. Government of the Netherlands, *The Coalition Agreement: New Accents in the Arms Export Policy* (Den Haag: Ministry of Economic Affairs, 1998), 2.
60. Undisclosed interviewee 2003.
61. Holger Anders, *Combating Small Arms & Light Weapons Proliferation: Scope for Action by the EU*, Briefing Paper No. 28 (Brussels: International Security Information Service-Europe, June 2003), 5–6.
62. Ibid., 6–7.

Part VI

Conclusion

Chapter 10

New Threats and New Actors in Security Governance: Developments, Problems, and Solutions

Elke Krahmann

Two key developments have been central to international security in the post–Cold War era: the emergence of new threats such as ethnic wars, terrorism, transnational crime, HIV/AIDS, and small arms, and the proliferation of non-state actors such as nongovernmental organizations (NGOs) transnational corporations, private security companies, and international regimes, in the provision of human, national, and international security. This volume has aimed to explore the relationship between these two trends. In particular, it has raised a number of questions, such as: What is the nature of these "new" security threats? To what degree are states unwilling or unable to address them? Are non-state actors more suited to dealing with nontraditional security threats? Finally, what are the advantages and what are the problems associated with the growing role of private actors in the making and implementation of security policy?

In addition, this volume has attempted to understand the changing relationships among state and non-state actors in security. Are states loosing their "monopoly" on the legitimate provision of security, or are states merely using non-state actors for their own purposes? To what extent are NGOs and private companies independent security actors? To what degree are non-state actors able to influence governments?

Both sets of questions point to a fundamental transformation of security policy-making in the new millennium. States remain a key focus in international security. However, neither are interstate wars the predominant security concern of our times nor is security provision limited to the policies and actions of governments. Security studies should reflect these changes, and this volume has attempted to make a contribution to this aim.

The purpose of this conclusion is to integrate the findings presented in the preceding chapters and to provide some answers to the questions raised above.

In addition, it seeks to position these answers within the theoretical context of the shift from "government" to "governance" outlined in the introduction to this volume. In particular, the following suggests that the evidence and conclusions presented in the preceding chapters can be understood in relation to three concepts: the emergence of "security governance"; the problems or "governance failures" that can arise from it; and the role that standards of "good governance" can play in resolving these failures.

To achieve these aims this chapter is structured in three parts. The first part examines the relationship between the rise of non-state threats and actors, and new forms of networked coordination in security governance. It also turns to the important question of the utility of non-state actors and the changing role of the state from a direct security provider to an enabler and employer. The second part summarizes and seeks to explain the problems and governance failures that can emerge as the result of these new structures, including the challenges of transnational terrorist, criminal, and small arms networks to sovereignty-bound nation-states, the lack of accountability among non-state actors, and the difficulties of public–private cooperation in security governance. Finally, the third part discusses how the notion of "good governance" can help address these problems and contribute to improving contemporary security governance.

Between Government and Governance

The introduction to this volume has suggested that the growing contribution of private actors such as NGOs, transnational corporations, and private security firms to global security can be theoretically conceptualized as a shift from government to security governance.[1] Within this framework government and governance are viewed as ideal types at opposite ends of a continuum ranging from centralized to fragmented political coordination in seven dimensions: geography, function, distribution of resources, interests, norms, decision making, and policy implementation.

The findings presented in the preceding chapters appear to confirm this shift. However, they suggest that the transformation from government to governance is neither complete nor uniform across these seven dimensions. States retain a, if not the most, central position in security governance. States shape the geographical scope of security regimes. They delegate specific tasks to non-state actors, while preserving what they consider to be "core" functions. States fund NGOs and employ private military companies and assert their interests vis-à-vis advocacy NGOs. State actors promote neoliberal norms such as privatization and marketization, and states continue to dominate decision making in multilateral organizations. Finally, the state is the single actor capable of implementing international interventions such as in postwar Iraq that involves 130,000 military personnel and a budget of 4 billion U.S. dollars per month.

Yet, as most of the contributors to this volume have argued, it is also, or specifically, because of the central role of states and their actions that non-state actors are posing new threats and becoming important contributors to security. Thus,

Michael Kenney illustrates in chapter 4 on terrorism and transnational drug trafficking that state strategies to combat these threats have facilitated the development of fragmented, decentralized criminal networks as a response. In chapter 6, Stefan Elbe suggests that states' delayed identification of HIV/AIDS as a national and international security threat may have contributed to the spread of the epidemic. Mike Bourne (in chapter 8) even points to the collaboration of corrupt state officials in and conduciveness of some states' regulations to the contemporary proliferation of small arms and light weapons (SALW). In sum, public policies have directly and indirectly played a role in the emergence of contemporary transnational security threats, either because states have failed to develop suitable responses or because their actions have encouraged adaptations that are designed to escape the authority and reach of the state.

States have also been key agents in promoting the rise of non-state actors as new security providers. Driven by the neoliberal New Policy Agenda that proposed the reduction of state bureaucracy, market reforms, and privatization in order to increase cost-effectiveness and efficiency, states have delegated security functions to NGOs and private companies. In chapter 2 on NGOs in peacebuilding, Loramy Conradi Gerstbauer thus concludes that states find NGOs useful actors in security governance because of their reputation for political neutrality, their expertise, and their grassroots linkages. She fears that "some NGOs are in danger of becoming delivery mechanisms for governments."[2] Since many NGOs accept or are even dependent upon government funds for their operations, states can influence where and how these funds are used.

Carrie Sheehan observes a similar development with regard to HIV/AIDS in chapter 7. In 2001, she argues, 70 percent of the USAID's own budget of $284 million for the fight against HIV/AIDS, Tuberculosis, and Malaria, was distributed through NGOs.[3] Government funds are thus an important condition for NGO work in international security. The negative consequence is that increased competition among NGOs for public funding reduces their willingness to criticize donor governments. Moreover, Sheehan finds that some NGOs can be tempted to "securitize" HIV/AIDS, that is, present it as a national security threat, in order to obtain financial support.

In addition, states are increasingly seeking the help of private corporations in global security. As Christopher Spearin observes in chapter 3, states and NGOs have been hiring private military personnel for security and logistical support in international intervention such as in Afghanistan and in Iraq. Other authors, such as Robert Mandel, suggest that Western governments might even consider employing private security forces in their fights against terrorism and transnational crime.[4]

Another form of public–private cooperation is the topic of chapter 5 on targeting money laundering by Eleni Tsingou. She argues that states need to work in collaboration with private financial institutions in order to combat money laundering as part of the fight against transnational crime and terrorism. Although states can impose national and international regulations and reporting requirements, she argues, private corporate responsibility is crucial for the effective implementation and functioning of these controls.

The central contribution of states to the emergence of "dark networks"[5] among terrorists and transnational crime, and to the shift from governments to private security providers outlined by these authors, however, does not deny that non-state actors are to some extent autonomous agents with their own interests, aims, and capabilities. In particular, the chapters on non-state actors as causes of security threats illustrate how private actors can circumvent and undermine the authority of the state. Michael Kenney's analysis of terrorist and drug trafficking networks suggests that these actors constantly adapt their internal structures and operating rules in order to evade state controls.[6] Similarly, Mike Bourne observes that small arms traffickers take advantage of legal loopholes and poorly controlled areas such as international private air and sea transport. Moreover, illegal arms brokers exploit the weaknesses of a regulation and control system based on national authority by transferring SALW through several countries before they are ferried to their final destination.[7]

It follows that states' superior resources and authority are not necessarily sufficient to contain contemporary security threats. Guerilla groups, terrorists, transnational crime networks, and arms traffickers are learning the art of "asymmetrical warfare," that is, to avoid state strengths and seek out its weaknesses.[8] Instead of facing an overwhelming military enemy, they target civilians; instead of using central kingpins, they work in small independent groups; and instead of facing governmental controls, they move to offshore safe havens.

Moreover, although NGOs can receive funding from governments, private security companies can be employed by states, and financial institutions can be subject to governmental regulation, the contributions to this volume have demonstrated that non-state actors also make independent contributions to security. Furthermore, by means of their specific expertise and resources, and through formal and informal networks with officials, both NGOs and private firms are capable of influencing governments in their turn. Accordingly, Gerstbauer suggests that state funding for NGO peacebuilding is only one explanation for the proliferation of NGO operations in this area. Another is the argument that development NGOs recognized that "giving aid would be futile unless long-term conflict issues were addressed."[9] Peacebuilding thus became "a natural outflow"[10] of their development activities. Moreover, Gerstbauer finds that development NGOs that used to be service providers are moving toward advocacy and seeking to exert pressure on governments because of the political content of their peacebuilding work.

In chapter 3 on the emerging relationship between peacebuilding NGOs and private security companies, Christopher Spearin finds further evidence for this new autonomy. He observes that NGOs that are concerned about working alongside national and international military forces or want to operate in regions where states are not interested in intervening are increasingly considering employing private security personnel for their own protection. Although this gives rise to problems that will be discussed in more detail below, private protection enables NGOs to operate more independently from states in conflict management.

Concerning the fight against HIV/AIDS, Carrie Sheehan illustrates that NGOs might conform to government policies, not because of the overwhelming influence of states, but in order to use governments. Specifically, she argues that most NGOs do not view the epidemic as a national security threat, but have strategically linked the two issues in discussions with the U.S. government in order to obtain additional funding. Once these funds are secured, however, the majority of U.S.-based NGOs use them in conventional ways targeted at child health, reproductive health, and HIV/AIDS education rather than projects with armed forces in developed and developing countries.

Turning to advocacy NGOs, chapter 9 by Holger Anders on private efforts to control the proliferation of SALW demonstrates how non-state actors can also sometimes help shape government policies. Specifically, he demonstrates that European NGOs were able to organize a campaign for the construction of a *European Union Code of Conduct on Arms Exports*, including SALW. They succeeded by gaining allies among the involved European governments and by providing expertise and drafts for a code that influenced government agendas.

In sum, the empirical evidence suggests that, despite imbalances of authority and capability, state and non-state actors are increasingly locked into a system of security governance in which neither is entirely independent from the other and cooperation becomes crucial. However, since the shift from government to security governance is uneven and complex, cooperation among state and non-state actors is not unproblematic. The following section examines what kinds of challenges emerge from the studies presented in this volume.

Challenges and Problems in Security Governance

While the growing involvement of private actors in security governance can help to lower the pressures on the resources of governments, it has also been linked to a range of problems or "governance failures."[11] This section suggests that the theoretical framework for the analysis of government and governance proposed in the introduction to this volume can contribute to understanding some of them. Specifically, it suggests that governance failures can arise when a shift from government to governance in some of the identified seven dimensions—geography, function, resource distribution, interests, norms, decision making, and policy implementation—is not matched by congruent changes in the other dimensions. This can lead to two types of problems in particular: normative and structural. The first type arises when policy processes and structures are not consistent with the norms and beliefs of the actors involved, and the second emerges from a mismatch among the scope, resources, decision making, and policy implementation processes within security governance arrangements. The contributions to this volume thus identify four key governance failures: the loss of governmental control, the politicization of non-state actors, the lack of transparency and accountability among private actors, and insufficient coordination between public and private agents.

Loss of governmental control specifically refers to the challenges which transnational security threats such as terrorism pose for national security policy. These challenges were highlighted by the devastating attacks on the World Trade

Center on September 11, 2001. They also include the rise of transnational crime, the proliferation of weapons of mass destruction, and the spread of HIV/AIDS over the past decades. The transnational nature of these threats means that borders and national armed forces are increasingly unsuited for the provision of human, national, and international security. Moreover, they put into question the foundations of a security system based on the norms of national sovereignty and a state monopoly of the legitimate use of violence.

However, most governments and citizens continue to subscribe to these norms even though they might lead to ineffective policies or might no longer be accurate perceptions of contemporary security governance. This leads to a tension between existing norms and the current security environment and policies. As the contributions to this volume have illustrated, new threats such as terrorism, transnational crime, diseases, and proliferation frequently escape the full reach of the state. Transnational terrorists and criminal networks adopt structures that evade national controls; arms traffickers disguise their tracks by channeling their exports through multiple countries; and HIV/AIDS escapes detection at immigration controls by long incubation periods. At a practical level this means that governments are increasingly forced to seek collaborative solutions either with other states through multilateral institutions or with non-state actors such as NGOs, private military companies, and multinational corporations. At a normative level, it suggests that states have to accede to the pooling their sovereignty and accept the fragmentation of the legitimate provision of security.

However, the traditional norms of national autonomy and the state as key security provider persist in spite of these developments leading to a mismatch between new security policy arrangements and underlying norms. In the public mind, national governments are almost exclusively believed accountable for combating threats such as proliferation, terrorism, and transnational crime although they increasingly have to collaborate and compromise when working with other states or private security actors to address these security concerns. The result is a perception of "governance failure" as states are in incomplete control of strategies and outcomes that involve multiple agents and cross national boundaries, yet remain the actor that is held politically responsible.

Non-state actors face the opposite problem. While many private actors have perceived themselves and have been perceived as neutral, their growing involvement in security is contributing to their politicization. Thus Gerstbauer observes that in particular development NGOs that have traditionally subscribed to the norms of impartiality and independence are faced with a dilemma. On the one hand these NGOs observe a growing need for their contribution to security operations, on the other hand they find that participating in politically contentious interventions, working alongside military forces, and accepting government funding, puts their reputation of political neutrality in jeopardy and can undermine the effectiveness of their missions. In addition, Gerstbauer argues that concern about security leads some development NGOs to engage in explicit political action by turning to advocacy roles.[12]

Although Spearin suggests that NGOs can attempt to limit the dependence and need for collaboration with states and international peacekeeping forces by hiring private security firms, this only partially resolves the problem of politicization. Specifically, Spearin argues that private security companies themselves operate in a market regulated by governments and some countries, such as the United States, require licensing of contracts with public and private actors abroad. In addition, private security firms usually work for multiple employers and hire local personnel who can indirectly involve NGOs into the conflicts that they are trying to alleviate.[13]

Sheehan's analysis of NGOs in the fight against HIV/AIDS complements these findings by illustrating how some private voluntary organizations are encouraged to engage in the political strategy of "securitizing" HIV/AIDS, for example, by proposing projects directed at HIV/AIDS education in the armed forces, in order to obtain funding.[14] However, most NGOs at the same time seek to maintain their key focus on the general population. What emerges from these studies is a picture of private actors transforming into political actors as they take on state, and thus inherently political, functions. However, their own norms and the public perception of private actors will have to change accordingly—particularly with regard to public accountability.

Lack of transparency and accountability has been increasingly noted as a problem linked to private actors becoming involved in the making and implementing of security. If these actors are accepting political roles by advocating or providing security policies, democratic norms suggest that they should also be publicly and politically accountable. The shift from government to governance is challenging these expectations since the fragmentation of security policy-making contributes to the dissolution of clear lines of responsibility. While under "government" political responsibility rests with the legislative and executive, in "governance" it is distributed among a multiplicity of state and non-state actors. As these actors cooperate in the making and implementation of security policies, it is difficult to hold one single actor accountable for the outcomes of this process.

Moreover, as Gerstbauer, Spearin, Tsingou, and Anders point out, states, international organizations, NGOs, private military companies, and transnational corporations have traditionally been accountable to different audiences.[15] Governments are answerable to their electorates; international organizations to their members; NGOs to their donors and the recipients of their aid or services; and private companies to their shareholders and customers. Only the former three are primarily accountable to the general public and democratic processes.

However, the loss of transparency and accountability due to the outsourcing of security functions to NGOs, private security companies, and transnational businesses is not always unwelcome. Thus, several chapters observe that some governments take advantage of the fragmentation of security policy-making to avoid public debates over controversial international interventions. According to Gerstbauer, NGOs offer alternative channels for government influence in politically risky areas, and have been used as sources of informal diplomacy where direct involvement might be politically contentious.[16] Similarly, it has been suggested that some governments employ private security firms to intervene in regional conflicts without public scrutiny.[17]

Finally, there is the structural problem of coordination among the growing number of state and non-state actors operating in security governance.

These cooperation failures can be explained by the fragmentation of security policy-making in terms of geography, function, and resource distribution, which is not always sufficiently reflected by suitable adaptations of state-centric decision-making and implementation processes. In particular, coordination problems in security governance arise from three factors. The first is a lack of formal and informal institutional structures to ensure sufficient communication and coordination among governments, international organizations, NGOs, and private firms. Thus, Spearin observes that both states and NGOs have been slow to establish cooperative structures. According to his findings, "NGOs, for their part, have so far placed operational and organizational independence ahead of developing standardized policies that would collectively allow NGOs to have input into the uniform structuring of contemporary security governance".[18] However, states, too, have been lagging behind in the institutionalization of relations with non-state actors such as NGOs and private security companies. Tsingou agrees in her study of money laundering that financial regulators, law enforcement agencies, and the private banking sector "need to reach an improved understanding of the goals and policies of combating money laundering and engage in closer cooperation"[19] in order to be successful.

A second factor is differences in the interests of governments, NGOs, and private firms. These differences mean that congruence and compatibility in the making and implementation of security policies cannot be assumed. New structures and processes are needed to coordinate policies and to resolve disagreements. Illustrative of the divergent interests of public and private security actors is Sheehan's study of the "securitization" of HIV/AIDS and state agencies' focus on the spread of the disease among military personnel, while NGOs view the epidemic in terms of its cost for "human" security and development.[20] Gerstbauer concurs with regard to peacebuilding that "[s]tate actors have tended to define the peacebuilding enterprise with a narrower scope and time frame [than NGOs]. If the central purpose of U.S. foreign policy is to protect and promote U.S. interests, it is natural that certain conflicts will receive more attention than others and that the attention will seek to maximize marketable results."[21] Spearin further observes the differences, the goals, and concerns of NGOs, states, and private military companies in peacebuilding that range from neutrality and impartiality to cost-efficiency and profit.

Finally, coordination problems among governments, NGOs, and private companies are compounded by divergent organizational cultures. The hierarchical organizations of governmental agencies, in particular that of the military, frequently find it difficult to collaborate with the more flexible and horizontal organizational structures of NGOs or private firms. Moreover, while governmental and intergovernmental institutions primarily rely on formal channels of communication, private security actors frequently use personal and informal networks to coordinate their operations.[22] Tsingou finds that private sector money laundering measures rely on "persuasion, cooperation, [and] self-regulation," while state law enforcement agencies stress top–down policies such as "prosecution, external regulation, and public justice and punishment."[23] Observing comparative differences between states and peacebuilding NGOs, Gerstbauer fears that the increasing cooperation between state and non-state agents might "[wipe] away the very attributes for which the NGOs are praised,"[24] such as their close and informal relations with local actors.

If the incomplete and uneven transformation from government to governance in security policy-making can help explain the resulting normative and structural problems, it can also contribute to answering the question of how such governance failures might be addressed. The following examines the concept of "good governance" that has been proposed as a guiding principle for governance arrangements that include state and non-state actors at the national, transnational, and international levels.

Security and Good Governance

The concepts underlying the notion of good governance first emerged in the United States and the United Kingdom in the 1980s in the contexts of the neoliberal New Policy Agenda and New Public Management. These agendas proposed the introduction of competition, performance incentives, and internal auditing within a decentralized and customer-oriented structure in order to increase accountability, transparency, and civil-society participation in public sectors such as education, health, and transportation.[25] Redefined as "good governance," the same principles have subsequently been adopted by the World Bank and the IMF as conditions for development aid in the Third World[26] and have been applied to a growing range of policy areas. The ideals promoted by good governance aim to provide alternative norms and more appropriate political processes for sectors that are being transformed from government to governance. In particular, they offer a replacement for the state-centric model of public service provision.

However, the notion of good governance is not entirely uncontroversial. In development, World Bank policies that endorsed good governance principles, such as decentralization and privatization, have been accused of further weakening already failing states that can contribute to instability and conflict.[27] Similarly, some of the contributions to this volume suggest that competition among state and non-state actors in the provision of public services is not necessarily advantageous. NGOs that have to compete with each other for state monies are less likely to question inefficient governmental policies. And peacebuilding NGOs that bid alongside private firms for post-conflict reconstruction funds are prone to focus on more obvious material development projects, rather than underlying social and cultural issues.[28]

Nevertheless, some of the ideals underlying the concept of good governance are worth considering in relation to the findings and conclusions presented in the preceding chapters. They include the quest for the greater transparency and accountability of non-state actors in global security; the need for improved regulation and self-regulation; and the political and practical involvement of those who are immediately affected by the "new" security threats. This section examines how each of these measures can contribute to resolving the governance failures discussed above.

One of the core principles of good governance is enhancing the transparency and accountability of the state and non-state actors engaged in governance. Good governance thus aims to counter the diffusion of political authority and the possibility of "blame avoidance" that has above been identified as one problem of the shift from government to governance in security. In particular, it calls for more transparency and accountability of the private sector as non-state actors increasingly participate in the making and implementation of security policies. The argument behind these demands is the observation that private actors are becoming politicized. NGOs and private firms that are part of the policy process and implement public services are by definition not private, but political actors. However, contrary to governments, non-state actors rarely disclose information about their political operations or accept public responsibility for their actions.

The notion of good governance reflects a recognition that policy processes are changing. As the shift from government to governance involves a growing number of non-state actors in policy coordination, it suggests, that our understanding of politics itself has to adapt. Traditional forms of democratic decision-making and public policy implementation that revolve around parties, parliaments, and governments, are in need of being transformed in order to accommodate the growing role of private actors. In particular, they need to be complemented by nonelective procedures of accountability and a redrawing of the lines between the public and private spheres that has so far inhibited the public scrutiny of private firms and other non-state actors.

The concept of good governance is part of this adaptation. It suggests that NGOs and private firms should be accountable not only to their donors and shareholders, but also to the stakeholders in their operations. Moreover, good governance demands the disclosure of information that relates to public concerns. In both areas, there appears to be some progress. The contributors to this volume observe a number of instances in which the transparency and accountability of state and non-state actors has been improved by regulative and voluntary measures in security governance.

The role of governmental regulation in fostering good governance and increasing the transparency and accountability of non-state actors is illustrated by Anders' study of the *European Union Code of Conduct on Arms Exports*. In this case, European governments have tightened their controls of private arms exports and have begun publishing annual reports about the quantity and destinations of governmental arms export licenses granted to private firms.[29] Although most armaments firms continue to resist publishing crucial information about their exports and contracts themselves, these public measures represent the recognition that private arms transfers are of political concern since they contribute to maintaining or endangering contemporary security. Spearin appears to agree in chapter 3 on peacebuilding NGOs and private security companies that governments should seek to safeguard the public interest in the behavior of private security services by legal means such as regulations.[30]

However, even among private military firms there are efforts to enhance their reputation and public image by institutionalizing voluntary codes of practice where governmental regulation is lacking in order to show their commitment to public transparency and accountability. Thus, the International Peace Operations Association that includes among its members major private security companies such as Sandline International, Military Professional Resources Inc., and ArmorGroup, has published a Code of Conduct for private security operations.[31]

Gerstbauer and Spearin observe similar voluntary measures among NGOs that tend to be "self-monitoring agencies whose performance evaluation is subject to their own reporting standards." Following questions about the efficiency and accountability of NGO projects in peacebuilding and other areas, some NGO organizations have sought to develop best practices such as the "do no harm"— guidelines that seek to improve NGO responsibility toward recipients and stake-holders.[32] Another is the "Reflecting on Peace Practice" project run by Collaborative for Development Action that collects and assesses experiences from conflict-focused programs and encourages learning and good governance practices among NGOs.[33] Moreover, Spearin finds, NGO forums such as the InterAction Security Advisory Group are also attempting to set standards for NGO interaction with private security companies.

Regulation and self-regulation not only apply to transparency and accounta-bility, but also to other aspects of good governance such as safeguarding the public interest by controlling financial transfers with regard to money laundering, and limiting the export of SALW. The chapters 8 and 9 by Bourne and Anders, respec-tively illustrate that governmental licensing of arms exports remains the key mechanism through which the proliferation of small arms is contained. It is particularly in this sector that private self-regulation and self-control are still missing. Partly this appears to be due to the fact that arms producers so far lack a sense of corporate and public responsibility. In the financial sector, as Tsingou demonstrates, this sense of business responsibility is in the process of developing. Thus, she reports that banks "have adopted a series of procedures to combat money laundering and comply with regulatory requirements."[34] These voluntary procedures range from identification to monitoring, and the implementation of auditing procedures and accountability measures. Some banks have even set up their own anti-money laundering units. Moreover, a selection of major banks have set up the Wolfsberg Group of Banks that has published a private code of conduct of anti-money laundering measures for the finance sector.

In addition to increasing transparency, accountability, and the restraint of private actors, good governance endorses greater stakeholder involvement in the making and implementation of security policies. The aim of this principle is to ensure that security policies primarily serve the interests of the affected groups rather than the state and non-state actors that implement them. Moreover, stake-holder involvement favors "enabling" approaches aiming to help actors to provide, in the long term, for their own security instead of relying on international public and private interventions. By doing so, good governance indirectly addresses the problems of public–private coordination in security governance that have been outlined above. In particular, decentralized and stakeholder-focused security governance provides a common principle around which the policies of state and non-state actors can converge. It also alleviates differences of interest among public and private agents by putting those of the recipients first.

The benefits of decentralized, "customer-oriented," and participatory security governance are demonstrated in a number of chapters in this volume and involve both the making and the implementation of security policies. Projects directed at encouraging civil society participation in defining national and international security issues have traditionally included the work by advocacy NGOs that seek to influence the behavior of states, international organizations, and private firms by informing and mobilizing the general public. Chapter 9 on the role of NGOs in the creation of the *EU Code of Conduct on Arms Exports* illustrates this strategy and the increasing involvement of non-state actors in agenda setting and policy formulation. Key to the impact and success of advocacy NGOs appears to be the belief that transnational security concerns such as crime, terrorism, and infectious diseases, in spite of global effects, can best be addressed locally. Thus, Anders points out that over recent years many European countries have been pressured to accept their special responsibility for global peace and security as major arms producers and exporters.

The principles of stakeholder involvement play an even greater role in reforming the implementation of security policies, as illustrated by the fight against HIV/AIDS. Sheehan specifically highlights the positive effects of CARE's "Urban HIV/AIDS Control and Prevention Project" in Addis Ababa that seeks to reduce mother-to-child transmission of HIV/AIDS by offering support for community-based groups dealing with the epidemic. She further observes the spread of stakeholder-focused projects among other NGOs such as Catholic Relief Services that concentrates on training local volunteers in providing home care for people infected by HIV/AIDS.[35]

What these good governance principles have in common is the transformation of the norms and processes that define security policy-making. Although current notions of good governance do not address all problems that can be linked to the shift from government to governance, they help to alleviate in particular the normative concerns related to public transparency and accountability, public and private control, and "customer" satisfaction. Other issues, such as lack of coordination among state and non-state actors, still need to be integrated into good governance. In particular, formal and informal guidelines should be established that ensure sufficient consultation of and communication among all relevant public and private actors involved in security governance at the local, national, regional, and global levels.

Conclusion

This chapter has sought to summarize and analyze the findings presented in this volume within the theoretical context of the emergence of security governance. Specifically, it has argued that the fragmentation of capabilities, expertise, and functions between state and non-state actors engaged in security can be understood as the result of a shift from government to governance. As a consequence of this shift, this chapter did not observe the dissolution or weakening of the state, but its increasing collaboration and interdependence with non-state actors. Moreover, it suggested that the role of the state might be shifting from a "monopoly" security provider to that of an enabler, employer, and regulator of private actors in complex networks of security governance.

Both developments can be interpreted as a reaction to the rise of transnational security threats that stretch the resources and challenge the reach of sovereignty-bound governments. Transnational threats such as terrorism, crime, proliferation, and infectious diseases cannot be effectively fought by national armed forces. They require more differentiated and comprehensive measures that transgress national borders and incorporate capabilities and expertise from multiple sources. Moreover, transnational security threats are best addressed at the local level with the involvement of those who are directly affected.

In conclusion, the proliferation of new threats and new actors in security governance are closely connected. They are the reflection of important changes of security in the twenty-first century.

Notes

1. For an extensive discussion of this framework see Elke Krahmann, "National, Regional and Global Governance: One Phenomenon or Many?" *Global Governance* 9, no. 3 (2003): 323–46; Elke Krahmann, "Conceptualising Security Governance," *Cooperation and Conflict* 38, no. 1 (2003): 5–26.
2. Loramy Conradi Gerstbauer, chapter 2 in this volume, 23.
3. Carrie Sheehan, chapter 7 in this volume, 131.
4. Christopher Spearin, chapter 3 in this volume, 45. Robert Mandel, "Fighting Fire with Fire: Privatizing Counterterrorism," in *Defeating Terrorism*, ed. R. Howard and R. Sawyer, 62–73 (Guilford, CT: McGraw Hill, 2003).
5. Jörg Raab and H. Brinton Milward, "Dark Networks as Problems", *Journal of Public Administration and Theory* 13, no. 4 (2003): 413–39.
6. Michael Kenney, chapter 4 in this volume.
7. Mike Bourne, chapter 8 in this volume, 261.
8. For the growing literature on asymmetric warfare see for instance Colin S. Gray, "Thinking Asymmetrically in Times of Terror," *Parameters* 32, no.1 (2002): 5–14; Roger W. Barnett, *Asymmetrical Warfare: Today's Challenge to U.S. Military Power* (Dulles, VA: Brassey's, 2002); Anthony H. Cordesman, *Terrorism, Asymmetric Warfare, and Weapons of Mass Destruction; Defending the U.S. Homeland* (Westport, CT: Praeger, 2002).
9. Gerstbauer, chapter 2, 23.
10. Ibid., 23.
11. For studies which examine the problems emerging from the proliferation of NGOs and private security companies in international interventions see for instance Larry Minear, Ted van Baarda, and Marc Sommers, *NATO and Humanitarian Action in the Kosovo Crisis*, Occasional Papers (Providence, RI: The Thomas J. Watson Jr. Institute for International Studies, 2000); Alexander Cooley and James Ron, "The NGO Scramble: Organizational Insecurity and the Political Economy of Transnational Action," *International Security* 27, no. 1 (2002): 5–39. James Larry Taulbee, "Mercenaries, Private Armies and Security Companies in Contemporary Policy," *International Politics* 37, no. 4 (2000): 433–56, 436; Juan Carlos Zarate, "The Emergence of a New Dog of War: Private International Security Companies,

International Law and the New World Disorder," *Stanford Journal of International Law* 34, no. 1 (1998): 75–162, 77.

12. Gerstbauer, chapter 2,

13. Spearin, chapter 3, 45.

14. Sheehan, chapter 7, 131.

15. Gestbauer, chapter 2, 23; Spearin, chapter 3, 45; Eleni Tsingou, chapter 5, in this volume, 91; Holger Anders, chapter 9, in this volume, 177.

16. Gestbauer, chapter 2, 23.

17. See for instance Garry Cleaver, "Subcontracting Military Power: The Privatisation of Security in Contemporary Sub-Saharan Africa," *Crime Law and Social Change* 33, no. 1–2 (2000): 131–49.

18. Spearin, chapter 3, 45.

19. Tsingou, chapter 5, 91.

20. Sheehan, chapter 7, 131.

21. Gerstbauer, chapter 2, 23.

22. Minear, van Baarda, and Sommers, *NATO and Humanitarian Action.*

23. Tsingou, chapter 5, 91.

24. Gerstbauer, chapter 2, 23.

25. Martin Minogue, *Should Flawed Models of Public Management be Exported? Issues and Practices*, Working Paper No. 15 (Institute for Development Policy and Management, University of Manchester, February 2000); Kenneth Stowe, "Good Piano Won't Play Bad Music: Administrative Reform and Good Governance," *Public Administration* 70, no. 3 (1992): 387–94.

26. Cynthia Hewitt de Alcantara, "Uses and Abuses of the Concept of Governance," *International Social Science Journal* 50, no. 1 (1998): 105–13, 107–8; World Bank, *Governance and Development* (Washington, DC: World Bank, 1992).

27. de Alcantara, "Uses and Abuses of the Concept of Governance," 108, 111–12; Peter Blunt, "Cultural Relativism, 'Good' Governance and Sustainable Human Development," *Public Administration and Development* 15, no. 1 (1995): 1–9; George Philip, "The Dilemmas of Good Governance: A Latin American Perspective," *Government and Opposition* 34, no. 2 (1999): 226–42.

28. Gerstbauer, chapter 2, 23.

29. Anders, chapter 9, 177.

30. Spearin, chapter 3, 45.

31. IPAO, "Code of Conduct," http://www.ipoaonline.org/code.htm.

32. Mary B. Anderson, *Do No Harm: How Aid Can Support Peace—Or War* (Boulder, CO: Lynne Rienner, 1999); Koenraad Van Brabant, *Operational Security Management in Violent Environments: A Field Manual for Aid Agencies* (London: Overseas Development Institute, 2000), 58.

33. The Collaborative for Development Action, "Reflecting on Peace Practice Project," http://www.cdainc.com.

34. Tsingou, chapter 5, 91.

35. Sheehan, chapter 7, 131.

Selected Bibliography

Aall, Pamela. "Non-governmental Organizations and Peacemaking." In *Managing Global Chaos: Sources of and Responses to International Conflict*, edited by Chester A. Crocker, Fen Osler Hampson, and Pamela Aall, 433–44. Washington, DC: USIP Press, 1996.

Adler, Emanuel. "The Emergence of Cooperation: National Epistemic Communities and the International Evolution of the Idea of Nuclear Arms Control." *International Organization* 46, no. 1 (1992): 101–45.

Alexander, John B. *Future War*. New York: Thomas Dunne Books, 1999.

Allenby, B.R. "Environmental Security: Concept and Implementation." *International Political Science Review* 21, no. 1 (2000): 5–21.

Anderson, Mary B. *Do No Harm: How Aid Can Support Peace—Or War*. Boulder, CO: Lynne Rienner, 1999.

Anthony, Ian. "Current Trends and Developments in the Arms Trade." *The Annals of the American Academy of Political and Social Science* 535 (1994): 29–42.

Anthony, Ian. "Causation and the Arms Trade, with Reference to Small Arms." In *Small Arms Control: Old Weapons, New Issues*, edited by Jayantha Dhanapala, Mitsuro Donowaki, Swadesh Rana, and Lora Lumpe, 59–75. Geneva: UNIDIR, 1999.

Arquilla, John, and David Ronfeldt. "The Advent of Netwar (Revisited)." In *Networks and Netwars: The Future of Terror, Crime, and Militancy*, edited by John Arquilla and David Ronfeldt, 1–25. Santa Monica, CA: RAND Corporation, 2001.

Arquilla, John, David Ronfeldt, and Michele Zanini. "Networks, Netwar, and Information-Age Terrorism." In *Countering the New Terrorism*, edited by Ian O. Lesser, 39–68. Santa Monica, CA: RAND Corporation, 1999.

Atkinson, M.M., and W.D. Coleman. "Policy Networks, Policy Communities and the Problems of Governance." *Governance* 5, no. 2 (1992): 154–80.

Baldwin, David A. "The Concept of Security." *Review of International Studies* 23, no. 1 (1997): 5–29.

Barabási, Albert-László. *Linked: The New Science of Networks*. Cambridge, MA Perseus, 2002.

Barnett, Roger W. *Asymmetrical Warfare: Today's Challenge to U.S. Military Power*. Dulles, VA: Brassey's, 2002.

Benson, William. *Light Weapons Controls and Security Assistance: A Review of Current Practice*. London: Saferworld and International Alert, 1998.

Berdal, Mats, and David Malone, eds., *Greed and Grievance: Economic Agendas in Civil Wars*. London: Lynne Rienner, 2000.

Bergen, Peter L. *Holy War, Inc.: Inside the Secret World of Osama bin Laden*. New York: The Free Press, 2001.

Betts, Richard K. "The Soft Underbelly of American Primacy: Tactical Advantages of Terror." In *Terrorism and Counterterrorism*, edited by Russell D. Howard and Reid L. Sawyer. Guilford, CT: McGraw-Hill/Dushkin, 2003.

Beyrer, Chris. *War in the Blood: Sex, Politics and AIDS in Southeast Asia*. London: Zed Books, 1998.

Biersteker, Thomas J. "Targeting Terrorist Finances: The New Challenges of Financial Market Globalization." In *Worlds in Collision*, edited by Ken Booth and Tim Dunne, 74–84. Basingstoke: Palgrave, 2002.

Blunt, Peter. "Cultural Relativism, 'Good' Governance and Sustainable Human Development." *Public Administration and Development* 15, no. 1 (1995): 1–9.

Boulding, Elise, and Jan Oberg. "United Nations Peacekeeping and NGO Peacebuilding: Towards Partnership." In *The Future of the United Nations System: Potential for the Twenty-first Century*, edited by Chadwick F. Alger, 127–54. New York: United Nations University Press, 1998.

Boutros Ghali, Boutros. *An Agenda for Peace*. New York: United Nations, 1992.

Boutwell, Jeffrey, and Michael T. Klare. *Light Weapons and Civil Conflict: Controlling the Tools of Violence*. New York: Carnegie Commission on Preventing Deadly Conflict, 1999.

Brauer, Jurgen. "An Economic Perspective on Mercenaries, Military Companies, and the Privatization of Force." *Cambridge Review of International Affairs* 13, no. 1 (1999): 130–46.

Buzan, Barry, Ole Wæver, and Jaap de Wilde. *Security: A New Framework for Analysis*. Boulder, CO: Lynne Rienner, 1998.

Byman, Daniel L. "Uncertain Partners: NGOs and the Military." *Survival* 43, no. 2 (2001): 97–114.

Chow, Jack. "Health and International Security." *The Washington Quarterly* 19, no. 2 (1996): 63–77.

Clark, Anne Marie. "Non-governmental Organizations and Their Influence on International Society." *Journal of International Affairs* 48, no. 2 (1995): 507–25.

Cleaver, Garry. "Subcontracting Military Power: The Privatisation of Security in Contemporary Sub-Saharan Africa." *Crime Law and Social Change* 33, no. 1–2 (2000): 131–49.

Commission on Global Governance. *Our Global Neighbourhood*. Oxford: Oxford University Press, 1995.

Cooley, Alexander, and James Ron. "The NGO Scramble: Organizational Insecurity and the Political Economy of Transnational Action." *International Security* 27, no. 1 (2002): 5–39.

Cordesman, Anthony H. *Terrorism, Asymmetric Warfare, and Weapons of Mass Destruction; Defending the U.S. Homeland*. Westport, CT: Praeger, 2002.

Croall, Hazel. "Combating Financial Crime: Regulatory versus Crime Control Approaches." *Journal of Financial Crime* 11, no. 1 (2003): 45–55.

Crocker, Chester, Fen Osler Hampson, and Pamela Aall. "Introduction." In *Managing Global Chaos: Sources and Responses to International Conflict*, edited by Chester Crocker et al., xiii–xx. Washington, DC: USIP Press, 1996.

Cucovaz, Silvia. "Interrelationship between Illicit Trafficking in Small Arms, Drug Trafficking, and Terrorist Groups in South America." In *Curbing Illicit Trafficking in Small Arms and Sensitive Technologies: An Action-Oriented Agenda*, edited by Péricles Gasparani Alves and Daiana Belinda Cipollone, 33–47. Geneva: UNIDIR, 1998.

Cusimano, Maryann K., Mark Hensman, and Leslie Rodrigues. "Private-Sector Transsovereign Actors–MNCs and NGOs." In *Beyond Sovereignty: Issues for a Global Agenda*, edited by Maryann K. Cusimano, 253–82. Belmont, CA: Wadsworth, 2000.

Czempiel, Ernst-Otto. "Governance and Democratization." In *Governance without Government: Order and Change in World Politics*, edited by James N. Rosenau and Ernst-Otto Czempiel, 250–71. Cambridge: Cambridge University Press, 1992.

Davis, Ian. *The Regulation of Arms and Dual-Use Exports: Germany, Sweden and the UK*. Oxford: Oxford University Press, 2002.

Davis, James R. *Fortune's Warriors: Private Armies and the New World Order*. Vancouver: Douglas & McIntyre, 2000.

de Alcantara, Cynthia Hewitt. "Uses and Abuses of the Concept of Governance." *International Social Science Journal* 50, no. 1 (1998): 105–13.

Desch, Michael C., Jorge I. Domínguez, and Andrés Serbin, eds., *From Pirates to Drug Lords: The Post-Cold War Caribbean Security Environment*. Albany, NY: SUNY Press, 1998.

Deutch, John, and Jeffrey H. Smith. "Smarter Intelligence." *Foreign Policy* 128, no. 1 (2002): 64–9.

Donini, Antonio. "Asserting Humanitarianism in Peace-Maintenance." In *The Politics of Peace-Maintenance*, edited by Jarat Chopra, 81–96. Boulder, CO: Lynne Rienner, 1998.

Duffield, Mark. "Globalization, Transborder Trade, and War Economies." In *Greed and Grievance: Economic Agendas in Civil Wars*, edited by Mats Berdal and David Malone, 69–89. London: Lynne Rienner, 2000.

Duffield, Mark. "The Political Economy of Internal War: Asset Transfer, Complex Emergencies and International Aid." In *War & Hunger: Rethinking International Responses to Complex Emergencies*, edited by Joanna Macrae and Anthony Zwi, 50–69. London: Zed Books, 1994.

Edwards, Michael, and David Hulme, eds., *Beyond the Magic Bullet: NGO Performance Accountability in the Post-Cold War World*. West Hartford, CT: Kumarian Press, 1996.

Edwards, Michael, David Hulme, and Tina Wallace. "Increasing Leverage for Development: Changes for NGOs in a Global Future." In *New Roles and Relevance: Development NGOs and the Challenges of Change*, edited by David Lewis and Tina Wallace, 1–14. Bloomfield, CT: Kumarian Press, 2000.

Elbe, Stefan. "HIV/AIDS and the Changing Landscape of War in Africa." *International Security* 27, no. 2 (2002): 159–77.

Elbe, Stefan. *Strategic Implications of HIV/AIDS*. Adelphi Paper 357. Oxford: Oxford University Press for IISS, 2003.

Enders, Walter, and Todd Sandler. "The Effectiveness of Antiterrorism Policies: A Vector-Autoregression-Intervention Analysis." *American Political Science Review* 87, no. 4 (1993): 829–44.

Evangelista, Matthew. *Unarmed Forces: The Transnational Movement to End the Cold War*. Ithaca, NY: Cornell University Press, 1999.

Farmer, Paul. "Social Inequalities and Emerging Infectious Diseases." *Emerging Infectious Diseases* 2, no. 4 (1996): 259–69.

Fidler, David P. "The Globalization of Public Health: Emerging Infectious Diseases and International Relations." *Indiana Journal of Global Legal Studies* 5, no. 1 (1997): 11–52.

Finkelstein, Lawrence S. "What Is Global Governance?" *Global Governance* 1, no. 3 (1995): 367–72.

Fourie, Pieter, and Martin Schönteich. "Africa's New Security Threat: HIV/AIDS and Human Security in Southern Africa." *African Security Review* 10, no. 4 (2001): 29–57.

Garrett, Laurie. "The Return of Infectious Disease." *Foreign Affairs* 75, no. 1 (1996): 66–79.

Ghils, Paul. "International Civil Society: International Non-governmental Organizations in the International System." *International Social Science Journal* 133, no. 4 (1992): 417–29.

Gillard, Emmanuela. "What's Legal? What's Illegal?" In *Running Guns: The Global Black Market in Small Arms*, edited by Lora Lumpe, 27–52. London: Zed Books, 2000.

Gordenker, Leon, and Thomas G. Weiss. "Pluralizing Global Governance: Analytical Approaches and Dimensions." In *NGOs, the UN, and Global Governance*, edited by Leon Gordenker and Thomas G. Weiss, 17–47. London: Lynne Rienner, 1996.

Gordenker, Leon, Roger A. Coate, Christer Jönsson, and Peter Söderholm. *International Cooperation in Response to AIDS*. London: Pinter, 1995.

Gray, Colin S. "Thinking Asymmetrically in Times of Terror." *Parameters* 32, no. 1 (2002): 5–14.

Greene, Owen. "Examining International Responses to Illicit Arms Trafficking." *Crime, Law & Social Change* 33, no. 2 (2000): 151–90.

Gunaratna, Rohan, *Inside Al Qaida*. New York: Columbia University Press, 2002.

Haas, Peter. "Introduction: Epistemic Communities and International Policy Coordination." *International Organization* 46, no. 1 (1992): 1–35.

Heinecken, Lindy. "AIDS: The New Security Frontier." *Conflict Trends* 3, no. 4 (2000): 12–15.

Helleiner, Eric. "State Power and the Regulation of Illicit Activity in Global Finance." In *The Illicit Global Economy and State Power*, edited by H. Richard Friman and Peter Andreas, 53–90. Lanham, ML: Rowman and Littlefield.

Hoffman, Bruce. *Inside Terrorism*. New York: Columbia University Press, 1998.

Hoffman, Bruce. "Rethinking Terrorism and Counterterrorism Since 9/11." *Studies in Conflict and Terrorism* 25 (2002): 303–16.

Hoffman, Bruce. "A Nasty Business." In *Terrorism and Counterterrorism*, edited by Russell D. Howard and Reid L. Sawyer, 339–44. Guilford, CT: McGraw-Hill/Dushkin, 2003.

Holsti, K.J. *The State, War, and the State of War*. Cambridge: Cambridge University Press, 1996.

Homer-Dixon, Thomas. "Environmental Scarcities and Violent Conflict." *International Security* 19, no. 1 (1994): 5–40.

Homer-Dixon, Thomas. *Environment, Scarcity, and Violence*. Princeton, NJ: Princeton University Press, 2001.

Howe, Herbert M. *Ambiguous Order: Military Forces in African States*. Boulder, CO: Lynne Rienner, 2001.

Janice E. Thomson, *Mercenaries, Pirates, and Sovereigns: State-Building and Extraterritorial Violence in Early Modern Europe*. Princeton, NJ: Princeton University Press, 1994.

Jönsson, Christer, and Peter Söderholm. "IGO-NGO Relations and HIV/AIDS." In *NGOs, the UN, and Global Governance*, edited by Thomas Weiss and Leon Gordenker, 121–38. Boulder, CO: Lynne Rienner, 1996.

Kaldor, Mary. *New and Old Wars: Organized Violence in a Global Era*. Stanford, CA: Stanford University Press, 1999.

Kalipeni, Ezekiel, Susan Craddock, Joseph R. Oppong, and Jayati Ghosh, eds., *HIV&AIDS in Africa: Beyond Epidemiology*. Malden: Blackwell, 2004.

Karp, Aaron. "The Rise of Black and Gray Markets." *The Annals of the American Academy of Political and Social Science* 535 (1994): 175–89.

Karp, Aaron. "Small Arms—The New Major Weapons." In *Lethal Commerce*, edited by Jeffrey Boutwell, Michael T. Klare, and Laura W. Reed, 17–30. Cambridge, MA: Committee on International Security Studies of the American Academy of Arts and Sciences, 1995.

Kartha, Tara, *Tools of Terror: Light Weapons and India's Security*. New Delhi: Knowledge World, 1999.

Kaul, Inge. "Public Goods: Taking the Concept into the Twenty-first Century." In *The Market or the Public Domain*, edited by Daniel Drache, 255–73. London: Routledge, 2001.

Kaul, Inge, Isabelle Grunberg, and Marc A. Stern. "Defining Global Public Goods." In *Global Public Goods*, edited by Inge Kaul, Isabelle Grunberg, and Marc A. Stern, 2–19. New York: Oxford University Press, 1999.

Keck, Margaret, and Kathryn Sikkink. *Activists beyond Borders: Advocacy Networks in World Politics*. Ithaca, NY: Cornell University Press, 1998.

Keen, David. *The Economic Functions of Violence in Civil Wars*. Adelphi Paper 320. Oxford: Oxford University Press for IISS, 1998.

Kenis, Paul, and Volker Scheider. "Policy Networks and Policy Analysis: Scrutinizing a New Analytical Toolbox." In *Policy Networks. Empirical Evidence and Theoretical Considerations*, edited by Bernd Marin and Renate Mayntz, 25–62. Frankfurt/Main: Campus, 1991.

Kenney, Michael. "When Criminal Organizations Out-smart the State: Understanding the Learning Capacity of Colombian Drug Trafficking Organizations." *Transnational Organized Crime* 5, no. 1 (1999): 97–119.

Kerry, John. *The New War: The Web of Crime that Threatens America's Security*. New York: Simon & Schuster, 1997.

Kindleberger, Charles P. "Dominance and Leadership in the International Economy." In *The International Economic Order—Essays on Financial Crisis and International Public Goods*, edited by Charles P. Kindleberger, 185–95. Hemel Hempstead: Harvester Wheatsheaf, 1988.

Klare, Michael T. "Light Weapons Diffusion and Global Violence in the Post-Cold War Era" In *Light Weapons and International Security*, edited by Jasijit Singh, 1–40. London: BASIC, 1995.

Klare, Michael T. "The Global Trade in Light Weapons and the International System in the Post-Cold War Era." In *Lethal Commerce*, edited by Jeffrey Boutwell, Michael T. Klare, and Laura W. Reed, 31–43. Cambridge, MA: Committee on International Security Studies of the American Academy of Arts and Sciences, 1995.

Klare, Michael T. "The International Trade in Light Weapons: What Have We Learned?" In *Light Weapons and Civil Conflict: Controlling the Tools of Violence*, edited by Jeffrey Boutwell and Michael T. Klare, 9–28. New York: Carnegie Commission on Preventing Deadly Conflict, 1999.

Krahmann, Elke. "Conceptualising Security Governance." *Cooperation and Conflict* 38, no. 1 (2003): 5–26.

Krahmann, Elke. "National, Regional and Global Governance: One Phenomenon or Many?" *Global Governance* 9, no. 3 (2003): 323–46.

Krahmann, Elke. *Multilevel Networks in European Foreign Policy*. Aldershot: Ashgate, 2003.

Krause, Keith, and Michael C. Williams, eds., *Critical Security Studies: Concepts and Cases*. Minneapolis, MN: University of Minnesota Press, 1997.

Kriesberg, Louis. "Social Movements and Global Transformation." In *Transnational Social Movements and Global Politics: Solidarity Beyond the State*, edited by Jackie Smith, Charles Chatfield, and Ronald Pagnucco, 3–10. Syracuse, NY: Syracuse University Press, 1997.

Laqueur, Walter. "Postmodern Terrorism." *Foreign Affairs* 75, no. 5 (1996): 25–36.

Laurance, Edward. *Light Weapons and Intrastate Conflict; Early Warning Factors and Preventive Action: A Report to the Carnegie Commission on Preventing Deadly Conflict*. New York: Carnegie Corporation of New York, 1998.

Lederach, John Paul. *Building Peace: Sustainable Reconciliation in Divided Societies*. Washington, DC: USIP Press, 1997.

Lesser, Ian O. "Countering the New Terrorism: Implications for Strategy." In *Countering the New Terrorism*, edited by Ian O. Lesser, Bruce Hoffman, John Arquilla, David F. Ronfeldt, Michele Zanini, and Brian Michael Jenkins, 85–144. Santa Monica, CA: RAND Corporation, 1999.

Lilly, Damian. *The Privatization of Security and Peacebuilding*. London: International Alert, 2000.

Majone, Giandomenico. "From the Positive to the Regulatory State: Causes and Consequences of Changes in the Mode of Governance." *Journal of Public Policy* 17, no. 2 (1997): 139–68.

Malvesti, Michele L. "Explaining the United States' Decision to Strike Back at Terrorists." In *Terrorism and Counterterrorism*, edited by Russell D. Howard and Reid L. Sawyer. Guilford, CT: McGraw-Hill/Dushkin, 2003.

Mandel, Robert. *Deadly Transfers and the Global Playground.* Westport, CT: Praeger, 1999.

Mandel, Robert. "The Privatization of Security." *Armed Forces and Society* 28, no. 1 (2001): 129–51.

Mandel, Robert. *Armies without States: The Privatization of Security.* Boulder, CO: Lynne Rienner, 2002.

Maoz, Zeev. *Paradoxes of War.* Boston, MA: Unwin Hyman, 1990.

Martin, Gus. *Understanding Terrorism.* Thousand Oaks, CA: Sage, 2003.

Massari, Monica. "Transnational Organized Crime between Myth and Reality." In *Organized Crime and the Challenge to Democracy*, edited by Felia Allum and Renate Siebert, 55–69. London: Routledge, 2003.

Mathews, Jessica T. "Redefining Security." *Foreign Affairs* 68, no. 2 (1989): 162–76.

Mathews, Jessica T. "Power Shift: The Age of Nonstate Actors." *Foreign Affairs* 76, no. 1 (1997): 50–66.

Mawlawi, Farouk. "New Conflicts, New Challenges: The Evolving Role for Non-governmental Actors." *Journal of International Affairs* 46, no. 2 (1993): 391–413.

McNeill, William. *Plagues and People.* New York: Doubleday, 1976.

Mearsheimer, John. "Back to the Future: Instability in Europe After the Cold War." *International Security* 15, no. 4 (1990): 5–56.

Meek, Sarah. "Combating Arms Trafficking: Progress and Prospects." In *Running Guns: The Global Black Market in Small Arms*, edited by Lora Lumpe, 183–207. London: Zed Books, 2000.

Mendelson Forman, Johanna, and Manuel Carballo. "A Policy Critique of HIV/AIDS and Demobilisation." *Conflict, Security & Development* 1, no. 2 (2001): 73–92.

Minear, Larry, and Thomas G. Weiss. *Mercy Under Fire: War and the Global Humanitarian Community.* Boulder, CO: Westview Press, 1995.

Mitchell, A., P. Sikka and H. Willmott. "Sweeping It under the Carpet: The Role of Accountancy Firms in Money Laundering." *Accounting, Organizations and Society* 23, no. 5–6 (1998): 589–607.

Mitchell, Daniel J. "US Government Agencies Confirm that Low-tax Jurisdictions Are Not Money Laundering Havens." *Journal of Financial Crime* 11, no. 2 (2003): 127–33.

Morris-Cotterill, Nigel. "Money Laundering." *Foreign Policy* 124, no. 3 (2001): 14–22.

Muni, S.D. "Arms and Conflicts in the Post-Cold War Developing World." In *Between Development and Destruction: An Enquiry into the Causes of Conflict in Post-Colonial States*, edited by Luc Van de Goor, Paul Sciarone, and Kumar Rupesinghe, 197–216. London: Macmillan, 1996.

Mussington, David. *Understanding Contemporary Arms Transfers: An Analysis of the Post-Cold War Arms Trade and Supplier Strategies for Limiting Conventional Weapons Proliferation*, Adelphi Paper 291. London: Brassey's for IISS, 1994.

Myers, Norman. "Environment and Security." *Foreign Affairs* 70, no. 3 (1991): 115–31.

Natsios, Andrew S. "NGOs and the UN System in Complex Humanitarian Emergencies: Conflict or Cooperation?" In *NGOs, the United Nations, and Global Governance*, edited by Leon Gordenker and Thomas G. Weiss, 67–81. Boulder, CO: Lynne Rienner, 1996.

Natsios, Andrew. "NGOs and the UN System in Complex Humanitarian Emergencies: Conflict or Cooperation?" In *NGOs, the UN, and Global Governance*, edited by Thomas Weiss and Leon Gordenker, 388–405. Boulder, CO: Lynne Rienner, 1996.

Natsios, Andrew. "An NGO Perspective." In *Peacemaking in International Conflict: Methods and Techniques*, edited by I William Zartman and J. Lewis Rasmussen, 337–64. Washington, DC: USIP Press, 1997.

Natsios, Andrew. "The Politics of Saving Lives." *Foreign Service Journal* 75, no. 12 (1998): 16–22.

Navias, Martin. "Finance Warfare and International Terrorism." In *Superterrorism: Policy Responses*, edited by Lawrence Freedman, 57–79. Oxford: Blackwell, 2002.

Naylor, R.T. "The Insurgent Economy: Black Market Operations of Guerrilla Organizations." *Crime, Law and Social Change* 20, no. 1 (1993): 13–51.

Naylor, R.T. "Loose Cannons: Covert Commerce and Underground Finance in the Modern Arms Black Market." *Crime, Law and Social Change* 22 (1995): 1–57.

Naylor, R. Thomas. "Mafias, Myths, and Markets: On the Theory and Practice of Enterprise Crime." *Transnational Organized Crime* 3, no. 3 (1997): 1–45.

Nye, Joseph S. Jr. "The American National Interest and Global Public Goods." *International Affairs* 78, no. 2 (2002): 233–44.

Ostergard, Robert L., Jr. "Politics in the Hot Zone: AIDS and National Security in Africa." *Third World Quarterly* 23, no. 2 (2002): 333–50.

Palan, Ronen. "Tax Havens and the Commercialization of State Sovereignty." *International Organization* 56, no. 1 (2002): 151–76.

Paris, Roland. "Human Security. Paradigm Shift or Hot Air?" *International Security* 26, no. 2 (2001): 87–102.

Passas, Nikos and Richard B. Groskin. "Overseeing and Overlooking: The US Federal Authorities' Response to Money Laundering and Other Misconduct at BCCI." *Crime, Law and Social Change* 35 (2001): 141–75.

Patrick, Stewart. "The Donor Community and the Challenge of Postconflict Recovery." In *Good Intentions: Pledges of Aid for Postconflict Recovery*, edited by Shepard Forman and Stewart Patrick, 35–66. Boulder, CO: Lynne Rienner, 2000.

Philip, George. "The Dilemmas of Good Governance: A Latin American Perspective." *Government and Opposition* 34, no. 2 (1999): 226–42.

Pieth, Mark and Gemma Aiolfi. "The Private Sector Becomes Active: The Wolfsberg Process." *Journal of Financial Crime* 10, no. 4 (2003): 359–65.

Poku, Nana, and David T. Graham, eds., *Redefining Security: Population Movements and National Security*. Westport, CT: Praeger, 1998.

Posen, Barry R. "The Struggle Against Terrorism: Grand Strategy, Strategy, and Tactics." In *Terrorism and Counterterrorism*, edited by Russell D. Howard and Reid L. Sawyer, 391–403. Guilford, CT: McGraw-Hill/Dushkin, 2003.

Powell, Walter W. "Neither Market nor Hierarchy: Network Forms of Organization." *Research in Organizational Behavior* 12 (1990): 295–336.

Prendergast, John. *Frontline Diplomacy: Humanitarian Aid and Conflict in Africa*. Boulder, CO: Lynne Rienner, 1996.

Price-Smith, Andrew T. "Infectious Disease and Global Stability at the Turn of the Century." *International Journal* 54, no. 3 (1999): 426–42.

Price-Smith, Andrew T. *The Health of Nations: Infectious Disease, Environmental Change, and their Effects on National Security*. Cambridge, MA: MIT Press, 2001.

Pugh, Michael. "Civil-Military Relations in the Kosovo Crisis: An Emerging Hegemony?" *Security Dialogue* 31, no. 2 (2000): 229–42.

Raab, Jörg, and H. Binton Milward. "Dark Networks as Problems." *Journal of Public Administration Research and Theory* 13, no. 4 (2003): 413–39.

Ranstorp, Magnus. "Interpreting the Broader Context and Meaning of Bin-Laden's *Fatwa*." *Studies in Conflict and Terrorism* 21 (1998): 321–30.

Rasmussen, Lewis J. "Peacemaking in the Twenty-First Century: New Rules, New Roles, New Actors." In *Peacemaking in International Conflict: Methods and Techniques*, edited by I. William Zartman and J. Lewis Rasmussen, 23–50. Washington, DC: USIP Press, 1997.

Rees, Wyn. "Transnational Organized Crime, Security and the European Union." In *Organized Crime and the Challenge to Democracy*, edited by Felia Allum and Renate Siebert, 112–25. London: Routledge, 2003.

Reinicke, Wolfgang. "Global Public Policy." *Foreign Affairs* 76, no. 6 (1997): 127–38.

Reno, William. "War, Markets, and the Reconfiguration of West Africa's Weak States." *Comparative Politics* 29, no. 4 (1997): 493–510.

Rieff, David. "Humanitarianism in Crisis." *Foreign Affairs* 81, no. 6 (2002): 111–21.

Risse-Kappen, Thomas, ed., *Bringing Transnational Relations Back In: Non-state Actors, Domestic Structures, and International Institutions.* Cambridge: Cambridge University Press, 1995.

Roberts, Adam. "The Crisis in UN Peacekeeping." In *Managing Global Chaos: Sources and Responses to International Conflict,* edited by Chester Crocker, Fen Osler Hampson, and Pamela Aall, 297–320. Washington, DC: USIP Press, 1996.

Roberts, Adam. *Humanitarian Action in War: Aid, Protection and Impartiality in a Policy Vacuum.* Adelphi Paper 305. London: International Institute for Strategic Studies, 1996.

Rosenau, James N. "Change, Complexity, and Governance in Globalizing Space." In *Debating Governance. Authority, Steering and Democracy,* edited by Jon Pierre, 169–200. Oxford: Oxford University Press, 2000.

Rosenau, James N. *Turbulence in World Politics: A Theory of Change and Continuity.* Princeton: Princeton University Press, 1990.

Rosenau, James N. "Governance, Order and Change in World Politics." In *Governance without Government: Order and Change in World Politics,* edited by James N. Rosenau and Ernst-Otto Czempiel, 1–29. Cambridge: Cambridge University Press, 1992.

Rothschild, Emma. "What is Security?" *Daedalus* 124, no. 3 (1995): 53–98.

Roy, Olivier. *The Lessons of the Soviet/Afghan War,* Adelphi Paper 259. London: Brassey's for IISS, 1991.

Salomon, Lester. "The Rise of the Nonprofit Sector." *Foreign Affairs* 73, no. 4 (1994): 109–22.

Sandler, Todd. "Global and Regional Public Goods: A Prognosis for Collective Action." *Fiscal Studies* 19, no. 3 (1998): 221–47.

Sandoz, Yves. "Private Security and International Law." In *Peace, Profit or Plunder? The Privatisation of Security in War-Torn African Societies,* edited by Jakkie Cilliers and Peggy Mason, 201–26. Pretoria: Institute for Security Studies, 1999.

Sankey, John. "Conclusions." In *The Conscience of the World: the Influence of Non-governmental Organizations in the UN System,* edited by Peter Willetts, 270–6. Washington, DC: Brookings Institution, 1996.

Schneider, Mark, and Michael Moodie. *The Destabilizing Impacts of HIV/AIDS.* Washington, DC: Center for Strategic and International Studies, 2002.

Seagrave, Sterling. *Lords of the Rim: The Invisible Empire of the Overseas Chinese.* New York: Putnam, 1995.

Shearer, David. *Private Armies and Military Intervention.* Adelphi Paper 316. Oxford: Oxford University Press for IISS, 1998.

Shearer, David. "Private Military Force and Challenges for the Future." *Cambridge Review of International Affairs* 13, no. 1 (1999): 80–94.

Shelley, Louise L. "Transnational Organized Crime: An Imminent Threat to the Nation-State?" *Journal of International Affairs* 48, no. 2 (1995): 463–89.

Shutz, Richard H., and Andreas Vogt. "The Real Intelligence Failure on 9/11 and the Case for a Doctrine of Striking First." In *Terrorism and Counterterrorism,* edited by Russell D. Howard and Reid L. Sawyer. Guilford, CT: McGraw-Hill/Dushkin, 2003.

Singer, Peter W. "Corporate Warriors: The Rise and Ramifications of the Privatized Military Industry." *International Security* 26, no. 3 (2001): 186–220.

Singer, Peter W. "AIDS and International Security." *International Security* 44, no. 1 (2002): 145–58.

Singer, Peter W. *Corporate Warriors: The Rise of the Privatized Military Industry.* Ithaca, NY: Cornell University Press, 2003.

Sislin, John, Frederic S. Pearson, Jocelyn Boryczka, and Jeffrey Weigand. "Patterns in Arms Acquisitions by Ethnic Groups in Conflict." *Security Dialogue* 29, no. 4 (1998): 393–408.

Small, Michael. "Peacebuilding in Postconflict Societies." In *Human Security and the New Diplomacy*, edited by Rob McRae and Don Hubert, 75–80. Montreal: McGill-Queen's University Press, 2001.

Smillie, Ian. "Changing Partners: Northern NGOs, Northern Governments." *Voluntas* 5, no. 2 (1994): 155–92.

Smillie, Ian. "NGOs: Crisis and Opportunity in the New World Order." In *Transforming Development: Foreign Aid for a Changing World*, edited by Jim Freedman, 114–34. Toronto: University of Toronto Press, 2000.

Smillie, Ian, Lansana Gberie, and Ralph Hazleton. *The Heart of the Matter: Sierra Leone, Diamonds and Human Security.* Ottowa: Partnership Africa Canada, 2000.

Smith, Brian. *More than Altruism: the Politics of Private Foreign Aid.* Princeton, NJ: Princeton University Press, 1990.

Smith, Chris. "Light Weapons and Ethnic Conflict in South Asia." In *Lethal Commerce*, edited by Jeffrey Boutwell, Michael T. Klare, and Laura W. Reed, 61–80. Cambridge, MA: Committee on International Security Studies of the American Academy of Arts and Sciences, 1995.

Smith, Jackie. "Transnational Political Processes and the Human Rights Movement." *Research in Social Movements, Conflict and Change* 18 (1995): 185–219.

Smith, Jackie, Charles Chatfield, and Ronald Pagnucco, eds., *Transnational Social Movements and Global Politics: Solidarity beyond the State.* Syracuse, NY: Syracuse University Press, 1997.

Spearin, Christopher. "A Private Security Panacea? A Specific Response to Mean Times." *Canadian Foreign Policy* 7, no. 3 (2000): 67–80.

Spearin, Christopher. "Private Security Companies and Humanitarians: A Corporate Solution to Securing Humanitarian Spaces?" *International Peacekeeping* 8, no. 1 (2001): 20–43.

Stern, Jessica. *The Ultimate Terrorists.* Cambridge, MA: Harvard University Press, 1999.

Storey, Andy. "Non-Neutral Humanitarianism: NGOs and the Rwanda Crisis." *Development in Practice* 7, no. 4 (1997): 384–94.

Suhrke, Astri. "Environmental Change, Migration, and Conflict: A Lethal Feedback Dynamic?" In *Managing Global Chaos: Sources of and Responses to International Conflict*, edited by Chester A. Crocker, Fen Osler Hampson, and Pamela Aall, 113–28. Washington, DC: USIP Press, 1996.

Taulbee, James Larry. "Mercenaries, Private Armies and Security Companies in Contemporary Policy." *International Politics* 37, no. 4 (2000): 433–56.

Tuathail, Gearóid Ó, Andrew Herod, and Susan M. Roberts. "Negotiating Unruly Problematics." In *An Unruly World? Globalization, Governance and Geography*, edited by Andrew Herod, Gearóid Ó Tuathail, and Susan M. Roberts, 1–24. London: Routledge, 1998.

Tucker, Jonathan B. *Scourge: The Once and Future Threat of Smallpox.* New York: Atlantic Monthly Press, 2001.

Tvedt, Terje. *Angels of Mercy or Development Diplomats: NGOs and Foreign Aid.* Trenton, NJ: First Africa World Press, 1998.

Ullman, Richard H. "Redefining Security." *International Security* 8, no. 1 (1983): 129–53.

Van Creveld, Martin. *The Transformation of War.* New York: The Free Press, 1991.

Vaux, Tony, Chris Sieple, Greg Nakano, and Koenraad Van Brabant. *Humanitarian Action and Private Security Companies: Opening the Debate.* London: International Alert, 2002.

Wæver, Ole. "Securitization and Desecuritization." In *On Security*, edited by Ronnie D. Lipschutz, 46–86. New York: Columbia University Press, 1995.

Wallensteen, Peter, and Margareta Sollenberg. "Armed Conflict 1989–2000." *Journal of Peace Research* 38, no. 5 (2001): 629–44.

Walt, Stephen M. "The Renaissance of Security Studies." *International Studies Quarterly* 35, no. 2 (1991): 211–39.

Weiss, Thomas, and Cindy Collins. *Humanitarian Challenges and Intervention*. Boulder, CO: Westview Press, 1996.

Weiss, Thomas G., and Leon Gordenker, eds., *NGOs, the UN, and Global Governance*. Boulder, CO: Lynne Rienner, 1996.

Whiteside, Alan, and Clem Sunter. *AIDS: The Challenge for South Africa*. Cape Town: Human & Rousseau and Tafelberg, 2000.

Willetts, Peter, ed., *The Conscience of the World: The Influence of Nongovernmental Organizations in the UN System*. Washington, DC: Brookings Press, 1996.

Williams, Phil. "Transnational Criminal Organizations and International Security." *Survival* 36, no. 1 (1994): 96–113.

Williams, Phil. "Organizing Transnational Crime: Networks, Markets and Hierarchies." *Transnational Organized Crime* 4, no. 3–4 (1998): 57–87.

Williams, Phil. "Transnational Organized Crime and the State." In *The Emergence of Private Authority in Global Governance*, edited by Rodney Bruce Hall and Thomas Biersteker, 161–82. Cambridge: Cambridge University Press, 2002.

Williams, Phil, and Gregory Baudin-O'Hayon. "Organized Crime and Money Laundering." In *Governing Globalization*, edited by David Held and Andrew McGrew, 127–44. Cambridge: Polity, 2002.

Wolfers, Arnold. "National Security as an Ambiguous Symbol." In *Discord and Collaboration*, edited by Arnold Wolfers, 147–65. Baltimore, MD: Johns Hopkins University Press, 1992.

Young, Oran. *International Governance: Protecting the Environment in a Stateless Society*. Ithaca, NY: Cornell University Press, 1994.

Zangl, Bernard, and Michael Zürn. "The Effects of Denationalization on Security in the OECD World." *Global Society* 13, no. 2 (1999): 139–61.

Zanini, Michelle. "Middle Eastern Terrorism and Netwar." *Studies in Conflict and Terrorism* 22 (1999): 247–65.

Zanini, Michelle, and Sean J.A. Edwards. "The Networking of Terror in the Information Age." In *Networks and Netwars*, edited by John Arquilla and David Ronfeldt, 29–60. Santa Monica, CA: RAND Corporation, 2001.

Zarate, Juan Carlos. "The Emergence of a New Dog of War: Private International Security Companies, International Law and the New World Disorder." *Stanford Journal of International Law* 34, no. 1 (1998): 75–162.

Zartman, I. William. "Introduction: Posing the Problem of State Collapse." In *Collapsed States: The Disintegration and Restoration of Legitimate Authority*, edited by William Zartman, 1–14. Boulder, CO: Lynne Rienner, 1995.

Index

ActionAid, 33
Afghanistan, 71, 76, 78, 81, 84, 85, 94, 169, 201
    Mujahedeen, 74–5, 146, 165
    Northern Alliance, 165
    Taleban, 166, 171
Africare, 139
"Agenda for Peace", 27, 31
aid, 11, 15, 16, 23–43, 48, 132, 202
    development, 24–5, 207
    humanitarian, 8, 11, 13, 14, 49
    military, 157, 159, 164–6, 166, 168, 171
    NGOs, 23–43, 47, 52–53, 132
AIDS, *see* HIV/AIDS
Albania, 32, 35
Algeria, 76
al Qaeda, 5, 74–90, 170–1
    committees, 76
    leadership, 82
    Osama Bin Laden, 75, 76, 80, 81, 83, 84, 86
    Shura council, 76
American Jewish World Service, 139–40
Amnesty International, 15, 185
Angola, 8, 62, 94, 118, 188
    Movimento Popular da Libertacao de Angola (MPLA), 166
    Unión Nacional para la Independencia Total de Angola (UNITA), 164–6, 169
Anti-Ballistic Missile Treaty, 178
Argentina, 104
ArmorGroup, 52, 54, 209
arms trade, 155–76, 177–96
    see also SALW
    black market, 162, 163, 168–71
    brokering, 159, 160, 163, 167, 182, 188–90, 192
    grey market, 162

licensing, 183, 189, 209: End User Certificates, 159, 166–8, 170
    trafficking, 158, 160, 162, 167, 171, 180–2, 186, 188, 190, 192
Austria, 97, 104, 127, 180, 188

Bin Laden, Osama, 75, 76, 80, 81, 83, 84, 86
    see also Al Qaeda
Bahamas, 114
Bahrain, 169
Bali nightclub bombing, 83
Bangladesh, 125
Belgium, 104, 180, 181, 183, 185, 187, 188, 189
Bolivia, 71, 72, 145
Bosnia-Herzegovina, 82, 85, 124
Botswana, 112, 118, 119
bubonic plague, 114
    see also diseases
Burkina Faso, 167
Burundi, 36, 52, 62
Bush, George W. (President, USA), 71, 135, 136, 142

Cambodia, 62, 113, 123, 124, 145, 147, 165, 169
    United Nations Transition Authority in Cambodia (UNTAC), 123
Cameroon, 144
Canada, 31, 104, 116, 127
    Canadian International Development Agency (CIDA), 31
CARE, 15, 27, 31, 47, 52, 139, 140, 145–6, 147, 210
Caribbean, 112, 113, 114
Caritas, 47, 52
cartels, 71, 73, 81, 88
Catholic Relief Services (CRS), 31–3, 36, 39, 139, 210

Central America, 77, 174
Central Africa, 112, 123
Central Asia, 113, 114, 168
Central Intelligence Agency (CIA), USA,
    79, 81, 82, 133, 136, 164–5, 174
China, 104, 113, 121, 136, 164, 165
Christian Peacemaker Teams, 33
Church World Service, 139–40
civil society, 11, 15, 17, 24, 26–8, 31–2, 35,
    38, 156, 172, 207, 210
civil war, 4, 6, 8, 29, 94, 156, 166, 179
Clinton, Bill (former President, USA), 84,
    134–5
cocaine production, 69–70, 73, 79, 82
Cold War, 4, 6, 7, 164–6, 177–8, 182
Collaborative for Development Action,
    37, 209
Colombia, 38, 69
    Cali cartel, 71, 72, 74, 84, 88
    drug industry, 70–74, 94, 155
    insurgents, 74, 155, 166, 169
    law enforcement strategies, 70–3, 81–2
    Medellín cartel, 71, 72, 74, 84, 88
communism, 26
complex humanitarian emergencies, 23,
    31, 34, 42
conflict
    management, 23–43, 155
    resolution, 15, 23, 48–9, 54
    statistics, 3–7, 10, 33, 50, 115, 155, 157
Conflict Management Group (CMG),
    38–39
Congo-Brazzaville, 118, 166
Congo, Democratic Republic of, 52, 118,
    166
consumerism, 24
Contras, 164–5
corruption, 72, 94, 106, 161
Croatia, 123
Cyprus, 169
Cuba, 26

democracy, 25, 27, 32, 35, 86
democratization, 24, 26
Denmark, 104, 183
development
    aid, 24–5, 141, 207
    organizations, 23–7, 30–9, 131, 139–46,
        179, 180, 202, 204
    sustainable, 157, 179, 180

United Nations programs,
    115–16, 132
diamonds, 94, 162, 167–70
diseases, 126, 134, 137, 142, 201
Drug Enforcement Administration (DEA),
    USA, 70, 73, 82
drugs
    cartels, 71, 73, 81, 88
    cocaine, 69–70, 73, 79, 82
    heroin, 71–3, 76, 82
    marijuana, 72, 76
    trafficking, 69–90

East Africa, 76, 78, 80, 84
Eastern Europe, 9, 14, 32, 112–13, 114,
    123, 145, 163
East Germany (German Democratic
    Republic), 164
Economic Community of West African
    States (ECOWAS), 124, 171
Ecuador, 71
Ecumenical Advocacy Alliance, 140
education
    AIDS, 35, 126, 145–6, 203, 205
Egypt, 104, 164, 174
    Egyptian Islamic Jihad, 76
Eisenhower, Dwight D. (former President,
    USA), 142
El Salvador, 165, 174
environment, 25
    degradation, 4, 11, 30
    global warming, 132
    threat, 4
environmental security, 11, 26, 115
Eritrea, 118, 123, 125, 145
Escobar, Pablo, 73, 82
Ethiopia, 62, 125, 136, 146, 152
European Political Co-operation
    (EPC), 118
European Union (EU), 9, 11, 12
    arms control, 177–96, 203, 208
    Conventional Arms Exports Working
        Group (COARM), 181–3,
        185–7, 189
Executive Outcomes, 55

Family Health International (FHI),
    144–5, 148
Farabundo Marti National Liberation
    (FMLN), Nicaragua, 165

Federal Bureau of Investigation (FBI),
    USA, 70, 78, 80, 81
Federation of Red Cross and Red
    Crescent Societies, 55
Finland, 104, 124, 188, 189
France, 82, 104, 180, 183, 187–9

Geneva Convention, 35
German Agro Action, 47
Germany (Federal Republic of Germany),
    76, 78, 104, 171, 180, 181, 183–5,
    188, 192
Ghana, 33
globalization, 7, 13, 25, 70, 160, 161, 168
Gore, Al (former Vice President, USA),
    134, 136
Great Britain, see United Kingdom
Guatemala, 72, 104
Gueï, General Robert (former President,
    Ivory Coast), 167

Hague Conventions, 57
Hague Peace Conference, 178
Haiti, 114
HIV/AIDS, 111–30, 131–52
    children, 117, 147
    education, 126, 134, 137, 147
    fatalities, 7
    human security, 115–17
    infection rates, 6, 112–14
    international security, 122–52
    military, 117, 118
    mother-to-child transmission (MTCT),
        137, 146, 147, 210,
    national security, 117–22
    pandemic, 112
    peacekeeping, 122
    prevalence rates, 111, 112–14
    programs, 131, 133, 137, 144, 146
Honduras, 165, 174
humanitarian assistance, 141
    contract culture, 48
    militarization, 51
    neutrality, 50
    politization, 49
human rights, 11, 125, 126, 187
    NGOs, 23, 24, 25, 28, 31, 178
    United Nations Universal Declaration
        of, 35, 86
    violation, 50, 85, 155, 179, 188

immunization, 134
India, 112, 113, 121, 124, 136, 147, 150,
    164, 174
Institute for Democracy, South Africa, 121
Institute for Security Studies, South
    Africa, 121
InterAction, 15, 57, 138, 139, 142–5,
    151, 209
International Action Network on Small
    Arms (IANSA), 178–9, 194
International Alert, 57, 59
International Committee of the Red Cross
    (ICRC), 47, 52, 55, 59
    see also Federation of Red Cross and
        Red Crescent Societies
international law, 172, 178, 183
    humanitarian and human rights
        law, 179
international organizations, 5, 8, 9, 11, 12,
    31, 45, 131, 205, 206, 210
interventions
    humanitarian, 9, 29
    military, 200
Iran, 5, 165
    Iran-Contra affair, 100
Iraq, 9, 13, 62, 86, 155, 181, 187, 200, 201
Ireland, 104, 127, 183, 187
Islamic terrorism, 71, 75, 76, 83–7
Israel, 75, 86, 164, 174
Italy, 17, 82, 104, 167, 180, 181, 183

Japan, 5, 17, 104, 116, 171
Jihad, 75, 76, 83, 84
Jordan, 82, 127

Kenya, 113, 120, 122, 144, 152
kingpin strategy, 73–4
Kosovo, 13, 14, 34, 42, 62

Latin America, 86, 113, 114, 145–6, 165,
    168
    see also Central America; South America
Lebanon, 164, 174
Lesotho, 118, 119, 152
liberalization
    finance, 91, 93
    markets, 160, 163
Liberia, 165–9
Libya, 181
Lifeguard, 54, 55

Local Capacities for Peace framework, 32
Lutheran World Relief, 139

Macedonia, 32, 82
mafia, 171
malaria, 126, 137, 142, 201
   see also diseases
Malawi, 118, 119, 152
Medecins du Monde (MDM), 47
Medecins sans Frontières (MSF), 8, 15,
   47, 49
mediation, 28, 33, 35, 39
Mennonite Central Committee (MCC), 33,
   34, 39
mercenaries, 15, 45–65, 69
Mercy Corps, 31, 39
Mexico, 72, 74, 98
Middle East, 35, 75, 83, 85–6, 113,
   165, 170
migration, 11–12, 24, 132, 204
military, 34–5, 49, 74, 117, 126, 131, 134,
   139, 143–5, 148, 155
Military Professional Resources
   Incorporated (MPRI), 8, 209
modernization, 25
money laundering, 16, 91–107, 159,
   201, 209
Mozambique, 124
Movimento Popular da Libertacao de
   Angola (MPLA), 166
Mujahedeen, 74–5, 146, 165
multinational corporations, 12, 45, 204
Myanmar (Burma), 113, 147, 169

Namibia, 118–19, 124
narcotics, see drugs
narco-trafficking, see trafficking
national interest, 30, 38, 133, 142, 187
nationalism, 30
natural resources, 167–9, 179
Netherlands, 72, 180–1, 183–5, 187–8, 192,
networks, 3, 10–11, 50, 92, 141, 160, 163,
   166, 168–70, 177–9, 200–2, 204, 206,
   211
   and security governance, 14–17
   information, 14, 24
   structures, 72–4, 76, 80, 83–4
"New Policy Agenda", 26–7, 201, 207
"New Wars", 160
Nicaragua, 164–5

Contras, 164–5
Farabundo Marti National Liberation
   (FMLN), 165
Niger, 167
Nigeria, 112, 118, 122, 124
non-governmental advocacy networks,
   177–9
non-governmental organizations (NGOs)
   and private security companies (PSCs),
      8–10, 15, 45–65, 200, 204–6
   and peacebuilding, 15, 201–2, 206–9:
      involvement, 210; mandate, 15,
      23–4, 30–3, 37–8; problems, 33–4
   and conflict prevention, 28, 32
   and preventative diplomacy, 27–8
   and peacemaking, 27, 34
   and conflict resolution, 23, 28–9, 34,
      38–9, 48
   and mediation, 28, 33, 35–6, 39
   and reconciliation, 8, 32, 35–6, 38
   and education, 33, 35, 138, 145–7,
      203, 205
   and democratization, 24, 26
   and partnering organizations, 29
   and private development corporations,
      35
   and the United Nations, 12, 15, 27–8, 32,
      35–6, 59–60, 131
   and the development community, 32
   as civil society organizations, 15, 17, 24,
      25–8, 31–2, 38, 172, 210
   as pressure groups, 20, 25, 33–4, 38–9,
      45, 177–9, 183–5
   as service providers, 25, 202
   as security actors, 11, 178–9, 199, 204,
      206
   accountability, 36–7, 52–4, 58, 200, 203,
      205, 207–8
   advantages, 27, 199
   "Agenda for Peace", 27, 31
   apolitical, 26, 33, 48, 60
   arms control, 8, 177–9, 184–5, 190–3,
   "associational revolution", 23
   autonomy, 27, 57, 139, 202
   definition, 24
   domestic, 23
   effectiveness, 27, 37–8, 204
   environmental, 24–6, 30
   evaluation, 32, 36–7, 146, 209
   faith-based, 140

funding, 27, 30–3, 35–6, 38, 48, 51, 139, 142–5, 148, 201–5
grassroots, 27–9, 32, 38, 201
humanitarian, 24–7, 32–3, 35, 37, 45, 47–8, 60
human rights, 15, 23–5, 28, 31
impartiality, 29, 48, 50, 52, 54, 204, 206
international, 8, 23, 25, 138–9, 143–5
mandates, 15
neutrality, 15, 33–4, 37, 48, 50, 52, 54, 201, 204, 206
"New Policy Agenda", 26–7, 201, 207
Northern (western), 24, 26
number, 23–25
"Peacebuilding Initiative", 31
refugees, 11, 13, 30, 32, 35
relief and development, 27
relationship with state actors, 15, 37, 57, 138–9, 142–5, 151, 209: shared agendas, 3, 31, 177; promotion by states, 25, 30; weakening of third world states, 13, 27; as agents of the state, 25, 30, 38–9
"track-two diplomacy", 28
women's issues, 25
North Africa, 113
North Atlantic Treaty Organization (NATO), 9, 11–14, 34, 38
North Korea, 5, 98
Northern Alliance, 165
Norway, 116
Norwegian Peoples Aid, 47
Nuclear Test Ban Treaty, 178
nuclear weapons, 5–7, 178
control, 6, 178
disarmament, 178
proliferation, 5, 204

oil corporations, 166
Operation Anaconda, 83
Operation Enduring Freedom, 83
Organization of American States (OAS), 180
Inter-American Convention Against the Illicit Manufacturing of and Trafficking in Firearms, Ammunition, Explosives and Other Related Materials, 171, 180

organized crime
see transnational criminal organizations
OXFAM, 56, 185

pacifism, 34
Pakistan, 71, 76, 81–3, 85–6, 165, 171
Palestine, 86
Palestine Liberation Organization (PLO), 164–5
Panama, 100
peacebuilding, 23–43, 45–65, 155, 201–2, 206–9
"Peacebuilding Initiative", 31
peacemaking, 14, 27, 34
Pentagon, 75, 78, 83
Peru, 71–2
Philippines, 26, 71, 85
Partiya Karkaren Kurdistan (PKK), Turkey, 165
Population Services International (PSI), 144–5
poverty, 23, 38, 85–6, 120, 123, 131, 140, 146, 157
Powell, Colin (Secretary of State, USA), 135–6
preventative diplomacy, 27–8
private development corporations, 35
private military companies (PMCs)
see, private security companies
private security companies (PSC), 3, 8–10, 11–13, 15, 34, 45–7, 50–5, 57–61, 199, 200–6, 208–9
private voluntary organizations (PVAs), 136, 205
see also non-governmental organizations
privatization, 26, 47, 94, 98, 200–1, 207
security, 12, 47, 55, 98, 157, 200, 201

RAND Corporation, 79
Reagan, Ronald (former President, USA), 69–70, 164
Reagan Doctrine, 164
Reflecting on Peace Practice (RPP), 37, 209
refugees, 11, 13, 24, 28, 30, 32, 34–5, 50, 138
Revolutionary Armed Forces of Colombia (Fuerzas Armadas Revolucionarios de Colombia, FARC), 74, 166
Revolutionary United Front, Sierra Leone, 55, 165

Rumsfeld, Donald (Secretary of Defense, USA), 86
Russia, 5, 98, 100, 112, 114, 121, 165, 171
Rwanda, 31, 33, 119, 165–6
  genocide, 38, 155, 166

Saferworld, 185, 187
Save the Children, 47, 139, 185
Saladin, 55
sanctions, 169
Saudi Arabia, 75–6, 85–6
Second World War
  see World War II
securitization, 11, 132–3, 138, 141, 147, 206
security
  definition, 4, 10–2
  human, 115–16, 145–7
  traditional, 131–2, 136, 143–5
  military, 13, 132
  national, 132, 134
  international, 132
  environmental, 11, 26, 115
  privatization, 12, 47, 55, 98, 157, 200, 201
security governance, 3, 11–15
security sector reform, 155
September 11, 2001, 5, 70, 76, 78, 80, 83, 92, 94–6, 101–2, 111, 142–3, 204
Serbia, 169
Sierra Leone, 8, 54–5, 94, 117, 122–5, 165–7, 169
  Revolutionary United Front (RUF), 55, 165, 167, 169
Singapore, 82
Small arms and light weapons, 155–76, 177–96
  see also arms trade
  availability, 179
  brokering, 165–8
  covert military aid, 164–5
  demand, 157
  export controls, 177–96
  legal trade, 163–4
  production, 163
  proliferation, 156–63
  stockpiles, 160
  supply, 163–8
Somalia, 9, 34, 38, 54, 75, 84
South Africa, 26, 54, 57, 58, 113, 117–18, 121–2, 125, 165–6, 182

Institute for Democracy, 121
Institute of International Affairs, 125
Institute for Security Studies, 121
Mbeki, Thabo (President, South Africa), 121
Regulations of Foreign Military Assistance Act, 57
South Asia, 83, 165, 171
Southeast Asia, 6, 83, 113, 123
Southern African Development Community (SADC), 120, 125, 180
Southern Cross, 55
sovereignty, 8–9, 13, 30, 51, 60–1, 81, 87, 98, 200, 204, 211
Spain, 72, 112, 180
Spanish influenza, 114
Sub-Saharan Africa, 6, 112–13, 117–20, 135–6, 147–8, 165, 182
Sudan, 76, 165, 168–9
Swaziland, 118–19
Sweden, 180–1, 184–5, 187–9, 192
Syria, 165, 181

Tajikistan, 165
Taleban, 166, 171
  Army of the Islamic Emirate of Afghanistan, 171
Tanzania, 76, 118, 144
  Dar-es-Salaam embassy bombing, 75
terrorism
  attacks, 5, 10, 69, 76, 80, 82, 83, 84, 86, 101, 102, 111, 156
  bioterrorism, 134
  intelligence, 16, 70–3, 79–82, 84–5, 87
terrorist organizations, 69–90, 165, 170
  funding, 76
  networks, 76–7
  training camps, 76, 84
Thailand, 113, 147, 165, 169
Togo, 145
"track-two diplomacy", 28
trafficking, 16, ch.4, 91, 94, 101, 132, 157–62, 167, 169, 171, 180–2, 186, 188, 190, 192, 201–2
  drugs
  arms
"transnational advocacy networks", 14, 177

transnational criminal organizations,
17, 161
see also arms trade; cartels; mafia;
trafficking
tuberculosis, 126, 134, 137, 142, 201
see also diseases
Tunisia, 83
Turkey, 82, 97, 164–5

Uganda, 55, 144, 147, 165, 168
Ukraine, 114, 167
Unión Nacional para la Independencia
Total de Angola (UNITA), 164–6, 169
United Kingdom (UK), 54, 57–8, 100, 178,
180–1, 183–5, 187, 207
United Methodist Committee on Relief,
139–40
United Nations (UN), 9, 12, 15, 27, 28, 32,
35–36, 50, 59, 97, 131
arms embargoes, 158, 172, 188
Children's Fund (UNICEF), 35, 59,
139–40
Conference on the Illicit Trade in Small
Arms and Light Weapons in All Its
Aspects: Programme of Action on
Small Arms, 161
Convention against Transnational
Organized Crime, 180
Declaration of Human Rights, 35, 86
Development Program (UNDP), 32, 35,
132: Human Development Report,
115, 132
Disarmament Commission, 157
General Assembly, 136, 171
High Commission for Refugees
(UNHCR), 50, 59
International Convention against the
Recruitment, Use, Financing and
Training of Mercenaries, 59
Joint United Nations Programme in
HIV/AIDS (UNAIDS), 131
Office for the Coordination of
Humanitarian Affairs, 60
Panel of Governmental Experts on
Small Arms, 155, 157, 158
Protocol against Illicit Firearms, 180
Security Council (UNSC), 134–5, 142
Transition Authority in Cambodia
(UNTAC), 123
World Food Program (WFP), 59

United States of America (USA)
Agency for International Development
(USAID), 26, 32, 35, 136–9, 147–8,
201
Advisory Committee on Voluntary
Foreign Aid (ACVFA), 141–3, 148
Air Force (USAF), 165
Bernard, Dr Kenneth (Special Assistant
to the President for International
Health Affairs), 134–5
Bush, George W. (President), 71, 135–6,
142
Centers for Disease Control and
Prevention, 136–8, 147–8
Central Intelligence Agency (CIA), 79,
81–2, 133, 136, 164–5
Clinton, Bill (former President), 84,
134–5
Congress / Senate, 5, 70, 80, 100, 134,
136, 140, 142–3, 148
"Debt Relief Enhancement Act" HR
4524, 140
Department of Agriculture
(USDA), 136–7
Department of Defense (DOD), 134,
136–8, 142, 145, 147–8
Department of Labor, 136–7
Department of State, 133, 137
Drug Enforcement Agency (DEA), 70,
73, 82
Eisenhower, Dwight (former President),
142
Federal Bureau of investigation (FBI),
70, 78, 80–1, 101
Global AIDS program (GAP), 137, 148
Global HIV/AIDS Workplace
Initiative, 137
Gore, Al (former Vice President), 134–6
International Traffic in Arms
Regulations (ITAR), 58
Leadership and Investment in Fighting
an Epidemic initiative (LIFE), 136
National Intelligence Council, 118, 120,
133, 135–6
National Security Council (NSC), 134–5
Naval Health Research Center, 137
Pentagon, 75, 78, 83
Powell, Colin (Secretary of State), 135–6
Rumsfeld, Donald (Secretary of
Defense), 86

United States of America—*Continued*
  Tenet, George (Director, CIA), 136
  Wolfowitz, Paul (Deputy Secretary of
    Defense), 80
  World Trade Center, 75, 78
Uruguay, 123–4

Venezuela, 77
Vietnam, 27, 164
violence, 37, 49–50, 56, 70, 75, 85, 156–7,
    160, 178–80, 204

warlords, 141, 166, 169
wheel networks, 72–4, 76, 80, 83–4
Witness for Peace, 33
Wolfowitz, Paul (Deputy Secretary of
    Defense, USA), 80
women, 25, 94, 113, 138, 146, 179

World Bank, 32, 97, 114, 137, 207
World Food Program (WFP), 59
World Health Organization (WHO),
    111–12, 120
World Trade Center attack
    (1993), 75
World Vision, 31, 33–5, 49, 52, 139–40,
    145, 147
World War II, 7, 26, 31

Yemen, 71, 75, 82, 85
  USS Cole Destroyer attack, 80
Yugoslavia, 9, 12, 169
  see also Bosnia-Herzegovina, Croatia,
    Serbia

Zaire
  see Democratic Republic of Congo